THE GLORY AND THE GRANDEUR

Today the physical remains of the vast historical phenomenon that was Greco-Roman civilization are little more than scattered ruins whose beauty is but a faint echo of their original splendor. But the artistic, intellectual, and moral legacy of classical culture is an integral part of the living fabric of the Western World. It is the purpose of Hellas and Rome *to illumine to the fullest extent the glory that was Greece, the grandeur that was Rome, and the greatness that has been passed down to us.*

ROBERT DOUGLAS MEAD, *the general editor, is a free-lance writer who has published works on subjects ranging from ancient music to Milton's poetry to contemporary affairs. Planned companion volumes to* Hellas and Rome, *under his direction, will treat other great ages of world civilization, including the culture of the United States.*

Contributors

Meyer Reinhold, *University of Missouri*
Norman Austin, *University of California, Los Angeles*
Henry C. Pitz, *Professor Emeritus, Philadelphia College of Art*
Harold L. Geisse, Jr., *Wesleyan University*

Consultant on the Humanities

Adele Stern, *Vice-Principal For Curriculum, Paramus High School*

HELLAS AND ROME

The Story of Greco-Roman Civilization

Robert Douglas Mead
Series General Editor

College Library, Wayne, Nebr.

A MENTOR BOOK from
NEW AMERICAN LIBRARY
TIMES MIRROR
New York and Scarborough, Ontario
The New English Library Limited, London

Copyright © 1972 by Robert Douglas Mead
All rights reserved
Library of Congress Catalog Card Number: 72-75007

Photo Acknowledgments

The Lion Gate, Mycenae: reproduced by permission of the Hirmer Fotoarchiv München

Figure of Dionysus from the Parthenon, Athens: reproduced by permission of the Trustees of the British Museum

Boy Jockey: reproduced by permission of the National Archaeological Museum, Athens, Greece

Boy Jockey (detail): reproduced by permission of the National Archaeological Museum, Athens, Greece

The Alexander Mosaic: reproduced by permission of Fratelli Alinari and the Art Reference Bureau

The Hermes of Praxiteles: reproduced with the kind permission of the Archaeological Museum, Olympia, Greece

The Apoxyomenus: reproduced by permission of the Vatican Museums, Rome

The Venus de Milo (detail): reproduced by permission of the Musée de Louvre and the photographer, Maurice Chuzeville

The Victory of Samothrace: reproduced by permission of the Musée de Louvre and the photographer, Maurice Chuzeville

The Laocoön: reproduced by permission of the Vatican Museums, Rome

Frieze from the Altar of Zeus, Pergamum (detail): reproduced by permission of the Staatliche Museen zu Berlin

The Altar of Zeus, Pergamum: reproduced by permission of the Staatliche Museen zu Berlin

The Pantheon, Rome: reproduced by permission of Fratelli Alinari and the Art Reference Bureau

Interior of the Pantheon, Rome: reproduced by permission of Fratelli Alinari and the Art Reference Bureau

The Arch of Constantine, Rome: reproduced by permission of Fratelli Alinari and the Art Reference Bureau

Mummy Portrait of a Man: reproduced by courtesy of the Trustees, The National Gallery, London

 MENTOR TRADEMARK REG. U.S. PAT. OFF. AND FOREIGN COUNTRIES
REGISTERED TRADEMARK—MARCA REGISTRADA
HECHO EN CHICAGO, U.S.A.

(The following page constitutes an extension of this copyright page.)

SIGNET, SIGNET CLASSICS, SIGNETTE, MENTOR and PLUME BOOKS
are published *in the United States* by
The New American Library, Inc.,
1301 Avenue of the Americans, New York, New York 10019,
in Canada by The New American Library of Canada Limited,
81 Mack Avenue, Scarborough, 704, Ontario,
in the United Kingdom by The New English Library Limited,
Barnard's Inn, Holborn, London, E.C. 1, England.

First Printing, September, 1972

PRINTED IN THE UNITED STATES OF AMERICA

300949

CONTENTS

Introduction: Hellas and Rome	13
I : GREEK AND ROMAN CIVILIZATION	19
Greek Origins	19
The Mycenaean Age and After	24
The Epics of Homer	28
The Greek City-State	29
The religion of the city-state	33
The rebirth of literature and art	35
Greece and Persia	39
The Golden Age of Athens	45
The arts in Athens	48
The Greek enlightenment	50
Socrates	51
The Peloponnesian War and Its Aftermath	52
The Coming of Alexander the Great	55
The Hellenistic Age	58
The Beginnings of Roman Civilization	63
The Roman Kingdom	67
The Roman Republic	68
Republican institutions	69
The Growth of Empire	73
The transformation of Roman society	76
Early Roman literature and art	79
The city of Rome	83
The Roman Revolution	83
Julius Caesar	86
The death of the Republic	87
The Golden Age of Roman literature	88
The Augustan Age	89
Augustan literature	90
The Roman Empire Fully Formed	92
Imperial dynasties	92
The Silver Age	93
The good Emperors	95
The quality of Imperial life	98
The Decay of Empire	102
The crisis of the Empire	104
Regimentation and totalitarianism	106
The Triumph of Christianity	108
For Further Reading	111

II : THE LITERATURE OF GREECE AND ROME — 114

- The Beginnings of Greek Literature — 114
  - The epic world of Homer — 114
  - Lyric poetry — 117
- The Golden Age of Athens — 121
  - Athenian tragedy — 122
  - Comedy — 131
  - The age of prose — 134
- Hellenistic Literature — 139
  - The Alexandrian period — 141
- How Roman Literature Began — 143
  - Early Roman comedy — 145
  - Literature at the end of the Republic — 146
- The Age of Augustus — 151
  - Virgil and *The Aeneid* — 153
  - Horace — 156
  - Three elegiac poets — 157
- The Silver Age — 160
  - Satire in the Silver Age — 161
- In the Twilight of Pagan Rome — 163
- *For Further Reading* — 165

III : HISTORIANS AND BIOGRAPHERS — 168

- Myth and Legend — 169
- The Great Greek Historians — 171
  - Herodotus — 171
  - Thucydides — 176
  - Other works of history — 182
- Greek Biography — 184
- The Hellenistic Period — 186
  - Polybius — 187
- Early Roman Historians — 189
- Revolution and Empire — 191
  - Julius Caesar — 191
  - Sallust — 193
  - Biography — 195
- The Augustan Age and After — 196
  - Livy — 196
  - History under the Empire — 198
  - The great biographers — 201
- *For Further Reading* — 204

IV : THE ARTS OF GREECE AND ROME — 206

- The Early Greeks — 207
  - The renewal of civilization — 210
  - Early Greek architecture — 213
  - Early Greek sculpture — 214
  - Vase-painting techniques — 215
- Classical Greece: The Crest of a Civilization — 217
  - The rebuilt Acropolis of Athens — 219
  - Classical Greek sculpture — 224
  - The art of the brush — 227
  - Art in a postwar era — 230
- The Art of the Hellenistic World — 237
  - Sculpture — 239
  - Painting and architecture — 244
- The Triumph of Rome — 246
  - The growth of Greek influence — 247
  - Roman architecture — 249
  - Sculpture — 253
  - Painting and mosaic — 256
  - The death of classical art — 258
- *For Further Reading* — 260
- *Some Technical Terms* — 261

V : ANCIENT MUSIC AND ITS INSTRUMENTS — 265

- The Golden Age: How the Greeks Valued Their Music — 267
  - General characteristics of Greek music — 269
  - Greek musical performance — 271
- The Instruments — 273
  - Greece — 273
  - Rome — 276
  - The sound of ancient music — 278
- *For Further Reading* — 279

VI : PHILOSOPHY, RELIGION, AND SCIENCE — 281

- Where It All Began: Classical Greek Religion — 281
  - Greek religious ideas — 281
  - Greek gods — 284
- The Beginnings of Rational Thought — 287
  - The Milesian philosophers — 288
  - Pythagoras — 290

New Ideas of the Universe	293
Heraclitus	294
The Eleatic philosophers	295
Other fifth-century philosophers	296
The Fifth Century: The Breakdown of Values	301
The Greek mystery-religions	303
Humanism: Socrates and the Sophists	305
The Fourth Century: Greatness in Defeat	309
Plato	310
Plato's Theory of Reality	312
Plato's Social and Political Thought	314
Aristotle	315
The Hellenistic World	319
Epicureanism	319
Stoicism	320
The Final Flowering of Ancient Science	322
Mathematics	323
Medicine	325
Astronomy	326
Religion and Philosophy Under the Romans	327
Roman religion	327
The end of philosophy	331
For Further Reading	
Some Technical Terms	336
Index	341

ILLUSTRATIONS

TIME LINES

Greek Civilization, 2000–1400 B.C.	20
Greek Civilization, 1400–800 B.C.	26
Greek Civilization, 800–200 B.C.	46
Roman Civilization, 1200–600 B.C.	64
Roman Civilization, 600 B.C.–0	74
Roman Civilization, 100 B.C.–A.D. 500	94
Greek Literature, 800–200 B.C.	120
Roman Literature, 300 B.C.–A.D. 300	152
Greek Historians, 700–100 B.C.	178
Roman Historians, 400 B.C.–A.D. 200	194
Greek Art, 700–100 B.C.	222
Roman Art, 200 B.C.–A.D. 400	250
Greek Thought, 700–100 B.C.	302
Roman Thought, 100 B.C.–A.D. 500	328

LINE DRAWINGS, MAPS, CHART

The Greek Alphabet (*chart*)	36
Greece and the Persian Wars (*map*)	41–43
A Roman Private House in the Time of the Republic (*Fig. 1*)	82
The Roman Empire at Its Greatest Extent (*map*)	96–97
A Roman Private House of the Imperial Period (*Fig. 2*)	100
The three Orders of Greek Architecture (*Fig. 3*)	212
The Acropolis at Athens (*Fig. 4*)	218
The Agora at Athens (*Fig. 5*)	226
Plan of the City of Priene (*Fig. 6*)	236
A Basic Arch Form (*Fig. 7*)	248
Basic Vault Forms (*Fig. 8*)	252

HALFTONE PLATES

The Lion Gate, Mycenae (*Plate 1*)	209
The Figure of Dionysus from the Parthenon, Athens (*Plate 2*)	221
Boy Jockey (*Plate 3*)	225
Boy Jockey, *detail* (*Plate 3A*)	225

The Alexander Mosaic, *detail* (*Plate 4*)	231
Hermes Carrying the Infant Dionysus (*Plate 5*)	232
Apoxyomenus (*Plate 6*)	235
Venus de Milo, *detail* (*Plate 7*)	238
Victory of Samothrace (*Plate 8*)	241
Laocoön (*Plate 9*)	243
Frieze from the Altar of Zeus, Pergamum, *detail* (*Plate 10*)	246
The Altar of Zeus, Pergamum (*Plate 10A*)	247
The Parthenon, Rome (*Plate 11*)	254
Interior of the Parthenon, Rome (*Plate 11A*)	255
The Arch of Constantine, Rome (*Plate 12*)	257
Mummy Portrait, Roman Egypt (*Plate 13*)	259

INTRODUCTION:

Hellas and Rome

ROBERT DOUGLAS MEAD

THIS IS A BOOK about civilization—specifically, about two great civilizations of the past which, more than any others, have shaped both our ideas of civilization and our civilization itself. Yet just what we mean by the word *civilization*, so fundamental to this book, is not easy to say, in part because the word has not one but several meanings. In English and in other Western languages, for example, it is connected with a group of words—*civil, civilian, citizenship*—all of which point toward one social form: the city. And, as we shall see in Chapter 1, the beginning, the growth, and ultimately the death of civilization in the ancient world corresponds with the growth and decay of its cities. By *civilization*, then, we mean those kinds of things that men have been able to do by virtue of being gathered together in the unity, cooperation, and mutual trust that city life requires; especially the arts of literature, sculpture, painting, music—and the equally necessary urban arts of politics, finance, commerce. This is one reason that this book is organized as it is, with separate chapters on each of these aspects of ancient civilization.

But these things, the products of a civilization, depend in turn on a whole cluster of ideas that make civil life possible: above all, perhaps, the agreement of a group of people as to what is important, what things they will lend their labor to, coupled with enough respect for human differences so that they can live and work together in the close life of a city. These ideas are called values: Civilization—and a particular civilization—is defined both by what it does and by the values that its people hold in common. And that is another way of saying what this book is about: Our concern is both with civilization and with those values, human and humane, that underlie civilization. There are a number of reasons for making this exploration by way of the great civilization of the past.

Two thousand or more years separate us from the great

age of classical civilization, yet it remains a living part of our own tradition, our own civilization. In important ways, all of us who participate in twentieth-century Western civilization have, inescapably, something of Greek in us, something of Roman. That is one of the reasons for studying the past, this particular past: for what we can learn about ourselves.

The Greek and Roman civilization with which we are concerned in this book extended in time over nearly two thousand years, one culture, one society, merging into, being absorbed by, the other. Historians use the term *Greco-Roman* to emphasize that two-thousand-year continuity, but the closer one gets to it, the more one knows, the more the two cultures seem separate and distinct. That is why this book has a double title: *Hellas and Rome*. And that is why it is Hellas, not Greece.

Greece as a nation came into existence in the nineteenth century after hundreds of years of occupation by the Turkish Empire. In classical times, the people we know as Greeks called their land Hellas, but they did not mean by that a clearly defined geographic entity. By the fifth century B.C., there were independent Greek cities not only on the Greek mainland but everywhere in the Mediterranean basin, from the shores of the Black Sea to what are now Spain, France, and — importantly — Italy. Wherever the Greek language was spoken, the ideals of Greek culture shared, was Hellas. But in spite of their loyalty to Hellas, the Greek cities remained fiercely independent, never able to unite except briefly, in times of great common danger, until finally foreign conquerors forced unity upon them. Throughout the great ages of her history, Greece — Hellas — remained not so much a place as an idea.

This is the first of the great contrasts that one discovers between Greece and Rome, two cultures that at this distance in time may seem rather similar, with much in common. But where the Greeks — the ancient people who above all others valued ideas — could give supreme allegiance only to an idea, Rome was always a solid fact, measurable at any point in history by the clear-cut borders of her empire. And of course it was the existence and relative stability of the Roman Empire that permitted the cluster of ideas called Hellas to circulate freely, to enter into the consciousness of peoples as far removed, in every sense, as Egyptians and Britons, and, ultimately, to be transmitted to ourselves.

At whatever point we touch the Greek and Roman cultures, we find contrasts like this basic one: the Greeks —

imaginative, artistic, creative, self-confident, skilled in political theory, scientific, rational; the Romans—practical in every area where the Greeks were theoretical, with the conqueror's mask of assurance concealing dark inner doubts. But knowing the cultures of Greece and Rome has broader uses than simply to illuminate these two strands of Western civilization, important as that is. Knowing them, we are compelled to ask how two cultures, starting with much in common, could have developed so differently. In trying to answer that question, we can learn much about the nature and meaning of civilization itself, about that body of knowledge and values that we call "the humanities," and ultimately about man himself. For us, Hellas and Rome are like two specimens of civilization in a laboratory. Most of the facts about them are in our hands, abundantly known. From them, making our own interpretations, drawing our own conclusions, we can learn much about what civilization is, about the kinds of values we call civilized, humane.

For when we go back to the beginnings of Greek and Roman civilization, we find some interesting parallels. The Greek and Italian mainlands are in fact physically close, with similarities of climate and geography. Both were settled, in the darkness of prehistory, by wandering peoples who sprang from a common Eurasian homeland, with a common or related language, customs, beliefs. Both Rome and Athens, the supreme example of Greek civilization, enter recorded history as city-states ruled by hereditary kings, and both at an early date threw off their kings in favor of the earliest forms of democracy in the ancient world, a system that permitted the governed to decide their rulers, and how they would be ruled, for themselves. And yet the two cities, Rome and Athens, were already moving along quite different paths. If we can understand the nature of these differences and the ways in which they developed, we shall know much about human civilization itself—and about ourselves.

There is much to be learned, then, from comparing the two civilizations which are the subject of this book. But there is another kind of usefulness in learning about the past, especially the Greek and Roman past, for inevitably such knowledge drives us back to our own present time. It may be true that the past does not repeat itself, but in similar situations, similar events happen in similar ways: with allowances for obvious differences, there is much to learn here. History, indeed, was invented by the Greeks, and the earliest Greek historians set about their patient recording and interpretation of their own recent past primarily for the benefit of future generations, so that those who came after—including even those of the twentieth century—might understand what happened to them and avoid their mistakes.

Reading about Greek civilization and its history in broad outlines is like watching a movie in which a likable and talented hero repeatedly makes a disastrous mistake. *We* know when he is going wrong—it seems so obvious now, at this distance—and we cry out, "Don't! Stop! Come back!," but it's no use. In barely a century, between the fifth and fourth centuries B.C., Athenian society rose to one of the highest points of human civilization—and then fell apart in the attempt to unite the warring Greek city-states under her own rule (and for her own benefit). Hardly ever can a society have been so rewarding for its citizens as fifth-century Athens—so united, so self-assured, so rich in all the arts, above all so free. And yet in the last third of the fifth century, it all went to pieces, in a war that involved most of the Greek city-states and large parts of the Mediterranean, that lasted *nearly thirty years* and in Athens set class against class, generation against generation, brought out the selfishness and irresponsibility that are the greatest threat to any democracy, and ultimately impoverished all of Greece and prepared the way for conquest, first by the unified kingdom of Macedonia, finally by Rome. For an American living in the final third of the twentieth century, the parallels are disturbing—and instructive.

For a time, the Greeks seemed able to solve every problem of human society by the use of reason, by their wonderful inventiveness, by courage, by their sheer delight in living. Yet in the big problem, they failed: The qualities that made life so rich for the individual citizen seem inseparable from the jealously guarded independence of the many city-states, maintained by constant warfare; they could find no way of reconciling the two.

Looked at from this distance, in its simplest terms, the Roman failure was also a political one, but of a very different kind. In the matter of unity, of reconciling conflicting local interests over a large area and a long period of time, the Roman Empire was impressively successful. The famous *Pax Romana* (Roman Peace) was indeed a reality, providing the diverse peoples within the boundaries of Western civilization with periods of peace, stability, and prosperity longer than at any stage of Western history before or since. But the human costs were great.

The authority of the state over the individual (especially authority supported by efficient military power) played a large part in the lives of individual Romans, compared with Hellas—even though that authoritarianism was regulated by a reasonable and well-administered system of law. The system provided great economic opportunities: among the Romans, we encounter the first private millionaires in history, the first great private consumers of all the arts (but little of the creativity in sculpture, architecture, music, science, and philosophy in which the Greeks were such constant innovators). And we also find, again for the first time, a welfare system that provided food, clothing, money, entertainment—but no useful work—for large numbers of impoverished citizens, both in Rome itself and in the great cities of the Empire. The political forms of the Roman Republic had been well suited to the needs of a small, tightly knit city. But in the nearly six hundred years that it endured, the Empire never succeeded in adapting those forms to the needs of a multinational state on a continental scale. Again, for those of us who live day by day with the realities of the twentieth century, the parallels are disturbing.

This book has been designed to provide a framework within which the reader can explore, as fully as he wishes, issues such as these and others like them. For this purpose, we have brought together specialists in each of the areas in which Greco-Roman civilization expressed itself—literature, historical writing and biography, art, music, philosophy, and science. The opening chapter, "Greek and Roman Civilization," is a kind of road map of the whole, sketching in broad strokes the two-thousand-year cultural history of Greece and Rome and suggesting some of the important ways in which these several areas are related to one another and to the whole. The result, it is hoped, will be read for pleasure in just that way, as an introduction to a fascinating era of human history, marvelous in its achievements, tragic in its failures. But it is also meant to help the student or the general reader to carry out his own explorations, make his own discoveries, in any or all of these areas, to whatever depth his interests lead him. Thus, teachers and students can use this book in a variety of ways: as an outline for systematic study of Greek and Roman civilization or as a starting point for comparing and appreciating, in their cultural context, particular works of art, literature, or philosophy, according to their own needs and interests. And there are many possibilities in between.

Ultimately, as the reader comes to know and appreciate the art and the thought of classical civilization, he can construct his own answers to the questions with which we began: What is civilization and what are its values? Having identified these values, how can we apply them in our own lives, our own society? For something that Robert Frost often said of poetry also describes our experience of the other arts or, perhaps, of any real achievement of the human mind and spirit: that it begins in delight and ends in wisdom.

By its nature, this book could only have been possible through the enthusiastic work and cheerful cooperation of many people: the four contributors, Meyer Reinhold, Norman Austin, Henry C. Pitz, and Harold L. Geisse, Jr.; Adele Stern, a brilliant teacher who has been among the pioneers of the new interdisciplinary approach to the teaching of the humanities in American schools and colleges; the editors of New American Library, particularly Ward Mohrfeld, who had the imagination to see the usefulness of this book when it was no more than an outline in the general editor's typewriter; and, not least, the general editor's wife and sons, who for more than a year have tolerated his obsession with past civilizations. To all of them, I express my thanks.

CHAPTER I

Greek and Roman Civilization

MEYER REINHOLD

UNIVERSITY OF MISSOURI

THE WONDER and excitement we all share at the awesome discoveries and inventions of our century are blighted by our anxiety for the future of mankind. Man in the past has erected splendid civilizations that sooner or later disintegrated, leaving their skeletons in the graveyard of history. Many now extinct cultures took pride in their accomplishments, yet, glittering as they were in their heyday, once they died these civilizations swiftly vanished from the memory of man. The mighty Hittite Empire that flourished in the Near East in the second millennium B.C. has only recently been rediscovered. Others, like the Assyrian Empire, remembered for its militarism and brutality, left little or no legacy to the societies that followed. The ancient civilizations that have bequeathed the most lasting heritage to modern man are the Chinese, Hindu, Hebrew-Christian, Greek, and Roman. The vitality of these age-old but ageless cultures still seems contemporary and basic. This is why we are constantly drawn back to them for enlightenment and guidance, for we recognize in their views of life fundamental continuities with and relevance to our own culture. It is particularly in the heritage of Europe and America that we recognize our enormous debt to the cultures of the Greeks and the Romans.

Greek Origins

The focus of Greco-Roman civilization was the Mediterranean Sea (the Great Sea, it was usually called by the ancients), one of the world's most splendid natural highways

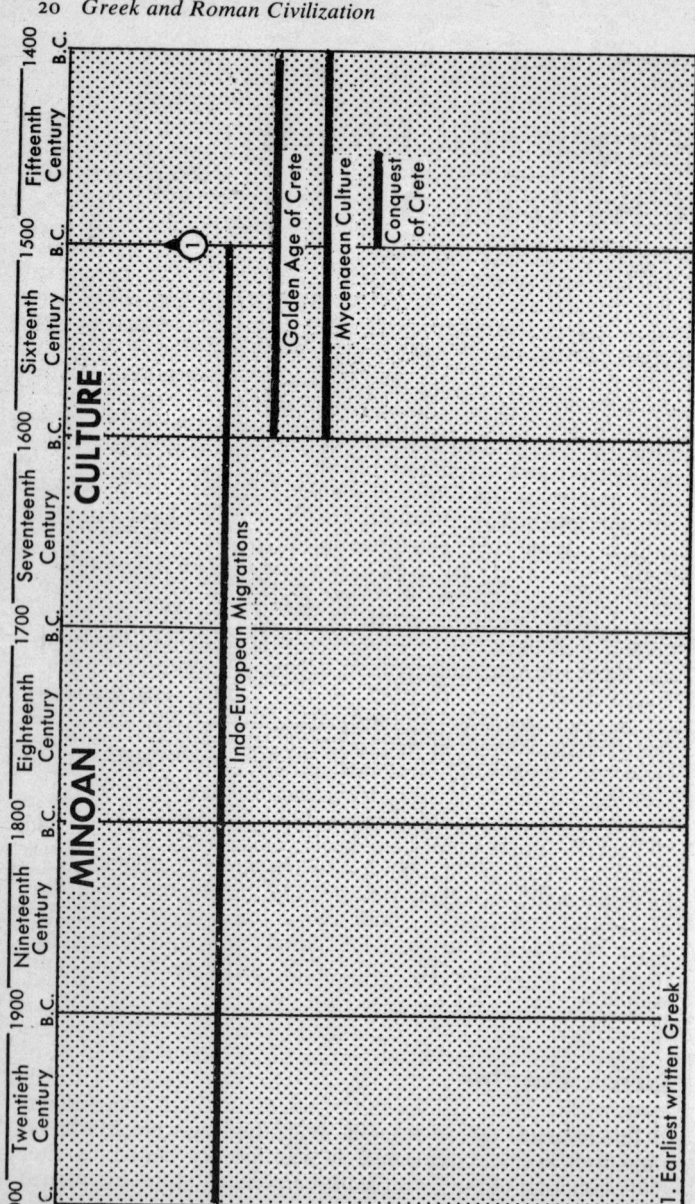

linking many lands on three continents. It provided the means through travel of breaking away from the localism that is characteristic of most early communities. The first part of the continent of Europe to attain the level of civilization — with settled, ordered, and lasting communities — was the large eastern peninsula reaching into the Mediterranean: Hellas, as the Greeks came to call their land.

At first sight, this region seems a most unlikely place to support a settled, growing society. Hellas is extremely limited both in its natural resources and in the amount of land suitable for food production. What, then, attracted settlers to this barren, rocky land? It was the nearness to and ease of communication, via the Aegean Sea, with the immemorial and affluent civilizations of the Near East, such as Babylonia and Egypt. Many peoples at lower levels of culture flocked to the shores of the Aegean so as to enjoy the advantages of the high civilizations created in the richly endowed lands of the Near East and the Egypt of the pharaohs.

From the beginning, Greece faced east, and its debt to Near Eastern cultures was in many respects as great as the debt of the Romans later was to the Greeks. Thus, Greece, in borrowing from earlier cultures, was the mediator between East and West, just as the Romans later were to become the transmitters of Greek culture to Western Europe. As the course of civilization has moved westward step by step over the last five thousand years, there is an unbroken continuity in many aspects of cultural tradition from the Near Eastern birthplaces of mankind's civilization to our own.

About 2000 to 1500 B.C., there took place one of those periodic migrations that have been characteristic of crowded Europe. From Central Europe hordes of migrants moved southeastward to richer lands — some into India, some into Asia Minor, some into Greece. All these peoples, and many others, originally spoke a language that, for want of a better term, we call Indo-European. Those who settled in Hellas were the users of the earliest form of the Greek language. Since Greek is now known to have been spoken and written as early as 1500 B.C., it has had, along with Chinese, the longest known continuous existence as a language in mankind's history. The invaders, who were not the first inhabitants of the peninsula, gradually absorbed the original population, along with their religion, many words of their language, and their skills in cultivating the soil and in navigation. After this blending of peoples, the population of Hellas remained quite stable (compared, for example, with Italy) for over two thousand years.

Hellas proper is a small country—the area in antiquity was about fifty thousand square miles, roughly the size of Illinois or of England. There are no rivers of any size, and none of them is navigable. It is, moreover, a highly mountainous country, with massive ranges and high peaks that in the north cut Hellas off from the rest of Europe. Overland travel was extremely difficult. The mountains, the many small valleys, and the islands that dot the sea off the coast combined to produce one of the most distinctive characteristics of Greek culture: From earliest times, it was fragmented into numerous completely independent communities. A fierce love of local self-government became indelibly ingrained in the Greek consciousness. The Greeks were the first people in history who proclaimed freedom as the basis of political life.

To the sharp contrasts of land, mountains, and sea were added the ambitions of numerous independent small states motivated by intense local patriotism, mutual suspicions, and competitive rivalries of all kinds. This separatism was to remain the glory and the curse of the Greeks. Their rivalries generated a degree of creativity rarely equaled in human history; but hatreds and disputes unleashed interminable wars that ultimately exhausted the wealth, manpower, and spirit of the Greeks. Collective action among groups of Greek communities was rare and temporary; unity was not finally achieved until it was imposed upon them by foreign powers such as those of the Macedonian kings Philip and Alexander and, finally, the Romans.

The local vigilance of Greek communities against outsiders, whether Greek or non-Greek, was also motivated by the extreme barrenness of the land. Only about one-quarter of Greece is cultivable, and the land is, moreover, not suitable for grain or cattle. The farmer's life was indeed hard in Greece compared with lush Egypt and Mesopotamia. Making a virtue out of necessity, the Greeks came to terms with nature's stinginess by elevating into a way of life the concepts of simplicity, frugality, austerity, self-restraint, and moderation in everything. "Greece has always had poverty as her companion," the Greek historian Herodotus tells us. The Greeks indeed would have been sentenced to eternal poverty and cultural insignificance had they not opened up outlets across the sea to supplement their meager resources. Thus, there was always a high degree of insecurity, tension, and challenge in Greek life; they rarely had the opportunity to become accustomed, as the Romans did in Italy, to self-satisfied enjoyment of material things. They found compensation in perfection on a small scale, particularly in their temples, the human body, and the human mind.

Nature, while withholding worldly goods from Greece, endowed her with exquisite beauty — in her profusion of hills, mountain ranges, and peaks, her lovely valleys, vivid colors, crisp clarity of atmosphere, and ever-present glimpses of the sea. Indeed, access to the sea is primarily what made Hellas so desirable to her inhabitants — not only for fishing but also for commerce, at first with Near Eastern civilizations, later with the Black Sea region and the entire western Mediterranean. Greece has one of the most highly indented seacoasts in the world, with numerous peninsulas, bays, harbors. No part of Greece is more than fifty miles from the sea, and with its many islands, no part of the Aegean Sea is more than fifty miles from land. As a result, travel by sea became more natural to the Greek than travel by land, which was arduous and costly. Indeed, the Greeks eventually became the principal traders and travelers of the ancient world, the most adventurous and enterprising seafarers in world history until modern times. Such venturesomeness away from their homelands was in time to give the Greeks worldwide perspectives — greater knowledge and sophistication and broader horizons than any people in man's previous history.

In addition to the Near East, a major force shaping early Greek life was the large island of Crete, which formed the southern border, as it were, of the Aegean Sea. Here, from about 2000 to 1500 B.C., flourished the remarkable Minoan culture (so called, after the mythical kings of Crete named Minos, by Sir Arthur Evans, the Englishman who discovered this civilization in 1900). During Crete's Golden Age (1600–1400 B.C.), this pre-Hellenic culture was a very affluent society — the leading maritime power, with trade routes throughout the Mediterranean. The Cretans, in contrast to the Greeks, were apparently a peaceful, pleasure-loving people who did not fear internal disorders and relied on the sea for defense. In many parts of the island, there were great palaces of kings, but no other large-scale architecture (such as temples or tombs, already found in Egypt) and no fortifications to protect the royal palaces. The largest and most famous Cretan palace is located at Knossos near the north-central coast of the island. It was a vast complex covering about six acres, and it served not only as royal headquarters but as the religious, social, economic, and manufacturing center of the small kingdom.

Crete had an art unique in world history. The principal subject was nature: Scenes of plant, animal, and sea life are caught in full movement, giving the artistic style a dynamic quality unsurpassed until modern times. The human figure, which was to become the dominant concern of the later Greek artist, was of little interest to the Cretan. Moreover, in Cretan art there are no scenes from history or mythology, no portraits of kings or nobles, no monuments honoring the kings. In their religion, the Cretans worshiped especially a mother goddess as representing fertility. The Cretans invented a form of writing (today called Linear A script) that employed a large number of symbols, each representing a syllable. Despite the claims of some to have deciphered this script, we cannot as yet read their language. This pre-Hellenic society — optimistic, affluent, international in its contacts — was the precursor of Greek culture, the earliest formative influence on the Greeks of the mainland.

The Mycenaean Age and After

About 1500 to 1450 B.C., Greek invaders conquered Crete. But they had little time to adopt the higher Cretan culture, for about 1400 B.C. disaster overwhelmed the island. There is evidence of great fires everywhere in Crete, but we do not know whether they were caused by an earthquake or a great volcanic eruption or by internal revolutions of the Minoans against their Greek conquerors. Whatever the cause, the peaceful civilization of Crete had received a mortal blow, and it gradually faded away, becoming one of the many lost cultures rediscovered by modern archaeologists. In a few hundred years, the culture of the island became completely Greek, and it has remained so ever since.

With the collapse of Crete began the Mycenaean Age of Greece (1600–1200 B.C.), so called from Mycenae, the most powerful Greek kingdom of the time. The Mycenaean Greeks were not only supreme in the Aegean Sea but maintained active commercial relations by sea in many parts of the Mediterranean and beyond. Mycenaean wares have been found in Egypt, Phoenicia, Palestine, Italy, Sicily, even as far away as England. The Golden Age of Mycenaean Greece (about 1400–1200 B.C.) developed a monumental architecture never again seen in ancient Greece: huge palaces, massively walled, and grandiose tombs of royalty and nobility. The most famous and best preserved of the Mycenaean palaces are those at Mycenae, Tiryns, and Pylos. The presence of great protective walls is striking evidence that we now are in the midst of a warrior society.

That the Mycenaeans were a literate people has been proved by the numerous inscriptions on clay tablets found at Mycenaean sites and also at Knossos in Crete. These were in a new script (so-called Linear B) adapted from the Cretan syllabic writing to the Greek language. Many of the gods and goddesses of the later Greek pantheon are already mentioned in Mycenaean inscriptions. It is clear that from the beginning the principal god of the Greeks was the sky-god Zeus. His numerous "marriages" with the pre-Hellenic mother goddess under various names are evidence of the amalgamation of the Greek people with their predecessors.

The ruling class of the Mycenaean Age was a warrior aristocracy: Their principal interests were war, seizing of booty, making piratical raids, hunting, and feasting. We find a new element in the Mycenaean society that is by and large absent from the older Near Eastern cultures: the yearning of the individual aristocrat for personal glory, especially as demonstrated by prowess and physical perfection. The highest form of such recognition was to become the subject of a literary composition that narrated his glorious deeds.

The numerous small independent Mycenaean kingdoms formed a kind of loose confederacy. In this manner, a degree of Hellenic unity existed through the allegiance of the various kings to the king of Mycenae as their overlord. The Greek kings were actively involved in diplomatic relations with the Near East and were known to the Hittites and Egyptians, the two leading powers of the time. So impressed were later Greeks of the Classical Age that they called this period the "Heroic Age" of Greece. Memories of the Mycenaean Age survived among the Greeks as a glorious age filled with heroes and exhibiting a degree of unity and cooperation that vanished in the Classical Age of the Greek city-state.

The greatest coordinated exploit of the Mycenaean Age was the siege and destruction of Troy (or Ilium, as the Greeks called it), inspiring two of the most famous and enduring works of world literature—*The Iliad* and *The Odyssey* of Homer. Located in the northwestern corner of Asia Minor, about four miles from the entrance to the Hellespont (the modern Dardanelles), the fortress palace of Ilium was destroyed by human violence about 1250 B.C. according to modern archaeologists. (The Greek scholar Eratosthenes

26 *Greek and Roman Civilization*

| 1400 B.C. | Fourteenth Century | 1300 B.C. | Thirteenth Century | 1200 B.C. | Twelfth Century | 1100 B.C. | Eleventh Century | 1000 B.C. | Tenth Century | 900 B.C. | Ninth Century | 800 B.C. |

MYCENAEAN CULTURE

Mycenaean Golden Age

① — 1. Trojan Wars
② — 2. Settlement of Sparta

GREEK DARK AGES

calculated the date to be 1184 B.C.) We do not know who the Trojans actually were or why the Greeks mobilized in such numbers in the Trojan War. In Greek tradition, the reason was the abduction of Helen, wife of Menelaus, brother of King Agamemnon of Mycenae, by Paris, son of King Priam of Troy.

The Mycenaean Age of Greek culture did not long survive its most famous exploit, the Trojan War. Soon after the fall of Troy, the Mycenaeans' civilization was destroyed. From about 1200 to 1100 B.C., hordes of invaders swarmed over all the great centers of Near Eastern civilization. In terror the Mycenaeans evacuated Hellas, and the refugees settled in the eastern part of the Aegean, along the coast of Asia Minor and on the large islands of Cyprus and Crete, all of which resemble Greece in climate and geography. The latter islands became, and still remain, integral parts of the Greek world. But Hellas did not long remain unoccupied, for a new wave of Greek-speaking people, the Dorians, soon moved in from the north and settled especially in the southern part of Greece known as the Peloponnesus. The Dorians were a more backward part of the Greek people who had thus far had little contact with the higher civilizations to the south.

The stricken land of Hellas now entered a Dark Age (about 1100 to 750 B.C.), one of the most severe steps backward in the history of mankind's civilization. For about four hundred years, life throughout Hellas and the entire Aegean area was at a level drastically lower than in the Mycenaean Age. For the Aegean world, communication with the outside ceased, and the Hellenic aristocracy turned to landowning, farming, and grazing as the bases of their wealth and power. Writing disappeared—the only time in the history of European civilization that literacy, once achieved, was completely lost. The arts, too, were in a deep recession: There were no sculpture, no wall painting, no monumental palaces or large tombs. Only one significant development, a minor one, took place in the field of the arts: the invention of a new type of pottery decorated with geometric patterns (triangles, circles, zigzags), apparently created in the area of Athens and spread from there to other parts of the Greek world. This absorption in purely abstract patterns was a forerunner of the later Greek preference for creating the human figure in art in accordance with mathematical formulae of design.

While kings continued to rule, government regressed from the Near Eastern type of monarchy, with its palace administration and society, to the earlier, more primitive tribal monarchy. The Greek king (called *basileus*) now had limited powers, checked by a triple division of authority and the consent of the governed. Everywhere in the Greek world there was now, side by side with the king, a local council of aristocratic elders, who advised the king, and an assembly of the people to whom reports were given periodically. We can recognize in this new development the germs of modern types of government, far different from the arbitrary power exercised by most Near Eastern kings. The code of life of the hereditary landowning nobility stressed the honor and glory of the individual aristocrat in the display of physical prowess in war, hunting, or feats of strength. But another way of displaying the excellence of the individual now emerged—athletic competition, a cultural manifestation that was to become one of the most distinctive characteristics of Greek life. A favorite type of entertainment for the nobles was the recital by traveling minstrels of stories about the glorious heroes of the Mycenaean Age.

One extremely important technological development took place in the Hellenic Dark Age—the spread of the use of iron in Greece, displacing the more expensive bronze in everyday life. Ready access to iron made weapons available to all, creating a revolution in warfare and reducing the dependence of the lower classes on the nobility for defense. The number of small kingdoms greatly increased through fragmentation of the earlier Mycenaean kingdoms.

The Epics of Homer

During the dormant centuries after the destruction of the Mycenaean society, a new Greek culture was slowly taking root. Suddenly, in the eighth century B.C., there burst forth two of the most exquisite masterpieces of world literature, *The Iliad* and *The Odyssey* of Homer. These are the first great creations in a literature that still exerts a deep influence on our own culture. Homer's works are mankind's first large-scale literary creations, and Homer, the first articulate European, is the first author anywhere whose name is known. Nothing by earlier Greek poets has survived; these men were pygmies beside the extraordinary genius of Homer. The principal topic had been myths, stories composed orally and handed down by memory for centuries. Though Homer inherited these age-old stories of the Heroic Age and the traditional manner of telling them, he was a poetic genius of the highest order, one of the world's greatest storytellers and a sophisticated literary artist.

But Homer was also a product of the dawning of the new Classical Age of Greece. Though we can trace many influences of Near Eastern literature in Homer's epics, they are unmistakably products of Greek genius. Almost immediately after their composition, *The Iliad* and *The Odyssey* became classics; and they have remained literally among the best sellers of all time. They were the most read, studied, quoted, and imitated works of Greek literature, the nearest the Greeks ever had to a Bible. At the same time that Homer's epics told of heroes and values of a bygone age, his magnificent stories illuminate the national character. The Homeric hero is an individualist striving for glory. Keenly aware of the shortness of life, he concentrates on the quality of life, not its length, preferring, like Achilles, the hero of *The Iliad*, to be a young dead hero long remembered by posterity rather than an ordinary person of long life but soon forgotten. To attain this form of immortality, the heroes of the Homeric poems seek honor and fame through victory in combat, conquest, plunder, and feats of physical prowess.

Yet the drive for personal glory often conflicts with the hero's obligations to friends, family, people. In the telling of his stories, Homer reveals the suffering caused by this extreme pursuit of personal fame and power and holds up as an object of deep concern the welfare of one's group and community, which often requires that the individual's personal ambitions be curbed. Indeed, in the figure of Odysseus —the epitome of the Greek national character—Homer created an alternative to the warrior victors of the Trojan War, a new type of hero whose greatness lay not in physical prowess as such but in his intelligence, balance, and above all in his concern for the community. In effect, Homer was questioning the heroic code of the past and elevating the group to a new level of importance. And already in Homer's own time, a new kind of Greek social organization was coming into being: the city-state, whose very existence depended on curbing the violence and excessive personal ambitions of the individual.

The Greek City-State

While he looked back nostalgically to the Heroic Age, Homer sensed the emergence of a new way of life that gave priority to the community and required cooperation and social commitment: the *polis,* or city-state. About 800 to 750 B.C., there occurred a new phenomenon in world civilization—the creation of the *polis,* the political masterpiece of the Greeks and the most distinctive characteristic of their culture. Each of the earlier Greek kingdoms was at this time transformed into an autonomous city the size of a county but with the population of a small city.

The city-state came into being when the aristocracy of each kingdom put an end to the rule of hereditary kings and substituted the control of the community by the aristocratic leaders acting as a group. To provide administrators, the election of officials was introduced; magistrates holding office for limited terms (eventually the common practice was to limit the term to one year) were elected, at first by the aristocracy from among their own numbers, in time, in many cities, by the votes of all citizens. Since magistrates came and went, laws, not men, were sovereign. (By 600 B.C. there were already published law codes in Greek cities.) Matters of public concern became every citizen's concern, and constant vigilance was needed to prevent any one man from acquiring too much power or wealth. We thus see taking form the central values of the Greek way of life: civic humanism in small, independent cities; the doctrine of moderation in every aspect of life. By way of contrast, at this time power was increasingly centralized in the Near East, where empires composed of many nations and races were ruled by one autocratic lifetime king whose decisions were often arbitrary and unchecked.

The political revolution that established the city-state took place not only because the body of aristocrats in each city was growing in affluence and self-confidence but because the older method of fighting, in which the aristocracy went to battle in chariots and fought duels with the enemy, had become obsolete. The ready availability of iron weapons produced a new type of fighter—heavy-armed foot soldiers, called hoplites, who fought as a coordinated battle unit in a compact formation called a phalanx. As a consequence, the hereditary king as war leader was displaced by aristocratic generals (called *strategoi,* "army leaders") who planned the movements and led the massed troops.

In addition to elected magistrates chosen on the principle of rotation in office, there was a council of aristocrats and a popular assembly, just as under the kings. What was basically new was the concept of limited terms for officials, the practice of voting for officials and laws. Moreover, for the first time in history, decisions by majority vote were considered binding on the whole community. In time, more and more inhabitants were involved in the affairs of each city, so that direct government by numerous persons developed. To provide security and public buildings, the heart of the city-state (which also possessed sufficient land for food production) was an urban center, with government buildings, a public meeting place (the *agora*), and a low hill (called *acropolis*) serving as a religious center. This is the beginning of the urbanization of Europe. So long as there were cities, Greek and Roman civilization carried on its special way of life, an entirely new conception of what life is for.

Such a way of life involved consent of the governed and continuous free discussion of public affairs. The benefits were many, and in such a participatory government there were also many obligations: military service for all men, who formed a citizen militia; payment of taxes; public services of many other kinds. The *polis* thus enlarged the scope of individual equality, at first among the aristocrats, later among all citizens. Each person was thought to possess an *arete*, or special excellence, which it was society's duty to allow to express itself to the full. Thus, for the first time in world history, we begin to find recorded the names of numerous individuals. More Greeks are known by name in the Classical Age than the total number of all human beings anywhere before since the beginning of time.

From their experience with life in the city-state, the Greeks were the first to proclaim freedom as the birthright of man. This meant both independence for each *polis* and freedom of the citizens from tyranny in their own midst. There are many expressions of the high value the Greeks placed on freedom, but both its meanings are found in the oath taken in 480 B.C. by the Greeks who united to oppose the Persian invasion: "I will not hold life dearer than freedom."

At the same time, the very existence of such an atmosphere of freedom among hundreds of independent city-states brought the Greeks their greatest weaknesses: frequent wars among themselves and an inability to unite in the face of common danger from foreign powers. Plato said, "Every city is in a natural state of war with every other, not indeed a proclaimed war, but everlasting." The cry of "peace" was frequently heard among the Greeks, but the priorities and realities were a state of war.

An enormous thrust was given to the Greek renaissance

by the great colonization movement that took Greeks in great numbers to faraway places between 750 and 550 B.C. Naturally, the effects of overpopulation in such a barren region as Greece would be felt very quickly. One safety valve was infanticide, which became a distinctive trait of Greek culture. But the unrest and suffering caused by excess population and land hunger mounted, for the technology to increase food production did not exist. The crisis led to a deliberate policy of siphoning off excess population by sending out colonies wherever suitable places could be found on the shores of the Mediterranean and the Black Sea.

This colonization movement was the first great planned population shift in world history. Many Greek colonies were founded in the western Mediterranean: on the large island of Sicily; on the coast of southern Italy; in southern France and on the east coast of Spain; on the shores of the Black Sea; and at a few places in North Africa, including the city of Naucratis (which means "Sea Power") in the Nile Delta in Egypt. Some of these Greek colonial foundations still exist today: Marseilles, Monaco, Naples, Syracuse, Istanbul (originally named Byzantium), to name only a few. The new Greek colonies became at once independent new city-states (for instance, Naples was called by the Greeks Neapolis, meaning "New City"); they retained cultural but not political ties with their mother city.

The by-products of this colonization movement were more important than the easing of the problems of land hunger at home: large-scale, long-distance trade and travel were revived on a scale never before known to man; the previously severed connections with the Near East and its cultural treasures were resumed; wealth increased tremendously; new horizons and new levels of sophistication followed; there was a greater sense of independence among these pioneering individuals. Thus, the lives and thinking of the Greeks were revolutionized. This first massive expansion of the Hellenes found them living from as far west as Spain to as far east as the ends of the Black Sea—a range of about three thousand miles. Thus, Hellas in antiquity really had no fixed frontiers: wherever Greek was spoken and Greek ways of living existed, there was Hellas. By 550 B.C., the expansion had stopped because there simply was no more suitable land available along the shores of the Mediterranean. Besides, strong powers, such as the Carthaginians and Etruscans, blocked further Greek settlement. New solutions for the feeding of more mouths had to be resorted to: conquests, empire, booty, and tribute. Not until the time of Alexander the Great two centuries later were new lands opened up to the Greeks—vast territory in the heart of Asia as far as India.

The Religion of the City-State

Each Greek city had its own special religious institutions maintained by the state for the well-being of the entire community. Polytheism (belief in many gods) was taken for granted; atheism was almost unheard of in antiquity, and devotion exclusively or excessively to one god was likely to be regarded as irreligious. On the whole, Greek religion was a cheerful religion, for the gods were highly anthropomorphic: that is, they were thought of as looking like and behaving like humans, though on a grander scale. Mere faith in the gods and living by a code of moral behavior had no relevance in Greek religion. Everything depended on what one said and did in dealing with the gods, that is, on proper prayers and sacrifices. A prayer was essentially a request for a favor of some sort—rainfall, success in business, protection in war, good health, the blessing of children. A sacrifice was something offered to a god in return for the favor granted, usually some food, such as an animal, a bird, or wine. To perform the ritual, the worshiper stood before a statue of the particular god or goddess in whose power lay the boon requested. The image of the god was ordinarily housed in a temple, which served as the home of the god. The last stage of the ritual was the sacrifice offered by the worshiper on the altar in front of the temple.

Greek religion was rather flexible: It had no dogmas, no Bible, no powerful priests. Among the many hundreds of gods and goddesses, a group of twelve, the Olympian gods, were thought to be the most significant divinities of the Greeks. They formed a kind of exclusive club living on top of Mount Olympus, the highest peak in Greece. Here, in a palace lived the king of the gods, the sky-god Zeus, with members of his family, each with specific functions—Hera (Zeus's queen), Hestia, Demeter, Poseidon, Athena, Apollo, Artemis, Hephaestus, Ares, Aphrodite, Hermes.

Life in a land like Hellas led to the sanctioning of the basic virtues of austerity and restraint by the threat of divine punishments. The belief was that there was a borderline in every aspect of life that a human might not cross without evoking the anger of the gods. The gods, it was thought, were jealous of humans, and so constantly kept a sharp eye on all of them. Anyone who overstepped the bounds of moderate behavior was said to be guilty of the sin of *hybris,* or excess. Whether such excess was willful (excessive ambition, pride, power, wealth) or involuntary (beauty, high intelligence), the sin of excess threatened the possessor. Therefore, the most Hellenic of all virtues was *sophrosyne,* or moderation, which implies self-control and caution concerning the consequences of all one's acts. The frequency with which the Greeks repeated the warning of moderation in everything is an indication of how difficult it was to maintain a nice balance between the yearning of the individual for personal distinction and the overall welfare of the community. The Greek city-state tended to level everybody within prescribed limits.

The religion of the city-state did not concern itself with the spiritual needs of the individual. To satisfy these needs, there grew up a number of so-called mystery-religions, which promised a happy afterlife to those initiated in them. The most important mystery-religions among the Greeks were the Eleusinian mysteries and the Orphic mysteries, which began to be popular in the seventh and sixth centuries B.C. These cults both involved special initiation ceremonies, including purification (sometimes by baptism), a communion meal, and the revelation to the initiates of certain carefully guarded secrets. It is surprising to find among the Greeks a widespread craving for purification, an indication of great insecurity and guilt feelings. Ceremonies were devised to free guilt-ridden persons from many sorts of taints.

A different side of Greek religious life is apparent in the various practices whose purpose was to reveal the future, an intriguing matter for men in any age. Among the Greeks, all sorts of signs and omens were studied for clues. Persons gifted with inner sight, called prophets and prophetesses, were believed to be inspired by a god, usually Apollo, with knowledge of the future. The most important sources of prophecy were oracles at temples, especially at Dodona and Delphi. At Dodona, the oldest Greek oracle, Zeus, in the form of a sacred oak tree, was thought to speak to humans through the rustling of the leaves, whose meaning was interpreted by priests and priestesses. The city of Delphi in the mountains of central Greece became almost a national religious authority for the Greeks because of the fame of its oracle of Apollo, god of prophecy. Questions were addressed to a priestess, the Pythia, sitting on a tripod, after sacrifices and the payment of temple fees, and her mysterious replies were interpreted by the priests. Even such an intellectual as the philosopher Socrates did not despise the wisdom of the oracle.

Despite the separateness of the Greek city-states, the Greeks possessed a strong Pan-Hellenic ("all-Greek") awareness, a realization that all Greeks shared a distinctive culture. Besides their common customs and language, Greeks everywhere shared a reverence for the great Pan-Hellenic festivals. Periodically, Greeks from all over the Hellenic world flocked to religious festivals held at Olympia, Delphi, Nemea, and the Isthmus of Corinth. The oldest and largest was the one held every four years in honor of Zeus at Olympia, in the northwest part of the Peloponnesus, which was believed to have been held for the first time in 776 B.C. A truce in all wars was declared three months before the festival began, to enable Greeks to travel to Olympia from the far-flung Greek lands, not only to honor Zeus but to participate in games held in this connection. For among the attractions at all the great festivals were athletic competitions for prizes.

The Greeks tended to view many human activities as occasions for competition to determine who were foremost in excellence in a particular field. Such competition might test excellence in horse racing, chariot racing, playing a musical instrument, singing, dancing, literary composition, athletics. The Greeks placed a higher valuation on athletic competition than any civilization in history, and they were the first people to develop organized sports.

There were no professional athletes among the Greeks in the Classical Age. The popular sports were boxing, wrestling, the *pancration* (a combination of boxing and wrestling), foot races, the *pentathlon* (a combination of five events), the discus throw, the javelin throw, and chariot racing. The prizes, much coveted as status symbols, were purely symbolic—a wreath of leaves. But victory in a Pan-Hellenic game brought fame to the athlete and to his native city.

The Rebirth of Literature and Art

About 750 B.C., the Greeks once more became a literate people when they borrowed the Semitic alphabet from the Near East. In adapting the Semitic alphabet, which had twenty-two consonants but no vowels, the Greeks changed some letters to vowel sounds and added several new letters to make a total of twenty-four. The Greek form of the alphabet soon spread widely, wherever Greeks lived, espe-

The Greek Alphabet

This table shows the final form of the Greek alphabet, with two earlier stages in its development; the classical form of the alphabet is similar to that adopted by Athens in 403 B.C. In the list of Latin/English equivalents, the letters in parentheses differ in form or in phonetic value from the Greek letters because they were transmitted to Rome through the dialects of Magna Graecia and through Etruscan. All letters are shown in their capital (majuscule) form. Small (minuscule) letters began to be used in Greek as early as the third century B.C. In Latin, majuscule letters continued to be used exclusively for inscriptions and for literary classics (Virgil, for example) until the end of the fifth century A.D.

EARLY GREEK (written from right to left)	A	ᗺ	⅃	⊲	ⱻ	Ⅎ	I	⊠	ⵑ	ꓘ	⅃	ꟽ
LATER GREEK (written from left to right)	A	B	Γ	Δ	E	F	I	⊗	ᛌ	Κ	L	⌐
CLASSICAL AND HELLENISTIC GREEK	A	B	Γ	Δ	E	—	Z	Θ	I	Κ	Λ	M
THE GREEK NAME	alpha	beta	gamma	delta	epsilon	digamma	zeta	theta	iota	kappa	lambda	mu
LATIN/ENGLISH EQUIVALENT	A	B	(C,G)	D	E	(F,U)	Z	(H)	I	K	L(I)	M

EARLY GREEK (written from right to left)	Ͷ	Ƹ	O	Γ	Ϙ	ꟼ	Ƹ	⊥	Y	Φ	X	Ψ	—
LATER GREEK (written from left to right)	И	Ξ	O	Π	Ϙ	P	M	T	Y	Φ	X	Ψ	Ω
CLASSICAL AND HELLENISTIC GREEK	N	Ξ	O	Π	—	P	Σ	T	Y	Φ	X	Ψ	Ω
THE GREEK NAME	nu	xi	omicron	pi	koppa	rho	sigma	tau	upsilon	phi	chi	psi	omega
LATIN/ENGLISH EQUIVALENT	N	(X)	O	P	Q	R	S	T	(U,V)	—	(X)	—	—

cially in the western Mediterranean. Here, it was eventually adopted by the Romans, whose form of the letters, with some changes, we still use today. Publication of the laws of many Greek city-states became possible, and in time literacy among the Greeks reached a higher level than in any previous civilization. Despite the emphasis on physical fitness and sports, intellectual excellence was valued in most Greek cities, especially in Athens. In Greek education, both mental and physical fitness were stressed, producing the ideal of the whole man. The older distinction between a hereditary aristocratic elite and the common man faded, for intellectual and athletic excellence might be found in any social class.

The unprecedented changes of the Greek renaissance, beginning about 750 B.C., stimulated individualism as well as enormous interest in the present, its triumphs, problems, conflicts. The appeal of epic poetry, with its stories of a bygone Heroic Age, began to wane. The aristocrats of the new age, proud of their own achievements and bursting with their own thoughts and feelings, were eager to speak for and of themselves in a manner suitable to the new times. Thus, lyric poetry—short poems expressing personal emotions and reactions to the contemporary scene—replaced epic as the aristocratic literature of the Greek renaissance.

About 800 B.C., a new motif began to appear among the geometric vase designs that had prevailed since the end of the Mycenaean Age: the human figure. This is the beginning of Greek humanism in art. Soon, the old geometric patterns were entirely displaced by scenes depicting human beings.

Renewed contact of the Greeks with Egypt in the seventh century B.C., after a lapse of five centuries, revolutionized Greek art. The Greeks traveling and living in Egypt were simply overwhelmed by the time-honored civilization. To this influence can be attributed the revival of monumental architecture in Greece—above all, the building of temples—and the introduction of lifesize sculpture.

No other people in history has devoted more of its creative energies and treasure to sculpture than the Greeks. Most Greek cities had so much public sculpture that they were virtually outdoor museums. Greek sculpture was created not for private homes but as community art, for social and religious purposes: statues of gods and goddesses, athletes, decorative reliefs on temples and tombs. The human figure, considered the most beautiful subject to model, served to portray timeless ideal types—gods, mythical heroes, athletes—rather than individual persons or actual historical scenes.

Archaic Greek art, whose favorite subjects were the nude male figure (*kouros*) and the standing draped female (*kore*), was deeply influenced by the stiff, mathematically designed Egyptian statues, with their symmetry of torso, fixed smile, and patterned hair. This stylized Egyptian art accorded with the Greek instinct for order, symmetry, and balance. But the Greeks, not bound by Egyptian tradition, were soon to create one of the great revolutions in the history of art.

As Greek genius in sculpture was asserting itself, the great glory of Greek architecture, the Greek temple, also made its appearance. Like the inspiration for sculpture, that for the "houses of the gods" came from Egypt, but the Greek national genius, resources, and requirements produced a new architectural form, the small temple. The idea of using columns in architecture also came from Egypt. To give elegance to the blank wall of the temple room, the Greeks often surrounded it with a row of columns, of the Doric, Ionic, or Corinthian order (or style). The white marble of the Greek temple was customarily painted with bright colors: blue, red, green, yellow, gilt. Today, very little of the ancient color has survived, so that we do not see Greek temples as the Greeks did.

Together with its famous marbles, Greece also possessed an abundant supply of clay of excellent quality. The designing and painting of vases became one of the outstanding Greek arts. For the first time in world art we know the names of ceramic artists, of potters and painters who proudly put their signatures on their creations. About 600 B.C. a new style — black figured vases — was invented in the city of Athens, from which it spread to all parts of Greece. In this style, the painter painted black figures on a red background, usually scenes from myths. Later, about 530 B.C., the color scheme was reversed, beginning the long line of famous red-figured vases with scenes on a black background that became the most popular style in Greece.

In the midst of this ferment, which brought with it a breaking up of the traditional patterns of society, we begin to hear the voices of the small farmer and the successful merchant and businessman crying out against the hardness of life, against injustice and the corruption of officials. In cities governed by hereditary aristocracies, where was one to seek redress of grievances? By 650 B.C. there was great unrest and instability in many Greek cities as a result of the failure of the aristocracy to keep pace with the rapidly changing times. The discontented among the nonaristocratic classes agitated for justice and political and economic reforms. To avert revolutions, the aristocrats in some cities chose respected arbitrators to work out a package of acceptable concessions.

Elsewhere, revolution led to a coup d'état by one of the aristocrats acting as leader of the disadvantaged classes. Such unconstitutional rulers were called *tyrants*. Yet the Greek tyrants were advantageous rulers who maintained peaceful regimes, lowered many social barriers and expanded the civil rights of the lower classes, and brought prosperity and brilliance to their cities. They were builders and patrons of the arts and literature. Tyrants ruled for life and passed on their power to their sons, but the system rarely lasted more than two generations anywhere. Tyranny was a transitional type of government among the Greeks. Later, the institution got a bad name, and Greeks of later generations glorified tyrant-slayers as heroes.

Greece and Persia

Greek city-states exhibited great variety in their traditions and institutions. Sparta, early frozen into a static military society, was unique. Coming as Dorian settlers in the southern part of the Peloponnesus about 1100 B.C., the Spartans organized their city-state about 750 B.C., and, like other Greek cities of the time, it was an affluent, aristocratic city with an interest in art and literature. When overpopulation led to land hunger, instead of sending out colonies (except for one at Tarentum in southern Italy), the Spartans solved their survival problem by invading and annexing the Messenians, fellow Greeks of the very fertile neighboring plains. The conquered Messenians were turned into serfs (called *helots*), compelled to work the land as sharecroppers for their masters the Spartans.

About 650 B.C., a rebellion of the Messenians alarmed the Spartans to such a degree that they mobilized themselves in a state of permanent military readiness. To keep the Messenian nine-tenths of the population in subjection, they approved a constitution (said to be the work of Lycurgus) that required all Spartan citizens, about nine thousand, to remain soldiers all their lives. The conservative nature of this society is underlined by several facts: that Sparta retained hereditary kings as figureheads of the state; that the minimum age for membership in the Senate (called *gerousia*) was sixty; and that Spartans were denied the right to vote until they were thirty.

Sparta escaped tyranny and maintained a stability often

envied in other Greek city-states—a stability that lasted without significant change for about three hundred years. But this highly regimented Greek society, in which all individualism was suppressed, was a political fossil. Most significantly, to achieve its ends of economic security, Sparta renounced many of the graces of Greek civilization—art, literature, philosophy. The bleak, drab city was virtually a military barracks. Boys began their training—exclusively military—at the age of seven, were subjected to harsh discipline, became soldiers at about eighteen, and remained in barracks until they were sixty. It was said in other Greek cities that Spartans were willing to die in battle because life was so unpleasant at home. Spartan women were also severely disciplined and subjected to gymnastic training to equip them for motherhood in a stern society.

Spartan foreign policy was isolationist, aimed simply at maintaining security at home through fear of the powerful Spartan army. Thus, Sparta gradually became the most powerful city in the Peloponnesus and solidified its position by military alliances with almost all Peloponnesian cities. Possessing the largest territory of any Greek city and the best army, it was the most powerful Greek city in the sixth century B.C.

The second largest city in Greece was Athens. By 700 B.C., the entire peninsula of Attica had peacefully united in voluntary union as a city-state, with Athens as its political center. The early aristocratic city-state of Athens was ruled by annual magistrates, called *archons,* selected from among the aristocrats. Like Sparta, Athens did not send out colonies. When economic and political unrest mounted, the aristocracy, to avert revolution, chose one of their number, Solon, to act as mediator, for the purpose of modernizing Athens. Solon's middle-of-the-road philosophy is summed up by his declaration, "I gave the common people such privilege as is sufficient for them. . . . I stood with a strong shield thrown before rich and poor, and would have neither prevail unrighteously over the other." His appeal and policies were typically Greek: reason, compromise, harmony, social justice. In place of political rights limited to those of aristocratic birth, Solon substituted the principle of wealth, and thus a major step was taken to upgrade the importance of each citizen in the political process. Solon sought principally to reduce friction and strengthen the city-state of Athens by involving more classes of citizens in government.

But many serious problems remained unsolved, and continued unrest led to the seizure of power by Peisistratus (560–528 B.C.), the great tyrant of Athens. He brought prosperity to Athens, made the city an important international power, and was a patron of artists and poets. His sons Hippias and Hipparchus, ruling after him as joint tyrants, were of lesser stature. They sought to continue the policies of their father, but when Hipparchus was assassinated, Hippias became arbitrary and despotic. A revolt in 510 B.C. led to the exile of Hippias and the restoration of the aristocracy to power.

In 508 B.C., Cleisthenes led a second revolution. To prevent both the restoration of the aristocracy and the return of tyranny, he established the first democracy in the world. He did this by making the entire citizen body the ultimate source of power, by creating election districts based on residence, opening up offices to all citizens, and establishing equality of electoral rights. Basic to this new form of government were equality before the law and equality of speech for all citizens. One remarkable provision of the Athenian democracy was ostracism—a device by which excessively powerful political leaders might by vote of the citizens be exiled from the city for ten years, as the punishment of the people for political *hybris*.

Beginning about 600 B.C., the Lydian Empire gradually forced the Greek cities of Asia Minor under its rule but left their cultural traditions undisturbed. (Indeed, the Ionian Greeks were the leaders of world culture; in the Ionian cities, particularly Miletus, occurred the great intellectual revolution that gave birth to philosophy and science.) An entirely new atmosphere was created, however, when Cyrus the Great in 550 B.C. founded the Persian Empire, launching a series of whirlwind conquests that were to unite most of the Near East under Persian rule. Among the areas the Persians conquered and annexed were Lydia, the Ionian Greek cities, Egypt, and the entire Middle East as far as sections of western India. With this unification of the East there was established the "Persian Peace" that brought stability and prosperity to western Asia for two hundred years, until it was shattered by Alexander the Great. But in democratic circles among the Ionian Greeks, intense anti-Persian feeling developed. The requirement of military service in the great international armies of Persia, the exaction of heavy taxes, and the imposition of one-man rule in every Greek city—a system the Persians regarded as more efficient—stirred them to rebellion. Aid was forthcoming from several Greek cities in Hellas, notably Athens and Eretria.

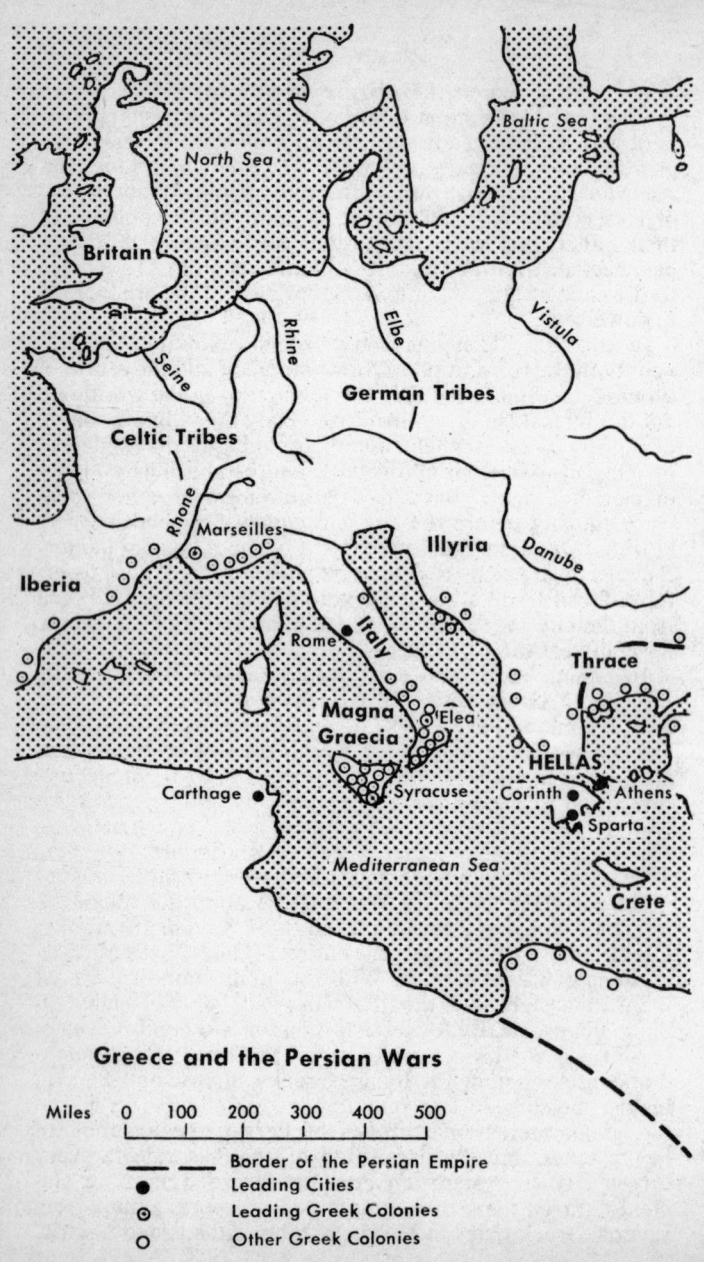

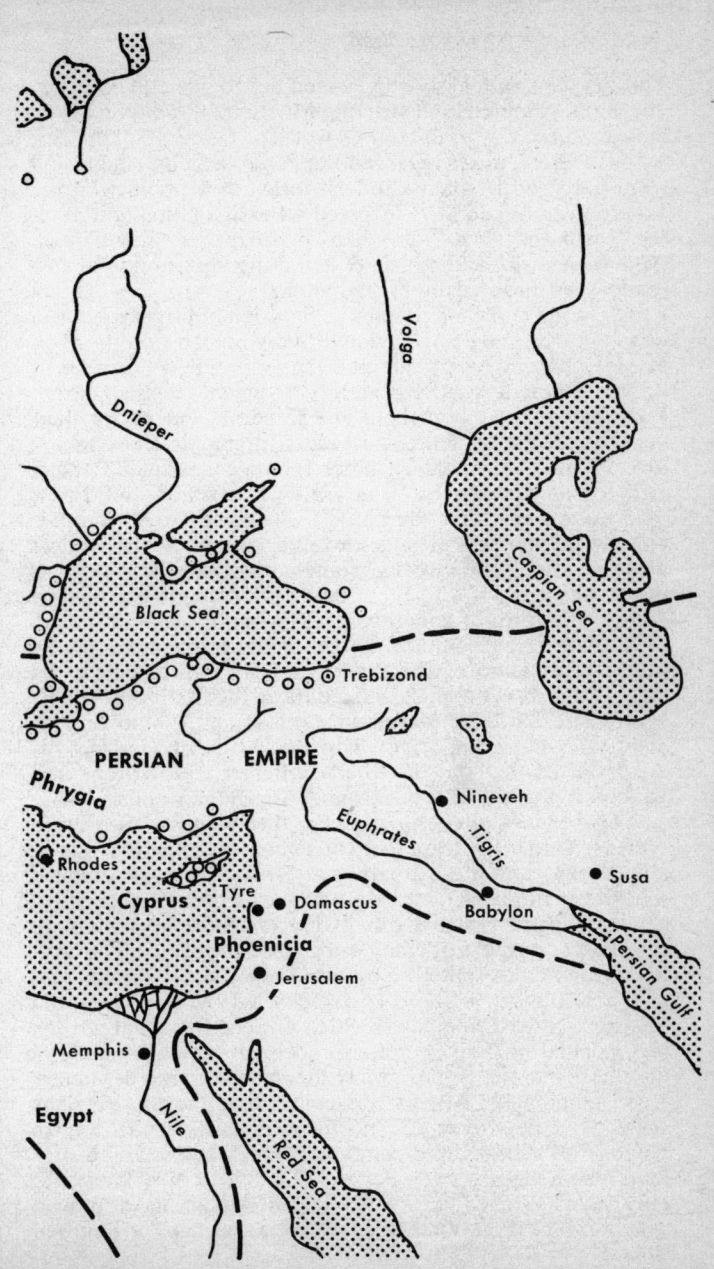

The Persians ruthlessly suppressed the Ionian Revolt (499–494 B.C.), completely destroying Miletus, the wealthiest and most cultured city of the Greek world.

Most Greek cities regarded Persian rule as inevitable and were prepared to make the best terms they could with the superpower. When they received a Persian ultimatum to offer "earth and water" as tokens of surrender, they agreed. Athens, Eretria, and Sparta rejected the very notion of surrender and ordered mobilization. In 490 B.C., the Persian King Darius launched a punitive invasion of Greece. Eretria was captured and destroyed, but the Athenians, on the plain of Marathon in Attica, about twenty-six miles northeast of Athens, won a stunning victory over the Persian army. Fighting for their homeland and freedom, indeed for their very survival, the Athenian citizen militia in the phalanx formation was more than a match for the conscripted Persian army. (The Spartans sent an army of two thousand, but it reached Athens after the battle.) The victory over the previously invincible Persians elevated Athens to the highest prestige among the Greeks. Some interpreted the victory as the result of the spirit generated by the recently established democratic form of government. The battle's significance in preserving Greek culture as one of the foundations of the future civilization of the West has been expressed by the great English economist and political theorist John Stuart Mill: "The Battle of Marathon, even as an event in English history, is more important than the Battle of Hastings. If the issue of that day had been different, the Britons and Saxons might still have been wandering in the woods."

Preparedness was now given the highest priority in Athens. Under the leadership of Themistocles, Athens built a huge navy and a great harbor at Piraeus, thus becoming a sea power in a few years. In 480 B.C., Darius's successor, his son King Xerxes, personally led a massive invasion with the express purpose of conquering all of Greece. Only thirty-one Greek cities united to oppose the Persians. At the Pass of Thermopylae, a force of Greeks led by three hundred Spartans under Leonidas shielded Greece for about a week in a suicidal holding operation, repelling wave after wave of the finest Persian troops. After the valiant Greek defenders were annihilated, Athens was evacuated, and the Persians seized and destroyed it. Shortly afterward, in the Bay of Salamis off Athens, the combined Greek ships won a brilliant naval victory over Persia. The Battle of Salamis not only saved Greece but swiftly ended Persian naval power. The next year at Plataea in Boeotia, perhaps a hundred thousand Greek soldiers inflicted an overwhelming defeat on the Persian force. About the same time, the Greeks in the western Mediterranean also faced mortal peril, at the hands of the powerful Phoenician colony of Carthage, which invaded the Greek island of Sicily. The defeat of the Carthaginians by Syracuse matched the triumph over Persia that preserved Greek freedom in the East. It was Greece's finest hour in her struggle for freedom and cultural integrity.

Athens, the "savior of Hellas," strove to maintain the unity that the Greek cities had achieved for the first time since the Trojan expedition, but Sparta withdrew into her customary isolation. Thus, the decisive factor in Greece was now Athenian naval power. The Athenians continued to maintain the largest navy of the time (two hundred to three hundred warships) and perfected the port of Piraeus as the greatest military and commercial harbor of the time. Under the leadership of Athens, a hundred and fifty Greek cities formed the Delian League as an alliance against Persia. Each member contributed ships or money to the war chest of the league, which met regularly at Delos.

When the threat of Persia was long a thing of the past, some cities of the Delian League announced their intention to withdraw. Athens compelled them to remain and used her power to force still other cities to join. In 454 B.C., by vote of the Athenian Assembly, the treasury of the Delian League was transferred to Athens, presumably for safekeeping. Even after a peace treaty was signed with Persia in 449 B.C., Athens held together about a hundred and fifty Greek cities, which continued to pay contributions into the treasury in Athens. Thus was born the Athenian Empire, the smallest in size and the shortest lived among the imperialisms of ancient times. The mastermind behind the Athenian Empire was the Athenian statesman Pericles, the highest elected official of the Athenian democracy.

The Golden Age of Athens

The period that followed the solidifaction of the Athenian Empire was dominated by Pericles and is thus often called the Periclean Age. This Golden Age of Athens, from about 460 to 430 B.C., was moulded by his creative personality, his faith in democracy and the common man, and his policies of making Athens both a showplace of beauty and the cul-

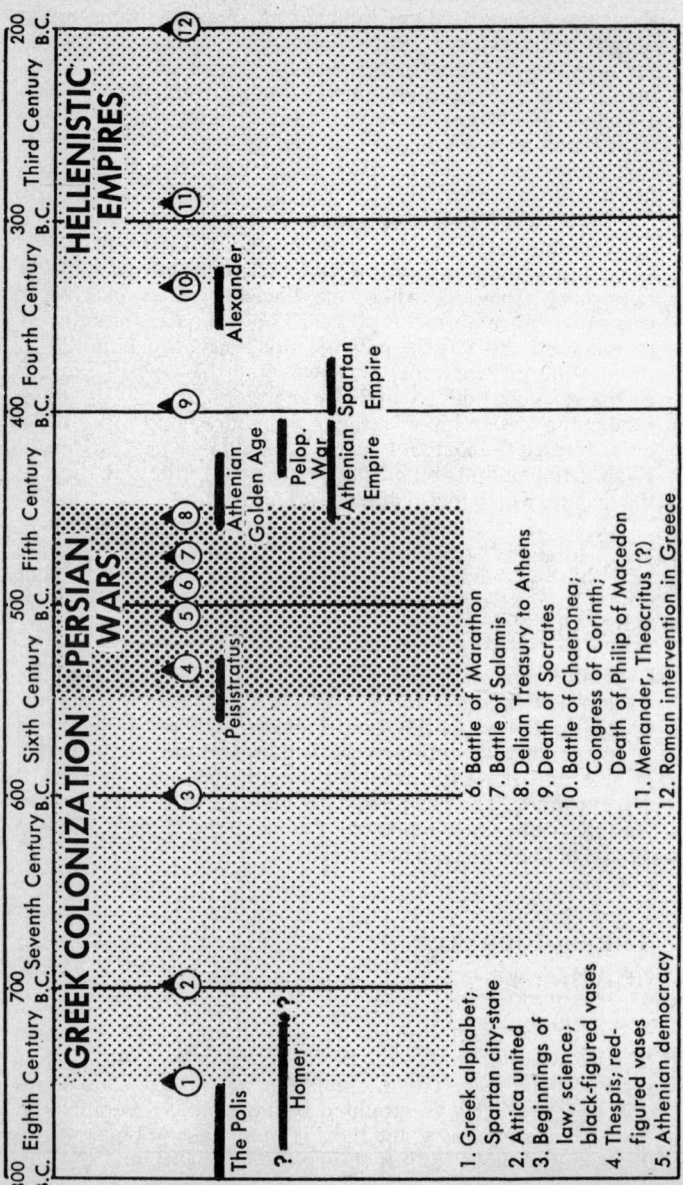

tural, political, and economic leader of Greece. The post he held was that of *strategos* (general), an annual office to which he was elected many times. To supply the manpower for Athens' far-flung naval empire, Pericles expanded Athenian democracy still further. His policy was based on the view that the ordinary man was capable of assuming political responsibilities to a degree not previously conceived. The ideal of Pericles was a versatile body of citizens, to be fostered by awakening the talents and abilities of every citizen, so that each could attain his own excellence. The needs of the community and the empire would thus be served, while at the same time the pursuit of personal happiness would also be fostered. In this way a society would be created in which a balance existed between the needs of the community and the individual.

Under the democratic constitution of Athens, perfected by Pericles, the ultimate power was in the hands of the entire citizen body (the *demos*). Every male citizen had the right to vote at the age of eighteen and participated actively in the mass meetings of the Assembly. Here, all laws and important decisions were determined by majority vote. The Athenian citizens were selected for many offices and public duties by lot rather than by formal election. Only the board of ten generals was actually elected.

Active participation in the Athenian democracy took up at least two days a week of an ordinary citizen's time, but citizenship was the privilege of only a small part of the total population—hardly ten per cent out of about three hundred and fifty thousand. Of the rest, perhaps one-third were slaves who did housework or manual labor both public and private. Athens also had numerous resident aliens whose principal activities were business and banking, which Athenian citizens tended to shun. Athenian women, the wives and daughters of citizens, were secluded at home, sharing neither the political democracy nor the social life of the male-dominated society. Altogether, the drastic limitation of the rights and responsibilities of citizenship was a serious defect in Athenian democracy. Moreover, those who *did* exercise the responsibilities of citizenship often showed themselves capable of serious blunders and of inefficiency and corruption in the conduct of the government. The Greeks, who invented democracy, were also the first to demonstrate how fragile and fallible an institution it is.

To make the Athenian democratic system work—it lasted for about two hundred years—leisure and the funds to provide it were indispensable. These were assured by slavery, the inferior status of Athenian women, heavy taxation of the rich, and tribute from the Athenian Empire. Without the wealth that poured into the treasury, their direct democracy could not have lasted very long. But because the system provided a high quality of life for its citizens, most Athenians believed in the empire and were prepared to risk their lives to preserve it.

Yet the priorities in the budget of the Athenian government during the Periclean Age were not given to war but to many social and public services. There were support for war orphans, war widows, and injured veterans; payments for many public services; expenditures on public festivals of all kinds and on public art and public buildings. Pericles did not strive to make Athens a great military power but rather to beautify it and make it the cultural center of the civilized world.

The educational aims of Athens, in contrast to Sparta's, were directed at developing the whole man as a versatile member of the democracy. While there was no public-school system, it was expected that all future citizens would receive at least an elementary education to the age of fourteen. Thus, Athens achieved in the Periclean Age the highest degree of literacy thus far attained in mankind's history. Jurors and many public officials were expected to know how to read and write, and everywhere in the city there were inscriptions and public notices on display as nowhere else previously in history.

Under the unique conditions in Athens in the fifth century, the harmony between the generations was shattered. There were many reasons for this loss of respect for tradition and the authority of the fathers and the older generation: the priority of the *polis* over the family, the political equality of youth at eighteen, the unprecedented pace of change, the liberating effects of education, growing esteem of knowledge, the respect for reason and dialogue in the democratic process. For the first time anywhere the generations were polarized. We can still read, in the *Antigone* of Sophocles, the intransigent defiance of idealistic youths against the arbitrary authority of parents, the older generation, and the government.

The Arts in Athens

Athens is the birthplace of tragedy and comedy. One way of worshiping the god Dionysus (or Bacchus), god of wine and the potency of nature, was the performance of a choral lyric (known as a *dithyramb*), sung and danced by a chorus in a circular dancing place, the Greek word for which is *orchestra*. Out of this literary protoplasm the Athenian Thespis, about 535 B.C., created the drama by adding an actor and thus composed the world's first tragedies. The tyrant Peisistratus promptly made the production of plays an official function of the government as part of festivals honoring the god Dionysus.

In democratic Athens, drama was a form of community art, produced for a citizen audience in the public Theater of Dionysus. In the fifth century the writers and performers were not professionals but citizens who gave their services, competing for prizes for the best play and best performances. Out of the hundreds of plays written—each intended for a single performance—only thirty-three tragedies (by Aeschylus, Sophocles, and Euripides) and eleven comedies (by Aristophanes) have survived. All these plays explore important contemporary problems and conflicts in dramatic form, with almost unlimited freedom of expression. Greek drama was thus less a form of entertainment than a medium of continuing adult education.

It was on the Acropolis, the low hill that served as the religious center of Athens, that Pericles chose to pour out the energy and wealth of his city in the beautification program that was to make Athens a showplace for all time. There was built the Parthenon (the temple of Athena, patron goddess of Athens), the architectural masterpiece of the Greeks. In its sculptured decorations, it commemorated the triumph of Athens over Persian despotism and the devotion of the entire community to its patron divinity. Near the Parthenon still stand the exquisite little temple called the Erechtheum and the small temple of Athena Victory. The monumental gateway at the entrance to the sacred precinct is called the Propylaea.

Elsewhere in Athens were public buildings like those to be found in other Greek cities: many temples and shrines; the Agora, both meeting place and market place; stoas, all-purpose colonnades with roofs as protection against sun and rain; the Council House; the Theater of Dionysus; the Odeum, a small covered theater for musical performances; the stadium, for athletic competitions; and the gymnasia, which served as both exercising grounds and educational centers. Most Greek cities were protected by walls, ever-present reminders of the constant wars. For the same reason, there were no aqueducts leading into Greek cities. The water supply came from the immediate area, from wells, springs, and cisterns, and each city was equipped with many fountains from which the people drew their water. Greek cities—even Athens—had no sewers, either, so that sanitary conditions were primitive. Their homes, even those of the wealthiest, were quite unpretentious, crowded together amidst narrow streets. The Greek spent most of his time out of doors in public places. The drabness of his home was one of the prices he paid for the advantages of urban life and civic involvement.

The beginning of the fifth century B.C. witnessed what was to be a revolution in world art as well as Greek art: the Greek sculptor discovered how to portray natural movement in the human figure. All archaic traits were soon eliminated, and the distinctive traits of Greek classical idealism became dominant: concentration on ideal beauty and the typical rather than the individual; balance, symmetry, and rhythm; harmony achieved through mathematical proportions; restraint, simplicity, majestic dignity, serenity, grandeur.

The Greek Enlightenment

Freedom of thought and speech prevailed in Athens during the fifth century as nowhere else before. Even so, the reliance on reason met with opposition when it led to conclusions that clashed with venerable traditions in religion or with the institutions of society. Among the mass of the people, there was indeed suspicion and hostility toward science as destructive of religion. Even among the intellectuals, the bewildering variety of systems devised to explain the universe, each based on reason and each claiming to have all the answers, eventually led to widespread skepticism.

Those who sought a higher education in Athens attended the schools of the Sophists ("men of wisdom"), the equivalent of college professors. The Sophists were all aliens; their teaching was very much in demand, and they received enormous fees for their instruction. The Sophists were basically rationalists, and in the name of reason they opposed traditional Greek religion and morality. All persons, the Sophists maintained, obey law and tradition only through fear of punishment. In morals there are no standards or principles that should be followed at all times and under all circumstances: In ethics there is only relativity. The fundamental characteristic of human nature, the Sophists held, is that each man does and believes in only what benefits his own self-interest. Thus, everyone is in a permanent state of war with everyone else for power and wealth. Similarly, in each state classes of people with common interests are constantly struggling with each other for advantage, and between states the guiding policy is power: Power triumphs, not principle. The Sophists taught the knowledge and skills useful for public officials and citizens under the democratic imperialism of Athens: public speaking and sophistic reasoning, a method of rhetoric calculated to win over any audience by clever argumentation without regard for truth. On the whole, the Sophists were ahead of their times in many respects. But the effect of their teaching was to stimulate the drive for personal power on the part of individuals, a tendency that ultimately was fatal to the city-state way of life. Among the Greeks there was always suspicion of intellectuals. Even during the Periclean Age, under a new law against irreligion, such men as Protagoras and Anaxagoras, two of the intellectual giants of the Greeks, were expelled from Athens, and some offending books were publicly burned—the first time in history that we hear of public burning of books.

Socrates

The principal opponent of the teaching of the Sophists was the Athenian philosopher Socrates. He was not a professional teacher like the Sophists and took no fees, but in the memory of man he remains as one of the greatest teachers of all time. He taught people to think more critically in one area, ethics. Countering the views of the Sophists, Socrates argued that there are moral truths and that the laws of ethical conduct—universal, unchangeable standards of behavior—can be discovered by the use of reason. To act virtuously one must first possess the knowledge of what is right and what is wrong. Conversely, affirmed Socrates, no one ever does wrong intentionally but only through ignorance of what is right. Therefore, when one learns what is right one will live a life of virtue, not one devoted to material things, bodily pleasures, and power. Such a life is true human happiness, and the practice of virtue is its own reward. Thus, not power but virtue triumphs, and the individual must always live in accordance with firm, reasoned ethical principles, even in the face of popular opinion and in defiance of the government.

In 399 B.C., in a period of national hysteria following the defeat of Athens by Sparta, Socrates at the age of seventy was indicted on charges of religious impiety and corrupting the youth. His conviction and execution by the Athenian democracy made him one of the greatest martyrs in the cause of human freedom. The stilling of his voice is also a symptom of the growing crisis of the city-state that was to result in the loss of all Greek freedom before the end of the fourth century. We must now turn our attention to the war that brought this crisis to a head.

The Peloponnesian War and Its Aftermath

The aggressive efforts of Athens to protect her imperial interests and win new political and economic advantages generated intense hostility in many of the freedom-loving Greek cities. Their fear drove them into the arms of the other major Greek power, Sparta, which also felt a growing alarm at Athenian might. Eventually, two powerful blocs of cities confronted each other — Athens and her empire, Sparta with her allies. Acting in the name of Greek freedom, authoritarian Sparta appeared as the "liberator" of Greece. When Pericles rejected a Spartan ultimatum demanding that Athens free all the cities under her control — tantamount to dissolving her empire — the Peloponnesian War broke out, in 431 B.C.

This disastrous war lasted, with intervals of truce, until 404 B.C. It was a war that pitted Athenian naval power against Spartan infantry. Unable to protect their farmlands, the Athenians evacuated the entire populaton of Attica into Athens, which relied on its fleet and harbor for supplies. In the second year of the war, a plague broke out in overcrowded Athens. One-third of the population died, including Pericles. New, more aggressive leaders stepped into his shoes, and the war went unrelentingly on, broken by a period of uneasy peace for a few years. Within Athens intense conflict developed between those who favored the war and those who opposed it. In 416 B.C., the more aggressive leaders of Athens embarked on a daring new policy, the conquest of the great island of Sicily in the west. But the huge naval force sent there in 415 B.C. was by 413 B.C. overwhelmingly defeated and practically wiped out. Almost every family in Athens was affected.

Soon, internal tensions, verging on chaos, tore Athens apart; portions of the empire revolted; the resources and spirit of the Athenians were not equal to the crisis. The defeat of Athens became inevitable when Sparta formed a military alliance with Persia. After great naval losses, Athens was blockaded by a fleet supplied to Sparta by the Persians, hereditary enemies of the Greeks. In 404 B.C., Athens surrendered unconditionally. The allies of Sparta demanded the total destruction of the conquered city, but Sparta, out of respect for the victors in the Persian Wars, saved the city from annihilation. But Athens lost her empire, her fleet, and for a time even her democratic constitution. Though her democracy was restored in 403 B.C., and she slowly recovered her economic strength, Athens was never again a great power. Yet she remained the cultural leader of Greece. The loss of life and wealth during the war was incalculable: Greece never really recovered from this disaster. After thirty years of pitiless warfare, the Greeks were impoverished and disillusioned, particularly with the institution of the city-state, which seemed to have failed them.

One of the effects of the war was to intensify the conflict of generations discussed earlier. After the disastrous conclusion of the war, many of the affluent and educated Athenian youth — the natural leaders of the postwar generation — refused to take any role in public affairs, or showed their rejection of the traditional way of life by antisocial activities of all kinds: excessive drinking, sexual looseness, squandering of wealth, idleness. The reaction of the older generation was a kind of backlash against freedom and democracy. This conflict was to last until the end of the fourth century when Athenian democracy was dead, and with it the respect for reason, the ancient civic humanism. Yet the decline of the city-state was not without some good side-effects, for with it went an enrichment of some aspects of Athenian culture.

The disillusionment, turbulence, and restrictions on freedom after the Peloponnesian War gave the death blow to classical Athenian tragedy and comedy, which were social functions of a confident democracy. The major interests in the fourth century changed to efforts to explain and understand the troubled history of the times. This shift was heralded late in the fifth century by the work of Thucydides, the first scientific historian, who wrote his *History of the Peloponnesian War* so that future statesmen might avoid the Greeks' mistakes. Oratory reached new heights as a highly practical skill in the shifting politics of an age of crisis. The greatest teacher of Greek oratory, Isocrates, and the greatest orator, Demosthenes, belong to the fourth century.

But it was Greek philosophy that achieved its greatest triumphs in this troubled age. Aware of the decay that was eroding the culture of the Greek city-state, Plato, a pupil of Socrates, and Aristotle, Plato's own prize student who became the tutor of Alexander the Great, devoted their lives to a fundamental rethinking of the foundations of their culture. Both Plato and Aristotle were imbued with Hellenic idealism. Both reflect the disappointments of a disillusioned age in their questioning of democracy. Both were profoundly rooted in traditional Greek values, convinced of the superiority of the Greek city-state over all other forms of government, the racial superiority of the Greeks, and the validity of slavery.

Plato's greatest work, the *Republic*, shows the influence of Spartan authoritarianism. The more realistic Aristotle, in his influential *Politics*, believed that the best practical state was one in which the middle class was dominant. Aristotle was especially a systematizer of knowledge, the founder of the sciences of biology, zoology, psychology, logic. Though limited by Greek perspectives, the achievements of Plato and Aristotle, two of the most extraordinary geniuses of all time, have profoundly influenced human thought and action ever since.

The fourth century, besides Platonism and Aristotelianism, also produced two other systems of thought and conduct as responses to the troubled times. Cynicism, founded by Diogenes, distrustful of all human motives, rejected all social obligations and material things, all conventions, and urged people to drop out of organized society to live a natural life. Similarly, Cyrenaicism advised people to concentrate on the search for happiness through the pleasures of the senses.

If the fourth century was a great age for Greek philosophy, it was also notable for a deepening and refinement of the arts. Throughout the century, typical Greek public buildings continued to be built in Greek cities in the traditional manner. In the field of sculpture, Greek idealism was somewhat modified by individualizing trends, as the ideals of the city-state declined. In response to the changing mood, artists began to portray softer human qualities, especially human weaknesses: compassion, sadness, pathos, suffering. In turning aside from the values of the male-dominated city-state, artists now gave greater scope to the female figure. Although by the fourth century the classical style in art was beginning to lose its former assurance, Greek genius was still capable of producing a remarkable number of great works of sculpture. To this century belongs, for example, probably the best known Greek artist, Praxiteles, whose nude Aphrodite (goddess of love) at Cnidos, standing in soft, languorous beauty, was the most famous ancient statue next to Phidias' Olympian Zeus and Athena Parthenos, created at the height of the Athenian Golden Age.

The Coming of Alexander the Great

Before the end of the fourth century, a solution of sorts to the Greeks' problems would impose itself through the power of Philip and his son, Alexander the Great, rulers of Macedon, the semibarbarous kingdom immediately north of Hellas. In the meantime, the Greeks tried various expedients to extricate themselves from their difficulties.

The Greek cities had paid a ruinous price for their narrow patriotism and their jealously guarded independence. The Peloponnesian War had revealed and deepened the Greeks' fatal weakness: their inability to end the intercity warfare or to form a united Greece. As the century unrolled, warfare and fierce internal struggles between rich and poor, democrats and oligarchs, continued to drain the cities' manpower, wealth, and inner strength. The results were a decline in civic spirt and an avoidance of public responsibilities: many turned their backs on politics and sought to evade military service.

When masses of citizens withdraw from involvement in their cities, "strong men" arise to fill the vacuum. For the first time in Greece, professionals appear in many fields: professional soldiers, generals, politicians, even athletes. As brutalizing intercity warfare and internal disorders increased in the fourth century, three possible solutions were proposed: the establishment of regional federal leagues of cities, each of which would relinquish some of its jealously prized autonomy; the negotiation of a general peace treaty guaranteeing freedom and autonomy to all Greek city-states (a plan never realized); and, finally, a massive invasion of the Persian Empire that would solve Greek economic problems by obtaining Persia's wealth and siphoning off large numbers of Greeks into Asia.

In 404 B.C., Sparta, the "liberator" of Greece, had stepped into Athens' shoes and attempted to rule large areas of Greece. The Spartan Empire was short-lived. The Spartans' ineptness and brutality alienated many Greek cities, which formed a military alliance against her. Overwhelmingly defeated in the Battle of Leuctra (371 B.C.), Sparta was forever reduced to a second-rate power; and after 350 years of subjugation to Sparta, the Messenian helots finally regained their freedom.

The city of Thebes succeeded to Sparta's position as the leading Greek power but survived only ten years of empire when a new coalition of Greek cities destroyed its power (362 B.C.). Greece lay utterly prostrate, exhausted and dispirited. The yearning for peace was very strong, but the tradition of sovereign independence for each city was stronger. Many Greeks felt that only a leader from outside Greece could save their society from extinction.

Such a leader appeared in King Philip of Macedon. Macedon was a tightly unified monarchy with a powerful army, outstanding generals, and a politically astute, ambitious king. By shrewd diplomacy and by bribery ("I can take any city into which I can drive a donkey loaded with gold," he once said), Philip made formidable inroads into Greece, and pro-Macedonian factions sprang up everywhere.

Resistance was finally organized by the Athenian statesman Demosthenes, who, attacking the Macedonians as barbarians and Philip as a despot, organized support for the freedom and autonomy of the Greek city-states. The coalition of cities mobilized under Demosthenes' leadership was, however, no match for the Macedonians. At the fateful Battle of Chaeronea in Boeotia in 338 B.C., Philip became master of Greece. The Athenian orator Lycurgus said of those who fell at Chaeronea: "They alone in all Greece had the freedom of Greece in their bones; for they died as Greece fell into slavery; with their bodies the freedom of Greece was buried."

At the Congress of Corinth in 337 B.C., a united Greece finally came into being at the command of Philip, and thus a foreign king was chosen commander-in-chief of the combined Macedonian and Greek armies. Philip proposed to solve the Greeks' problems by conquering the Persian Empire. An invasion force of fifty thousand was mobilized, and war was declared. In 336 B.C., before he could embark on his ambitious program, Philip was assassinated. At the age of twenty, his extraordinary son Alexander inherited his power and his plans.

When Alexander succeeded his father, he had already absorbed the Greeks' hostility to the Near East and their sense of racial superiority. Indeed, his tutor Aristotle had advised Alexander to consider non-Greeks as "animals and plants." But this prejudice was to be profoundly altered by his contacts with the great Persian civilization. At twenty, Alexander assumed his father's position as commander of the Macedonian-Greek armies and promptly invaded Persia. One of the greatest military and organizational geniuses of all time, in thirteen years he would conquer and unify Greece, Egypt, and the entire East as far as western India. Fighting only four pitched battles, he and his armies marched over twenty thousand miles; his plan was to continue until he reached the ocean, but his troops mutinied in India and refused to go any farther.

Reluctantly, he returned to organize the largest empire thus far in the history of the world, supplanting the Persian Empire that he had destroyed. Alexander's policy was to establish a lasting world empire based on the cooperation of the Macedonians, Greeks, and Persians. Wherever he went, he built new cities in the Greek style as centers of the new culture. (His most famous foundation, Alexandria in Egypt, is still one of the great cities of the world.) He sought to develop a corps of army officers and administrators and by his policy of racial fusion to create a new interracial ruling class. He ordered his officers to marry Persian women, and he himself took as his wife the daughter of an Eastern noble. Alexander became convinced that he was of divine origin and demanded worship in his lifetime. To such a concept of a god-ruler on earth the Near East was long accustomed, but for the Greeks it was a difficult adjustment, though they had long worshiped dead benefactors as demigods.

Alexander brought a new epoch to world history. He ended the autonomous city-state as an institution. Greek cities continued to exist as urban centers, but with little or no independence, like cities in modern nations. One of the great achievements of Alexander's conquests was the spread of Greek civilization to Egypt and to Asia as far as India. A new world civilization extending from the Aegean Sea to India had been created and was to last a thousand years until the Arab conquests of the seventh century A.D. This new culture — a blending of Greek culture with the civilizations of the Near East — soon spread to the West. The most important beneficiaries were the Romans, who eagerly adopted it and spread it thoughout Western Europe. Alexander's conquests and policies Hellenized the world.

The Hellenistic Age

This new culture we call Hellenistic, to distinguish it from the previous Hellenic civilization, by this time virtually extinct. Hellenistic culture is Greek culture adapted to and modified by other cultures, and we call its varieties Greco-Egyptian, Greco-Indian, Greco-Roman, and so on. It involved a mixture of races and cultural values, though always with the Greek predominating. The centers of Hellenistic culture were great cities such as Alexandria, Ephesus, Pergamum, Syracuse, Antioch, the island of Rhodes; in this new era, the cities of Hellas were no longer of much account. A new form of Greek called *koine* (the "common" language) became an international tongue. Because of the general uniformity of Hellenistic culture, such ideas as the brotherhood of man and cosmopolitanism as an attitude of life developed, as compared with the previous more narrow localism of the Greek *polis*.

In the rapid Hellenization of the East, even the Jews were affected by the diffusion of Hellenism. A Jewish holiday, Chanukah, still commemorates the liberation of the Jews from Greek domination in the second century B.C. Far to the East, many Greeks came to India as travelers, explorers, settlers, artists, even rulers—in greater numbers than any European people until the British conquest. Hindu art is Greco-Buddhist: the first statues of Buddha were created under Greek influence in imitation of the Greek god Apollo. A Greek king, Menander, conquered a large empire in India about 200–150 B.C., was converted to Buddhism, and is still venerated today in India as a Buddhist saint under the name of Milanda. Today, in the Punjab of India the word for philosopher is *aflatoon*, a corruption of the name Plato. An early Hindu work says of the Greeks: "They are barbarians, but the science of astronomy originated with them and for this reason they must be revered as gods."

Alexander's dream of the unity of the known world ended with his early death in 323 B.C., after which his empire was torn apart by his successors and generals. The characteristic governments of the Hellenistic Age in the East were powerful monarchies supported by the theory of the divine right of kings and by large bureaucracies. Severe controls over freedom were imposed, and the Greek cities everywhere had little power, however much they liked to maintain the semblance of freedom. Such leading Greco-Macedonian kingdoms as Egypt, Seleucid Syria, Pergamum, and Macedonia left a legacy of international instability in their jockeying for power. There was continuing international tension marked by frequent wars, economic distress, and revolutions.

Unrest and confusion ravaged the whole world for hundreds of years, engulfing the western Mediterranean. In this world crisis, about 200 B.C., the Romans, whom some Greeks called "the barbarians of the West," intervened in the turbulent affairs of the Hellenistic states. The Romans were the best soldiers, organizers, and administrators in the world, already masters of the western Mediterranean. As Rome's international commitments grew, she intervened more and more in the East. Through protectorates, spheres of influence, treaties, and outright conquest, Rome gradually absorbed into her own empire the entire Hellenistic East. In 196 B.C., Rome proclaimed the freedom of the cities of Hellas, but intercity warfare soon broke out again. Exasperated, the Romans increased their direct control of Greece and, in 146 B.C., destroyed Corinth, one of the great Greek cities, as a terrifying warning to the eternally quarrelsome Greeks. Finally, all of Greece was converted to a province of the Roman Empire. Step by step, other parts of the Hellenistic East were annexed by Rome; in 30 B.C., with the death of Egypt's last Macedonian ruler, the famous Queen Cleopatra, and the annexation of Egypt, the Roman absorption of the entire Hellenistic world was complete. Peace finally came to the Mediterranean, and under Roman power for the first time in history the region was unified as *mare nostrum* ("our sea"). It was to remain so for about five hundred years.

The insecurity of the Hellenistic world and the destruction of the Greek city-state as a way of life left most Greeks with a feeling of alienation, loneliness, and anxiety. Extreme individualism became the dominant value, for the individual felt lost in the immensity of the vast monarchies, with no sense of real belonging, no social values, no confidence in controlling his own destiny. A Greek philosopher of the age, Timon of Phlius, said of Hellenistic man:

As the individual walked through the streets of the great cities, he was lost in the crowd, become a simple number in the midst of an infinity of human beings like himself, who knew nothing about him, of whom he knew nothing, a man who stood alone in bearing the weight of life without friends, without reason for living. . . .

Yet so traditional was the Greek love of freedom that this yearning now took the form of a search for inner freedom in an unstable, unpredictable world.

One system of thinking and living in response to this need was created by Epicurus of Athens. Epicureanism, which had a powerful appeal throughout antiquity, was basically a revolt against the city as a focus of injustice and the anonymity and anxieties of the individual. To secure peace of mind, Epicurus forbade participation in politics, marriage, having children. In place of conventional living, he urged friendship, a concept involving love of one's fellow man rather than distrust and competition. This idea swept the world. "Friendship," said Epicurus, "goes dancing around the world bidding us all awake and pass on the greetings of happiness to each other." "The Friends," as Epicureans were called, offered each other hospitality all over the world wherever they went.

For peace of mind, the Epicurean was advised to live in the country, practice moderation, and study science. The Greek atomic theory was the basis of Epicurean science; the universe, Epicurus taught, is made up entirely of matter, consisting of atoms, and empty space. Man should try to understand the universe in these material terms so as to overcome fear of the gods and of death. Epicurus taught that the gods have no power, that the soul is not immortal, and that there is no afterlife. Because Epicurus taught them how to eliminate fears and live with peace of mind, his followers called him the "savior of mankind." He was indeed a kind of missionary to the Hellenistic world, a Greek predecessor of St. Paul.

The competing philosophy, also concerned with individual peace of mind, was Stoicism, founded by Zeno, whose system took its name from a *stoa* in Athens where he conducted his school. Appearances to the contrary, taught Zeno, this is the best of all possible worlds. Therefore, people should not turn away from it but accept it. Everything that exists and happens in the world is part of universal nature, which is itself God, the Father of all. Each person's soul is thus part of God and therefore divine and immortal, and in this sense all men are brothers. All that happens in the world is predetermined by God, and since all is fated, we must accept and endure everything, even the most intense suffering. Actually, in such a perfect world there can be no evil. If one lives by reason, that is, understands the world as a prearranged machine, suppresses all emotions toward other people and material things, the reward is peace of mind. Marriage, children, doing one's duty in some commitment to society are natural and proper.

In place of politics, the Greek intellectuals were now devoting themselves to scholarship and science. In Alexandria in Egypt, under royal patronage, the brains of the civilized world were gathered together in a research institute known as the Museum. Scholars in the humanities and science were subsidized to lend glory to the kingdom of Egypt as a center of Greek culture. A library of seven hundred thousand volumes, the greatest in the world until modern times, was collected for their use. Here, they studied "The Classics" of Greek literature, already considered models of perfection. The scholars of the Museum did research mostly into the past, organizing knowledge, writing encyclopedias, literary criticism, and commentaries on Homer's epics and other treasured works of Greek literature.

The Hellenistic Age was also the golden age of Greek science, one of the most memorable periods in the history of science. The period produced Euclid's *Elements of Geometry,* a textbook still used today; the discoveries of Archimedes, the greatest scientist of the ancient world and one of the world's great mathematical geniuses; the theories of Aristarchus, the first to maintain that the sun, not the earth, is the center of our world, and that the earth moves around the sun; the discoveries of Eratosthenes, who accurately calculated the circumference of the earth and proclaimed that the earth was a sphere, stating that if one sailed West across the ocean one would reach India. Many brilliant discoveries in medicine were made in the Hellenistic period. (Greek medical knowledge was systematized several centuries later by the Greek physician Galen, and his views remained the basis of Western medicine for over a thousand years.) Similarly, the astronomical system of the scientist Ptolemy, based on Hellenistic thought, dominated the human mind until the Renaissance. Despite this explosion of scientific knowledge, the Hellenistic scientists, like their Greek predecessors, did not put their knowledge to practical use, and again almost no technological progress was made by Greek science.

In this new age, with so much study and imitation of "The Classics," there was little original literature. Most of what was written tended to be artificial and bookish, unrelated to real life. Shorter poems were preferred to large works. A new direction was given to literature by contemporary interest in the country and in home life with all its realistic everyday concerns.

In two literary forms, however, there was a renewal of creativity: in pastoral poetry (about the lives and loves of shepherds) and realistic comedy. Theocritus is the "Father of Pastoral Poetry," author of the famous *Idyls* ("Little Pictures"), which has influenced this branch of literature ever since. The most important new branch of Hellenistic literature was the New Comedy. This was so called to distinguish it from the previous Old Comedy concerned with the civic life of Athens. New Comedy, written solely for entertainment, dealt realistically with the everyday affairs of middle-class Greeks, mostly their love affairs. Of the many plays written in this period by about seventy writers, only those of the Athenian Menander have survived, rediscovered in the twentieth century when they were brought to light on papyrus rolls found in Egypt. It is characteristic of the age that for all of Menander's wit, elegant style, and good plots, there is not a single reference in his plays to the momentous events of his time, which was the period of the struggle for Alexander's empire. Yet these plays of the New Comedy had an enormous influence, especially on the Roman writers of comedy Plautus and Terence, who transmitted this literary form to the Western world. The New Comedy is the basis of modern comedy.

Few changes in Greek architecture occurred; and at the end of the fourth century Greek vase painting lost its appeal and came to an end. New centers of sculpture arose in the Hellenistic period: Pergamum, Alexandria, Rhodes. Sculptors worked principally for the kings and the rich, not for their cities. The sculpture of the age now glorified the Hellenistic kings in realistic portraits. In addition to the traditional public uses of sculpture to portray gods and goddesses, athletes, and scenes from mythology, much sculpture was created to decorate the private homes of the wealthy. New subjects made their appearance: scenes of everyday life and historical events. The restraint, calm dignity, and concentration on the typical that had characterized classical Greek sculpture were displaced by individualism and the portrayal of strong emotion and violent action. Famous Hellenistic statues, the pride of European museums today, are: Aphrodite of Melos (the so-called Venus de Milo); the Victory of Samothrace, a masterpiece of intense movement and energy; the Laocoön group, once considered by Michelangelo to be the greatest work of art ever made; and the sculptures of the Great Altar at Pergamum, depicting the victory of the Greeks over barbarians, the largest composition of ancient art.

With the writings of Menander and Theocritus in the early part of the third century B.C., Greek creativity in literature may be said to cease. A century later, about 150 B.C., all creativity in Greek sculpture suddenly came to a halt. It was in Rome that the wealth and the art patrons were now concentrated; and Greek sculptors seeking their fortune migrated in great numbers to the new capital of the world. Here, the new masters of the Mediterranean world employed them to beautify their city and their homes and villas. Greek artists lost their Greek individuality. The victory of Rome sounded the death knell not only to the last tatters of Greek freedom but also to Greek originality. But this gifted people handed on the torch of Greek culture to the Romans, and that is one of the basic reasons why the Romans became so important in moulding the fabric of our own civilization.

The Beginnings of Roman Civilization

When we turn from Greece to Rome, we do not find anything to match the Greek genius for artistic creation and speculative thought. Nor do we find the fatal flaw of Greek civilization, the inability to achieve lasting unity that ultimately cost the Greeks their freedom. The mark of Roman culture is a sense of order, a masterly talent for organizing both themselves and others. If Rome lacked the creative richness of Greek culture, what the city of Rome accomplished was unprecedented in human history: the unification not only of Italy but of much of the known civilized world under an acceptable government that endured for five hundred years. For the *Pax Romana* ("Roman Peace") was a reality: an era of relative peace such as the world had not known before and has never attained since.

The style of life and thought that the Romans spread throughout their world has remained one of the foundations of Western civilization. But it was Greek culture that humanized this style of life and makes it deserving of our attention today. The creation of Greco-Roman culture was a slow process of adaptation of Hellenic achievements to the Roman national character and needs. As everyone knows, Rome was not built in a day.

64 *Greek and Roman Civilization*

| 1200 B.C. | Twelfth Century B.C. | 1100 | Eleventh Century B.C. | 1000 | Tenth Century B.C. | 900 | Ninth Century B.C. | 800 | Eighth Century B.C. | 700 | Seventh Century B.C. | 600 B.C. |

ITALIC MIGRATIONS

ETRUSCAN MIGRATIONS

ROMAN KINGDOM

Greek Colonization in Italy

①

1. Founding of Rome

The peninsula of Italy was well endowed with agricultural and pasture land to support a large population. Yet though Italy lies only fifty miles west of Hellas—at the Strait of Otranto off the southeastern tip of the Italian peninsula—civilization and its urban life did not come to Italy until about 750 B.C. Rome itself did not become a city until about 625 B.C., almost seven hundred years after the height of the Mycenaean Age of Greek culture.

The late development of Italy was partly due to its distance from the birthplaces of civilization in the Near East. Furthermore, the fertile plains of Italy are on the western side of the peninsula, cut off on the east by the Apennine Mountains, which retarded the westward flow of civilization. Like Greece, Italy is highly mountainous and has few rivers of any size. But unlike Greece, in its two hundred miles of coastline, Italy has only a few good harbors. Italy did not develop a commercial culture. For a long time the Italic peoples were not affected by contact with the varied cultures overseas.

About 1200 to 1000 B.C., the Italic tribes had migrated to Italy from Central Europe in a western thrust of the great population shifts that brought about, as we have seen, the destruction of the Hittite Empire and the Mycenaean culture. Like the Greeks, the Italians spoke various dialects of the Indo-European family of languages.

The first people of Italy to develop an urban civilization were the Etruscans, who migrated by sea from Asia Minor about 1000 to 900 B.C. They were soon followed by the Greeks, who established themselves in southern Italy and in Sicily, founding colonies on the coasts. Later, about 400 B.C., marauding Gauls (Celts from what is now France) invaded Italy and reached as far south as Rome but withdrew across the Apennine Mountains and settled the great Po Valley. Thus there was a great diversity of racial stock, languages, and cultural patterns in Italy. It was one of the great achievements of the city of Rome that it succeeded in unifying this patchwork of peoples.

We are somewhat handicapped in our knowledge of the remarkable culture of the Etruscans, who occupied central Italy. We have been unable thus far to decipher their language, though it was written in an alphabet borrowed from the Greeks and we possess some ten thousand Etruscan inscriptions. It was through the Etruscans, and soon the Greeks, that the West first became literate. The Etruscans were pioneers in still another way: They introduced the city to Italy. Etruscan culture had a highly developed art, distinguished by its monumental tombs, grandiose temples, wall painting, and sculpture, including realistic sculpture. Etruscan art was the dominant art in central Italy for about six hundred years, just as Greek art prevailed in the south, until Roman art became established. The Etruscans were a very superstitious people, obsessed with gloom about death and with efforts to forecast the future by examining the entrails of animals, especially their livers.

An extensive Etruscan Empire grew up, extending into the Po Valley in the north and as far south as the plain of Campania. (Among their conquests was the plain of Latium, settled by the Italic Latin people that embraced the region of Rome.) But by 400 B.C., revolts within and the invasion by the Gauls had destroyed their empire, and their power and affluence waned. The Etruscans' greatest achievements were in engineering. Their most serious shortcoming was the inability, like that of the Greeks, of the Etruscan cities to unite for common purposes. The Etruscans, who ruled Latium for a century, had an enormous influence on many aspects of Roman culture.

The other great influence on Roman culture was, from the beginning, Greek. The Greek colonization movement throughout the Mediterranean from 750 to 550 B.C. brought numerous Greeks to southern Italy and Sicily. There were so many Greek city-states in southern Italy that the Italians in the north called this area *Magna Graecia* ("Great Greece"). Like those in Hellas, the numerous Greek cities in Italy were incapable of taking common action or eliminating frequent intercity warfare. The Romans were fortunate to have as their nearest neighbors such highly civilized peoples as the Etruscans and the Greeks. From the Greeks, in time, the Romans were to borrow and adapt to their needs many aspects of the higher civilization of the Hellenes.

There was a third important influence on Rome's beginnings, though of a different kind. After the decline of the Etruscans, the most powerful force in the western Mediterranean was Carthage, a Phoenician colony on the coast of North Africa, less than a hundred miles from Sicily. The Carthaginians, a Semitic people, were a commercial power, with colonies in many places in the western Mediterranean, in Sicily, Corsica, Sardinia, Spain. For about three hundred years, Carthage, for the benefit of its merchant princes, closed the Straits of Gibraltar to all but its own shipping. Carthage was to affect the destiny of Rome enormously.

The Roman Kingdom

Though the origins of the Roman kingdom are Italic, Rome bears an Etruscan name. About 625 B.C., Etruscan conquerors transformed into a city the villages the Latin and Sabine tribes had built on a group of seven low hills about fifteen miles from the mouth of the Tiber River. The spot was a strategic one, with great advantages for trade and military security. For over a hundred years, Rome had Etruscan kings, the Tarquins, until about 500 B.C., when a patriotic revolution drove them out. To the Etruscans, the Romans owed the draining of the swampy area near the Tiber, the establishment of the great Temple of Jupiter, the Roman sky-god, on the Capitoline Hill, and the introduction of the alphabet, the sport of gladiators, and many religious rites and customs.

In Roman tradition, the city's origins are a little different: Rome was believed to have been founded in 753 B.C. by Romulus, the first of her seven kings, who, with his twin brother Remus, was said to have been nursed by a she-wolf, one of the most famous symbols of Rome. Romulus was thought to be a descendant of the Trojan prince Aeneas, who wandered the Mediterranean with a few faithful companions after the fall of Troy until he settled near the future site of Rome. Our knowledge of the period when Rome had kings is unreliable, but we do know that the Romans, like the Greeks in general, had a triple division of government: an executive, a Senate (council of elders), and an assembly of the people. The king was elected for life by the heads of the aristocratic families and, in keeping with the Roman feeling for order, had almost unlimited authority in the political, military, and religious spheres.

We can observe, in the earliest period of Roman society, a strong concept of authority and seniority. The term *patres* for Senators, *patria* for fatherland, *patricians* for the upper class, *pater familias* as the title of the head of each family, *pater patriae* ("father of his country") as a title of honor for some distinguished Romans later—all these testify to the concentration of authority at the top of the Roman social pyramid.

Roman myths and traditional stories of this early period developed relatively late compared with those of Greece. The best-known Roman tales are patriotic rather than religious or heroic in theme, as the Greeks' tended to be, and emphasized discipline, courage in battle, seriousness of behavior, a sense of duty, and similar values that were to be important throughout Roman history. Among these values, the Greek ideal of individual excellence had no place.

The Roman Republic

About 500 B.C., the Roman Republic was established; it was to endure for about five hundred years. The founding fathers of the Republic were Roman aristocrats who united to drive out their Etruscan king. In place of a king who held power for life, they now elected two magistrates with equal authority called consuls, who held office for just one year. The concept of checks and balances was thus introduced. Additional checks on the consuls' power were provided by the Senate, which now consisted of ex-magistrates with the function of advising the consuls; and by the people, who as before gathered in assemblies but had very limited power.

The founding of the Republic, which we shall examine in detail presently, proved to be the first step in the city's evolution toward world domination. In a little over a hundred years (400–272 B.C.), the Republic brought all Italy under its power. After the expulsion of the Etruscans, Rome went through a critical period, struggling for survival at the very time when Athens was at the height of its great age. By 400 B.C., Rome had made itself the most powerful Latin city. Under Roman leadership, the rights of trade and intermarriage were shared among all the Latin cities on the plain of Latium, which gradually developed a common culture.

In their march to victory, the Romans developed many of their institutions. Long periods of warfare required a standing army, which began to receive pay for military service. Accordingly, the Romans established the policy of looting conquered cities for the benefit of the Roman public treasury. Usually, also, a portion of the conquered area was annexed to Rome and became public land.

The Republic suffered an almost fatal setback in 390 B.C. when the city was captured and destroyed by the semicivilized Gauls. Within fifty years, however, Rome was again strong enough to overwhelm all the Latins with her military might. New policies then introduced served as guidelines to future Roman treatment of conquered territory: Latin cities that surrendered were spared destruction and looting, and some were even granted full or partial Roman citizenship. To prevent them from ever uniting against her, Rome now employed for the first time her famous tactic of "divide and rule." Each city was compelled to sign an individual treaty with Rome, which forbade treaties with other cities and provided for trade and intermarriage only with Rome. Most important, the Latin cities were obligated to provide contingents of soldiers for the Roman armies.

In conquering the aggressive Samnites, an Italic people in the central Apennines, Rome began its policy of road building. (The first great Roman road was the Appian Way, built for rapid military communication with southern Italy.) After defeating the Samnites about 293 B.C., the Romans, now masters of central Italy, created still another effective technique of control: They sent out colonies of Romans and Latins to serve as permanent farmer-soldier garrisons. These Roman colonies did not, like the Greek colonies, become independent cities but were closely tied to Rome politically.

Rome completed the unification of Italy by conquering the Greek cities of southern Italy in 272 B.C. The looting of Tarentum, the leader of the Greek cities, brought untold wealth to Rome, including famous works of art. Thus, in a little over a century Rome had unified all of Italy and in so doing had become a world power.

One of the important factors that had made this possible was the Roman army. At first sight this is surprising, for the Roman armed forces were a citizen army led by inexperienced generals who changed every year—the annually elected consuls. But the crack Roman infantry legions were trained under harsh discipline. The penalty for many types of offenses was execution by stoning. Sometimes entire units were decimated as punishment—every tenth man was counted off and executed. By 270 B.C., Rome could mobilize in Italy over half a million men, the largest army in the world.

Republican Institutions

At this high point in Rome's development, the Republic's very success in the relatively limited sphere of the Italian mainland was about to launch her into conflicts on a world scale with other great powers that rimmed the Mediterranean. The conflicts that lay ahead would transform utterly the Republic and all its institutions—government, social structure, religion—even though leaving the outer forms largely intact. It is appropriate, therefore, that we turn our attention to these institutions as they were in their fully developed and most successful form.

The constitution of Rome, like that of England today, was

not a written one; it consisted of an accumulation of laws passed over the centuries. Its basic structure involved a triple division: executive, advisory council, popular assemblies. At the head of the government were about forty-four elected officials, holding office for only one year and always numbering two or more in each office. The chief magistrates were the two consuls, who also served as generals in wartime. Other officials were: praetors (judges); aediles (supervisors of public works and festivals); quaestors (public treasurers); tribunes (protectors of citizens). The priests were public officials of the state religion and were later elected to their positions, including the head of the state religion (the *pontifex maximus*), who held office for life.

The Senate, consisting of about three hundred members, at first exclusively patricians, was in principle made up of elder statesman whose duty was to advise the consuls. The senators held their positions for life. The people met in various assemblies to elect officials and vote on bills proposed by the consuls. Since the two permanent bodies of the constitution were the Senate and the people, the official designation of the Roman Republic was S.P.Q.R. (meaning "The Senate and the Roman People").

The revolution of 500 B.C. at first meant no advantages for the Roman plebeians. Rich and poor plebeians alike had no right to office or to membership in the Senate or the various priesthoods. The patricians, moreover, had a monopoly on lawmaking and kept the laws secret. Intermarriage between patricians and plebeians was actually illegal. Most serious of all, the authority of the higher magistrates was unchecked: Anyone might be arrested and executed without charges or a trial. The growth in population and in private debts, for which plebeians might be sold into slavery, led to serious unrest. There were demands for civil rights and economic improvements, including access to ownership of public land, which had long been controlled for the exclusive advantage of the patricians. Most of these controversies were solved not by revolution and bloodshed but by compromises with a minimum of violence.

To win concessions, the plebeians would stage a walkout (called *secessio*) during military crises. Realizing the need for leaders of their own, the plebeians annually elected out of their own number officials called tribunes to serve as their defenders. Backed by the masses, the tribunes assumed the power to say *veto* ("I forbid") in protecting the plebeians against the arbitrary power of the patrician magistrates. The first great achievement of this patrician-plebeian struggle was the publication of the Twelve Tables in 450 B.C., bronze tablets on which were displayed the code of Roman law and custom. This first landmark in the long history of Roman law assured uniform law for all. Other victories won by the plebeians included the right to ownership of public land to satisfy their land hunger; admission to all public offices and priesthoods; the end of debtor slavery; the right of appeal, which provided that no Roman citizen could be beaten or executed by magistrates without an appeal to the assembly of all Roman citizens; intermarriage between the two classes; and, most important of all, the right of the people to pass laws without the approval of the Senate.

These many advances did not convert Rome into a democracy. Instead, a new aristocracy was created, the *nobiles* ("well-known men"), through a political coalition of rich plebeians with patricians. A very limited number of leading families, through their prestige, wealth, and numerous clients among the plebeians, were now able to maintain a monopoly over the magistracies. The Roman Senate, a body of ex-magistrates, became the leading power in the Roman Republic, controlling the army, public finances, and foreign affairs.

For many centuries, the group—the family and the state—was supreme among the Romans. Standards of morality and discipline were so high in this early period that the great Roman historian Livy later wrote of it, "I do honestly believe that no country has ever been greater or purer than ours or richer in good citizens and noble deeds, none has been so free for so many generations from the vices of avarice and luxury, nowhere has there been such high esteem for thrift and plain living." The Romans were a hardy, industrious, unsentimental people, distinguished by their conservatism, distrust of change, veneration for order, and practical realism. The sober Roman was disciplined in duty (*pietas*), which involved obligations to the family, the gods, and the state, as well as dignity and seriousness in every aspect of life. Every Roman acquired a profound devotion to tradition (*mos maiorum,* "customs of the ancestors"), embodied in the ways of his predecessors and respect for the authority of the head of the family.

The head of the Roman household (*familia*), the *pater familias,* ruled like a king over many people related to him. The father's power was at first absolute, including life and death; gradually, it was limited by custom. Yet to the end of

Roman civilization, this total power of the father remained part of Roman law, the most extreme form of parental control in the ancient world. The father's power did not cease when a young man came of age, as it did at Athens. Such a system offered little freedom, little opportunity for change. Each new generation for more than a thousand years was molded in the image of the fathers and ancestors.

Roman women, though never granted legal independence (they were all their lives under the control of a male, either father, husband, or guardian), yet had the highest status among women in the ancient world. "We Romans," said the stern Cato, "rule the world, but our wives rule us." The Roman matron was the honored mistress of her household; the Romans were the first to set aside one day of the year as "Mothers' Day."

Early Roman religion reflected the importance of the family and the state in Roman culture. The Romans believed in a great number of vague divine forces that affected every aspect of life and must therefore be dealt with constantly for the welfare of the group. Each family conducted its own religious rites, the father acting as the family's priest. Similarly, the Roman state religion conducted prayers and sacrifices to many spirits of more general scope (the sky, war, fertility of the soil, fire) for the preservation of the entire Roman people. Among the great priestly bodies were the pontifs, augurs, and fetials (who presided over declarations of war and treaties), and the Vestal Virgins, who looked after the sacred fire of Rome symbolizing the permanence of the state. The most important center of the Roman state religion was the Temple of Jupiter on the Capitoline Hill in Rome. It housed a triple shrine of Jupiter, Juno, and Minerva. As among the Greeks, there was an urgent, ever-present concern with forecasting the future. Among the Romans, there were priests who interpreted omens and augurs who took the auspices (that is, watched the flight of birds for divine signs).

Under the influence of the Etruscans and Greeks, anthropomorphism was adopted by the Romans—the belief that gods have human shape and behave like humans. Many anthropomorphic gods were taken over by the Romans and correlated somehow with their older Italic spirits. Jupiter, the spirit of the sky, was related to the Greek Zeus, king of gods and men; Juno to Hera; Minerva to Athena; and so on. But anthropomorphism and the sometimes irreverent myths of the Greeks tended to destroy the awe the early Romans felt toward the divine.

The Growth of Empire

By changing the balance of power in the western Mediterranean, Rome's conquest of Italy set her on a collision course with the great naval and commercial power Carthage. A colony of Phoenicians, this once famous city on the coast of North Africa, near modern Tunis, was founded long before Rome. While Rome was occupied with affairs in Italy, Carthage was methodically building up a naval empire and an affluent commercial civilization extending throughout the western Mediterranean to the Straits of Gibraltar and beyond.

After centuries of peaceful coexistence, the two Western powers now found themselves rivals, and they confronted each other on the island of Sicily, just off the coast of southern Italy. There, in 264 B.C., Rome intervened "in defense of allies," and the first of the fateful Punic Wars broke out (so called because the Roman name for the Carthaginians was *Punici*). Though expert only in land warfare, in the course of this conflict the Romans transformed themselves into a sea power. Off the coast of Sicily, Rome and Carthage fought the greatest sea battles thus far in world history. (It has been calculated that about a hundred thousand Italians lost their lives in storms at sea and in naval battles.) With final victory in 241 B.C., Rome was catapulted into the position of a great naval power, her empire* enlarged by the overseas provinces of Sicily, Sardinia, and Corsica. Sudden new wealth poured into the Roman treasury.

Carthage recouped her losses with naval bases and a new empire in Spain, and within less than twenty-five years Rome and Carthage were again at war. In the Second Punic War (218-201 B.C.), the great Carthaginian general Hannibal succeeded in leading a huge professional army through Spain and southern France and over the Alpine passes into Italy.

For fifteen years Hannibal roamed freely, the Romans powerless to defeat him. Both sides destroyed cities and villages all over Italy, especially in the south. At the Battle of Cannae in southern Italy in 216 B.C., Hannibal inflicted Rome's greatest disaster, one of the supreme tactical tri-

---

* The Roman empire was a practical reality under the Republic long before the accession of the first Emperor, Augustus, in 27 B.C. To distinguish Rome's possessions under the Republic from the Empire and political system organized by Augustus, we shall capitalize the latter: Roman Empire.

74 Greek and Roman Civilization

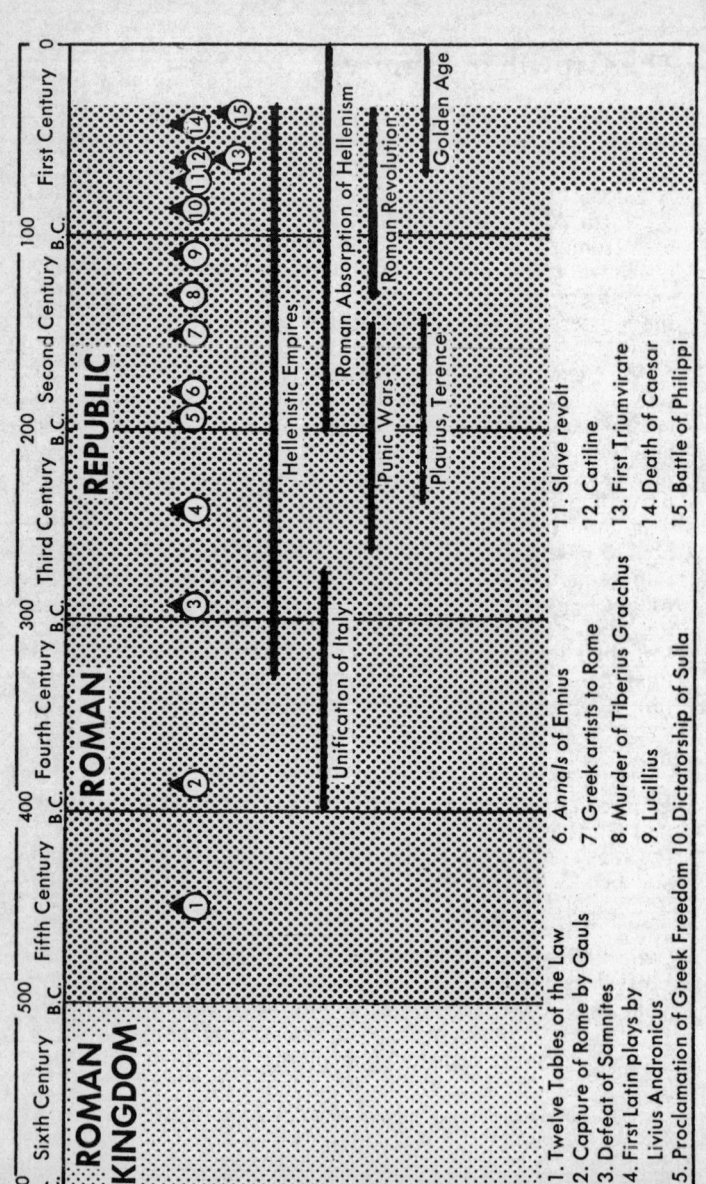

umphs in military history. Yet though Hannibal soon after stood at the gates of Rome, he did not have the resources to capture it and turned aside, never to regain the opportunity. Many of Rome's allies deserted her, but most remained loyal. Most important, the dogged Romans were still capable of a superhuman effort to survive and retake the initiative. The tide was finally turned with the appointment of the first really great Roman general, Publius Cornelius Scipio, the youngest man thus far in Roman history to hold a military command. Diverting the war to Spain and Africa, he crushed Hannibal at the Battle of Zama in North Africa, winning for himself the honorary title *Africanus*. Rome not only annexed all of the Iberian peninsula but reduced Carthage to a powerless ally of Rome. Rome was now the greatest military power in the world, but the price was disastrous. Most of southern Italy was devastated: The decline in population and prosperity there was so catastrophic that the region has not even to this day recovered.

Rome's overwhelming power brought new responsibilities, temptations, and opportunities. The remnants of Alexander's once great empire in the eastern Mediterranean looked with anxiety at the growing might of the "barbarians in the West." Rome soon began to intervene in the East. As elsewhere, the Roman Senate applied the policy of "divide and rule," forming alliances, supporting weaker states, and trying through diplomacy to prevent the stronger powers from uniting. When Roman legions defeated Philip V of Macedon, the country that had supplied the nucleus for Alexander's invincible armies, an era in world history ended. Six years later, in 190 B.C., Roman legions under Scipio Africanus crossed over into Asia and inflicted a humiliating defeat on the Seleucid Empire of Antiochus the Great, who had intervened in Greece. (The Seleucid Empire, stretching from Asia Minor to Afghanistan, was another highly civilized Hellenistic descendant from Alexander's conquests.) Thus, in the decade after the defeat of Carthage, Rome had become the greatest power in the world, and for the first time in history the entire Mediterranean was controlled by a single power.

The foreign policy of the Roman Senate, at first a cautious one relying on diplomacy and avoiding annexations, became ruthless in response to the endless intrigues among the Eastern states, a great rebellion in Spain, and massive slave revolts in Sicily. Thus, for example, Rome first divided the once mighty kingdom of Macedon into four independent republics forbidden to communicate with one another, then annexed the country outright as a Roman province. So great was the loot from Macedon alone that direct taxes on Roman citizens were henceforth abolished. In 146 B.C., Carthage was seized by Roman legions and so methodically destroyed that archaeologists today can find little or nothing of that once mighty city. Similarly, Numantia in Spain and Corinth in Greece were destroyed to terrorize the populations into submission. Peace was being imposed by the use of terror. The burdens of empire had brutalized the Romans.

Conquered lands outside Italy were called provinces and were heavily taxed for the expenses of occupation and administration. The taxes were collected by private companies that made high profits by all sorts of illegal methods. To govern the provinces, the Senate sent out members of its own body, all ex-magistrates, who were called proconsuls or propraetors and were changed annually. They had enormous arbitrary powers, acting almost like kings, and many used their position to plunder the provinces. The whole world cried out in anguish against this small handful of greedy, ruthless Roman nobles. "Words cannot express," said the Roman orator Cicero, "how bitterly we are hated among foreign peoples because of the outrageous conduct of the men whom in recent years we have sent to govern them."

The Transformation of Roman Society

Rome's sudden emergence as the world's leading power wrought profound changes in the austere farmer-soldier society. The wars had proved highly profitable to the upper classes: Vast quantities of booty, slaves, and tribute poured in, altering the quality of life and destroying many traditional Roman values. Eminent Romans now began to build magnificent town houses in Rome and villas in the country that they filled with masterpieces of Greek art. This extravagant life served to highlight the widespread poverty among lower-class Romans and Italians. Because of the enormous destruction in Italy during the wars with Carthage and the drain on their time and property in the numerous wars that followed, many small Italian farmers could no longer make a go of it. They abandoned their land or sold it to absentee landlords, especially Roman senators, who thus built up huge estates (called *latifundia*).

These enormous tracts of land were suitable for the large-scale commercial agriculture and cattle grazing that great numbers of slaves made profitable. Hordes of slaves, mostly war captives, were drained to Italy from all over the Mediterranean. Italy for the next few centuries was the largest center of slavery in world history until the introduction of slavery in the Americas. The decline in the number of free farmers was to have a long-range effect on Rome's vigorous citizen-army, which by tradition was drawn from those who owned land, above all the small farmers. Moreover, the Senate's harsh policy was now directed against Rome's Italian allies, limiting a potential source of manpower; those who failed to meet the growing Roman demands were punished by seizure of their land and restrictions on the coveted Roman citizenship.

The Senatorial class had become all-powerful. About twenty-five prestigious families maintained a monopoly of the offices through their clients, connections, and political machines. Even the tribunes of the people now conducted their duties in complete harmony with the Senate. Instead of their previous readiness to introduce reforms by practical compromises, the Senators now obstinately resisted change. Their monopoly of power was, however, soon challenged by a new social class, the Equestrian Order, which came into being because Senators were forbidden by law to engage in overseas commercial ventures. The Equestrians made fortunes in banking, commerce, construction of public works, and tax-collecting.

The masses of Romans and Italians had no share in these golden opportunities. They flocked to the cities of Italy, especially Rome, in search of means of survival. Unemployed all their lives, they crowded into the city slums, living on occasional handouts and, in time, on government welfare allotments, courted for their votes, with bribes and lavish amusements, by the Senators. The Roman plebs, as the lowest class of citizens was now known, were steadily increased by ex-slaves who, in accordance with Roman law, became Roman citizens as soon as freed.

In its conquest of the world, Greek culture won its greatest triumph among the Romans, who for the rest of their history were never free of Hellenic influence. The Roman nobility was dazzled by the brilliant culture of the conquered Greeks. All educated Romans learned to read and write Greek; precious Greek libraries and an enormous number of original works of Greek art were transported to Rome. Numerous Romans traveled in the East to savor Greek culture. And numerous Greeks—artists, teachers, philosophers—flocked to Rome to seek their fortune. The teachers of Roman boys were mostly Greek slaves and freedmen. Greek philosophers introduced the Romans to the intricacies of Stoicism, Epicureanism, Cynicism, and Skepticism. When the Greek philosopher Carneades, in public lectures in Rome, argued one day that justice was the basic principle of the world and the next day that injustice was, the troubled Roman Senate expelled him from Rome. (In 161 B.C. all philosophers were ordered out of Rome as a menace to public morality.)

Having no literature of their own, the Romans became avid readers of the Greek writers. They also began to take pleasure in seeing plays and in watching sports. But for all their interest in athletics from this time forth, the Romans, unlike the Greeks, were spectators rather than participants. In music also, closely associated in Greek life with athletic and literary excellence, the Romans departed from the Greek model; while most educated Greeks learned to play a musical instrument, the Romans regarded such an interest as unmanly.

In the early period of the Republic, Roman boys had been trained by their fathers in basic knowledge and skills. Under Greek influence, upper-class boys now undertook formal study, especially of law and public speaking, to prepare themselves for government careers. Roman education, conducted by private teachers, mostly Greeks, stressed Greek literature, oratory, and philosophy. Most eminent Romans also sent their sons for a period of study in Athens, the great university center of the world.

The new life style and training shifted Roman values from group solidarity to individual happiness, and wealth and personal power displaced *pietas*. Family solidarity began to crumble; for the first time, divorce became common. Yet the basic institutions of Roman society continued to be group-oriented, causing tensions and conflicts.

The mounting individualism had a disastrous effect on the traditional religion, which had served the interests of the family and the state. Moreover, the great war crises, the mounting external and internal problems, and the use of religion as a political tool by the Senate tended to undermine respect for the old religion. There was a growing skepticism toward the Roman gods and a widespread desire for an individual relationship with a personal divine force. The Senate had permitted the importation of foreign cults and gods to satisfy popular feeling: Aesculapius from the Greeks, a personal god of medicine and healing, and Isis from Egypt, whose worship promised a happy immortality. When the Greek cult of Bacchus began to spread in Italy early in the second century B.C., however, the Senate became alarmed. Bacchus was the god of wine and the potency of nature, and drunkenness and sexual freedom were practiced in his worship. The Senate determined to stamp it out. Accordingly, it declared the worshipers of Bacchus dangerous political subversives, proclaimed a national emergency and martial law, and instituted a witch hunt that lasted for five years. Thereafter, the suspicious Roman Senate tended to regard unauthorized meetings of any sort as seditious conspiracies. It was in this context that the early Christians were to become the victims of Roman fear of private allegiances.

Early Roman Literature and Art

For all their growing importance in the world, the Romans had no literature of their own until 240 B.C. In that year, when the defeat of Carthage had made Rome the strongest power in the West, the Senate decided to encourage the creation of a national literature by commissioning a Greek freedman from Tarentum, Livius Andronicus, to write two plays in Latin. A Roman national literature was thus suddenly brought into existence as a deliberate creation—an act unparalleled in the history of literature. Early Roman literature was in every respect second-hand: It was written in Latin but was the work of non-Romans from among the conquered peoples. And it was for the most part simply an adaptation of Greek literary forms to the Latin language. For a long time this literature was merely the Latin equivalent of Greek literature.

In the hundred years following Livius Andronicus, many Latin tragedies and comedies appeared, mostly adaptations or translations from famous Greek plays. The most famous writers of Roman comedy were Plautus and Terence, twenty-seven of whose plays have survived, all based on Greek models, all Greek in their scenes and characters. The proud Romans were not inclined to laugh at themselves.

The earliest important work on a Roman theme was the *Bellum Poenicum (Punic War)* by Naevius, an epic poem that launched Roman history as a major theme, comparable to the Greek preference for mythological subjects. This was followed early in the second century B.C. by another Roman historical epic, the *Annals* of Ennius, the "Father of Roman Poetry." In contrast to the Greek epics, Ennius's poem had no central hero; the unifying theme was the greatness of Rome itself.

Roman creative talent was as slow to appear in the visual arts as it was in literature. As late as the third and second centuries B.C., Etruscan art was still dominant in central Italy, Greek art in the south. Suddenly, the Romans became collectors of Greek art, especially painting and sculpture. They began by plundering Greek cities and bringing the looted works of art to Rome for display in public, and in private town houses and villas. An enormous number of classics of Greek art thus found their way to Italy. The demand was so great that an important statue-copying industry developed, made possible by Greek artists, who, beginning about 150 B.C., flocked to the world capital to seek their fortunes. This migration marked the end of creativity in the Greeks' national arts, but it launched a new Roman art at the same time. This new native Roman art was not strikingly original; it was the work of Greek stylists seeking to satisfy the political, social, and religious needs of the Romans and is properly called Greco-Roman.

By contrast with Greek idealism, the outstanding characteristic of Roman art is realism. The distinctive subjects of Roman sculpture were realistic portraits and historical reliefs. After 100 B.C., anyone who could afford it could have himself immortalized in a realistic portrait bust, and thousands of these portraits, ranging from the Roman great to insignificant persons, have been preserved; world museums are full of them. Roman relief sculpture provided a realistic visual documentation of Roman military victories and other events from recent and contemporary history that satisfied Roman national pride. The Greeks would have depicted the same types of events symbolically, in appropriate scenes from their mythology.

The Romans were the greatest builders in world history until the nineteenth century. One is at once struck by the vast size of Roman structures. This massiveness was necessary in part to meet the public needs of a great city like Rome, which at its height had a population of about a million. But the monumental structures that characterize Roman architecture were also the consequence of Rome's wealth and of its inferiority complex before the exquisite beauty of many Greek cities.

The invention of concrete and cement in Italy in the second century B.C. (unmatched until Portland cement in the nineteenth century) set off a technological revolution. An inexpensive building material, concrete poured in prepared moulds greatly extended the range of architectural shapes and made possible the huge scale of Roman building. As a result, the arch, the vault, and the dome—all distinctive characteristics of Roman architecture—became widespread. The Romans faced the crude concrete with well-nigh indestructible kiln-baked bricks or with marble veneers.

Under Etruscan influence, Rome built its most famous temple, the Capitol, on the Capitoline Hill, as the center of the Roman state religion, especially for the worship of the principal Roman god, Jupiter Optimus Maximus ("Jupiter the Best and Greatest"). Etruscan practice, which the Romans followed, was to build temples on a high platform with a long flight of steps in front. From the Etruscans the Romans also borrowed the circular temple of which the earliest famous example is the temple of Vesta in the Roman Forum.

From the Greeks, the Romans borrowed not only the basic Greek temple design but the three orders of architecture (Doric, Ionic, and Corinthian). From Greek practice the Romans also borrowed or adapted a number of typical public structures. The Greek *stoa,* termed a basilica by the Romans and used for law courts and business purposes, was built all over the Roman world. (Many were later converted by the Christians into churches.) Roman theaters, inspired by Greek theaters, were built not on the slopes of hills but on level ground. The Greek stadium became the Roman circus, used mostly for chariot races. Roman amphitheaters were a new type of construction, for gladiatorial games. Another type of Roman structure, adapted from Greek sources but elaborated by the Romans into vast buildings, were the huge public baths, which served also as social clubs.

Roman building owed more to the science of engineering than to the art of architecture. The famed Roman roads, some of them still in use today, were built as straight as possible—over arched viaducts, over rivers by bridges, and through mountains by tunnels. Roman engineering skill is also revealed in the numerous bridges over the Tiber (some still used today) and all over the empire, and in the great aqueducts that supplied water to the major cities, especially Rome itself. Roman aqueducts were constructed in part underground, in part on arches and viaducts, which can still be seen in Rome and the surrounding countryside. The vast underground sewer system of Rome, the first in the world, made Rome a model of sanitation compared with Greek and Near Eastern cities.

82 Greek and Roman Civilization

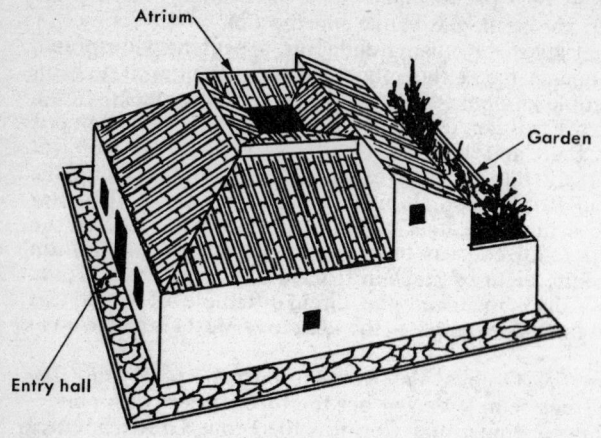

Fig. 1. *A Roman Private House in the Time of the Republic.* This is the kind of house (*domus*) that a well-off Roman gentleman would have lived in during the fourth or third century B.C. The house is designed for the small lots and close quarters of a city and looks inward—there are almost no windows, and the interior gets its light from the opening in the roof of the atrium. The floor plan (below) makes clear how this design grew out of earlier and simpler forms. The earliest Roman house was a single large room (the *atrium*) with an opening in the roof to let light in and smoke out; a pool (the *impluvium*) was placed below this opening to catch rain water. To the atrium were added an entry hall at the front (the *vestibulum*); bedrooms and storerooms at the sides under a shed roof; and a study (the *tablinium*) in a lean-to at the back. The garden shown here is unusual; most Roman houses at this time did not have gardens. (See also the illustration of a later house, Fig. 2.)

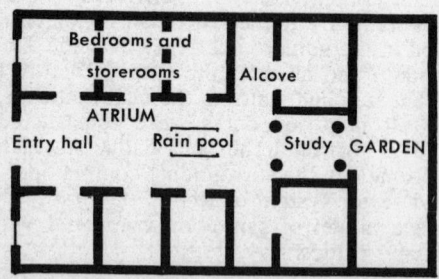

The City of Rome

The world capital was built on seven low hills, the two most important being the Capitoline and Palatine. Through the city flowed the Tiber River, navigable from Rome to the Tyrrhenian Sea about fifteen miles to the west. Between the Capitoline and Palatine was the Roman Forum, the counterpart of the Greek *agora*, crowded with such revered temples as those of Vesta, Concord, and Castor and Pollux; the speakers' platform, the Rostra; the Senate House (the Curia); an open-air meeting place for public assemblies (the Comitium); basilicas; commemorative statues, arches, inscriptions. North from the Forum ran the major street of Rome, the Via Lata (Broad Way). Between the Broad Way and the Tiber stretched the famed Campus Martius (Field of Mars), a military training ground where eventually there were many public buildings.

The Roman government was concerned only with public structures and made no provision for public housing. As a result, most of Rome, with its narrow, irregular streets, was like a huge slum. The very rich owned town houses (such a home was called a *domus*) designed for elegant living in crowded cities. These houses were not detached and had no windows; they received their air and light from the open sky in the interior. The front portion of the *domus* was the *atrium*, a large reception room with a hole in the roof (rain was caught in a pool in the floor). In this large room visitors were entertained and images of the family ancestors displayed. The family quarters were in the rear, in rooms arranged around an open courtyard called the peristyle. Interior decorations of the walls and floors were permanent—mural paintings on the walls and mosaics on the floors.

The Roman Revolution

In gaining the whole world, Rome became a sick society, slowly decaying internally. In the midst of unparalleled affluence, there was unparalleled poverty in Italy, the heart of the empire. Discontent welled up everywhere—in Rome, Italy, the provinces. Meanwhile, the Senate blindly maintained the status quo—and methodically fleeced Rome's subjects.

In 133 B.C., with the murder of Tiberius Gracchus, began a great crisis that was to last a century and bring the civilized world to the brink of chaos. Some liberals in the Senate sought to cure the illness of Roman society by tackling the problems of mass idleness and poverty, the methods of recruiting the Roman armies, and the quality of life in Rome and Italy. The first of these reformers was Tiberius Gracchus, grandson of Scipio Africanus, the conqueror of Hannibal. To provide farms from the public land for landless citizens, he broke with tradition: As tribune, he went directly to the people for the enabling legislation. When the Senate obstructed this program, he proposed to apply the income from the rich new province of Asia to finance it. This introduced a new factor into Roman public life: The lowest class, the plebs, came to expect as its birthright a share in the economic benefits of the empire. Henceforth, no Roman authority could ignore their claims. The Senate countered Gracchus' plan by bringing about his assassination, with many of his followers, on election day. This ominous event—the first open political bloodshed in Rome's history—marked the beginning of a hundred years of revolutionary violence during which naked force was to be the basic instrument both for control and change in Rome.

Ten years later, Tiberius Gracchus' younger brother Gaius Gracchus, now also a member of the Senate and a tribune, put together a more comprehensive program that would bring the benefits of the empire not only to the urban plebs but to the Equestrian Order and the Italians as well. Among the novel elements in his program were the government sale of wheat below the market price, the establishment of colonies of Romans in the provinces, and the granting of citizenship to all Italians. Riots broke out, martial law was declared, and Gaius Gracchus was murdered with thousands of his followers. Political violence, which breeds violence, was becoming more common.

The upheavals in Rome weakened the empire. Foreign powers and provincial leaders became more aggressive, and there was widespread incompetence, corruption, and greed among Roman generals and officers. Equally alarming, the traditional citizen militia of landowning farmers was too small, its loyalty questionable, its morale low. Vast powers were now given to one man, Gaius Marius, who broke all precedents by holding the consulship seven times. Drastically reforming the army, Marius threw open the legions to all volunteers, thus creating a professional army for the first time in Roman history. The new landless soldiers were promised a bonus in the form of land in Italy after a sixteen-year stint. The Roman armies were rebuilt, but the price was very high: henceforth, the army's loyalty would be to its general, not the government, and the ultimate power in Rome would belong to the military man.

Marius, a military genius, solved Rome's military problems by defeating the ambitious native prince of Numidia, Jugurtha, in North Africa, and annihilating the German barbarians in the north. As a statesman, however, Marius was ineffectual: He had no policy for reforming Rome's internal problems, and eventually he was forced to retire to private life. There followed a succession of staggering crises, wars, revolutions, civil strife, and power plays that convulsed Rome, Italy, and the world. When the Italian allies were denied Roman citizenship, they revolted, setting up a new independent state in Central Italy called Italia. Two years later, after thousands had lost their lives in the bloody war to crush this rebellion, the Senate did grant the Italians Roman citizenship. This extension of citizenship encouraged the spread of a uniform culture in Italy, but it also made Roman imperialism much more aggressive, increasing the exploitation of the provinces: A far greater number of Roman citizens were now entitled to relief and other advantages.

As oppression increased in the provinces, unrest also mounted. King Mithradates of Pontus, a kingdom east of the Roman province of Asia, came forth as the liberator of the provincials. In 88 B.C., Romans and Italians in the eastern provinces were massacred; in the province of Asia alone, about eighty thousand were killed. To meet this new challenge, the Senate gave a rising general named Sulla complete command of the East. He defeated Mithradates and ended the rebellion, but he also brought economic ruin by his huge fines, plundering for booty, and massacres of provincials. When Sulla returned to Rome, the first civil war in Roman history broke out, and Sulla, in an unprecedented move, made himself dictator for life. (He ruled only from 82 to 79 B.C.) To achieve political control and raise money, Sulla introduced the dreaded proscriptions: Certain individuals were declared enemies of the state; their names were published, and they were to be killed outright when seized and their property confiscated (to provide funds for the government and land for veterans). Ninety Senators, twenty-six hundred Knights, and thousands of others lost their lives and fortunes.

The general crisis continued; the empire was endangered both from within and without. Pirates controlled the Mediterranean, even cutting off Rome's food supply at will. In

70 B.C., a revolt of seventy thousand slaves led by the gladiator Spartacus terrified all of Italy. Mithradates again invaded Roman territory in the East. In these unprecedented emergencies, the Senate voted almost total power to a general named Pompey, who destroyed the pirates, suppressed the slave revolt (six thousand slaves were crucified along the Appian Way leading south from Rome), and decisively defeated Mithradates. After the death of Mithradates by suicide in 63 B.C., Pompey added many new provinces in the East, notably Syria, the last remnant of the Seleucid Empire, successor to Alexander's empire in the East. In his absence, Catiline, a Senator, organized a revolutionary plot whose political manifesto called for the overthrow of the nobility, the cancellation of all debts, and redistribution of the land of Italy. The plot was discovered through informers and suppressed by the consul of the year 63 B.C., Marcus Cicero, Rome's greatest orator.

Julius Caesar

Clearly, a dynamic new leader was needed, and in this crisis such a man was already rising to power. In 60 B.C., all power was seized by a military junta of three men: Pompey the Great, Julius Caesar, a popular politician, and Marcus Crassus, the wealthiest man in Rome. Thus was formed the First Triumvirate, whose purpose was to rule the world in place of the Senate. Under the First Triumvirate, constitutional government crumbled, but the Triumvirate itself slowly disintegrated. Crassus invaded Parthia, in the East, in 55 B.C., and lost his life in one of the most humiliating defeats in Roman history. Julius Caesar, lacking both wealth and a military reputation, began a vast program of conquests in the north, adding what are now France, Belgium, and the Netherlands to the Roman empire. He also crossed the Rhine into Germany and the English Channel into England, the first man since Alexander the Great to move the boundaries of the civilized world so far from its Mediterranean center. In so doing, Caesar determined the future and the culture of Western Europe for all time thereafter. It was to be Romanized, not Germanized.

The alliance between Pompey and Caesar broke apart, and Pompey joined forces with the conservatives in the Senate. Feeling threatened, Caesar led his victorious armies south across the Rubicon River into Italy in 49 B.C., thus beginning another civil war. The gamble paid off: He seized Rome and then in a series of whirlwind campaigns defeated all his enemies in battles all over the world. The defeated Pompey escaped to Egypt, a client kingdom of Rome, where he was immediately assassinated.

Caesar's policy in Rome, now that he had united the whole empire under his power, was clemency to his former enemies. He was self-confident, for his powers were without precedent in Roman history. Among other things, he was dictator for life. It is likely that Caesar planned to establish some sort of monarchy. He had many plans for reform, few of which he had time to put into effect. In general, these plans involved a more international and radical point of view than the Romans were accustomed to. For example, he not only spread Roman citizenship to an entire province, Cisalpine Gaul, thus uniting all of Italy up to the Alps, but he even admitted some provincials to the Senate. His most lasting reform was the establishment of the Julian Calendar of 365¼ days, which, with a minor revision in 1582 by Pope Gregory, is essentially the calendar in use today in most parts of the world.

The Death of the Republic

On March 15, 44 B.C., Caesar was assassinated by sixty conspirators within the Senate, including some whom he had pardoned. Their slogan was "Liberty," but they did not have a mass following and were soon crushed by Caesar's followers. In his will, Caesar left a small legacy to every single Roman citizen, but he made a young relative of his, Octavius, then only eighteen years of age, his principal heir and his son by adoption. This youth, whom we know as Octavian ("formerly Octavius") and later as Augustus, soon proved to be not only enormously ambitious but one of the master politicians of the world.

After much maneuvering, Octavian joined with Marcus Antonius and Marcus Lepidus, Caesar's principal aides, to form the Second Triumvirate. (It lasted from 43 to 33 B.C.) Like the First Triumvirate, it was a military junta whose purpose was to dominate the world. Its first act was to issue a proscription of three hundred Senators (Cicero included) and two thousand Equestrians. Vengeance was taken upon the assassins of Caesar at the great Battle of Philippi in 42 B.C. in Macedonia, where the leaders of the Senatorial party, Brutus and Cassius, committed suicide.

Relations among the Triumvirs were never good. In 36 B.C., Lepidus was dismissed. By clever propaganda, Octavian portrayed himself as the defender of law and order, of property rights and Roman traditions, and the champion of the primacy of Italy. Antony remained in the East, where he met Queen Cleopatra, fell madly in love, and as a result sent home his Roman wife Octavia, Octavian's sister. The national hostility of Italy mounted against Antony; incidents and accusations led to a declaration of war against Cleopatra. Finally, in 31 B.C. at the naval Battle of Actium off western Greece, Octavian's forces won an overwhelming victory. Shortly after, in 30 B.C., Antony and Cleopatra committed suicide in Alexandria. At the age of thirty-three Octavian was master of an empire twice the size of Alexander's.

After five hundred years, the Roman Republic was dead, and from a variety of diseases: the greed for personal wealth and the lust for power of the political leaders; the failure of the Senate and of liberal reformers to change the system; the loyalty of Roman armies to their generals rather than the state; the economic crisis that disrupted normal life and brought insecurity and poverty to millions; the discontent of many in Rome, Italy, and the provinces; the growth of extreme individualism in a chaotic world; moral decay; ruthless exploitation of the provinces; the inadequacy of a city-state form of administration for the governing of a vast empire. Everywhere for a century there had been anxiety, fear for life and property. Everywhere there had developed a desperate yearning for security and peace. As the price for these blessings, the Roman people themselves were prepared to sacrifice "Liberty," which meant much to the traditionalist Senators but little to them. After 31 B.C., all over the world Octavian was hailed as a savior, the god-sent leader who had brought peace to the world.

The Golden Age of Roman Literature

Despite the prolonged revolutionary turmoil, the finest creations of Roman literature were written between about 70 B.C. and the death of Augustus in A.D. 14. In the early part of this Golden Age of Roman literature, from 70 B.C. to 43 B.C., most persons felt a deep sense of alienation from existing society—yet the Roman tradition expected authors to write in the service of Rome, to glorify or improve it, at least to amuse the masses. Cicero, a great lawyer and politician, active in politics (he lost his life in the proscriptions of the Second Triumvirate), was also the first great Latin prose stylist. Among his works are speeches, philosophical essays, and an enormous body of private letters, not originally intended for publication, that provide a panorama of the great figures of the time.

The versatile Julius Caesar in the midst of his military campaigns wrote defenses of his policies and military adventures in his *Commentaries on the Civil War* with Pompey and in his *Gallic War*. A contemporary of Caesar's was Sallust, the first great Roman historian, who, after an active career as a Senator and a provincial governor, retired to write the history of his times. His *Catiline* and *Jugurtha* give us a grim but fascinating picture of the decline and fall of the Roman Republic. New literary directions were explored by Lucretius, who in his long, passionate poem *On the Nature of Things* attempts to persuade the Romans to adopt the escapist philosophy of Epicureanism. He was in fact urging people to follow an un-Roman way of life: avoidance of duty, of politics, marriage, children. Catullus, Rome's greatest lyric poet, expressed the same impulse. A young northern Italian from Verona, he was one of a group calling themselves the New Poets who rejected national purpose in literature and devoted themselves to self-expression for its own sake, with a freedom unknown before among the Romans.

Catullus died at thirty-one, a typical representative of an alienated younger generation driven to pleasure-seeking by a lack of social purpose. The reorganization of society by Octavian put firm controls on violence as a method of social protest and change, but pleasure as a way of life remained to plague the Romans, both old and young, until the end of their civilization.

The Augustan Age

That the Roman Empire not only survived the Republic but continued for centuries was due to the personality and policies of one man: Octavian—or Augustus, as he is known, according to the honorary title voted him by the Senate in 27 B.C. For over forty years—the longest reign in Roman history—Augustus was revered as an infallible leader, the "prince of peace" and savior of the world. Though Augustus proclaimed that he had restored Republican institutions, his reorganized Roman Empire (as we may now call it) was in reality a disguised constitutional monarchy. He did not take the title king—the Romans hated the word—but preferred to be called the *princeps* ("chief"). From this quite unofficial title, the next three hundred years of the Empire are known as the Principate. Though most of the power was in the hands of an Emperor chosen for life, the traditional Roman political system was retained: Senate, magistrates, popular assemblies. But the *princeps* dominated all. He was, for example, *imperator* ("commander-in-chief") and thus in control of the legions; he could initiate legislation, veto laws, try legal cases, and was the head of the state religion.

Under Augustus, efficient government was restored and a salaried imperial civil service established, with Senators and Equestrians holding the highest positions. Plebeians received farm land or were put to work. Many plebeians also became members of the new professional army of three hundred thousand that swore allegiance to the Emperor. Augustus' vision of one world under Rome, guided by one dedicated man, became a reality. He established the Roman Peace (*Pax Romana*) in the civilized world, assuring, for the next two centuries, order within the Empire and security along its borders. In foreign affairs, his aim was stability. There were wars during his reign, but their principal aim was consolidation and guarantee of the defenses of the borders rather than plunder.

In creating this new world order, Augustus hoped to restore Roman tradition, implanting old values on the new situations: He sought to reestablish the morals of the ancestors, revive family solidarity, renew respect for *pietas* (duty), and bring back life to the decaying Roman religion. But he also encouraged a new religious tendency—the desire to worship him as a god in his lifetime. Emperor worship remained a basic part of Roman religion until the triumph of Christianity about three hundred and fifty years later. For all his efforts and his own personal example, however, Augustus was unable to reverse the basic direction of Roman life, its materialism and pleasure-seeking. At his death in A.D. 14, the Roman Senate officially voted Augustus a god, providing funds for a temple and sacrifices. Thereafter, nearly every Roman Emperor was elevated to divinity at his death by decree of the Senate.

Augustan Literature

The Augustan Age is the high point of Roman achievement in literature, comparable to the Periclean Age in Athens and the Elizabethan Age in England. Despite the ever-watchful eye of the Emperor and the actual restrictions on freedom, there was an unparalleled outburst of creativity.

The Augustan Age 91

Many writers supported the new regime out of conviction; many were recruited to help glorify the new order. A wealthy friend of Augustus, Maecenas, became the patron of this pampered circle of authors, which included such great poets as Virgil and Horace. Their goal was the creation of exquisitely polished works of literature that would be worthy of the greatness of the age and elevate the Romans to the cultural leadership of the world. Many traditional Roman themes were stressed in Augustan literature: the past greatness and achievements of Rome; the patriotism of the great Romans; the ancestral virtues of *pietas,* discipline, *gravitas* ("seriousness"); military sacrifice for the country; the imperial mission of Rome to rule the world; love of Rome and Italy; and ancient family life and religion. But new themes, too, were needed for the new order: the peace and prosperity of the world under Augustus; the essential humanity of Rome toward its subjects; the virtues of Augustus and the imperial family.

All of these Augustan themes are embodied in the work of the poet Virgil, above all in his *Aeneid,* a new kind of epic poem in which myths of the coming to Italy of the Trojan Aeneas are recast to symbolize contemporary problems and achievements; Aeneas himself represents both the Roman people and Augustus. Aeneas is the hero whom destiny had chosen to bring the Trojans to Italy and build a city from which ultimately would arise Rome and the rulers of the world. He thus symbolizes the national ideals of the Augustan Age—service, religion, and the mission of Rome as the bearer of universal peace and humanity.

Virgil's best friend Horace, a voluminous poet, wrote a collection of *Satires,* essays in verse in an elegant style that avoided the fierce personal attacks of Lucilius, the creator of Roman satire. His *Odes,* imitations of Greek lyric poems, are exquisite gems of wit, sophistication, and technical perfection expressing commonplace ideas. The very sophisticated poet Ovid wrote a good deal of love poetry—*Amores* (*Loves*) and *Ars Amatoria* (*The Art of Love*), some of it verging on the obscene—that reveals the life of leisure and pleasure led by talented young Romans. He also wrote one of the most famous books about mythology in the history of literature—the *Metamorphoses,* a long poem in which he wittily retells many of the famous Greek and Roman myths. Not all the literature of the time was written in praise of Augustus and his policies. The great historian of the age, Livy, wrote a history of Rome from its beginnings down to the middle of the Augustan Age in which he idealized the past, the great men of Rome, and the virtues of the ancestors. His history is virtually a prose epic of Rome's greatness. The hero was Rome itself, not Augustus.

The Roman Empire Fully Formed

Imperial Dynasties

One problem Augustus faced and only partly solved was that of the continuation of his system—an orderly world with Rome at its head and one capable man at the summit. The alternative, in the history of the previous century, was chaos. Having no son of his own, Augustus sought a successor within his family, but first his sons-in-law and then his grandsons died, and finally he adopted his stepson Tiberius Claudius as his heir. The principle thus established—that the next Roman Emperor should be a relative or descendant of Augustus—was accepted without much ado to maintain order. The first four Caesars (as they are called from the use of his name in the imperial titles) were all members of two interrelated families and are therefore known as the Julian-Claudian dynasty. World society was henceforth dependent on one man as the source of policies and decisions. All went well so long as the Emperor was competent, but the practice of one man's holding power for life could also create serious difficulties. Since in fact the only sure remedy for an intolerable Emperor was assassination, many Emperors, ever insecure, started witch hunts and encouraged informers in order to maintain their power and protect their lives. Beginning with the reign of Augustus, there were frequent trials and convictions for treason—that is, for offenses against the "majesty" of the ruler.

Augustus' successor Tiberius was a very competent administrator but cynical, suspicious, and unpopular. It was during his reign that the Jewish religious reformer Jesus, in the Roman province of Judea, was arrested, tried, and convicted on the charge that he was being called "the King of the Jews," a treasonable situation. Caligula, who followed Tiberius, developed a mental disorder in the first year of his reign and became so cruel and despotic that he was murdered by his own bodyguard three years later. His uncle Claudius, who followed him to the throne, was an interesting, complex, scholarly man and a good ruler. It was in his reign that Britain was conquered and annexed to the Roman

Empire (A.D. 43) — so that Claudius might celebrate a triumph in Rome. He is said to have been poisoned by the last of his many wives, Agrippina, who wanted her son Nero to succeed him as Emperor. Nero squandered the wealth of the Empire recklessly, and after the great fire that almost destroyed Rome in A.D. 64, he built a vast new palace, the Golden House, among the ruins. When his mismanagement drove the Roman legions to revolt, he committed suicide to avoid capture. So ended the last of the Julian-Claudian dynasty, just about one hundred years after Augustus had achieved complete power.

In the confusion following Nero's death, Rome's various armies attempted to name the next *princeps*, and civil war again raged in the Empire. Finally the capable general Vespasian, a member of the family of the Flavii, took control and brought in a new era of order, peace, and prosperity, and economy and efficiency in government. The Flavian dynasty was brief, lasting only twenty-five years. Vespasian's reign was notable for the revolt in Judea in A.D. 70. In suppressing it, the Romans destroyed Jerusalem and deported the Jews all over the Empire, forbidding them to resettle their homeland. During the very brief reign of Vespasian's son Titus, a great volcanic eruption from Mount Vesuvius, near Naples, buried two nearby Roman cities, Pompeii and Herculaneum. These ancient cities were rediscovered in the eighteenth century; excavated and restored, they now give us our best picture of what life was like in Roman cities. The reign of Titus' brother Domitian was so unbearable that even his wife joined the conspirators who murdered him. Thus, for a second time a ruling dynasty was extinguished because the enormous power of the Emperor had fallen into unworthy hands.

The Silver Age

With the death of Augustus, the most creative period of Roman literature came to an end. In the century that followed, known as the Silver Age of Roman literature, writers avoided controversial subjects and in general tended to be merely amusing, to disguise their true thoughts or simply to be informative: Any work written with conviction and honesty might offend the Emperor and lead to a treason trial. In place of significant subjects, writers sought attention and fame by novel and witty ways of saying things. Manner became more important than content.

Petronius, a fashionable gentleman whom Nero called his

94 *Greek and Roman Civilization*

| B.C. 100 | First Century | 0 | A.D. First Century | A.D. 100 Second Century | A.D. 200 Third Century | A.D. 300 Fourth Century | A.D. 400 Fifth Century | A.D. 500 |

REPUBLIC | **ROMAN EMPIRE** | **EAST/WEST EMPIRE**

① ② ③ ④ ⑤ ⑥ ⑦ ⑧ ⑨ ⑩ ⑪

Roman Absorption of Hellenism

Golden Age — Silver Age

1. Battle of Actium, annexation of Egypt
2. Death of Augustus
3. Burning of Rome
4. Eruption of Vesuvius
5. Maximum extent of Empire
6. Death of Marcus Aurelius
7. Renewal of Persian Empire
8. Coronation of Diocletian
9. Legalization of Christianity, conversion of Constantine
10. Capture of Rome by Goths
11. Death of last Roman Emperor of the West

"minister of elegance," wrote a bawdy, realistic novel, the *Satyricon,* which displays a cynical panorama of contemporary life in Italy. Nero's tutor and chief adviser Seneca, a philosopher who expounded the Stoic system so congenial to the Roman upper class, wrote adaptations of Greek tragedies that stress Stoic fatalism and seek dramatic interest through scenes of horror and terror. They had enormous influence on later drama (including that of Shakespeare, who could read Latin but not Seneca's Greek models). Another first-century writer was Martial, a hanger-on of the rich and powerful in Rome, and, like Seneca, Spanish-born. The fifteen hundred short poems which make up his *Epigrams* form a biting commentary on leading persons and events of the age. Yet it is characteristic of this period that Martial also felt it necessary to season his insights with extravagant praise of the Emperor Domitian.

In the early part of the Silver Age, Pliny the Elder, an admiral of the Roman navy who lost his life investigating the eruption of Mount Vesuvius in A.D. 79, wrote a vast encyclopedia of science, *Natural History*. He drew his information from about a hundred Greek authors, intending the thirty-seven volumes as a practical handbook for the Romans. The practical Romans were not really interested in mastering scientific theory. Like Pliny, they merely compiled facts and crammed them into handbooks of information. Thus, they not only made no advances in scientific knowledge themselves but failed to preserve and hand down to posterity the great original scientific achievements of the Greeks. The decline in knowledge that resulted left the Middle Ages barren in the field of science for a thousand years. Not until 1600 did the modern age of science begin.

The Good Emperors

A century of government had revealed a major defect in the Principate—that the continuation of the highest power in the same family led to disaster. In the second century, a new principle was put into practice: Each emperor chose the man he considered best to succeed him and adopted him as his son. In this manner the so-called "Good Emperors" who followed Domitian—Nerva, Trajan, Hadrian, Antoninus Pius, and the philosopher Marcus Aurelius—maintained the Empire at a high level of order and prosperity for about a century. The English historian Gibbon called the middle of the second century A.D. "the period in the history of the world during which the condition of the human race was most

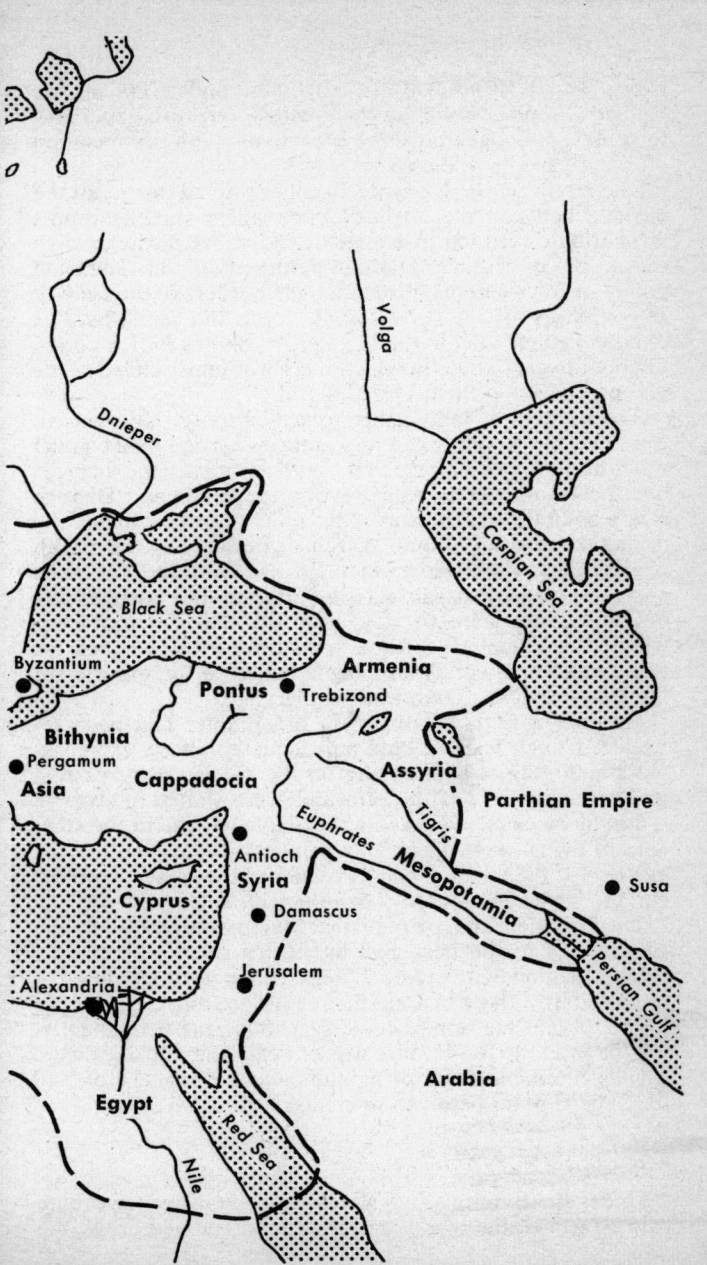

happy and prosperous." In A.D. 117, under Trajan, the Roman Empire stood at its greatest territorial extent—forty-five provinces on three continents, with a population of about seventy million.

The strain on the Empire's finances proved too great; the balance between the costs of imperialism and the profits from tribute resulted in a huge deficit. After the aggressive expansion of Trajan, Hadrian returned to the Augustan policy of fortifications, protecting the borders of the Empire by defenses of all sorts—walls, forts, ditches. The *Pax Romana* culminated in the reign of Antoninus Pius, a period of about twenty years in which there was unparalleled peace and prosperity in the civilized world.

The borders of the Empire remained tense, however. In the East, the Romans had for centuries carried on a conflict with the Parthian Empire that they had neither the finances nor the manpower to win. Beyond the Rhine and Danube rivers lived the vast hordes of the German tribes. Suddenly, during the reign of Marcus Aurelius, attracted by the wealth of the cities within the Roman Empire, both the Parthians and the Germans began massive attacks. The costs of war on two fronts were so staggering that the Emperor contributed his own vast fortune to the treasury. Moreover, for twenty years a worldwide plague added to the miseries of the Empire, killing countless people.

Another serious weakness in the Empire had been revealed. Could it afford both an adequate military establishment and a life of high quality for the civilian population in its far-flung cities? If the priorities were shifted in favor of the military cause, would the inevitable decline in the standard of living cause the civilian population to lose faith in the system? If the military budget remained the same, could the Empire survive the attacks from outside?

Disillusioned and pessimistic, Marcus Aurelius left the Empire not to the best man but to his son Commodus, a weak, incompetent ruler. When Commodus instituted a reign of terror, he was assassinated. Chaos and civil war followed. Again the armies took over, this time permanently, for the threat to the Empire was critical. The priorities were rapidly altered in favor of militarism at the expense of civil life. The Empire began to be militarized.

The Quality of Imperial Life

Under the Empire's *Pax Romana,* in exchange for tribute paid to Rome, the world was assured of law and order, the defense of civilized life against the barbarians outside, security of life and property, speed and convenience of travel, and toleration of cultural and religious differences. There still was a Senate in Rome, and the Senatorial Order, the highest social class, based largely on property, supplied the officials, provincial governors, and priests of the state religion—and also deified dead Emperors. To administer the Empire and collect revenues, the Emperors employed the largest salaried bureaucracy in the world's history until modern times.

Many Romans of the upper classes were extremely wealthy, and throughout the Empire there was a small upper class of rich provincials who lived on a level of affluence rarely enjoyed anywhere before except by royal families. The profits of the Empire were spent mostly in Rome for the benefit of the inhabitants. In addition to expenditures on public buildings, the government provided wheat and other foodstuffs at subsidized prices and distributed free monthly rations of wheat to about two hundred thousand heads of needy families, as well as free allotments of olive oil and meat. On special occasions, there were distributions of cash to all citizens. An important part of the budget was set aside for free public spectacles on Roman holidays and celebrations, which reached as many as 175 a year.

Rome itself was a special and extreme case, but the characteristic life everywhere was urban: The Empire was an aggregate of cities. The *Pax Romana* represents the highest degree of urbanization in history until the nineteenth century. For instance, the first cities in Britain were built under Roman planning, and even such a previously underdeveloped region as North Africa had about five hundred cities at the height of the Empire—more than at any other time in its history. Wherever there were Roman cities, the typical features of Roman life appeared: forums, theaters, amphitheaters, public baths, bridges, aqueducts. An integral part of Roman town planning was the construction of aqueducts. Indeed, it might be said that Roman civilization in many areas rose and fell with the water supply. And everywhere, safe, swift communication was facilitated either by sea or river or by the great network of Roman roads. Britain, for instance, by A.D. 150 had about 6,500 miles of paved highways.

The thousands of cities of the Empire were administered by public-spirited local rich who formed the municipal councils (like the Roman Senate, but consisting of one hundred men) and supplied the magistrates. The rich imitated the

100 *Greek and Roman Civilization*

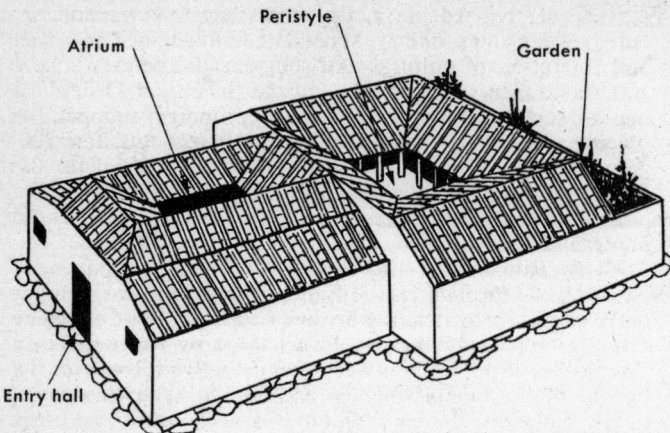

Fig. 2. *A Roman Private House of the Imperial Period.* The Roman house shown here is that of a well-to-do family of the first century A.D.—several like it have been preserved at Pompeii. This plan differs from earlier Roman houses (see Fig. 1) in having a large open courtyard (the *peristyle*) added on at the back, with bedrooms, baths, and a dining room built around it. The roof of the peristyle was supported by a colonnade, and there was often a fountain at the center of the open space, as shown here. This is an idea that the Romans borrowed from the Greeks. By this time, a walled garden at the back was also common, with a colonnaded porch, or *portico,* along the rear wall of the house. Often, small shops were built along the outside walls of the atrium, and the thrifty Roman businessmen rented them out to produce extra income. Most of the houses at Pompeii had shops built into the sides or front in this fashion.

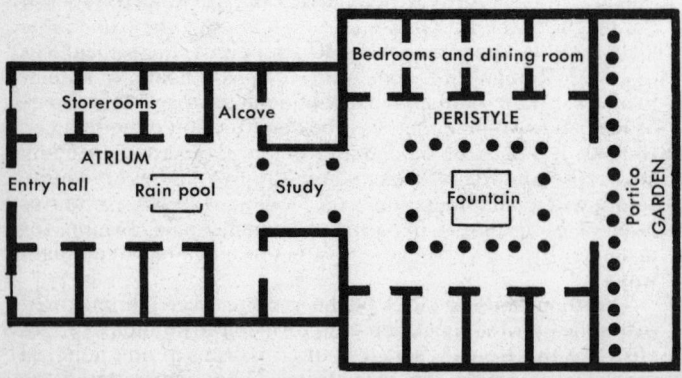

Roman multimillionaires by contributing to the erection of public buildings in their native cities and helping to feed and amuse the poor through welfare systems and public spectacles. Roman citizenship, which could be granted only by the Emperor, spread gradually to many individuals and even to whole regions. Everywhere in the West people dressed like Romans, lived like Romans, and spoke Latin. The older East, however, retained its age-old Greek traditions. (For example, both Latin and Greek were official languages, but Latin was the language of the West, Greek of the East.)

All over the Roman world careers and opportunities were open to men of all races and religions. The Roman government tolerated great cultural diversity, and competent men everywhere were absorbed into the imperial administration. In the third century A.D., North Africans, Syrians, and outstanding men from the Balkans ascended the throne as Roman Emperors. In all of Greco-Roman civilization, there were no obstacles to complete integration into society. From the time of Hannibal's invasion of Italy, for instance, there was a sizable number of blacks in the Roman Empire, some of whom rose to prominence.

Every Emperor left his mark on the public buildings of the capital city, which thus accumulated a greater proportion of public buildings than any modern city. New forums were added by Vespasian, Nerva, Trajan; new temples arose throughout the city. The Roman talent for immensity can still be seen in the remains of such buildings as the Circus Maximus, for chariot races, with seats for about one hundred and fifty thousand; the huge Baths of Caracalla and Baths of Diocletian, vast athletic-social clubs designed for leisure living in an affluent society. In the capital, most Romans lived in huge apartment houses, of which there were eventually about forty-five thousand, five stories high, provided with windows and balconies. The rich, as in the past, lived in elegant town houses or on their country estates.

The distinctive Roman art of sculpture, with its emphasis on realistic portraits and historical reliefs, spread all over the Empire, and Roman art became international as no other art until the twentieth century. The Emperors continued to commemorate, for Rome and humanity, the important events of their reigns. A famous example is the Column of Trajan in Rome, one hundred feet high, with its continuous spiral of sculptured scenes of Trajan's conquest of Dacia (modern Rumania). Trajan's message was clear—war as a means of achieving order and maintaining civilization. A similar but contrasting example is the Column of Marcus Aurelius, also in Rome and also one hundred feet high, which commemorates his wars with the northern barbarians: The continuous narrative of the wars against the Germans spiraling up the column stresses the horror and tragedy of war, the suffering and pathos for all, even the enemy. It is obvious in this monument and in many other aspects of their culture that the Romans were becoming deeply disillusioned and were losing faith in their society.

A similar note of foreboding began to appear in the literature of the second century when outwardly the Empire was at its height. In most of what was written, the loss of originality in thought and style is striking. Pliny the Younger, the rich and successful nephew of Pliny the Elder, wrote many charming letters, which were really miniature essays intended for publication. They give us a one-sided picture of the blessings of the age. The strongest voices are now those of protest, warning of corruption and decay. Tacitus, the greatest Roman historian, wrote his treatise *Germany* as a warning, contrasting the pleasure-seeking Romans with the more primitive, austere Germans. In his *Annals* and *Histories,* covering the first century A.D., Tacitus spreads before us a gloomy picture of evil Emperors, political and moral decay. It was Tacitus who put into the mouth of a native chieftain of northern Britain the famous words, "Empire is the name [the Romans] give to a policy of stealing, bloodshed, and plunder. And when they have created a desert, they call it 'Peace'." Similarly, Juvenal, the bitter author of sixteen *Satires* and the greatest satirist of all time, attacks Roman materialism, luxury, pleasure-seeking, sexual excesses, depravity, lack of values, and the discomforts and dangers of life in the capital. For Juvenal, vice and depravity in Rome had reached the climax in man's history, overwhelming him with hopelessness about the future.

The Decay of Empire

The *Pax Romana* had been won at a heavy price. By the second century, there was a widespread sense of gloom among the upper classes. Every person felt himself an insignificant speck in the vast Empire ruled by an all-powerful Emperor; people lived in the presence of public structures of such immensity that they dwarfed the individual to nothingness. Most people filled their lives with eating, drinking, sex, public games, gambling. There was little interest in government or the defense of the Empire.

With the rising costs of defense, the military, which always had the highest priority in the budget of the Empire, got an ever-larger slice. Cut off from further expansion in an age of world peace, the imperial economy could not stand the strain without destroying the quality of urban life. The increasing taxation to meet the military expenditures and the administrative costs of the central government gradually ended the relative affluence of the middle classes.

Besides the priorities given to the military budget, there were heavy expenditures for other unproductive purposes—for public buildings, public welfare, and entertainment. The financial requirements of the central government destroyed the prosperity and spirit of the cities of the Empire. The local rich found themselves more and more required to guarantee the payment of the ever-increasing taxes on their own communities; often they had to pay all the taxes due in advance, out of their own pockets. The city councils throughout the Empire thus became simply tax-collection agencies of the central government. The burdens were so heavy that many of the rich discontinued their customary benefactions or simply fled into anonymity. The results are visible in the changed appearance of the cities of the Empire after the middle of the second century—population decreased, and repairs and new construction came to a halt. Except for Rome, the cities of the ancient world—the very centers of classical civilization—received a mortal blow from which they never recovered.

In this atmosphere of anxiety and human powerlessness, resulting from loss of nerve and from rootlessness in the vast Empire, many persons turned inward in search of strength and a feeling of personal worth. Beginning in the second century, there was an explosion of religious feeling: more and more, the Greek tradition of reliance on reason was replaced by faith in divine forces, and the great interest became personal salvation, a yearning for a happy immortality. Magic practices and belief in miracles became quite common, and the desire for quick information about the future led to an almost universal belief in astrology, whose skilled practitioners claimed to interpret the heavenly bodies as controllers of each human's life. Even the Emperors had their horoscopes cast, and many kept official astrologers on their staffs. This growth of irrationality, of dependence on faith and mysticism, magic and astrology, was the death blow to the reverence for reason that, almost a thousand years before, the Greeks had made one of the bases of the classical way of life.

The polytheistic religions of the ancient world, with their many gods, no longer satisfied men's deep yearnings, nor, in the long run, did the worship of the Emperors, living and dead. More and more, the emotional and religious needs of the masses were being satisfied by so-called mystery-religions, all of Near Eastern origin. In all of these religions, converts offered themselves for initiation, were purified (sometimes by baptism), followed a set of moral rules, and were introduced to secrets known only to the initiates. What they gained was a promise of immortality and a happy afterlife.

The two most influential mystery-religions of the Roman Empire were Mithraism and Christianity. The former came from Persia and appealed mostly to men in the army who were initiated by having the blood of a bull (symbol of power and creativity) sprinkled over them. Christianity, developed from the teaching of Jesus, was the most democratic and inexpensive of all the mystery-religions: men, women, slaves, and children were admitted, and sacrifices were not required. The monotheism of Christianity (belief in one god rather than many) derived from the Jewish religion, and like Judaism was opposed to emperor worship; unlike it, Christianity actively sought converts. Because of this subversive combination of belief and practice, Christianity was early an illegal and persecuted religion, and so it remained, with some intermissions, for about two hundred and fifty years.

The Crisis of the Empire

The century from A.D. 180 to A.D. 284—from the death of Marcus Aurelius to the beginning of the reign of Diocletian—is one of the most fateful periods in the history of European civilization. A combination of civil wars within the Empire and massive attacks from outside did catastrophic damage to the normal civilian society to which people had been accustomed for hundreds of years. Widespread destruction of life and property, a sharp drop in the standard of living, and runaway inflation plagued the civilized world. In the face of these endless emergencies, the powers of the Emperor were steadily increased until they were virtually unlimited. The Emperor was now called "Our Lord," and the Imperial family "the Divine House." The *princeps* of the Augustan system had become a crowned king with absolute power.

In the face of these enormous threats, the Roman world was transformed into a military state. Because the armies were the principal source of the Emperor's power and the key to the survival of the Empire, soldiers now received preferential pay and privileges. Army officers became a new elite, and an increasing proportion of the income of the Empire went to the military budget, which rose to fantastic size.

In the third century A.D., Emperors reached the throne from many provinces. Among them were the great general Septimius Severus, a Romanized North African (married to a Syrian woman named Julia Domna) who brought a more international spirit and provincial perspectives to the policies of the central government. But he became Emperor principally because he was capable of preserving the Empire and controlling the armies. His son Caracalla, in A.D. 212/213, by decree made almost everyone in the Empire a Roman citizen so as to unify the laws and simplify tax collection and administration. In A.D. 226, in the reign of Alexander Severus, the Empire received a great shock when the Parthians were overthrown by a new and much more aggressive Persian Empire. A major war now broke out in the East. When Alexander Severus tried to buy time in A.D. 235 by seeking a negotiated peace with the threatening Germans and offering them cash subsidies, the army mutinied and killed him for arranging what they considered a dishonorable peace. Anarchy followed.

In the next fifty years, there were twenty-six Emperors, all but one of whom died a violent death. During this period of military anarchy, there were chaos, looting, killing, and destruction, especially in the cities of the Empire. The Empire was under siege on its borders, at the mercy of the Sassanid Persian Empire and the Germans. The famed Persian King Shapur I, the most dangerous enemy since Hannibal, even succeeded in capturing the Emperor Valerian and obtaining the surrender of his legions. Parts of the Empire were detached in both the east and the north. Invading German tribes, eager to loot the rich cities of the Empire, seized Gaul, Spain, part of North Africa.

The Empire was saved by a general of peasant origin from the Balkans, the Emperor Aurelian, who succeeded in restoring all the lost provinces except Dacia, which he abandoned. It was Aurelian who ordered the building of the great wall around Rome that bears his name. In his search for a unifying faith for the Empire, Aurelian established a new god as the supreme divinity of the Roman state religion, the Sun itself (called "the Unconquered Sun") as the eternal source of light, security, prosperity. One day of the year was set aside to celebrate the birthday of the Sun god, December 25, and Sunday was declared his sacred day each week.

Regimentation and Totalitarianism

The needs of the central government for defense were so enormous that the whole Empire was regimented for this purpose. The taxes on the civilian population were staggering: They included land taxes, trade taxes, head taxes, inheritance taxes, sales taxes, tolls on roads, imports, and exports; many products and services were simply requisitioned. All dissent was suppressed; compulsory services of all sorts were imposed on every person, as the government mobilized the entire population. All labor in the trades and the professions was conscripted: Persons were forbidden ever to leave or change their occupations. In desperation, to assure an adequate number of workers, the government even made trades and professions hereditary: Sons were required to follow their fathers in the same work. This was considered necessary to maintain the economy and essential supplies, especially to the armies and the city of Rome.

Trade associations (called *collegia*), which had long existed to represent the interests of those in the same occupation, were now nationalized and made to serve the interests of the state. To maintain vital agricultural production, farmers were deprived of their freedom to leave their land, to which they were attached by law, together with their descendants for all time. They are the forerunners of the serfs of the Middle Ages. Thus everywhere by the end of the third century compulsion was necessary to extract the taxes and services required to support the armed forces, without which the Roman state could not survive. The totalitarian state had come into being; state control over the individual was complete.

The serious danger to the Empire also explains why the Christians began to be more brutally persecuted in the third century by the Emperors and by panicky mobs. In A.D. 250, the Emperor Decius made an effort to abolish Christianity entirely by requiring every person in the Empire to take a loyalty oath to the Emperor as a god. Later, all Christian churches were ordered closed, priests were arrested, sacred books were burned, and even Christian cemeteries were closed down.

The expenditures for the military were so enormous that inflation could not be halted. In the Roman province of

Egypt in A.D. 301, one pound of gold was priced at 50,000 *denarii* (a Roman silver coin comparable, let us say, to our quarter); a few years later the price of gold rose to 100,000 *denarii* the pound. Between A.D. 300 and A.D. 400, the prices of some products rose 45,000 times. The government adopted an ill-advised economic policy: To replenish the treasury, pay for military supplies, and pay the restless armies, it debased the silver and gold coinage by mixing it with cheaper metals, so as to have larger quantities of money at its disposal. This caused a worldwide financial panic: People lost confidence in the cheapened Roman money and hoarded the purer coins. When this hoarding produced a steep rise in prices, the government countered by demanding payment of taxes in actual products, such as food and clothing, that were indispensable to the armed forces. The money economy that had characterized classical civilization for about a thousand years was now in ruins.

The previously affluent portions of the population were now impoverished; the standard of living declined radically. When the upper classes of the Empire sought to evade their responsibilities, the government made membership in the town councils compulsory and hereditary. The effect was further to impoverish the local rich who had kept the cities of the Empire thriving, providing them with their services and adorning them with their benefactions. Many persons of all classes who were accustomed to living in cities began to flee to the surrounding country districts.

Here, powerful landowners (Senators and army officers) offered them protection and security in exchange for their services in defense of their villas—a new form of the traditional Roman patron-client relationship. Because of the internal chaos of the Empire, more and more of these villas were transformed into fortresses to which all the rich landowner's vassals (called *villani, vassi,* or *coloni*) could flee for protection in time of danger. The country estates, the forerunners of the medieval manors and castles, thus became the new centers of life, providing luxurious living for a few and security for many. As a result, urban decay on a vast scale followed: The cities of the Empire declined steadily in physical facilities, appearance, size, and quality of life. For example, Alexandria by A.D. 260 had lost about sixty per cent of its population; by the seventh century, Rome's population had dwindled from about one million to twenty thousand. Thus, after a thousand years, the basis of classical civilization—life in urban centers—was being snuffed out. This was a death blow to classical culture.

The Triumph of Christianity

The totalitarian state was organized into a system of law by the Emperor Diocletian. Moreover, the Principate—the fiction that the Roman Republic still continued, though with a chief at its head—was replaced by an open monarchy called the Dominate, for the Emperor was now called Dominus ("Master" or "Lord"). Diocletian claimed his power not from the Senate or the armies but from Jupiter as a divine right.

With Diocletian, the state of emergency became a permanent institution, with everyone regimented for the defense of the Empire. The army was increased to half a million and made more efficient; the Empire was divided into four major areas, each with a separate capital and a co-Emperor and vice-Emperor. In A.D. 301, Diocletian attempted to stem the disastrous inflation by his Edict on Maximum Prices, which set price ceilings on every product and service in the Empire. This new attempt to regiment the economy also proved unworkable, for it only led to hoarding and black markets.

Diocletian's abdication and death led to civil wars, out of which finally one man emerged as sole Emperor: Constantine the Great. Despite the persecutions, the Christians had made numerous converts, even in very high places. Finally, in A.D. 311, after three hundred years of hardship, Christianity was declared a legal religion, and for the first time a man could be both a Christian and a loyal Roman. In A.D. 312, Constantine himself was converted to Christianity (though he remained *pontifex maximus* of the state religion) and launched a series of administrative and legal measures in favor of the Christian church. While Constantine did not abolish pagan worship or destroy pagan temples, his special favor and state subsidies made Christianity the dominant religion in the Roman state.

Constantine chose the Greek city of Byzantium (modern Istanbul in Turkey) as the site of a second capital of the Empire. Lying on the military highway connecting the two danger zones of the Empire, the Danube and Euphrates rivers, the new capital was designed from the start as a Christian Rome. When it was dedicated in A.D. 330 as Constantinople, the Second Rome was filled with Christian churches, typical Roman public buildings, the palace of the Emperor, and pagan works of art. Thus, the centuries-old tendency of the Empire to separate into a Latin West and a Greek East received new impetus. After five hundred years, the unity of the Mediterranean had come to an end. Constantinople soon became the new world capital and most important city of the Empire, putting Rome into the shade.

The great transformations of society and the human spirit in the third and fourth centuries are best seen in the historical reliefs and imperial portraits of the time. Roman realism was gradually displaced by a more primitivistic and symbolic art. The Emperor is no longer presented as a human leader of his people but as an awe-inspiring figure dominating in size and importance the masses of people around him. More and more, he is a symbol of absolute power, immobile and expressionless, like an idol. An early example of this new spirit is the sculptured group of Diocletian and his three co-Emperors: They all look alike and cling to each other like automatons, immobile, their eyes gazing upward in otherworldly contemplation. Thus does Greco-Roman classical art come to an end in this turning aside from the beauty and relevance of the human body and of human life. The new art is a spiritual art that, in an uncertain world, turns inward to the soul and outward to God.

After eight hundred years, the Eternal City had ceased to guide mankind's destiny. The disintegration of the Roman world, one of the longest enduring imperial systems in history, is one of the world's great disasters.

When did the Roman Empire fall? Various possible dates might be given. Symptoms of the decline were already visible about A.D. 150, in the decay of the cities. Territorially, the Empire began to be torn apart permanently in the fourth century A.D. as one by one its provinces were detached by invaders, especially the Germans. In A.D. 410, exactly eight hundred years after its first capture by the Gauls, Rome again fell to invaders, this time the Goths. In A.D. 476, Italy became a German kingdom when the last Roman Emperor in the West, with the astonishingly symbolic name of Romulus Augustulus, was deposed.

Yet the fall of the Roman Empire was not the result of the barbarian invasions, which for centuries the Romans were able to resist, but of many forms of internal decay. Some historians, like Gibbon, have said that the Empire was simply too big and so collapsed from sheer size; or that Christian otherworldly values undermined the Romans' determination to rule. Still others blame the fall of Rome on the decline of their morals; or on the institution of slavery; or on race mixture; or exhaustion of the soil; or even lead poisoning of the upper classes, who used lead-lined eating utensils. It is much more significant to inquire what was inherently wrong with the system itself that it finally ceased to respond to new demands and challenges.

The basic defect of the Roman system was that in the long run its priorities were self-destructive. The Roman world order was planned to provide a high standard of living for only a minority of the population while the masses remained paupers, kept alive and content by the "bread and circus games" of the Emperors. World peace of a sort did exist, but it was one enforced by the Roman armies. Rome was largely the world's policeman; it did not transmit a unifying sense of shared values. The resources of the Empire were used unproductively: They went largely into military expenditures, public buildings, urbanization, and public welfare. In the long run, the system required a constant transfusion of new resources that could only be obtained by fresh wars, and these came to an end with the *Pax Romana*. The resources within the Empire were not adequate for both defense and civilian needs, even those of the affluent minority. When, unable to continue expanding, the government began to expropriate the rich and the middle classes to guarantee its defense, people in great numbers lost faith in the system.

They fled from the cities into the favored army or into the clergy or to the estates of the great landowners, or they formed bands of brigands. The compulsion used by the government to force people to remain in their native places and their own occupations created a totalitarian state based on total regimentation. Confidence in the economy and the imperial currency was destroyed by the enormous loss of life and property, by confiscations, and by inflation. The far-flung cities of the Empire fell into physical and economic ruin and were gradually depopulated. The displacement of the population to the large estates (self-sufficient in their economic ability and in their security measures) fatally weakened the central authority. Eventually, it could no longer guarantee the safety of the Empire and proved incapable of holding back the barbarian invaders.

It is one of history's most important lessons that the great civilizations of the past have been destroyed not by external enemies but by their internal failures. No more instructive example can be found than the civilizations of the Greeks and the Romans, who contributed so much to the culture of mankind and whose legacy is woven into the fabric of our own culture.

FOR FURTHER READING

The books listed below are recommended for those who wish to study Greek and Roman civilization in greater detail. In addition, Edward Gibbon's eighteenth-century classic, *The Decline and Fall of the Roman Empire,* enormously vigorous and opinionated, is worth browsing through for the pleasure of it, even though modern historians disagree with him on both fact and interpretation. (A one-volume abridgement by D. M. Low was published by Harcourt, Brace in 1960.)

Since most of the books suggested are illustrated, mention is made of illustrations only if they are of unusual interest. The general works (first group) treat classical civilization or its Greek and Roman branches as a whole; those on special subjects are concerned either with limited periods of time or with aspects not presented separately in this book. For literature, history and biography, art, music, and philosophy, religion, and science, see the suggested readings following the appropriate chapters. An asterisk (*) indicates a paperback.

General Works

Roebuck, Carl. *The World of Ancient Times.* New York: Scribner's, 1966. A textbook of ancient Mediterranean history with the emphasis on Greece in its Near Eastern context and on Rome. Useful for reference; many black-and-white illustrations.

* Scullard, H. H., and van der Heyden, A. A. M. *Shorter Atlas of the Classical World.* New York: Dutton, 1967. Many useful maps, illustrations, plus a brief classical history.

Starr, Chester G. *A History of the Ancient World.* New York: Oxford University Press, 1965.

Greece

* Bowra, C. M. *The Greek Experience.* New York: New American Library, 1957.
* Finley, M. I. *The Ancient Greeks; An Introduction to Their Life and Thought.* New York: Viking, 1963, 1964. An interesting, very brief cultural history.

Hooper, Finley. *Greek Realities; Life and Thought in Ancient Greece.* New York: Scribner's, 1967. Emphasis on the Golden Age; well and abundantly illustrated.

* Kitto, H. D. F. *The Greeks,* rev. ed. Baltimore: Penguin, 1957. A good cultural history by a British scholar best known for his book on Greek tragedy. Chapters characterizing Greek thought, religion, and life.

Petrie, A. *An Introduction to Greek History, Antiquities, and Literature,* 2nd ed. New York: Oxford University Press, 1962.

Rome

* Dudley, Donald R. *The Civilization of Rome.* New York: New American Library, 1962.

112 Greek and Roman Civilization

* Fowler, W. W. *Rome,* 3rd ed. New York: Oxford University Press, 1967. Very brief historical account, old, but almost a classic.
* Grant, Michael. *The World of Rome.* New York: New American Library, 1961. Topical organization, with chapters on politics, social life, religion, literature, art, etc.

McDonald, A. H. *Republican Rome.* New York: Praeger, 1966.

* Petrie, A. *An Introduction to Roman History, Literature, and Antiquities,* 3rd ed. New York: Oxford University Press, 1963. Very brief; topical organization.

Special Subjects

Cary, M., and Haarhoff, T. J. *Life and Thought in the Greek and Roman World.* New York: Barnes & Noble, 1940. Old-fashioned but with chapters on food, clothing, recreation, and education that are still useful and make agreeable reading.

Greece

Agard, Walter R. *What Democracy Meant to the Greeks.* Chapel Hill: University of North Carolina Press, 1942. The development of democratic ideas from the Heroic Age to the high point under Pericles, the reaction following the Peloponnesian War, and the final suppression by Macedonia.

Burn, A. R. *The Warring States of Greece; From Their Rise to the Roman Conquest.* New York: McGraw-Hill, 1968. A brief, witty political history with unusual illustrations that emphasize the actualities of daily life (sports, clothing, weapons, portraits of the famous).

Flacelière, Robert. *Daily Life in Greece at the Time of Pericles.* New York: Macmillan, 1965.

Hadas, Moses. *Humanism; The Greek Ideal and Its Survival.* New York: Harper, 1960. Greek cultural values that have remained prominent in European civilization.

Jones, A. H. M. *Athenian Democracy.* New York: Praeger, 1958. Essays discussing the political practice of Athens and the usual criticisms brought against her form of democracy (that it was inefficient, rested on slavery, was made possible by the tribute paid by allies).

* MacKendrick, Paul. *The Greek Stones Speak; The Story of Archaeology in Greek Lands.* New York: New American Library, 1962. An account of the most important work on sites ranging in time from the Mycenaean to the Roman period, in chronological sequence; fairly technical.

Robinson, Charles A., Jr. *Athens in the Age of Pericles.* Norman: University of Oklahoma Press, 1959.

Zimmern, Alfred. *The Greek Commonwealth; Politics and Economics in Fifth-Century Athens.* New York: Modern Library (originally published in 1911). Leisurely and somewhat dated but still useful.

Rome

* Carcopino, Jerome. *Daily Life in Ancient Rome*. New Haven: Yale University Press, 1960.

Cowell, F. R. *Everyday Life in Ancient Rome*. New York: Putnam, 1961. If the preceding is not available, this offers quite good coverage of education, food, clothing, entertainment, chiefly for the first century A.D.

* MacKendrick, Paul. *The Mute Stones Speak; The Story of Archaeology in Italy*. New York: New American Library, 1960.

Rowell, Henry Thompson. *Rome in the Augustan Age*. Norman: University of Oklahoma Press, 1962. The political and social structure described, frequently in the Emperor's own words.

* Starr, Chester G. *The Emergence of Rome as Ruler of the Western World*, 2nd ed. Ithaca: Cornell University Press, 1953. A brief, clear account of Roman expansion to the consolidation of the Empire under Augustus and his immediate successors.

CHAPTER II

The Literature of Greece and Rome

NORMAN AUSTIN

UNIVERSITY OF CALIFORNIA,
LOS ANGELES

The Beginnings of Greek Literature

The Epic World of Homer

GREEK LITERATURE begins with two anonymous poems, *The Iliad* and *The Odyssey*. According to tradition, they were the work of Homer, a blind poet born in one of the Greek cities on the coast of Asia Minor who traveled from city to city as a wandering minstrel singing his poems of the Trojan War. But all this was later legend. No one knows with certainty who composed the poems nor when they were composed, and the methods of modern scholarship have brought us no closer to the secret of their authorship. For convenience, we fall back on the ancient tradition and refer to Homer as an historical person and to *The Iliad* and *The Odyssey* as his creations.

The ten-year-long Trojan War is the background for both poems, though in neither is it the central event. *The Iliad* narrates a major incident that occurred in the last year of the war. Agamemnon, the Greek commander, and Achilles, his best warrior, quarrel over the girl Briseis whom Achilles had obtained as part of his booty in a previous raid. Achilles, angered and insulted, withdraws from the battle, and in his absence the Trojans come close to routing the Greeks. Eventually, Achilles relents sufficiently to allow his friend Patroclus to go into battle dressed in Achilles' armor. Hector, the bravest Trojan warrior, kills Patroclus and thus brings about Achilles' return to battle. Achilles kills Hector in vengeance for Patroclus' death, and the poem ends with Hector's father Priam, king of Troy, going to Achilles' tent to plead for his son's corpse. We know that the war will continue after a period of mourning for Hector; we know, too, that Achilles will be killed and Troy destroyed, but these events are only foreshadowed in the poem.

The action of *The Odyssey* begins ten years after the end of the Trojan War. All the Greek survivors of the war have either reached their homes or have perished on their homeward journeys, except Odysseus. He alone is still at sea, detained against his will on Calypso's island, and in his long absence his wife Penelope fends off as best she can her many suitors. The poem narrates the journey that Odysseus' son Telemachus undertakes to gather news of Odysseus, and then the journey of Odysseus from Calypso's island back to his home in Ithaca. Eventually, both Odysseus and Telemachus are back at their palace in Ithaca, and together they slaughter Penelope's suitors, who have become progressively more arrogant and sacrilegious. Odysseus, after twenty years' absence, is king once again on his own island, and moral order is re-established.

From archaeological evidence, we know that there was a vast destruction of Troy about 1200 B.C. If the Trojan War is a historical event, it is probably to be dated to this time when all the great cities that Homer describes—Pylos and Mycenae in Greece, Troy in Asia—perished in some great holocaust. The Homeric poems, however, must have been written about the eighth century B.C. when the Greeks, borrowing the Phoenician alphabet, recreated their own system of writing. For centuries after the high civilization that Homer describes had perished, the memory of those cities and their heroic kings had been preserved not in written documents but in oral poetry.

The Homeric poems come as the culmination of a long oral tradition; their style, with its repetitions, betrays the strong influence of an oral culture. As the earliest Greek literary documents, they formed the Greeks' sense of their own past. At first, the authority of the poems was accepted with an almost religious faith, but in later times people became more critical of Homer's mixture of legend, mythology, and poetic exaggeration. Even then, however, the Greeks continued to see in Homer their spiritual history. Homer had defined their sense of honor, their religious values, their pride in individual achievement, and the Greeks honored him as the preserver of those ideals.

In the world that Homer depicts, the gods are powerful

beings who can be vengeful when offended. Even so, the emphasis is less on their anger than on the society that gods and heroes share in common. We see the gods appearing in mortal guise, cooperating with their favored heroes, advising or protecting them, grieving over their injuries. In few religions is the gulf between man and god as narrow as it is in Homer.

Homer's world is also one that honors art and the creative imagination. A hero must have more than mere proficiency in certain skills; he must excel, he must demonstrate finesse. Odysseus is renowned for his sound advice in the assembly, but he has more than good advice. His style of argument and his words have a beauty that charms his listeners. Manual crafts are no less honored than the aristocratic skills. Both Homer's heroes and his gods are moved by beauty. Homer himself stops often to comment on a beautiful piece of handicraft—a woven robe, a bow, even something as ordinary as Penelope's chair in *The Odyssey*. Homer looks realistically at the natural hazards threatening human life and at the cruelties of war, but there is always the other side, the ideal civilization in which men live in harmony with each other, using their skills to benefit the community and to give pleasure to themselves and others. Objects, persons, and skills are measured both by their utility and by their aesthetic grace.

Homer's creed is a deeply humanistic one. The gods impose inevitable duties and restraints, but throughout, the humans are the principal actors. Man striving to master his environment, man facing the inevitable fact of death with fortitude, man striving to assert his individuality—this is Homer's central drama. However different later Greek society was from Homeric society, however different the later literature, the Greeks continued to share with Homer that vision of the human potential.

At roughly the same time as Homer, there emerged another poet, Hesiod, from a relatively unimportant part of mainland Greece. Some of his poetry is epic but of a rather different kind from Homer's epics. His *Theogony*, an early attempt at recounting Greek mythology, is rather like an epic history of the world, of its creation from original chaos to the birth of the gods and eventually to the birth of mankind. In his *Works and Days,* we see a new kind of poetry emerging, something quite distinct from epic. The anonymity and detachment of the epic narrator is giving way to a more subjective style. Hesiod identifies himself and informs us that he is a small farmer eking out a bitter but honest livelihood from the soil. He does not hesitate to interject personal opinions, to offer advice to his friends, or to castigate his enemies. The poem itself is like a farmer's almanac in verse. It gives practical advice on agriculture, on the seasons for sowing, ploughing, or reaping. It emphasizes the farmer's need to observe the natural calendar provided by the stars and the seasonal changes. It is full of farmer's lore, both the practical kind and folk superstition.

Such a poem seems far removed from Homer. Even in Homer, however, the heroes are notable for their practical skills. Aristocratic women must weave, and warriors must run their estates. Odysseus is a warrior, an excellent athlete, a good public speaker, but he is also a carpenter and an accomplished navigator. He boasts that he can till the soil as well as any man. *The Odyssey* is a poem in praise of professionalism. Hesiod's *Works and Days* also asserts the necessity for professional knowledge and technique. *The Odyssey* is a tale of superhuman achievement, while Hesiod's poem brings us into the harsh reality of eighth-century Greece. The link between them is their belief in man's ability to master his environment by accurate knowledge and hard work. *The Odyssey* and *Works and Days* record the beginning of Greek science and technology.

Lyric Poetry

Hesiod's personal references—to himself, his own life and opinions—mark the beginning of a new form of poetry, lyric poetry, first written in the seventh and sixth centuries B.C. For the Greeks, lyric poetry was, as its name implies, poetry that was sung to, or accompanied by, music, especially a small harplike instrument called a lyre. For us, lyric has come to mean a certain style and subject, something small and subjective where the epic is objective and on a grand scale. Within our looser definition, we can also include elegiac and iambic poetry, which appears about the same time as lyric and has attitudes more in common with those of lyric than of earlier epic.

The seventh and sixth centuries were a period of rapid change in Greece as the Greeks began to emerge from the stagnation that had followed the fall of Mycenaean civilization. Two inventions, writing and coinage, were to have immense influence. Coinage in particular marked a great technological advance, and we can see the benefits of the new money economy in the general increase of prosperity in the Greek world. But the new economy was not an unmixed blessing. It created a new merchant class, it stimulated the arts, but it also began to open a gulf between the rich traders and the small landowners who struggled to earn a poor livelihood from agriculture.

The pattern of life was changing: It was a time receptive to new thoughts of every variety. It is our good fortune that many of the poets of the period were active in the political, artistic, and philosophical developments of their time and reflected on these developments in their poetry. Some were aristocrats drawn into the power struggles within their own cities. Others were philosophers and scientists searching for the principles by which to understand their world. Yet others were common soldiers, seeing the upheavals from the least privileged and most hazardous position. Lyric poetry, even though what has survived is but a fraction of what was written, still records for us the emotions and thoughts of the most diverse participants in the great events of the time.

Archilochus, a seventh-century foot soldier from the island of Paros, southeast of Athens, invented a new verse form and a new set of attitudes to go with it—anti-heroic to the point of ridiculing heroic values. He fought well and bravely but was not a man to surrender his life in a vain cause. Spartan mothers used to send their sons off to war with the traditional farewell: "Come back with your shield or on it." Come back a hero, whether dead or alive. Archilochus mocks such an ideal. In one poem, he admits freely that he dropped his shield on the battlefield and ran. Not for him the heroism that accepts the idea of future honor as compensation for death. He was also an effective satirist who, according to legend, drove an enemy to suicide by his ferocious lampoons. Archilochus not only shunned the heroic pose for himself but was able to assault other men's pretensions with devastating effect.

Very different from Archilochus in social position and temperament was Solon (640–558 B.C.). He is chiefly remembered for his reform of Athenian political life during a period of crisis in which he used the extraordinary powers granted him to resolve class antagonisms, adding a new dimension to the Greek theory and practice of democracy. As a poet, Solon reflected on those reforms and on the deeper questions behind them: the nature of society, the nature of justice in a society of conflicting classes and interests. He points the way to the political theories that were to be more fully developed in the sixth and fifth centuries.

The commonest themes of lyric poetry in the seventh and

sixth centuries were love and the pleasures of wine and good company. The two most famous lyric poets both came from the island of Lesbos: Alcaeus; and Sappho, the earliest known and most renowned woman writer in Western literature. Alcaeus' simple, forceful style made him popular in later antiquity, often imitated. His varied subjects included hymns to the gods, mythology, and politics, but his reputation rests more on his love poetry and drinking songs. The drinking song is really a kind of folksong, and his use of this form is an early example of the interest lyric poets have shown in popular song.

Sappho's works were known mostly from short quotations until the present century when papyruses of her poems were found in Egypt. Ignoring the interests of the male world—drinking and politics—Sappho devoted her poems to love or to the loneliness she felt when separated from the person she loves. Sappho could portray strong emotion, but she does so with gentle self-mockery. Although her poetry has that keen sense of visual beauty shared by all Greek writers, it is introspective, alert to the slightest inner vibrations, indifferent to heroism except when it stirs a response in her own imagination.

There was another kind of lyric poetry, public rather than personal: the choral lyric. It was poetry commissioned for special occasions, for festivals in honor of the gods or of victors in important athletic contests like the Olympic Games. While personal lyric was recited by the poet to his circle of friends, choral lyric was performed by a chorus before a large public gathering or a whole city. Choral lyric remained closer to its musical origins than personal lyric. The chorus, varying in size and make-up according to the occasion, sang or chanted the poem and probably also executed some kind of dance while singing. The poet generally had an important part in training and directing the chorus.

The most famous of all choral poets was Pindar (522–443 B.C.), who was born in a small town near the important city of Thebes. So great was the honor in which all Greeks held their great lyric poet that when, more than a century later, Alexander the Great captured Thebes and destroyed it, Pindar's house was the only one spared. Pindar's best-known poems are hymns to the gods and odes commemorating the victories of athletes. Since his victory odes were written to order for patrons from various cities, each praised the patron and the patron's native city. But more than any other Greek poet, Pindar expressed the ideal of Hellenism as a whole, undistorted by the constant, bitter

120 *The Literature of Greece and Rome*

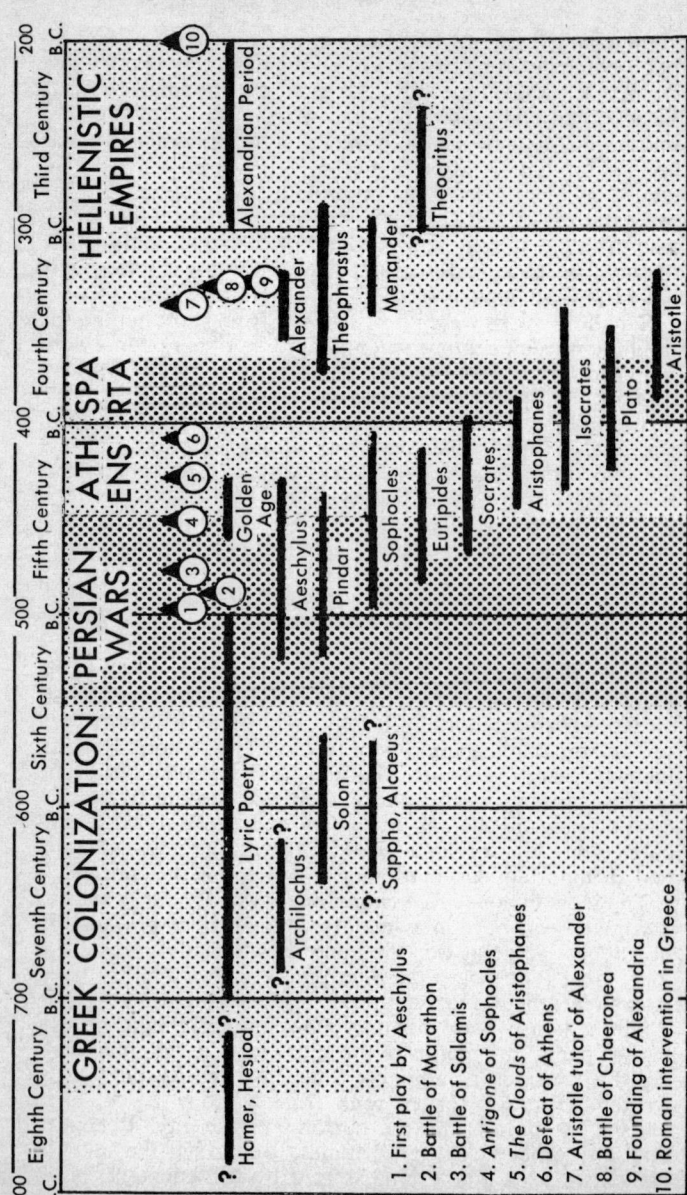

rivalries of the Greek cities: Whatever city or family supplied the subject for particular poems, each individual victor, each individual city with its own store of legends, was but one expression of the Greek spirit; it is always the common Hellenic heritage that Pindar praises. Pindar's choral odes, then, though they seem to concentrate on the mythological past, are really as much concerned with the present moment as the personal lyrics of Alcaeus and Sappho. Stressing the continuity of Greek achievement, Pindar called on his audience to honor the excellence of the ancient heroes now expressed in the athletes' victories.

The Golden Age of Athens

From the time of Homer in the eighth century through the sixth century, no one Greek city or region was pre-eminent in literature, although the most important works came more often from Asia Minor than elsewhere. The fifth century, however, belonged to Athens. Toward the end of the sixth century, Athens began to emerge as the cultural center of Hellas, and so it remained for the next two centuries: Even after the Peloponnesian War had destroyed the political dominance of Athens, her intellectual reputation continued. She became the chief university city of the Greeks and Romans and for centuries drew students to her philosophical schools from all over the civilized world. For the fifth and fourth centuries B.C., Greek literature is Athenian literature, and Athenian literature has remained so influential for our tradition that for most people today Greek literature means simply Homer and the Athenians.

The tyrants who ruled Athens in the latter part of the sixth century (see pages 39-41) contributed to Athens' creative spirit. Autocratic but enlightened, they fostered both economic and artistic progress, making Athens a magnet that drew poets and artists from all parts of Greece. After driving out the tyrants, moreover, Athens resolved her problems through energy-releasing constitutional reforms while other cities stagnated or were weakened by their internal conflicts. By the time of the Persian Wars early in the fifth century, Athens had developed a high level of prosperity, artistic achievement, and political consciousness. After the defeat of the Persians at Marathon (490 B.C.) and Salamis (480 B.C.), the supremacy of Athens as the protector of

Greece against the Persians brought an economic boom as money poured into the city's treasuries, and Athenians were kept in full employment building and manning ships as a deterrent force against the Persians. The victory of the small and rather disorganized Greek forces under Athenian leadership seemed to release unparalleled exuberance and energy. Intellectual speculation, innovation in the arts, historical and scientific research abounded. From now on, the Athenians would have the reputation recorded in the New Testament of spending their time "in nothing else but either to tell, or to hear, some new thing."

Athenian Tragedy

In this century of optimism and national pride, the art form that was to dominate all others in Athens was tragedy. Athenian drama was not staged daily through the year but was an important part of the city's annual religious celebrations. These religious festivals reflected the increase in personal and public wealth by becoming more elaborate and expensive. In the Athenian form of taxation, the wealthy citizens were required to contribute to civic projects, of which the festivals were one of the most prestigious. Tragedies were an expensive form of civic celebration. Underwriting them was one means by which prosperous citizens could demonstrate simultaneously their financial success, their civic conscience, and their artistic sensibility. Tragedy was born in affluence and rested on the foundation of affluence. The achievement of the Athenian dramatists was to turn that particular display of wealth into a most searching probe of purely material success.

Tragedy had its origin in rustic festivals in honor of Dionysus, the god of wine and agricultural fertility. The relationship between Dionysus and tragedy was always formally recognized in the staging of the plays. They were presented only at the two Dionysia, the city's annual celebrations of Dionysus. In the center of the orchestra stood the altar of Dionysus, and the priest of Dionysus sat in the center in the front row of the audience, flanked by the other civic officials.

In another way, too, tragedy recognized its relationship with Dionysus. Each dramatist presented not one play but a set of four plays: first a group of three deeply serious tragedies (a trilogy) and then a comic satyr play. The satyr play seems to have been a kind of burlesque of the themes or the legend presented in the tragic trilogy, in which the chorus, usually representing dignified citizens or counselors in the tragic trilogy, played their supporting role as satyrs. (The satyrs were half-human, half-animal attendants of Dionysus, much given to drinking and general carousing.) The playwright's work thus concluded with something like a tribute to the god of revelry, and in the satyr play we can perhaps see remnants of one original form from which tragedy grew.

Tragedy was really a continuation of the religious choral ode. In the choral ode there might be responses between the chorus leader and the chorus, and in this exchange we can see the beginnings of dramatic dialogue. In time, the chorus leader's role increased in importance until he became recognizably an actor conversing with the chorus.

We can pass from mere speculation with Aeschylus, the first Athenian tragedian who is more than a name. He was born at the shrine city of Eleusis in 525 B.C., began entering his plays in competition about 499, and won his first victory in 484. He wrote some eighty plays and won in the contests thirteen times. He is credited with one important technical innovation, the introduction of a second leading actor. Now it is no longer one man addressing the chorus but two characters in dialogue with each other, with the chorus beginning to withdraw into the background of the drama. This innovation marks the end of the choral ode and the beginning of drama in our modern sense.

In style, Aeschylus remained close to the earlier conventions of Greek drama. If we were to see an Aeschylean play staged as it was staged in his day, it might seem much closer to something like grand opera than to a modern play. There was almost no attempt at realism either in language or in stage scenes, but instead a deliberate artificiality. Massive figures in masks and regal costumes make long speeches in a highly ornate style. The chorus itself is still almost as important as the actors, entering into the action to express, in the loftiest poetry, its reaction to the events of the drama. Indeed, the themes of Aeschylean tragedy, divine power and justice, are ones that we would place within the realm of religion, just as the dramatic conventions, with their serious religious function, are far removed from everyday affairs.

In subject matter, too, Aeschylus might appear remote to us. His plots were drawn from mythology, principally from those two major groups of Greek myths, the one centering on the royal house of Oedipus in Thebes, the other on the rulers Atreus and Agamemnon at Mycenae, the center, a thousand years earlier, of Greece's first advanced civilization (see page 24). Athenian tragedy in general was to use ancient myth as a means of exploring current issues; in fact, Aeschylus provides one of the few exceptions to this rule. In a decidedly innovative move, he made a recent historical event the subject of one play. In 472 B.C., he presented his *Persians,* the story of Xerxes' invasion of Greece and his defeat at the battle of Salamis only eight years earlier. Aeschylus had fought in that battle, as had most of the adult males watching his play. The memory was fresh, as was the patriotic pride, and the play was highly successful. Yet his success did not tempt Aeschylus to repeat the experiment with another contemporary subject. Almost as if to avoid the narrow confines of a particular historical event, the tragedians turned back to myth and found there the relevance they needed for investigating contemporary problems.

If the words and the visual spectacle of Aeschylean plays seem remote, his thought is not. The myths he uses are primitive, full of hereditary curses, destructive oracles, violent murders, avenging furies. (A father sacrifices his daughter to gain a military victory. One man cuts up another man's children and serves them at dinner. A son chops his mother to death just as she had first murdered his father, her husband.) From such material Aeschylus was able to draw new psychological and religious meaning through the kind of poetic exploration of myth that has been influential in Western literature ever since. Through myth, Aeschylus examined the nature of moral law, the role of the gods in man's life, and the role man plays in shaping his own destiny.

Only one of Aeschylus's trilogies, *The Oresteia,* has survived complete, but it was the trilogy that was considered his masterpiece in antiquity, and it has remained one of the masterpieces of all literature. This group of three plays takes its name from the hero of the second and third plays, Orestes, son of Agamemnon, but the subject of the trilogy is much broader than that: It recounts the history of the house of Agamemnon in its attempt to understand the hereditary curse that brought catastrophe on the family one generation after another. In the first play of the trilogy, *Agamemnon,* we see Agamemnon's triumphant return from the conquest of Troy, followed immediately by his death at the hands of his wife Clytemnestra in revenge for sacrificing their daughter Iphigenia during the journey to Troy ten years earlier. In the second play, *The Libation-Bearers,* we see the consequences of the actions in the first play as Agamemnon's son Orestes, now grown to manhood, returns from exile to avenge his father's death. He kills his mother, as the primitive tribal ethic and Apollo's oracle demand, but in turn he is driven to madness for his crime. The final play, *The Eumenides*, attempts to find a resolution for this chain of vengeance.* The clan must yield its own harsh moral code to the larger society of the city as the agent of justice. Man must free himself from the drain of crime and personal revenge and accept a new concept of community and law.

Such a brief summary of the plot of *The Oresteia* suggests something of the political ideas expressed in the three plays, but it can give no idea of the variety and depth of the ideas nor of the emotional power of Aeschylus' poetry. His leading characters are not so fully portrayed that we can sense them as the unique human individuals of modern psychological drama. Yet *The Oresteia* is all psychological: Its concern is not individual psychology but human psychology in the broadest sense. Aeschylus is burdened by the problem of human freedom in a world where oracles can prophesy the future, and the gods can compel a man to perform acts that lead to his own destruction. While he recognizes that there remains always an element of necessity, that the gods can impose burdens that man cannot totally comprehend, he recognizes also that man is a free agent, even though limited in his freedom. In *The Oresteia*, we see those occasions when man is confronted by rival claims and forced to choose between them. No god compelled Agamemnon to sacrifice his daughter; he chose to do so voluntarily to gain smooth sailing for the Greek fleet on its way to Troy. Men bring the curse on themselves by their own decisions, sometimes willfully and sometimes through lack of foresight or sheer negligence.

As early as Homer we can see the beginning of the Greek concern with the relation of a man's character to the fate that befalls him. Oracles seem to foretell important events in Homer, and gods intervene to manipulate events in accordance with their desires, yet each event in the catastrophe portrayed in *The Iliad* is one step in a logical sequence determined by human error or arrogance. Aeschylus articulates the problem of human responsibility with greater precision and carries it to a new psychological level.

It has been common to view the later tragedian Euripides,

---

* The Eumenides of the title, also called Furies or Erinyes, were pitiless and much-feared demons who caused terrible mental and physical pain to those who committed a crime and went unpunished; the Greeks feared these avenging beings so much that they called them Eumenides, which means "well-intentioned," rather than use their actual name.

to whom we shall turn in a moment, as the radical innovator in Greek drama. Perhaps, however, it was Aeschylus who was the true radical: By his technical innovations he created the new form that we call Greek tragedy. It was Aeschylus, too, who raised the form above mere rhetorical bombast or extravagant spectacular, as it might easily have become, and made it the means for the deepest critique of life. Aeschylus created the new form and set its standards high, at the same time achieving great popularity that continued long after his death in 456 B.C. In his epitaph, however, there was not a word of this. Instead, it described him simply as an Athenian citizen who had fought against the Persians. That was honor enough.

The other two great tragedians of Athens' Golden Age followed Aeschylus by about a generation: Sophocles (495–406 B.C.) and Euripides (480–406 B.C.). According to tradition, Aeschylus fought in the battle of Salamis in 480 B.C., Sophocles sang in the boys' chorus that celebrated that victory, and Euripides was born on the day of the battle. The story may be an invention, but it reflects the relationship of the three dramatists' careers. Sophocles' earliest surviving plays were written within a few years of the death of Aeschylus, while those of Euripides began to appear perhaps fifteen years after that. Both were active until their death, which occurred in the same year toward the end of the fifth century. More than twice as many plays of Euripides, the radical overthrower of dramatic tradition, have survived as of Sophocles (probably nineteen compared with seven, including the only complete example of a satyr play).

Sophocles was responsible for three important technical innovations: increasing the chorus from twelve to fifteen members; adding a third leading actor to the drama, permitting a more complex action; and moving away from the trilogy form to three separate plays not necessarily connected in plot or theme. The Sophoclean play does not have the powerful effect of spectacle and grandiose language that we find in an Aeschylean play. Sophocles' style, though still quite formal, is simpler, less remote from everyday language. By abandoning the trilogy form, Sophocles moved closer to pure tragedy. The trilogy form seemed naturally to call for the presentation of the tragic problem in the first play, its development in the second, and its resolution in the third. Sophocles' best plays, on the other hand, are those in which the tragic situation is set forth without any resolution to lessen the force of the tragic experience. For example,

Oedipus the King, which we shall examine in detail shortly, ends with Oedipus' realization that he has indeed committed the horrendous crimes that the oracle had prophesied and which he had hoped to avoid. "The gods have preserved me for some still greater evil," he cries, and again, "Of all men I am the most hateful to the gods." It is the cry of anguish of a criminal, conscious that he is doomed by his own criminal act to a life of utter isolation from both men and gods. Parted from his children, ousted from his throne, he walks off the stage alone in a dramatic expression of his inner isolation. In *Antigone,* too, the tragedy is total. The king, Creon, stands alone at the end, conscious that by his decrees he has caused the death of his son Haemon and his niece Antigone. In Aeschylus, a man's wrongdoing meets with retribution — punishment by the gods — so that sooner or later his evil is paid for by suffering and the account is closed, the tragic situation resolved. In Sophocles, on the other hand, there is little of retribution in this sense. Instead, the tragic protagonist must endure the full consciousness of what he has done. Guilt has become more internalized in Sophocles, moving closer to our modern sense of personal conscience.

Aeschylus found the great subject for his poetic exploration in the fate of the ruling house at Mycenae. Sophocles found his ruling theme in the no less tragic history of the royal house at Thebes, a city northwest of Athens, a bitter rival of Athens throughout classical times until it was destroyed by Alexander the Great. Sophocles' three best known plays, *Oedipus the King, Antigone,* and *Oedipus at Colonus,* though not a trilogy like Aeschylus' *Oresteia,* portray a series of events from the myths centering on Thebes. The earliest written of the three was *Antigone.* It was produced about 442 B.C. when Athenian power was at its highest and shortly before Sophocles himself served as a commander (*strategos*) in the Athenian army. Before the action of the play begins, Thebes has been torn by civil war. Polynices has led an expedition against the city of which his brother was ruler. Both brothers have been killed in battle, and Creon, their uncle, has assumed power. Creon orders that Polynices' body must remain unburied, but Polynices' sister, Antigone, refuses to heed his command. When she is found trying to bury Polynices, Creon orders her walled up in a cave to die of starvation. Creon's son Haemon, who was to have married Antigone, chooses to share her fate. The play ends with Creon's realization that he has caused the death of his niece and his own son.

The play, coming at a time when the short-lived Athenian

Empire was supreme in Hellas, is a searching exploration of political power. The dramatic conflict is a stark confrontation between the autocratic but legitimate ruler of the city and a lone individual who willfully defies his decrees on the grounds of conscience—a higher authority, she claims, than that of any man. The problem was one that had scarcely surfaced in Athenian political life. Athenians took pride in their democracy and the freedom from state interference in their private lives that individual citizens enjoyed. But while Athens practiced democracy at home, elsewhere she was forcing a progressively more despotic rule on her one-time Greek allies, who had now become enforced subjects. In the mid-fifth century, the political conflict was not so much between individual and state as between small and powerless cities and the imperial might of Athens. But Sophocles showed prophetic insight. Scarcely forty years later, the Athenian democracy was to show itself capable of one of history's great crimes against individual freedom when it declared its sovereign will by executing Socrates, the most profound and humane of Greek moral teachers, a man who respected the state but respected his conscience more.

Several years after writing *Antigone*, Sophocles returned to the Theban material, this time to the figure of Oedipus, father of Antigone and Polynices. There are political implications in the play, but the focus is less on political questions than on man's realization of his personal destiny. Oedipus had fled from Corinth, where he had grown up, in fear of a prophecy that he would kill his father and commit incest with his mother. He became king of Thebes, married the queen of Thebes, whose husband had died about the time of his arrival in the city, and had ruled in prosperity until the moment when the play opens. Now the city was suffering from a plague sent by the gods for the unsolved murder of the old king. Oedipus sets about finding the unknown murderer and in pursuing this search slowly discovers that he was himself the murderer and that the old king was his father, the queen his mother. Everything had happened as the oracle foretold, and Oedipus is faced with the tragic irony that his every attempt to evade the prophecy had only brought him closer to its fulfillment. At the end of the play, he is a ruined man, an outcast from human society, and an outcast, too, as he believes, from the presence of the gods.

At the very end of his life, Sophocles again returned to Oedipus in another play, *Oedipus at Colonus*, which was produced by his son in 401 B.C., after his death. In this play, Oedipus has grown old after spending years in exile and dishonor. The play picks up the lament that Oedipus had made in the earlier tragedy, that the gods had singled him out for some extraordinary fate. *Oedipus at Colonus* turns the bleak end of the earlier play to a note of hope. Oedipus has been through extraordinary suffering, and now the gods elevate him to special honor. In his wandering, Oedipus has arrived at the Athenian grove of the Eumenides, the fearful avenging goddesses whom Aeschylus had made central to the last play of *The Oresteia* (see footnote, page 125). An oracle had prophesied that Oedipus would find peace among the Athenians. Theseus, the legendary ruler of Athens, comes out from the city to meet him, grants him asylum, and then accompanies Oedipus as he goes to meet his death. Oedipus dies, or rather he simply disappears from mortal life, and is recognized as a hero by Athens. The man who had left Thebes under a curse has undergone something close to Christian beatification, with the power, even after his death, to give blessings or curses to others. Sophocles wrote this play as his last reflection on the tragic destiny of the man who committed the worst of crimes without intending to. In *Oedipus the King,* Sophocles had focused on the discovery of that crime; in *Oedipus at Colonus,* he tells of the man who had lived through the anguish of that knowledge and reached a kind of purification through suffering.

Euripides carried Sophocles' developments still further. His overturning of the accepted dramatic conventions made him something of a scandal in Athens. He introduced daring changes in music; he worked toward greater realism by presenting unheroic characters on stage, by dressing them in ordinary clothes, even in rags, and by giving them a language still closer to that of daily life. In general, he seemed to be intent on replacing the tragic dignity with realism and with more contemporary philosophical speculation. It is hard for us today to find his stage conventions as revolutionary as his fellow Athenians did, but certainly we can see the shift in emphasis to the new skepticism of the century. The dialogue in Euripides becomes more a debate on an issue, argued in the style of the courtroom. The question of man's relation to the gods has become subordinate to the examination of political issues and human psychology.

The historical event that dominated the second half of the fifth century was the Greek civil war that we call the Peloponnesian War. The war itself continued for a quarter of a century, from 431 to 404 B.C., bringing no real gains even to the Spartans, who won it, and greatly weakening Athens. To this disastrous war Euripides reacted with outspoken vigor. The earlier dramatists had used incidents from the far-off Trojan War to express the tragedy of human existence. Euripides used the same kind of material more concretely as a means of protesting the particular war of his own time, the misguided politics that had led to that war. Aeschylus and Sophocles had both been active in the city's affairs: Aeschylus had been a soldier in the Athenian army, Sophocles a commander, but neither, so far as we know, had related his plays so intimately to his political life and views as Euripides did.

Euripides was a rationalist, the poet of Greece's Enlightenment, but he also probed human psychology in a new way and showed a special interest in irrational forms of behavior. Precisely because he abandoned the more traditional religious viewpoint, his drama could focus more on human character and motivation. His reputation as a dramatist has rested on his studies of consuming and destructive passion in such plays as *Medea* and *Hippolytus*. Passionate and vengeful women had never been lacking on the Athenian stage, but there had been none like Euripides' Medea or Phaedra, the tragic heroine of *Hippolytus*. Sophocles had presented two powerful portraits of passionate women, first in the figure of Antigone and then in Electra, Agamemnon's daughter, who, together with her brother Orestes, kills Clytemnestra as an act of vengeance for Agamemnon's death. Both women are defiant and determined, but both believe themselves answerable to higher laws and obey those laws even when obedience means their own death. Euripides' women cannot rely on that kind of external support; they know that they are acting entirely contrary to accepted moral standards.

Medea, a princess from the far-off Black Sea city of Colchis, had once saved Jason's life when he went there to carry off the city's great treasure, the Golden Fleece. Turning her back on her own people, she returned with Jason to Corinth, but Jason decided to marry Creusa, a princess of Corinth, and Euripides' play is the story of Medea's cruel revenge. In jealousy and rage, she kills both her own children by Jason and Jason's intended bride. She stands utterly alone, a stranger in Corinth and one who cannot hope to find the slightest sympathy for her terrible crime.

In *Hippolytus*, Phaedra also exacts a fearful personal revenge, but in a different way. She is married to Theseus but falls in love with Theseus' son Hippolytus. At first she conceals her love, but when Hippolytus discovers it and rejects it, she takes her own life to preserve her honor. At the same time, however, she leaves behind a letter that falsely incriminates Hippolytus. Theseus, reading the letter, calls down a curse on Hippolytus, and Hippolytus is killed shortly thereafter when his horses shy at the sudden appearance of a bull sent by the sea-god Poseidon. In Phaedra we have a subtle portrait of the struggle in one woman between honor and bitter frustration that turns to revenge.

In Euripides' *Bacchae*, the god Dionysus has an important role, a fact that has puzzled scholars. The Athenian dramatic festivals for which the tragedies were written were, of course, conventionally in honor of Dionysus, but here the god appears not merely as a convenient prologue or epilogue but as a full participant in the drama, sinister and powerful. He confronts the skeptical king Pentheus and proves his superior power by arousing the women of the city, including Pentheus' mother and sisters, to such frenzy that they tear the king to pieces. For some, this play, in which a god savagely causes the death of the man who disbelieved in him, reads like Euripides' apology for earlier disbelief in Dionysus. It is really a further development, however, of the interest Euripides had shown (in plays like *Medea* and *Hippolytus*) in what we should call the morbid state of mind. He recognized very clearly that men possessed by madness could be driven to savagery that would horrify them in their lucid state. In other plays, he had portrayed the morbid individual, like Phaedra torn by the conflict between her secret obsession and the moral code. In *The Bacchae*, he portrays a morbid individual, Pentheus, but also the mob that under obscure influences becomes deranged. In Euripides, the gods may not be so vividly personal as they had seemed in earlier Greek mythology, but behind them is a psychological reality that it is dangerous to ignore.

Comedy

The Persian Wars, which ushered in the fifth century B.C., gave an enormous lift to Athenian power, leadership, and wealth, and this had an important influence on the development of tragedy. It is ironic that toward the end of the same century, the ruinous and long drawn-out Peloponnesian War (431–404 B.C.) should have had an almost equally significant effect on comedy.

Comedy had existed before the Peloponnesian War, just as there had been some kind of tragedy before Aeschylus. In fact, tragedy and comedy were closely related in their origins. Both sprang from some kind of peasant ritual in honor of Dionysus, and both became central events in the Dionysian festivals in Athens. Comedy, however, seems to have remained for a longer period closer to its rustic origin in loosely organized improvisation and farce. Only in the middle of the fifth century did comedy come into its own as an art form to rival tragedy. We know by name a number of comic playwrights who lived and wrote in Athens in the second half of the fifth century and the early fourth century. The plays of only one of these comic writers have survived, however: Aristophanes. Eleven of the forty-four comedies he is known to have written have come down to us. The earliest of these, *The Acharnians,* a satire on inept Athenian diplomacy that demanded the end of the war with Sparta, won the prize at a festival of comedy in 425 B.C. when Aristophanes was barely twenty. (The dates of his birth and death are not known for certain, but he lived from about 445 to 385 B.C.)

Tragedy, no matter how relevant its themes to contemporary society, nearly always framed them in myths drawn from the distant past. Comedy, in contrast, was always directly topical. It seems to have begun as a vehicle for uninhibited caricature and criticism of the city's leading public figures. When comedy received official recognition in the annual drama festivals, it retained its original freedom for satire, extravagant invention, and bawdy language and incident. The social and intellectual changes of the latter part of the fifth century, the political tensions, the protracted war, and the violent conflict of generations added a sharp edge of bitterness to Athenian comedy. In Aristophanes, the wild extravagance of comedy was no longer merely a bold form of public entertainment; it expressed an underlying pessimism approaching despair.

Aristophanes' comedies generally place real people and real social and political problems in a frame of fantasy. In one play (*Lysistrata*) the women decide to stage a sexual strike against their husbands in order to force them to end the war. In another (*The Birds*), Aristophanes has given up on the human world altogether, and we are transplanted to a new world inhabited solely by birds, though we soon see in this animal parable that birds and humans are much alike. Another play (*The Frogs*) is set in the land of the dead where Dionysus, the god of the theater, serves as judge in a contest between Aeschylus and his modern successor Euripides. Aristophanes' plays are a comedy of exaggeration, of the absurd in the modern sense of the word. The language could be lewd in the extreme, and no doubt the stage business that went with it was even lewder. (We are told, however, that Aristophanes was rather more restrained in this respect than other Greek comic playwrights.) The attacks on political leaders were uninhibited, fierce, and often quite unfair. Anything in a politician's life was fair game for the comic stage. Slurs on his parentage, references to his sex life, personal gossip, true or false—all could provide useful material for the hostile playwright. (In *The Acharnians*, where the great tragedian Euripides also appeared as a character, he was repeatedly twitted because his mother was supposed to have been a vegetable seller.)

Political leaders were not Aristophanes' only target. He distrusted the new social and intellectual currents in Athens and saw in them a threat to Athens' inner strength. He attacked Euripides (in *The Frogs*) for reducing tragic grandeur to ignoble bathos. He ridiculed the Athenian assembly for voting according to momentary whims, for being taken in by the lying reports of pompous, overpaid ambassadors and other officials (*The Acharnians*). There is often in the plays a regret for the honest, self-sufficient life of the farmer that the Athenian citizens had abandoned for the debt-ridden existence of the urban capitalist. Aristophanes also attacked the loss of faith in the gods, the sophisticated arguments by which the new scientific thought of the time was overthrowing more traditional beliefs. And in one play, *The Clouds*, which most critics have found difficult to forgive, he combined all of these themes in a vicious attack on Socrates, the greatest and most humane of Greek philosophers.

The Clouds had a peculiar history. When it was first produced in 423 B.C., the Athenians apparently did not like it, and it failed to win the prize for comedy. Aristophanes seems later to have published the play with additions (the version that has survived) in which he defended it as the best thing he had written and denounced his rival playwrights. In the play, a boorish farmer is being driven bankrupt by his son, who can think of nothing but horseracing and is seeking some way of avoiding having to pay his creditors. He has the brilliant thought of seeking help from the new breed of professional teachers (called Sophists) who were stirring up controversy in Athens at the time, and the one to whom the farmer turns is called Socrates. In the figure of Socrates, portrayed as a bumbling, absent-minded professor, Aristophanes satirized many of the things that the average Athenian must have disliked about the Sophists—that they collected high fees for their teaching, enunciated improbable-sounding "scientific" theories that seemed as lacking in common sense as the old beliefs, and denied the existence of the gods; above all, that they used complicated arguments to persuade men to accept ideas that were impractical and immoral.

The portrait of Socrates in *The Clouds,* although very funny, is completely false (Socrates opposed the Sophists and their new "science" and never accepted money for his teaching), and that may have been why the festival audience rejected it. We might put the caricature down to the indiscretion and high spirits of a young writer of genius (Aristophanes was about twenty-two at the time) if it had not ultimately had a tragic sequel. For in 399 B.C., in the economic and moral bankruptcy that followed the loss of the Peloponnesian War, the Athenian government executed Socrates on a trumped-up legal charge—and it seems possible that the violent caricature by Aristophanes may have been at least a psychological reason for this result.

Comedy did not disappear with Aristophanes' death in 385 B.C., but it lost its political and social content and became quite different in form. It would be half a century, in the new context of Hellenistic civilization, before another notable writer of Athenian comedy appeared, in Menander. The "new comedy" that he wrote would be romantic, amusing, as concerned with love and marriage as a successful Broadway musical, but the dimension of political satire had disappeared.

The Age of Prose

When we read the comedies of Aristophanes—racy, topical, popular in the sense that both their subject and their audience were the Athenian people as a whole—we need to remind ourselves that in an age of poets he was a notable and often an exquisite poet. For the fifth century B.C. in Athens was an age of poetry—dramatic poetry—as the eighth century had been an age of epic poetry and the seventh and sixth centuries an age of lyric poetry. Yet something else of equal importance for Greek literature was happening in the fifth century: the development of prose as a major medium of communication and expression. Like the playwrights, the writers of prose owed much, directly and indirectly, to one man, Pericles, and to the marvelous Athenian achievements and failures in which he played a leading part.

In the fifth century, Greek literature began to produce

utilitarian prose works on a variety of subjects (medicine, geography, mythology, genealogy, local history). Now, also, under the impact of the century's two great wars, there appeared for the first time serious and reliable works of history. The two great Greek historians defined the ideals and the methods that historians have followed ever since, and both acted in the events they recorded and attempted to understand: Herodotus (484–425 B.C.), the "father of history," and Thucydides (460–395 B.C.).

History and biography are of such importance in Greek civilization that they will be discussed in detail in a separate chapter. But the books that Herodotus and Thucydides wrote are also literature, and some account of them must be given here.

Born in Asia Minor in the midst of the Persian Wars, Herodotus shared in the expansive optimism that so many Greeks felt at their great victories over the power of Persia. When he set out to record the wars for posterity, then, he saw them in the large context of the centuries-long conflict between East and West, Europe and Asia. His account opens with a discussion of the causes of the Trojan War, and both in style and in his sense of the greatness of the events he describes, he looks back to Homer. Unlike the epic poet, however, he was dealing with events that had occurred within living memory and did not have to rely on myth, legend, and the uncertainties of oral tradition. Herodotus traveled widely throughout Greece, Asia, and Egypt, seeing for himself the places where the conflict had occurred and collecting firsthand reports that he set down in a lively style. The modest title of his great book, *Histories,* means "researches" or "investigations" in Greek. By his careful and skeptical reporting of what he found, Herodotus established a new standard of historical truth. Before he wrote, the question of what actually happened could hardly have been asked of any historical event. By his example, he made it the primary question.

Herodotus is said to have read his *Histories* to great acclaim at the Olympic Games of 456 B.C. The heroic achievements at Marathon and Salamis were in the recent past; Greek greatness was on the rise, and above all the power and creativity of Athens, at the head of the Delian League and under the leadership of her greatest statesman, Pericles. By the end of the century, Athens had risen to the heights of her Golden Age — and fallen back again in the disaster of the Peloponnesian War. Both the grandeur and the ultimate ruin were in large measure the work of Pericles.

If Herodotus reflected the high hopes of the first half of the fifth century, Thucydides' *History of the Peloponnesian War* was a careful and objective account of the events that, by the end of the century, had destroyed those hopes. Athens under Pericles had reached extremes of greatness and decadence. In 454 B.C., the treasury of the Delian League, formed under Athenian leadership as a united Greek defense against the Persians, was highhandedly moved to Athens. Henceforth, Athens controlled this fund, using it both to build up the Athenian navy for the common defense and, directly and indirectly, to support the immense public building program of Pericles. In 449 B.C., when Sophocles was writing his earliest surviving plays, the long conflict with the Persians at last came to an end in a treaty of peace. But Pericles' aggressive foreign policy and the growing rivalry of the Spartan-dominated Peloponnesian League led, in 431 B.C., to the outbreak of the Peloponnesian War, which was to continue almost thirty years, until both sides, evenly matched, were exhausted. Pericles' strategy was to rely on the Athenian navy against the Spartan army. He encouraged the populace in the region around Athens to come into the city, leaving the Spartans free to ravage the countryside. Within a year of the beginning of the war, the crowded conditions in Athens resulted in an outbreak of plague; a year later, in 429 B.C., Pericles himself was dead of the disease.

These depressing events are important in our consideration of Thucydides for two reasons: first, the purpose of his *History* was to set down for posterity the errors that led to the disastrous war and the mistakes the Athenian people and their leaders made in its conduct—the book was to be a warning to future generations; and second, Thucydides was a commander in the Athenian navy. In 424 B.C., in punishment for a serious error in battle, he was condemned to twenty years' exile from Athens. He spent the rest of his life traveling throughout Hellas, gathering material for his *History*.

In contrast to Herodotus, Thucydides was careful to keep personal comment out of his work, but he made his views clear by his selection of events and the similarities and contrasts that he allowed them to demonstrate. For example, he includes the magnificent oration that Pericles delivered in tribute to those who had died in the first year of the war—a superb description of the virtues of Athenian citizenship and the democracy that, in large measure, he had helped Athens to achieve. But in Thucydides' account Pericles' oration is followed immediately by a description of the plague that decimated the Athenian population. Noble rhetoric and the sordid consequences of war, both physical and psychological, are placed in dramatic contrast, and the reader is left to draw his own conclusion.

The Peloponnesian War ended in 404 B.C., with Sparta victorious and, for a time, the dominant power in Hellas. Thucydides died in 395 B.C., leaving his *History* unfinished. In the meantime, a new, wartime generation had grown up in Athens, turning their backs on the public responsibilities that, at an earlier date, they would naturally have assumed. Plato (427–347 B.C.), a literary genius and one of the world's great philosophers, is the outstanding representative of this new generation.

As a young man, Plato came under the influence of Socrates (469–399 B.C.), and his writings were devoted to explaining and developing the thought of his great teacher. Of the more than thirty books by Plato mentioned in antiquity, all have survived, and in nearly all of them Socrates has an important role. Since Socrates himself wrote no books, nearly all that we know of him and his ideas is by way of Plato.

Almost all of Plato's philosophical works were written in a new literary form, the dialogue, modeled on the dramatic mode that dominated Greek literature in his time. (Before meeting Socrates, Plato tried writing plays, which he burned when he became interested in philosophy.) Embittered at the unjust execution of Socrates, Plato preserved a vivid and moving portrait of the master and his ideas in two short dialogues, the *Apology* and *Crito,* accounts of the trial and death of Socrates.

Plato founded a school of philosophy, the Academy, which met in a grove to the north of Athens and marked the beginning of the city's role as a center of higher learning, the first in European history. Among the several outstanding Greek philosophers who were his students, the most notable was Aristotle (384–322 B.C.), one of the greatest minds that humanity has produced. Taking philosophy in its broadest sense, he undertook to present all human knowledge in systematic form: ethics, logic, political science, biology, physics, astronomy, rhetoric, poetry, music. His scientific writings reflect direct observation and dissection of biological specimens. (His father was the physician to the king of Macedon, and Aristotle was probably trained in medicine.)

His *Poetics* remains an excellent summary of the aesthetic theory behind Greek tragedy and has been influential throughout the history of Western drama.

Aristotle had grown up at the Macedonian court before going to Athens to study under Plato, and it was therefore natural that in 342 B.C. Philip the Great should invite him back to instruct his brilliant young son, Alexander. Aristotle instilled in his pupil a love of Greek culture and thus, when Alexander became the ruler of the known world, had a direct role in the spread of Greek learning and the development of that new form of Greek civilization that we call Hellenistic. (The conqueror's respect for his teacher was large; on his marches through Asia, he collected biological specimens for Aristotle and sent them back to him in Athens.)

While philosophy was rising to these lofty heights (to be discussed in detail in a later chapter, "Philosophy, Religion, and Science"), there had been a parallel development that helped to make prose rather than poetry the characteristic literary form of the fourth century. The range of experience, feeling, and ideas that the Greek poets—above all, the tragic poets—were able to convey in verse was immense, but there were limits. Prose—the language of the law courts, of argument and refutation—emerged in the second half of the fifth century out of the need to express new ideas in a new form, particularly, perhaps, from the spiritual turmoil aroused by Athens' aggressive foreign policy and the crisis of the Peloponnesian War.

Representative of this new mode of thought and expression were the Sophists: professional teachers and public speakers, half lawyers, half philosophers. We have already noticed, in connection with the caricature of Socrates in Aristophanes' comedy *The Clouds,* the bad opinion that the ordinary Athenian citizen had of these men because of their willingness to persuade men of any proposition, regardless of its truth or falsehood. Although he was condemned for the skepticism that the Sophists promoted, Socrates opposed them, and Plato continued the opposition; the school Plato founded, the Academy, was in effect a rival to the Sophists' schools.

As Greek literature moved toward the time when it would no longer be purely Greek but Hellenistic, one man is of special interest as a transitional figure. In his long lifetime, Isocrates (436–338 B.C.), spanned the period from the high point of Athenian greatness to the submergence of Greece and its culture in the empire of Philip and Alexander of Macedon. (Isocrates is said to have starved himself to death out of grief at the Greek defeat by Philip at the Battle of Chaeronea in 338 B.C.). Like the Sophists, he conducted a school in which he taught the art of public speaking, and the more than thirty orations of his that have survived were written as models to be read rather than delivered in public. In speeches like the *Panegyricus* and the *Panathenaicus,* Isocrates expressed a lofty Athenian patriotism and a hope for resolving the ceaseless rivalries of the Greek city-states in a true Pan-Hellenic unity. Under Alexander the Great, this hope was about to be realized, though in a form that Isocrates and the other Athenian patriots could not understand or accept.

Hellenistic Literature

A year after the Macedonian defeat of the Athenian-led Greek forces at the Battle of Chaeronea, Philip of Macedon, at the Congress of Corinth in 337 B.C., imposed on the warring Greek city-states the unity that they had been unable to achieve for themselves. Before another year had passed, Philip himself was dead, and his twenty-year-old son and successor, Alexander, was ready to embark on the thirteen-year epic of conquest that would carry Greek culture, which his tutor Aristotle had taught him to cherish, to the limits of the known world—to Egypt in the south, to India in the East. This was the beginning of that mingling of Greek genius with the cultures of other peoples—Greco-Indian, Greco-Egyptian, ultimately, Greco-Roman—which we examined in Chapter I and which we sum up in the term Hellenistic.

Almost as significant as Alexander's conquests for the future of Greek literature and the new Hellenistic civilization was his building, in 331 B.C., of the new city in Egypt that he named for himself: Alexandria. For, a few years later, there was founded at Alexandria, under the patronage of the Ptolemaic Greek rulers of Egypt, that remarkable institution called the Museum, and with it the center of gravity of Hellenistic civilization shifted permanently away from Athens and Greece—first, for hundreds of years, to Alexandria itself, ultimately to Rome.

The Museum was dedicated to the advancement of scholarship in all fields. There, often as librarians assured of state support, were gathered the philosophers, scientists, and poets of the Greek-speaking world; and there, too, were collected and preserved virtually all the important writings of the known civilized world, in time a total of half a million volumes. Although much of this marvelous collection of books was scattered or destroyed in the upheavals of Hellenistic civilization (the Museum was finally destroyed in the seventh century A.D. when the Arabs conquered Egypt), it is to the Museum's existence that we owe most of what we know today of Greek literature.

In philosophy and in higher education generally, Athens continued to hold her high place for centuries after the rise of Alexandria to eminence. And throughout the fourth century B.C., in spite of all the dislocations, Athenian creativity persisted in literature, though with a difference. After the Peloponnesian War, the audience for literature in Athens was divided in two, popular on the one hand, serious and intellectual on the other. In the previous century, literature had had a universal appeal to all classes of citizens. Its roots were in popular forms, and it remained close to those roots. Aeschylus, for example, even at his most exalted, wrote essentially popular entertainment that reflected its important civic function, its integration with the general life of the city in which all citizens shared. By the late fourth century, however, tragedy had become largely a restaging of the classical plays of earlier dramatists. The biting satire and topical relevance of Aristophanes had been replaced by situation comedy. Now, one kind of public would find its entertainment in lighthearted comedy, while a smaller and more select audience turned to the polished political essays of a writer like Isocrates.

The comic playwright Menander (342–292 B.C.) illustrates both the changes that Athenian literature underwent at the beginning of the Hellenistic period and its continuing vitality. Menander had been a student of the philosopher Theophrastus (372–287 B.C.), who succeeded Aristotle as the head of the Lyceum, the school and research institute founded by Aristotle in the park of that name on the outskirts of Athens. In his lifetime, Menander wrote more than a hundred comedies and won the prize for comedy eight times. (The Athenian dramatic festivals continued.) At his death, he was held in a veneration second only to that accorded Homer in Greek literature. Curiously, his witty lines (more than fifteen hundred of them) were known from quotations in many other writers, but the plays themselves disappeared and were not rediscovered until the twentieth century. Today, apart from the many quotations and the imitations of the Roman playwrights Plautus and Terence (see page 146), Menander's work is known only from three rediscovered plays, all fragmentary but complete enough to give us an idea of his plots and the quality of his writing.

The Girl from Samos seems to be typical of Menander's work and of the New Comedy generally. Plangon, the daughter of a poor and ill-tempered Athenian, Niceratus, and Moschion, the adopted son of Niceratus' rich and genial neighbor Demeas, are secretly in love and want to marry, though Moschion boasts of his other romantic successes. The two parents at first favor the marriage, but innumerable, often very funny, complications get in the way, and every attempt at straightening things out only seems to add to the confusion—until the fifth act. (Among other things, Plangon and Moschion secretly have a baby, as does Demeas' mistress Chrysis—the "girl from Samos" of the title—and both must conceal the infants from Demeas and Niceratus.) The plot is more cleverly worked out than the plots of Aristophanes, but it is notable that unlike Aristophanes Menander makes only the most casual reference to the great events of his time (Chrysis, one of the Athenians expelled from the island of Samos after the defeat of Athens by Macedon, arrived in Athens destitute and unable to prove her citizenship, hence unable, under Athenian law, to marry Demeas, who fell in love with her and took her in). The satire was now no longer political but social. The world of the New Comedy has become the world of well to-do families with impertinent slaves, fathers successful in business, and rebellious sons who prefer their love affairs to business—a world in which money, success, and good marriages play an important part.

Yet if the old civic sense was dying out in Greek literature, there was a new breadth, a sense not just of shared Hellenic culture but of the common brotherhood of man. This new spirit is expressed in one of Menander's most famous lines, which has come down to us through a Latin translation by Terence: "I am a man; nothing in men's affairs I consider alien to me." The decline of power and wealth in Athens and in Hellas was not all loss.

The Alexandrian Period

The literature of the Alexandrian period shows the influence of the Museum. The poets of the third century were either librarians at Alexandria or were closely associated with the library. Their poetry is a conscious revival of ancient forms, but it is a scholarly kind of revival, written by scholars and librarians for an audience composed of men of similar tastes and occupations. The old civic function of poetry had disappeared and could not be revived.

The Alexandrian poets sifted through the literature of the past and yearned to be genuine successors to that tradition. They began to search for a new justification for poetry, a poetry that could embrace the past and yet speak to their contemporary society. Some attempted to recreate the epic, as Apollonius did in his *Argonautica,* a long poem narrating Jason's legendary quest for the Golden Fleece in his ship the *Argo.* For others, the epic poem seemed utterly unsuitable to the times. The librarian Callimachus opted instead for the smaller poem, with emphasis on elegance and refinement instead of epic grandeur.

Theocritus (born about 300 B.C. in Syracuse on the island of Sicily) turned to folk traditions hitherto ignored in literature. In the rustic life in Sicily, there were two popular traditions: the mime, a fairly loosely structured, even improvised, dramatic dialogue; and singing contests performed by shepherds and goatherds as they tended their flocks on the hillsides. The rustic songs were often laments for the fate of the mythical shepherd, Daphnis. They were as often concerned, however, with the daily affairs of the singers, with the shepherds' life out of doors, their work, their loves. Theocritus, himself a Sicilian of humble birth, created from these rustic sources a new form of poetry, the pastoral, peopled by shepherds or the humble city proletariat. His singing shepherds are literary shepherds, to be sure, but in their preoccupation with simple pleasures and their unpretentious language, we hear echoes of a genuine peasant life. Theocritus' pastorals are consciously literary, but at the same time they describe certain aspects of his world with an authenticity that no other poet of the time approached.

Through Alexandrian poetry runs a note of melancholy: The poets felt frustrated in their efforts to carry on the magnificent tradition with significant contributions of their own. "We need no new poets, Homer is enough for us," Theocritus laments, complaining that that is the common response that modern poets hear. That was the problem, that poetry no longer seemed necessary. The dilemma was one that neither the dedication of poets to their literary traditions nor their creative talent could entirely resolve. We may be thankful that the crisis produced a poet like Theocritus. Had he found the wealthy patron he sought, he might have been content to write rather artificial imitations of old choral odes. Instead, forced back on his own resources, with his eyes and ears open to the world around him, he created still another new poetic form.

The entire history of Greek literature is one of enormous creativity, of spontaneous new forms bursting forth at every period, even in the late day of Theocritus. Rarely can we make more than a guess about the origins of each form; suddenly the form appears in its perfection. Each form has its brief moment and then makes way for another. In the creation of new forms and in the ideas articulated through those forms, the Greeks showed a fertility of imagination hardly paralleled since. Europe has invented virtually no new literary forms since the Greeks. Indeed, European literature owes its very existence to Greece. Epic and lyric, drama, history, philosophy, oratory, even the novel and the essay — on every literary form practiced in modern times, we see the unmistakable imprint of the Greek mind.

How Roman Literature Began

Greece had discovered and exploited all its literary forms before there was anything in Rome that we could call literature. There were some official records, some religious and popular songs, proverbial sayings, but these were not literature. Not until the third century B.C. do we hear of writers consciously attempting to create a Roman literature. The first attempts, mostly translations from Greek literature, show the dependence with which Rome began her literary course and which she always acknowledged.

The earliest literary figures were not even Romans. Here we see a considerable difference between Greece and Rome. In Greece and the Greek settlements dotted across the Mediterranean, there were differences in dialect from place to place, but there was one common language and one common culture. Italy was not a nation in this sense but a land of many entirely distinct languages. Latin was at first the local language of the city of Rome and its environs, and only gradually, as Rome won political dominance, did it become established as the common language of Italy. The early writers came to Rome from other parts of Italy or from the Greek world, speaking a native language other than Latin. Latin was their second or even third language, since Greek was commonly their second language, and when they translated works from Greek into Latin, they were translating into their newly adopted tongue. The first chapter of Roman literature was thus the last chapter, in a sense, of classical Greek literature.

Livius Andronicus, from Tarentum in southern Italy, was brought to Rome as a slave in 272 B.C. and was the first to produce a play in Latin, at Rome in 240 B.C. Naevius, a playwright and poet of the same period, may have been a native Roman but was clearly well versed in Greek literature and in the folk traditions of southern Italy. The early epic poet Ennius (239–169 B.C.) also came from the south, where Greek influence had been strong for centuries. He claimed that he had three hearts because he spoke Greek and the two main Italian languages, Oscan and Latin. Plautus (254–184 B.C.), from Umbria in northern Italy, came to Rome probably as an actor. (Desperately poor, he worked as a stage carpenter before he began to write.) Lacking a literature of her own, Rome was thus beginning to come into contact with the Greek or Greco-Italian inheritors of a rich literary tradition extending back half a millenium. Borrowing was inevitable, and it was inevitable, too, that the middlemen in this transaction should most often be Italians from the Hellenized cities of southern Italy. Roman literature was doubly imported: its genres, or literary forms, were taken from Greek models, and its first practitioners were foreigners who were Romans only by adoption.

The late appearance of Roman literature and its dependence on Greek models allow us to watch the interesting process by which Rome created her own national literature. With the Homeric poems, Greek literature sprang into being fully formed. Predecessors to Homer there must have been, and influences from the non-Greek literatures of Asia Minor, but we know almost nothing of them. Homer himself gives no hint of earlier models, whether in Greek or in other languages. The history of Greek literature continues in this way, with each new genre making an instantaneous appearance as if by some electrical impulse. Only in the Alexandrian period do we see something of an experiment under way, with writers attempting this or that mode as if in doubt as to how to proceed.

Almost all of Roman literature shows the kind of uncertainty that we find in Alexandrian literature, and for somewhat the same reason. The past literary achievements, while they gave the Alexandrian poets an incentive to new creative efforts, were also a formidable threat. The Romans reacted in the same way to Greek literature; they were impelled to imitate and yet anxious to articulate their own experience. Roman literature is a continual experimentation, as writers worked toward the ideal balance between imitation and creativity. The modern world has seen many recurrences of this literary process. It appears in the nineteenth-century literature of small European countries as they tried to formulate their national identity. It has been perennial in American literary history, as American writers have taken literary forms from England while attempting to use those forms to convey authentic American experience. This has been, in fact, a problem common to all the Americas, as each colony, English-speaking, Spanish, or Portuguese, achieved independence and then sought to create a literature reflecting both its Old World and its New World ancestry. Roman literature is a laboratory where we can observe in detail this process of imitation, adaptation, and experimentation.

Most of early Roman literature has disappeared, but even among the fragments that remain we can trace the stages of development. First, there were direct translations, like Livius Andronicus' translation of *The Odyssey* into Latin, using a Roman verse form, the Saturnian. Then, still in the third century B.C., we find Naevius creating a Roman drama based on Greek models and writing his epic poem of the war with Carthage, *Bellum Poenicum,* in imitation of Homer. A writer like Ennius experimented with various genres—epic, comedy, tragedy—and developed a new form that he called *satura* ("a mixture," from which the later word *satira*, or "satire," derives). The *Annals* of Ennius, a long epic poem on Roman history and legend, became highly popular and stood as the national epic until it was superseded by Virgil's *Aeneid*. Only fragments of the *Annals* have survived. The poem was crude and unpolished compared with *The Aeneid*, but Virgil admired it and borrowed and improved passages from it.

Early Roman Comedy

With the comedies of Plautus, we come to literature that has survived in sufficient quantity to permit a clear understanding of the transformation of Greek into Latin. Plautus took his models from the Greek New Comedy of the Alexandrian period—situation comedies with stock characters and intricate, farcical plots. A limited number of formulas, with endless minor variations, sustained the plots. Mistaken identity figured prominently: slave girls at the beginning of the play turn out to be well-to-do ladies; orphans move from destitution to affluence when their fathers are discovered to be still living after all. Plautus took no pains to adapt the

Greek plays to Roman conditions. Imitation was still close to outright translation. His titles are Latin, but the plays are set in Greek cities; his characters generally have Greek names, often resort to Greek expressions, appear in Greek dress, and refer to Roman ways with the disparaging epithet *barbarus,* using the Greek perspective, which divided the world into Greek on the one hand and barbarian on the other. At the same time, his plays are also filled with allusions to Rome and to Italy, and the language, which relies for its effectiveness on Roman proverbs and puns, is clearly no translation. Plautus was content to let Greek and Roman elements jostle each other indiscriminately, with no concern for the incongruity. Several plays of Plautus provided plots for later writers, notably Shakespeare and the great French playwright of the seventeenth century, Molière.

Terence (about 195–159 B.C.), another comic playwright writing some fifty years after Plautus, attempted, surprisingly, to be more strictly Hellenic. He was a North African (from Rome's hated arch rival Carthage) who came to Rome as a slave. Ironically, after gaining his freedom, Terence became the close friend of the young noble Scipio, a descendant of the famous general Scipio Africanus (who defeated Hannibal and the Carthaginians in the Second Punic War) who would himself, in a few years' time, be responsible for the final and complete destruction of the city of Carthage. By Terence's time, a knowledge of Greek literature was almost an essential for educated Romans. Men like the aristocratic Scipio and the friends he had gathered around him had grown up familiar with Greek literature and valued it for its cultural and artistic standards. Terence wrote his plays for the public stage, but he was more intent on satisfying, as he said, the educated standards of his friends. The mixture of Greek and Roman allusions in Plautus evidently offended his sense of consistency, and his comedies remained true throughout to their Greek originals. All names, places, and allusions remained Greek. His plots, then, he proclaimed as Greek, but his language he made entirely Roman, refined and yet natural. Thus, while insisting on being more Greek than Plautus, Terence developed a Latin style so authentic that it became a model for study and imitation in later centuries.

Literature at the End of the Republic

Greek literature came to Rome through epic and drama, brought first by men of the lower class, slaves and freedmen, or, like Plautus, actors and stage managers. Slowly, as contact between Greece and Rome continued, Greek literature spread more widely among the Roman upper classes. It became fashionable for young Roman aristocrats to travel to Athens to study Greek literature in all its forms. Popular entertainment like comedy fell into neglect as literature became the property of the educated. Terence was able to bridge the gap between the cultured sensibility of the aristocrats and the less refined tastes of the growing city proletariat, but after Terence Roman literature was written by the educated and addressed to those who could be expected to appreciate subtle allusions or imitations of Greek rhythms. The first century B.C. became more consciously imitative of Greek forms, all the while, however, establishing a style that was distinctively Roman. Terence had shown how this could be done.

The Punic Wars had made Rome an imperial city with provinces, protectorates, and allies from the east Mediterranean to the west. Rome herself enjoyed great prosperity, but at the expense of her allies and subjects, who became increasingly restive. The first century B.C. was wracked by war: war between Rome and her Italian allies, then slave rebellions throughout Italy, and finally civil war, as the Roman Senate split into political parties, each forming military and political alliances to force the other party into subjection.

Literature reacted to this period of violence and change in two ways that recall what happened in Athenian literature as a result of the Peloponnesian War. Literary men turned either to rhetoric or to philosophy. Forced to make their reputations in the law courts and to advance their careers through political office, men of ambition became lawyers by necessity: the art of rhetoric—the essence of public speaking—became an essential part of education for public affairs, as it had been in Athens in similar circumstances. Others, however, seeing the personal risks for anyone in Roman politics—confiscation of property or death were common penalties for those who took their chances in the political arena—turned away from such involvement, preferring to find their satisfactions in quiet retirement or in contemplative philosophy.

In the last century of the Republic, two great literary figures stand out as representative of these opposing tendencies: Lucretius (about 94–55 B.C.) and Cicero (106–43 B.C.). Lucretius undertook to expound, in a long, didactic poem, *On Nature* (*De Rerum Natura*, literally, "*On the*

Nature of Things"), the scientific principles and moral philosophy of the Greek atomist Democritus. Through his later follower Epicurus, the philosophy of Democritus had been widely received throughout the Greco-Roman world as Epicureanism. (See Chapter VI for a full discussion of this philosophy.) Because Epicureanism attempted to explain all phenomena in purely material terms, it had gained the reputation of being a refuge for atheists for whom the pursuit of pleasure was the highest moral aim. Such hedonism went against the grain of the stern Roman character. There were Roman Epicureans, but it was a suspect, even ridiculed, philosophy.

Lucretius, seeing politics and worldly ambition as mere fantasies, tried to convey in Latin the essential doctrine of Democritus rather than the hedonism which generally passed for Epicureanism. The only pleasure Lucretius accepts is intellectual. To know the truth about the constitution of the universe and man's place in the order of nature is for Lucretius the true source of satisfaction. Most of what humans call pleasure he treats with sarcastic contempt. His aim was to replace superstition with true knowledge, but the picture he paints of man in nature would depress all but the most relentlessly honest. There are passages of lyric beauty in praise of nature in his poem, but man hardly fits into that nature. Man is born into isolation, unsustained by any gods yet not quite in harmony with nature, either. Lucretius turned the much-ridiculed Epicureanism into the sternest kind of scientific morality. With Lucretius, the dependence on Greek sources that we noticed in earlier Roman literature is no longer important. Lucretius was no nationalist, but his poem is thoroughly Roman, as true an expression of a national culture and language as any literary document can be.

Cicero was torn between his desire for a literary career—still a somewhat suspect occupation in Rome at that time—and his ambition to make his way through politics from the Equestrian class to which he was born into the privileged Senatorial class. He was hardly successful in trying to accommodate the two ambitions since he was executed for his politics and failed in his poetry. All the same, he wielded a wide influence on Latin prose style in his lifetime, and his works continued that influence in later centuries.

Cicero began his career as a lawyer, and by successful cases he gained sufficient publicity to get himself elected to political offices. In 70 B.C., he undertook for the Sicilians the prosecution of a propraetor who had plundered Sicily during his term as governor. Cicero's success in this case made him the foremost orator in Rome. By 63 B.C., he had achieved the highest office, the consulship, and during that year he discovered and successfully crushed a conspiracy by Catiline* and other dissident Senators to overthrow the Republic. It was a glorious moment for Cicero, but from that point his fortunes deteriorated as he became more and more embroiled in the political chaos of the Republic's last years. Despite his attempts to mediate between powerful opponents like Pompey and Julius Caesar and to establish an alliance between the Senators and the Equestrians, he was exiled through Caesar's machinations. Though his exile was revoked, Cicero continued as no more than a pawn in the designs of the First Triumvirate (see page 86). After Caesar's assassination, Cicero tried to wield political influence again, and in retaliation for his open attacks Antony had him assassinated in 43 B.C.

Cicero's varied writings include political speeches (such as the brilliant and impassioned orations delivered to the Senate by which he destroyed Catiline's conspiracy), philosophical essays, and some poetry. During his exile and afterward, when his political life was curtailed, he turned more to philosophy, and his essays became his personal interpretation of Greek thought. Cicero added no distinctive contribution of his own, but he was highly influential in transmitting Greek philosophy into Roman literature. In later centuries, when the Western Roman Empire went its own way and the Greek language was forgotten in the West, what the Western world knew of Greek philosophy came principally from Cicero. In the political sphere, Cicero had no sustained philosophy; he was motivated rather by a strong patriotism, acknowledged even by his enemies, and a fervent pride in the city's republican institutions. Despite his vanity, his indecisiveness, and his outright lapses in political judgment, he was guided by the idea of Rome as a community of shared interests. But though he reached the highest office, his calls for civic unity failed to impress the members of the Senatorial class, who looked on him as a mere upstart.

Despite his life of frustration, Cicero's influence on later Latin civilization was perhaps greater than that of any other

---

* The Roman historian Sallust wrote a detailed account of the conspiracy. In the period of Cicero and Lucretius, the writing of Roman history was also coming of age in the works of Julius Caesar, the dominant political figure of the time, and his friend and colleague Sallust. Both will be discussed in Chapter III, "Historians and Biographers."

single individual. His prolific writings form the most comprehensive set of documents for the last twenty or thirty years of the Republic. Beyond that, he perfected Latin prose style and scarcely found a competitor in the following centuries. Oratory had been a necessary art before Cicero, but he in effect created a new language, flexible, versatile, and forceful, and his became the standard of Latin wherever Roman civilization penetrated. Cicero's Latin modified the structure of languages as far removed as English. The excellence of his style, together with his pleas for civic unity above partisan loyalties and his dedication to the life of letters no less than to political activity, made him seem the best example of the concept that he himself had tried to formulate: *humanitas,* the concern for humane values.

Lucretius had taken one way out of political life, but there was another, exemplified by the poetry of Catullus (84–54 B.C.). Catullus belonged to a group of young writers who devoted their time to social pleasure and the study and practice of Greek poetry. They rejected the rugged style of early Roman poetry in favor of the elegance and personal immediacy they found in early Greek lyric or in Alexandrian poetry. They, too, were working new ground, for although the Roman orators and historians had created a literary language (in prose) of dignity and strength, it still lacked the delicacy that the Greek poets had achieved.

Catullus called his poems *versiculi* ("trifles in verse"). His attitude toward his poems is partly ironic, but he meant also that his poetry was not to be measured by the standards applied to poetry with a serious political or philosophical subject (like that of Lucretius). His *versiculi* might better be translated as "experiments in verse." Any occasion, however casual, could provide a subject for a poem: an individual's appearance or his pretensions, a guest's misbehavior at a dinner, a current piece of gossip about some familiar political figure. Catullus was continuing the tradition of Greek lyric, in which the poetic "I" is the central figure, but Greek lyric had a more limited repertory of accepted themes. Catullus knows no limits to what may be included in poetry. His work reads, more than most previous poetry, as a diary of his daily life and of his times. To what degree his poems reflect actual happenings or fictitious ones need not concern us since the vitality remains the same in either case.

The poems that Catullus addressed to his mistress, whom he calls "Lesbia," form the major and most memorable part of his surviving work. (Lesbia has generally been thought to be the infamous Clodia, who was under strong suspicion for many sinister crimes, for general profligacy, for poisonings, and for incest.) In this group of poems, Catullus actually achieved the new style and sensibility that he and his literary friends were aiming at. There had scarcely been so fervent an expression of love in Roman literature before. Catullus' literary models were, of course, Greek, but he went much farther in exploring the conflicting emotions aroused by passion, the play of love and hate, of repugnance and desire. What was particularly new, and of consequence for later literature, was that he had created a complete cycle of poems centered on a single affair. Catullus takes us through every conflict and change in his love for one person. In the Lesbia poems, we see lust become love, love gradually change to disappointment, then to repugnance and hatred. It is a chronicle as frank as a confession. The Lesbia poems are like love letters, full of the intensity of present emotion, the lover's joy, the lover's threats, his jealousy, his futile attempts to escape followed by apologies and reconciliation. The Lesbia poems form one long poem of the poet's love for Lesbia; that long poem is Catullus' unique contribution to the literature of the world.

The Age of Augustus

In 31 B.C., at the Battle of Actium, Julius Caesar's nephew Octavian (63 B.C.–A.D. 14) brought to an end the century of violence that marked the breakdown of the Roman Republic. As we saw in Chapter 1, it was Octavian (on whom the Senate now conferred the title Augustus by which he is known to history) who created the system that would prevail, with some modifications, until the death of the Roman Empire: The form of the republican institutions was preserved, though drained of their traditional content, with a single lifelong ruler at the head touching every aspect of Roman life with his power. The period corresponding with Octavian's lifetime has been called the Golden Age of Roman literature, and as Augustus the victor at Actium had an important direct influence on Rome's greatest writers.

Augustus had to find ways to prevent the eruption of old hostilities that would endanger his own position. Furthermore, he had to establish his legitimacy by presenting himself as the direct culmination of the old Roman tradition. Literature was a vital instrument for his purpose. Himself educated in the Greek classics, Augustus may have rec-

152 *The Literature of Greece and Rome*

ROMAN REPUBLIC / ROMAN EMPIRE

Timeline (300 B.C. – A.D. 300):

- Hellenistic Empires
- Punic Wars
- Plautus
- Ennius
- Terence
- Golden Age
- Cicero
- Lucretius
- Catullus
- Ovid
- Virgil
- Horace
- Livy
- Tibullus
- Propertius
- Silver Age
- Seneca
- Tacitus
- Pliny
- Suetonius
- Martial
- Lucan
- Quintillian
- Juvenal

Events:
1. First play in Latin
2. Proclamation of Greek freedom
3. Battle of Philippi
4. Battle of Actium
5. Exile of Ovid
6. Death of Augustus (?)
7. Death of Petronius
8. Accession of Hadrian
9. Coronation of Diocletian

ognized the civic function that literature had once fulfilled in Greece and envisioned a similar role for literature in Rome. Writers were now actively called into the service of the state, and literature was recognized with official favor. This policy gave Augustus the national literature he wanted, but it gave him something more, something far beyond a merely national voice.

Writers reacted to Augustus' encouragement in various ways. Many were understandably reluctant to adopt any political position. They had seen the rewards in the past for partisanship, and who was to say that a new strong man might not oust Augustus? The historian Livy (59 B.C.–A.D. 17 —see also Chapter III) accepted the task with few doubts. His long history of Rome, most of it now lost, praises the city and her ascent to world supremacy. He had read earlier authorities but was little interested in the primary research that Herodotus and Thucydides had made central to their method. Historical writing, under the influence of rhetoric, had become a form of belles-lettres used to advocate sound moral values. Livy's history is of this sort, a demonstration of the divine providence that had guided Rome's destiny from her humble beginnings to her imperial splendor under Augustus.

Virgil and The Aeneid

For Virgil (70–19 B.C.), the task of serving the Augustan policy created fierce conflicts. His epic poem *The Aeneid* is marked by the struggle between his doubts about Augustus' authority and his need to accept the New Order that Augustus claimed to have established. Virgil accepted the role of national poet more fully than any of his talented contemporaries, but yet with severe misgivings. No one could honestly claim that Augustus was in the republican tradition, but he had at least brought peace after seemingly endless war. There was really no other option.

Virgil was born near the city of Mantua in northern Italy, and a love of the country and of farm life formed an important element in much of his poetry. His farm was confiscated after the Battle of Philippi in 42 B.C. to provide bonus money for the victorious armies of the Second Triumvirate. By then, however, his first book of poems, the *Bucolics* (or *Eclogues*) had brought him to the attention of Octavian, who made good the loss. Virgil moved to Rome and became part of the circle of literary men gathered around Maecenas, the wealthy patron of the arts who helped Augustus apply his policies to literature. It was Maecenas who suggested that Virgil turn his talents to a patriotic theme.

Before attempting the epic, Virgil had developed his poetic craft in two collections of poems, the *Bucolics (Shepherd Poems)* and the *Georgics (Agricultural Poems);* both books took their titles from Greek words that the highly educated Virgil brought into Latin. The *Bucolics* are pastoral poems written in imitation of Theocritus, but with the scene changed to the Italian countryside. It is a scene further removed from real peasant life, from which labor is almost totally absent. Virgil's shepherds comment on political events and set the pattern for later European pastoral poetry in which intellectuals, thinly disguised as shepherds, discuss current politics, current theories of love and poetry. The later *Georgics* are reminiscent of Hesiod's almanac poetry. In them, Virgil takes us from the artificial landscape of the pastorals to the practical world of agriculture. The *Georgics* are poems full of the unpoetic concerns of farming, yet imbued throughout with the poetry that comes from Virgil's deep sense of piety toward the soil.

After these early works, Virgil committed himself fully to the New Order and gave Rome her national epic in *The Aeneid,* but if that poem shows chauvinism, it was hardly a chauvinism to please most political leaders. In *The Aeneid,* Virgil gives the legendary history of the founding of Rome by Aeneas, the Trojan hero who escaped from Troy after the Greeks had sacked the city. He traces the fortunes of Aeneas and his followers through their wanderings in the Mediterranean, their landing in Italy, and their war with the native Italian population, stopping just short of their reconciliation with the Italians, though that reconciliation is foreshadowed. By turning to the mythical past, Virgil was able to make topical allusions but avoided having to praise Augustus' accomplishments openly or mention events in recent history that might have a divisive rather than a unifying effect. The mythical framework permitted a more indirect approach. It also gave Virgil the opportunity to incorporate many old Roman rituals and legends, some of which Augustus himself was attempting to revive.

While giving Augustus his due as Aeneas' illustrious descendant, Virgil does not evade the brutal side of Roman history. The consul who had his sons executed for treason, the forcible eviction of peoples from their native soil, the cavalier behavior of Aeneas in accepting Dido's hospitality and then forsaking her, slaves brought to Rome in triumphal processions—these are as much part of *The Aeneid* as the more glorious achievements. In fact, the poem reads often more as criticism than as praise for Rome's conventional history. In place of that conventional history, which is largely a catalogue of battles and conquests, Virgil suggests another kind of history, a moral history, the development of a national conscience. The Romans prided themselves on virtues like self-control, dignity, and hard work, but Virgil suggests a new ideal: compassion.

The Aeneid is modeled on *The Odyssey* and *The Iliad*, with some influence also of the Alexandrian epic of Apollonius, the *Argonautica*, but the prevailing mood is one of deepest melancholy; there is little of the exultation that Homeric heroes feel in the heat of battle, little even of that hearty pleasure that Homer's warriors take in their daily lives. (Virgil seems not to have been robust, and at his death he directed that the almost completed manuscript of *The Aeneid* be burned; Augustus found out and saved the poem.) Aeneas and his band do what they must from a strong sense of duty to the future Rome, not from any hope for personal honor. Aeneas himself never lives to see the city that the gods have destined for his people, nor does he see peace established in Italy. It is in a distant future that Aeneas, and we with him, must believe. "We seek a land ever receding from us," Aeneas says during his wanderings, a statement that truly sums up his life and the poem.

Aeneas is a man well versed in suffering, and the people who befriend him have suffered equally. Much of the suffering is caused by civil wars. The Trojans and the Italians are, we are told, descendants from a common ancestor, so theirs was a civil war. Dido was in exile like Aeneas, herself also a victim of civil war. Aeneas' Italian allies are also exiles from a previous civil war. Aeneas and his allies have all experienced a common fate that makes them responsive to the suffering of others. That is the source of the compassion that Virgil portrays as the true Roman virtue. Rome's imperial destiny is not the reward for innate superiority; rather, her long history of suffering has, or should have, taught her how to rule with justice and mercy. *The Aeneid* expresses an almost desperate hope in the possibility of Rome's future greatness. Only a spiritual maturation could make Rome's past history tolerable. Because of that spiritual aspect of *The Aeneid* and a passage thought to prophesy the birth of Christ, Virgil in Christian times was regarded as a forerunner of Christianity, almost a pagan saint.

Horace

The other great poet of the Augustan age, Horace (65–8 B.C.), found it harder than Virgil did to adjust to Augustus' accession. A man of republican sympathies, as a student in Athens he had fought under Brutus against Octavian and Antony and had seen his father's house and estate in southern Italy confiscated under the Second Triumvirate. Through Virgil, Horace was introduced to Maecenas, the wealthy patron of the arts and influential friend of Augustus. With financial help from Maecenas, who gave him an estate, Horace was able to begin his literary career. When Augustus became *princeps* in 31 B.C., Horace had already established the personal style that he largely adhered to in his later writings. In time, Augustus won Horace over to friendship, and Horace reciprocated by writing certain political poems, by celebrating the victories of Augustus' stepsons, and by his choral hymn *Carmen Saeculare* for the Secular Feast that Augustus instituted in 17 B.C. His temperament did not run to epic.

Horace's early works were poems that he called *sermones* ("conversations"). In them, he revived the one literary form that the Romans claimed as distinctively their own, the *satura* (now *satira*) of Ennius. Greek poetry had often included satirical elements, but the Romans had created satire as a distinct poetic form. (Lucilius had used satire about a century before Horace as a vehicle for attacks on prominent individuals.) Horace directed his satire toward persons, perhaps fictitious, who offended his sense of moderation and propriety—a gourmand, a pompous philosopher, a bothersome individual trying to gain access to Maecenas. Behind his good-natured satire is the undogmatic philosopher trying to steer his own life between excesses. In Horace, satire is not simply the opportunity to vent one's indignation but a quiet form of self-examination.

From satires, Horace turned to the ode, a more sophisticated and rigorous poetic form but still one that allowed him his genial personal tone and the freedom to range over a wide field. In his odes, Horace goes back to the more disciplined forms of Greek lyric poetry. Several of the odes are adaptations from Greek poets, and there are, besides such adaptations, many echoes of their style. Some of the Horatian odes are on topical subjects, like his famous poem on Cleopatra's death, "Nunc est bibendum" ("Now is the time to drink"), but most are more subjective, exploring the poet's own thoughts on his poetic craft, his own behavior, some event in his life, or his approaching death. Horace's most famous single poem—certainly the most influential on European poetry ever since—is *The Art of Poetry*. It is a personal essay in poetic form in which Horace gives a history of Latin literature with his reflections on the styles of various authors and the relationship of Greek and Latin literature. *The Art of Poetry* forms part of Horace's *Epistles*, letters in verse that offer sensible advice on a great range of questions of life and conduct.

In antiquity, Horace was praised for the felicity of his style, and for centuries men have responded both to that style and to the congenial temperament behind it. His description of the fountain of Bandusia, of Mount Soracte covered in snow, his celebration of spring in his ode "Diffugere nives" ("The snows are fled" in the translation of the English poet A. E. Housman), his vision of dark Care seated behind the horseman—these and many other passages have remained the common property of our literary tradition. Horace boasted in one poem of being the first to "sing the Aeolian song" (the Greek lyric) in the Italian manner. We may go farther. Since Greek lyric was mostly lost and the Greek language itself forgotten in the West until the Renaissance, Horace was the poet who transmitted "Aeolian song" to Western culture. In the history of European lyric poetry, Horace's influence is scarcely equaled by that of any other ancient poet.

Three Elegiac Poets

The independence that Horace preferred was cherished even more by the elegiac poets of the Augustan period, Tibullus, Propertius, and Ovid. Tibullus (about 54–19 B.C.) associated with a circle that was decidedly republican in its sympathies, but in his poetry he carefully avoided the slightest reference to Augustus. He touches on some contemporary events—a journey undertaken by Augustus, the Battle of Actium, Augustus' victories—but in answer to Maecenas' request for a poem in praise of the Emperor, he replied that his poetic talent was inadequate for the task. Ovid (43 B.C.–A.D. 17), a man of independent means, needed no patron for support, but he was willing to include, as the climax of his long poem *Metamorphoses*, the deification of Augustus' uncle Julius Caesar. He thus gave his assent to an act that had been part of the Emperor's official program.

The elegiac poets were nonpolitical—or at least as nonpolitical as they could be. In choosing the elegiac form, they were reviving a Greek form from the period of early lyric poetry. The Greek elegy was the verse for epitaphs or for expressing political or philosophical sentiments, but the Romans used it as a form of personal lyric, mostly for love poetry. Although they took the form from early Greek models, in subject and style the Roman elegiac poets belong more in the tradition of their Roman predecessor, Catullus, and the Alexandrian poets. Like the Alexandrians, they sought to refine the poetic craft, and in their love poetry they continued certain conventions established by the Alexandrians. Both Tibullus and Propertius followed Catullus' example in creating a cycle of poems around their love for a single mistress; for Propertius, she is "Cynthia," for Tibullus, "Delia." (The second book of Tibullus' elegies is addressed to another mistress, "Nemesis," but her elevation in his poetry is, he makes clear, due to Delia's infidelity.)

A cycle of poems celebrating only one lover (or two, as in Tibullus' case) gives intensity to the portrayal of love. It emphasizes the obsessive, almost delirious nature of the poet's quest for love and his perpetual frustration. These qualities had become a convention in Roman poetry, and Tibullus and Propertius followed the convention, but in their poems the obsession comes through as real. There is a real anguish of men who are doomed to failure in love and yet can find no other purpose to engage their interest. The Augustan period seemed to allow only two subjects for poetry: political praise and love. If a poet excluded himself from writing about political events or undertaking a historical epic—the times had excluded him from the political process itself—then he had to make of love the substance of both his life and his art. There was a tension in the Augustan period that its love poetry indirectly reveals.

Ovid tried to escape from the narrow choice of his times. He began with love elegies celebrating "Corinna" as his mistress but then experimented with other forms which, though clearly influenced by earlier works in the Greco-Roman tradition, are entirely his own. He was not one to suffer delirium for unrequited love, and after his initial love elegies he treated love in a more jocular and cynical way in the *Ars Amatoria (Art of Love)*. The poem is a handbook of the technique of love, parodying the serious didactic poetry of the era (Lucretius, for example) and at the same time satirizing its sentimental love poetry. It is full of advice, some practical and some psychological, which Ovid, the amused and observant man of the world, has brought together for the beginner in the game of love. Ovid, in his poetic virtuosity, wrote several other kinds of poems: the *Fasti (Festivals)*, a highly informative work on the customs and legends associated with the festivals of the Roman calendar; and the *Tristia (Sorrows)*, poems written about his exile near the end of his life. It was, however, chiefly Ovid's long mythological poem, the *Metamorphoses*, that has assured his enduring reputation.

There were precedents for the *Metamorphoses*, but none had been particularly distinguished. Metamorphosis (the transformation of persons into other forms—animals, trees, stars) is a common element of mythology, and Ovid, by choosing that as his unifying theme, was able to include a vast quantity of Greco-Roman mythology in one coherent narrative. For many mythological tales, Ovid's account is our only source apart from brief allusions by earlier poets. If such stories as Phaethon and the chariot of the Sun, Echo and Narcissus, Daedalus and Icarus, Pyramus and Thisbe are familiar to us today, it is because Ovid's poem rescued them from obscurity. Ovid's success lies not only in the encyclopedic scope of his poem but in the narrative and psychological skill with which he tells his tales. Ovid's *Metamorphoses* ensured the preservation of Greek mythology in the Roman world until the Renaissance. Artists and writers who represented Greek mythological scenes in their art generally went to Ovid's account for their inspiration. In his quite different sphere, Ovid was to be as influential as Virgil.

Ovid seems to have kept on friendly terms with Augustus until in A.D. 8 he committed some offense—he refers to it cryptically as his *carmen et error* ("his poetry and his mistake"). For this, Augustus banished him to the remote city of Tomis in the province of Pontus on the Black Sea, about as far from Rome as it was possible to send him. (It seems possible that the reason for this was the sober Emperor's displeasure at the amused frankness of Ovid's treatment of love in the *Ars Amatoria*.) Augustus never revoked the ban, and there Ovid remained until his death, in spite of his pleas and his wife's efforts on his behalf in Rome. The penalty, which included the removal of Ovid's books from libraries, is a forceful reminder of the close personal interest that Augustus took in contemporary poets and of how far he could go to vent his displeasure. The Augustan period of Roman literature thus closes on a somber note, with the two works, *Tristia* and *Ex Ponto (From Pontus)*, which Ovid wrote in Tomis. These poems are filled with the bitterness of Ovid's fate. Augustus' vaunted New Order was short-lived, in literature, at least; it dies away in the pathetic notes of an exile's complaints. In A.D. 14, Augustus was dead, and Ovid soon followed him.

The Silver Age

If the period that ended with the death of Augustus was Rome's Golden Age in literature, the century that followed — to the accession of Hadrian as Emperor in A.D. 117 — was only slightly less productive. It is known as the Silver Age — valuable and interesting, but less so than the preceding century. For the Roman writers of the Silver Age, the problems were similar to those faced by the Greek poets of the Alexandrian period. Roman literature had reached its highest point in the Ciceronian and Augustan periods, and later writers felt the burden of that classicism, which seemed beyond imitation. There was much writing, but it lacked both the sense of national mission and the contact with Greek literature that had given earlier Roman poetry its creative excitement. It was a period of consolidation and review, a period in which encyclopedias, histories, and handbooks of various sorts abounded. Of these, some stand out conspicuously for their own merits and for their influence on later thought. Quintilian's (about A.D. 40–95) large work on rhetoric and education, *Institutio Oratoria (Oratorical Principles)*, or the *Natural History* of Pliny the Elder (A.D. 23–79) remained important for centuries for the wealth of information they contained, but neither professes to be literature to rival the Augustan classics. Some writers attempted original compositions more directly in the classical tradition. Lucan (A.D. 39–65), a Spaniard who for a time was taken up by the Emperor Nero, wrote an epic on the Roman civil war, the *Pharsalia* (named for the battle in which Julius Caesar defeated Pompey). It was a popular poem in its day and continued to hold a high place throughout later antiquity, but to us it seems to show precisely those faults of a literary epic that the *Aeneid* of Virgil successfully avoided. So, too, with the tragedies of the philosopher Seneca (about 4 B.C.–A.D. 65). His influence on later European drama was immense, but today Seneca's bloody adaptations of Greek tragedy seem less forceful than their Greek models. Interestingly, Seneca was Lucan's uncle, like him was Spanish, and had been Nero's tutor. Both suffered the penalty of Nero's favorites who incurred his displeasure: They were ordered to cut open their veins and bleed to death.

The historian Tacitus (about A.D. 55-120) is probably the one writer of the Silver Age whose works have maintained their reputation undiminished. As a historian, he will be discussed more fully in the following chapter, but here we may notice his two principal books, the *Annals* and the *Histories*, which were written about the beginning of the second century A.D. While concentrating on important figures in the biographical style, both aim for more than biography. In his skillful analysis, Tacitus shows himself in the tradition of the Greek historian Thucydides—and of Sallust, the Roman historian of the Ciceronian period. Though rhetorical in style, Tacitus' histories are an attempt to revive the high standards of historical writing, with the emphasis on accurate knowledge and intelligent analysis. We may find his heavy indictment of the Emperors less impartial than he claimed, but his histories remain valuable not only for their historical content but for the lonely integrity of a man who was willing to voice his hatred of the Imperial tyranny. While Tacitus, with his republican sympathies, despised the corrupt society of Imperial Rome, he admired the virility and democratic customs of the Teutonic tribes to the north, who remained fiercely independent of the Empire. His book *Germania* is the earliest account of the tribes that in time would spread throughout Europe and topple the Western Empire itself. (Letters to Tacitus from Pliny the Younger, a Roman governor and the nephew of Pliny the Elder, include the first references to the new Christian sect by a pagan.)

Satire in the Silver Age

Three satirists—Martial, Juvenal, and Petronius—have left us original and highly interesting portraits of the Imperial Rome of the Silver Age. Martial (about A.D. 40-104), like Lucan and Seneca a Spaniard from Cordoba, made his living by writing epigrams, short, witty, destructively critical poems. He wrote for various patrons and on any subject, trivial or serious, comic or obscene. His epigrams were not formal satire as the Romans knew it, but they are filled with satiric wit. In Martial's poems, we see the Roman epigram in its most finished form, ingenious, striking, and versatile.

Juvenal (about A.D. 60-140) wrote satires in the recognized satirical form. Of the five books that he published, we possess today only sixteen poems, but these sixteen give us a vivid sense of Rome in Juvenal's day and of Juvenal's reaction to his contemporary world. Working in the tradition of the early Roman satirist Lucilius, Juvenal raised the tone of satirical attack to a level of ferocity totally alien to the gentle kind of criticism we find in Horace. Juvenal had neither wealth of his own nor connections with the wealthy, and his satires are the poor man's lament for the inequity and corruption around him: the grossness and stupidity of the Emperors; the vast disparity between the poor, living in crowded tenements in danger at any moment of fire or collapse, and the rich carried in litters over the heads of the poor; the success of the cunning Greek businessmen. Juvenal's unbridled anger and pain strike out at all the reminders of the hardship of daily life in Rome for one who was not cunning or rich or subservient. There is literary exaggeration in Juvenal, but he adopted the one literary form that could still carry conviction. When Juvenal renames the Imperial city of Rome the Great Sewer, that is pure rage, beyond mere rhetoric.

Petronius (died A.D. 65) is remembered for two interesting reasons: He is the author of the *Satyricon*, a novel in prose that remained a ribald underground classic for nineteen hundred years and has only in our own permissive century come back into the open as a book (and as a distinguished film by the great Italian director Federico Fellini); and he is assumed to be the same Petronius named by Tacitus as Nero's friend and Arbiter of Elegance, the pacesetter at the Imperial court until he fell out of favor and suffered the same fate that the Emperor had prescribed for his two other literary courtiers, Lucan and Seneca. Tacitus' portrait fits the author of the *Satyricon*. Even without Tacitus, we would assume the writer of that book to be a cultured man, given to the enjoyment of life, highly observant, amused by human behavior but never moralistic. Petronius himself is highly sophisticated, but the milieu presented in the *Satyricon* is the opposite; it is the world of the lower classes, of pimps and prostitutes, of freedmen who have raised themselves almost overnight from slavery to the status of millionaires, wallowing in their new-found wealth.

The title *Satyricon* has nothing to do with the Latin word *satura*, or *satira* ("satire"), though there is satire in the work. The reference is to the Greek *satyrs*, the lecherous and carousing companions of the god Dionysus. Petronius' novel might well be called a satyr-novel, since it is the record of the picaresque adventures of a set of ne'er-do-wells who fall into one mishap after another, mostly for sexual reasons. The central characters are a trio of homosexuals, two older friends and an attractive youth who is the constant source of rivalry between them.

The novel is thoroughly vulgar and even frankly obscene, but behind the ribaldry is a serious artistic purpose. The world of the *Satyricon* is one that is mostly excluded from the serious literature of antiquity. Petronius takes that world as a serious subject for literature and treats it, in spite of obvious exaggerations, with honesty. He is true to its dialects, its conversational patterns, its modes of thinking and living. Nowhere in antiquity can we find another piece of literature that attempts such accurate realism. It was a bold experiment, but Petronius was hardly an edifying classic for the schools, and most of the *Satyricon* disappeared in the course of time. Not until the rise of the modern European novel do we see this kind of literary experiment repeated.

In the Twilight of Pagan Rome

With the end of the Silver Age, Roman literature began a decline that would continue, with brief outbursts of creative energy and talent, until the final collapse of the Western Empire and the disappearence of Latin as a language in daily use by the people. Interesting books did continue to be written, such as the biographer Suetonius' (about A.D. 69–140) *Lives of the Twelve Caesars,* but their interest today is more historical than literary. Henceforth, the greatest writers in Latin would be Christians like St. Augustine (A.D. 354–430) or St. Ambrose (A.D. 339–397), and their books would be among the doctrinal foundation stones of a triumphant Christianity.

In Hadrian's reign (A.D. 117-138), there was a revival of interest in the older classical literature, both Roman and Greek, and a conscious return to the earlier style. Much of the literature of the period is useful for the student of the classical world but makes no claim to great eminence. A notable exception is *The Golden Ass,* or *Metamorphoses,* of Apuleius (second century A.D.), a comic novel from which later novelists have freely borrowed episodes. *The Golden Ass* is an immensely long novel in the picaresque style, with one story strung onto another in a very loose structure.

Lucius, its hero, through his curiosity about magic, finds himself transformed (metamorphosed) into a donkey and condemned for a time to suffer all the physical indignities that are the lot of beasts of burden—with the added humiliation that he retains his human consciousness. After a series of adventures and trials, he regains his human form at a festival in honor of the Egyptian goddess Isis. (He eats some roses in the hands of the high priest.) The end of the novel is concerned with Lucius' advancement in the secret rites of the goddess.

Apuleius was a lawyer and a professional orator, and his novel betrays the flowery rhetorical style of his day, but it has other elements of cultural interest. Apuleius was an African of Greek descent who lived at various times in Africa, Greece, and Italy. His life is representative of the polyglot Roman civilization of the second century, and his novel reflects the extraordinary ethnic mixture of the Empire. The language of Apuleius is no longer the pure classical Latin. It borrows idioms and vocabulary from various contemporary sources. The novel form was one that the Alexandrian Greek writers had tried, but it had not hitherto found a place in classical Latin literature, with the one odd exception of Petronius' *Satyricon*. The worship of Isis that forms the novel's climax was not part of the official Roman religion but an importation from the East. Apuleius opens his work with an apology for his Egyptian themes and self-taught Latin.

Petronius and Apuleius, the one a Roman but interested in Italian dialects, the other an African of Greek stock, show Roman literature in the process of becoming Latin literature, not the literature of a single city but of the Mediterranean world. Foreigners had imported literature into Rome when the city was near the beginning of its international importance. At the end of the pagan period, five centuries later, when Rome had achieved that eminence, its writers again come from the far corners of the known world. This catholicity of Rome, so well illustrated by her literary history, enabled her to continue where Greece had left off. Perhaps because Rome began her intellectual life by absorbing the Greek experience, her literary history remained one of absorption—of the past from the Greeks, of the present from the diverse cultures within the borders of the Empire. By the end of the second century, by a final act of absorption from the East, Roman literature began to enter a new phase that would make it not only Latin but Christian.

FOR FURTHER READING

The basic works (first group) are recommended translations of the writings of the most important Greek and Roman authors, while the second group (Commentary) lists books about these authors and literary history and criticism in general that will be useful for the interpretation of particular works and for more detailed information about particular authors and periods. Reading lists for the classical historians, biographers, philosophers, and scientists are given after the appropriate chapters. An asterisk (*) indicates a paperback edition.

With the decline of the educated person's ability to read Latin or Greek, modern translations have multiplied. Nearly all of the major classical authors are available in a number of modern translations, mostly published in paperback. For an author in whom the reader is especially interested — particularly among the poets, all of whom, in varying degrees, are elusive in translation — it is worth reading more than one version; different translators, even when they are able poets in English, bring out different aspects of the original, and Homer and the Greek tragic playwrights in particular have been well and very differently translated by several different hands.

Basic Works

Greece

Aeschylus. *The Orestes Plays.* New York: New American Library, 1963. Verse translation by Paul Roche of the trilogy usually called The Oresteia (*Agamemnon, The Libation-Bearers, The Eumenides*).

____. *Prometheus Bound.* New York: New American Library, 1964.

* Aristophanes. *The Birds.* New York: New American Library, 1970. Translated by William Arrowsmith.
*____. *The Clouds.* New York: New American Library, 1970. Translated by William Arrowsmith.
*____. *The Frogs.* New York: New American Library, 1970. Translated by Richmond Lattimore.
*____. *Lysistrata.* New York: New American Library, 1970. Translated by Douglass Parker.
*____. *The Wasps.* New York: New American Library, 1970. Translated by Douglass Parker.

* Euripides. *Three Great Plays.* New York: New American Library, 1958. Verse translation by Rex Warner of *Medea, Hippolytus, Helen*.

Higham, Thomas F., and Bowra, C. M., ed. *The Oxford Book of Greek Verse in Translation.* London: Oxford University Press, 1928. A comprehensive anthology, chronologically arranged, many of the translations by major British poets of the past. Briefer collections of Greek verse have been translated by several notable twentieth-century American poets: Dudley Fitts (New Directions, outstanding); Richmond Lattimore (University of Chicago Press); Kenneth Rexroth (University of Michigan Press). All of the latter are available in paperback.

* Homer. *The Iliad.* New York: New American Library, 1950. A famous prose translation by W. H. D. Rouse that moves along as briskly as a novel. For a modern version that conveys something of the high poetry of the original, the verse translation by Richmond Lattimore (University of Chicago Press, 2nd ed., 1962, paperback) is recommended.

*———. *The Odyssey.* New York: New American Library, 1962. Prose translation by W. H. D. Rouse. Interesting English versions of Homer's epics have been made by several major British poets: John Chapman (sixteenth century, Shakespeare's contemporary); John Dryden (seventeenth century); Alexander Pope (eighteenth century). There are also good modern verse translations by Richmond Lattimore (Harper, 1967) and Robert Fitzgerald (Doubleday-Anchor, 1961, paperback).

* Pindar. *Odes.* Chicago: University of Chicago Press, 1947. Translated by Richmond Lattimore.

* Sappho. *Love Songs.* New York: New American Library, 1966. Translations by Paul Roche of all of Sappho's surviving poems.

* Sophocles. *The Oedipus Plays.* New York: New American Library, 1958. Translations by Paul Roche of the three plays (*Antigone, Oedipus the King, Oedipus at Colonus*) that, although written at widely separated intervals in Sophocles' life and not formally a trilogy, together present the main elements of the legends of Thebes and illuminate one another when read in sequence.

Theocritus. *Idylls.* Lafayette: Purdue University Press, 1963. Translated by Barriss Mills.

Rome

Apuleius. *The Golden Ass.* New York: Farrar, Straus, 1951. Translated by Robert Graves, an outstanding modern British poet.

* Catullus. *Poems.* New York: Grove Press, 1956. Translated by Horace Gregory, the only modern version that doesn't do violence to the anguished delicacy of Catullus' love poems.

* Cicero. *Nine Orations and the Dream of Scipio.* New York: New American Library, 1967. Translated by Palmer Bovie.

Godolphin, Francis R., editor. *Latin Poets.* New York: Modern Library.

* Horace. *Satires and Epistles.* Chicago: University of Chicago Press, 1959. Translated by Smith P. Bovie.

* Juvenal. *The Satires.* New York: New American Library, 1963. Translated by Hubert Creekmore.

* Ovid. *The Love Poems.* New York: New American Library, 1964. Verse translation by Horace Gregory.

*———. *The Metamorphoses.* New York: New American Library, 1960. Translated by Horace Gregory.

* Plautus. *Three Plays.* New York: New American Library, 1968.

Translations by Paul Roche of *Miles Gloriosus, Amphitryon, The Prisoners.*
* Virgil. *The Aeneid.* New York: New American Library, 1961. Verse translation by Patric Dickinson.
* ———. *The Georgics.* Chicago: University of Chicago Press, 1956. Verse translations by Smith P. Bovie of the shorter pastoral poems that preceded the *Aeneid.*

Commentary

* Hadas, Moses. *Ancilla to Classical Reading.* New York: Columbia University Press, 1954. An interesting supplement to the author's histories of Greek and Roman literature (see below): a compilation, largely in quotations from classical sources, of information about Greek and Roman authors and the circumstances of their lives (how professional Roman writers were paid, the making of papyrus, what constituted publication of a handcopied book, and so on); by a notable classical scholar.

Greece

* Flacelière, Robert. *A Literary History of Greece.* New York: New American Library, 1968. A rather detailed chronological account of Greek writers from Homer to the Roman period; useful for reference.
* Hadas, Moses. *A History of Greek Literature.* New York: Columbia University Press, 1950. A warmly appreciative account of the period from Homer to the second century A.D.
* Hamilton, Edith. *The Greek Way.* New York: Norton, 1942. A brief, simple, very readable appreciation of the chief writers of the Athenian Golden Age.
  Kitto, H. D. F. *Greek Tragedy; A Literary Study,* 3rd ed. London: Methuen, 1961. A classic discussion of the structure and meaning of all the dramatic works of Aeschylus, Sophocles, and Euripides, in the context of the origins and development of Greek drama.

Rome

Grant, Michael. *Roman Literature.* Cambridge: Cambridge University Press, 1954. Short, clearly organized, with the emphasis on the Golden Age.
* Hadas, Moses. *A History of Roman Literature.* New York: Columbia University Press, 1952. More detailed than the author's history of Greek literature, with greater emphasis on individual authors.
* Hamilton, Edith. *The Roman Way.* New York: Norton, 1932.
  Rose, H. J. *A Handbook of Latin Literature; From the Earliest Times to St. Augustine,* 3rd ed. London: Methuen, 1954.

CHAPTER III

Historians and Biographers

MEYER REINHOLD
UNIVERSITY OF MISSOURI

IN THE preceding chapter, we repeatedly touched on the Greek and Roman writers of history and biography. Their books form an important part of Greek and Roman literature, the first attempt by any people to separate fact from myth and legend, to set down a record of what had really happened in their past and to understand and explain it. By studying this record, we can learn to see the civilization of the Greeks and Romans as they themselves saw it, sharing their understanding of the great events that shaped it.

We cannot say with complete assurance why the Greeks should have had this special kind of self-awareness when other ancient peoples did not. But the need somehow to preserve one's own past and the past of one's race is a deeply human one that men have expressed in many different ways. We often hear of man's "death wish," but his will to live is infinitely stronger. There is in man an intense desire to be remembered after death and in this way to evade complete and permanent extinction. Yet of the countless billions who have lived on earth, only an infinitesimally small number have escaped total oblivion. What is more, there have been not a few entire civilizations that died and passed from the memory of man.

In order for such oblivion to be avoided, someone must care enough to collect and record information to preserve the memory of societies, events, and outstanding individuals. The first to do this were the Greeks. That is why our terms *history* and *biography* are Greek words, and that is also why the first periods of mankind's history that we know in considerable detail are those of the Greeks and of the Romans (who followed in their footsteps); and why the first gallery of mankind's great men consists of famous Greeks and Romans.

The poet Shelley, in his sonnet "Ozymandias," tells us of the traveler who saw

> Two vast and trunkless legs of stone
> Stand in the desert ...
> And on the pedestal these words appear —
> "My name is Ozymandias, king of kings:
> Look on my works, ye Mighty, and despair!"
> Nothing beside remains. Round the decay
> Of that colossal wreck, boundless and bare
> The lone and level sands stretch far away.

It is true that long before the Greeks and the Romans, Near Eastern kings and Egyptian pharaohs, as well as other eminent persons of the times, erected grandiose monuments and extensive inscriptions to commemorate their reigns and achievements. But these memorials — many of which have been discovered — belong to the category of what we would call propaganda today; for these commemorations, while they record some historical occurrences, were mostly intended to glorify rulers and officials in the eyes of their subjects and posterity.

In reading these inscriptions we usually see a ruler portrayed as a victor in a war, and this is explained as due to his greatness and the help of the gods of his people or country. These accounts, in fact, seem suspiciously alike. Before the Greeks, everywhere the tendency was to regard any significant event as a repetition, with changes of names and places, of events that had already happened. That is why battles and acts of rulers in these Near Eastern records tend to be described in the same general manner. In that way, those who recorded these events could liken them to known previous successes. Nothing that happened was regarded as unique. Such accounts are closer to myth than to true history.

Myth and Legend

The borderline between myth and history was for a long time a very thin one among the Greeks themselves. For instance, the events of the Trojan War as told by Homer in *The Iliad* and *The Odyssey* were regarded by the Greeks as history. Everyone believed that such men as Achilles, Agamemnon, Ajax, Diomedes, Hector, Priam, Odysseus, and many others were all real, historical persons, and that what Homer tells about them actually happened in just that way. For a long time, the Greeks did not distinguish between history and the imaginative literature inspired by their myths, and so they did not feel the need for history.

Looking back on the whole of past time, the Greeks thought it could be divided into five ages: Golden Age, Silver Age, Bronze Age, Heroic Age, and Iron Age. Except for their Heroic Age (which the Greeks equated with their Mycenaean Age), they thus believed that human society had steadily declined from a time of paradise in the Golden Age to the harsh conditions of their own time. This is, of course, similar to the way the Hebrews in the Old Testament portrayed the degeneration of man's life from the Garden of Eden to the evils of the present. Among the Greeks for a long time there were no written records of past events. All questions about the past were answered by tales surviving in popular memory, passed down by word of mouth, and by the stories in the epic poems of Homer and in similar poems that claimed to present the past in the form of myths. Thus, myths were regarded as history, and everything told about the past was saturated with myths. But myths are timeless stories told to illustrate a moral, teach a model of conduct to be imitated or avoided, or to explain some phenomenon of nature. They are not history.

But once the Greeks borrowed the alphabet from Asia Minor and began to travel widely around the Mediterranean, they were able to see things in a new way. Their expanded horizons and their growing respect for the use of reason to explain the world led, in the sixth century B.C., to the first great breakthroughs in philosophy and science in man's history. Moreover, the establishment of a multinational state by the Persian Empire interested all the Greeks enormously because they were its immediate neighbors. Thus there arose a group of Greek writers called logographers, who wrote between about 550 and 450 B.C. These men were the first authors to write exclusively in prose form; they were interested in many types of information and conducted investigations (the Greek word is *historia*). They collected their data partly through travel and partly through systematizing the popular memory of the past that existed in the form of myths. The logographers wrote collections of local legends, the pedigrees of leading families, descriptions of places they had visited or heard about, descriptions of and tales about foreign peoples (especially the Persians), and stories about the foundations of cities. Although none of the logographers' books have survived, we know their names, the titles of their books, and a good deal about them from references by other writers. Hecataeus and Hellanicus were the most famous of the logographers.

The Great Greek Historians

The works of these early collectors of myth and legend were merely preliminary to the writing of history. Men were learning to write interesting prose, to investigate and collect materials pertinent to a specific topic. And then an astounding historical event occurred that aroused immense curiosity among the Greeks and concerning which everyone sought to discover the true explanation: A handful of Greek city-states, threatened with the loss of their independence at the hands of the ever-expanding Persian Empire, fought back and succeeded in defeating the leading world power. In investigating the reasons for this totally unexpected outcome, Herodotus of Halicarnassus, a Greek city controlled by the Persian Empire, became the "Father of History."

Herodotus

Herodotus (about 484–425 B.C.) earned this title because he did several things that no one before him had ever done. To begin with, he did not start out with the idea of glorifying the Greeks but rather of explaining the cause and nature of the great Persian Wars. As a subject of Persia, he understood the Persian viewpoint; moreover, he had great respect for Persia and her culture, for he did not possess the national prejudices of superiority held by most Greeks. In addition, because he was exiled from his native city, he was able to travel extensively—seventeen years altogether—in search of information: in Hellas itself, the islands of the Aegean Sea, Egypt, Asia Minor, Babylonia, Scythia. Herodotus began to investigate the Persian Wars about thirty years after the victories of the Greeks at Marathon, Salamis, and Plataea. Although he had almost no written records to rely on, he managed to write the first history book that deserves the name.

Herodotus' *History* is a brilliant intellectual feat and also a generally trustworthy account of the Persian Wars and their background. His greatest achievement was to discover the main lines of what actually happened in a great event of the fairly recent past, and, just as important, to establish an accurate time sequence for things that happened in different places, something no one had ever done before. (This in itself was not easy; the system of dating events varied from place to place, making dates in different cities difficult to compare.) Actually, Herodotus investigated much more than the Persian Wars. For in seeking an explanation of the root causes of the wars, he went back in time almost two centuries, covering the period from about 650 to 478 B.C. in his systematic inquiry. It is thanks to Herodotus that we know this portion of human history as well as we do. Before that time, little is really known about the history of the Greeks or of any other peoples of the world.

Herodotus' method of investigation was closer to that used by a skilled newspaper correspondent: Since he was not an eyewitness of the events, he used his eyes and ears to find out and report what had happened. As he traveled about in his vast journeys on three continents (he has been called the Marco Polo of antiquity), he was tireless in interviewing people and in sightseeing. His curiosity and persistence were unending; he was rarely satisfied until he had checked and rechecked everything he could. He tells us, for instance, that when he was in Egypt he heard of a slightly different slant on some topic he was interested in, and so he traveled out of his way over a hundred miles to check this one point. Wherever he went, he took notes on what he saw and what people told him.

Herodotus spoke and read only Greek. In foreign countries such as Egypt, Persia, and Babylonia, he was thus at the mercy of interpreters, and more than once he was led into error by them. (He tells us that on some occasions he really did not believe what was told him, but he felt he ought to report what was said, anyway.) His task and his method were, obviously, difficult and laborious. Just as in such a simple matter as a highway accident, eyewitnesses, as everyone knows, will often contradict each other, so in major historical events it is even harder to find out the truth: Accurate understanding is clouded by the "official" versions of government authorities and by one or more opposition versions based on partisan politics and different systems of values.*

---

* Today, the oral method of Herodotus is used increasingly by writers of history, aided by collections of oral reports made by actual eyewitnesses and participants in important events. The best-known example of this approach is the Columbia University Oral History Project, which for many years has been recording the comments of leading statesmen on the events in which they participated.

Herodotus was the first person ever to make a thorough investigation of a war in all its aspects. What was his purpose? In the opening sentence of his preface, he tells us one of his aims:

> These are the researches of Herodotus of Halicarnassus, which he publishes with a view to preserving from oblivion the remembrance of what men have done. Thus, the great and wonderful deeds of the Greeks and foreign peoples will not lose the acclaim that is due them. At the same time, the reasons for their hostility will be put on record.

Thus, Herodotus was seeking to give an accurate account of events of the recent past and at the same time to understand foreign countries in their relations with the Greeks. On his canvas were not just the great battles of the Persian Wars but the whole Near East as well as Greece—the peoples of these regions, their geography, religions, customs, folktales, history. Though he was mostly interested in the events of the recent past, his curiosity was very broad. In the course of his oral research on the wars (which he was too young to have witnessed himself), Herodotus became interested in the still-earlier events that led up to them and in contemporary conditions in the Near East generally. Thus, his *History* turns out to be something really remarkable: both a history and a cultural survey of the entire known world in which the Greeks and the Asiatics fought.

Preserving a record of the past was, however, only one of Herodotus' interests. He also wanted his *History* to be a monument to the contrasts between the cultures of the Greeks and the Asiatics. Above all, he intended it as a series of practical lessons in the politics and morals that lead to success and failure.

In his investigations, Herodotus discovered a great deal about the rise and fall of civilizations; and, like the early Greek philosopher-scientists, he sought to find a single explanation of events—a kind of law of history. In fact, through his detailed study of the Persian Empire and the stunning defeat it suffered at the hands of a coalition of tiny Greek cities, he believed he had actually discovered a basic law of history—that excessive bigness inevitably leads to destruction. He observed that history reveals a recurring cycle of the rise and fall of great powers. One power rises to great heights and then decays; into the vacuum thus created, another power moves, only to undergo the same pattern of rise and fall. To explain this seemingly inevitable pattern, Herodotus fell back on the traditional Greek religious belief that the gods are jealous of human success. According to that belief, when humans, whether single individuals or entire peoples, become too big, they suffer divine retribution through Nemesis. That is the punishment of the gods for all who commit the sin of *hybris* (excess of any kind). The intervention of the gods in human affairs is seen repeatedly in Herodotus' *History:* The gods act both in person and by divine messages sent through oracles, dreams, and omens of all kinds.

In this manner Herodotus understood both the downfall of the Lydian Empire, the first foreign power to bring Greek cities under its control, and the rise and fall of the Persian Empire. Herodotus concluded that Lydia, in an affluent region of what is now Turkey, had collapsed because it expanded beyond the limits of moderation. Then Persia stepped into the shoes of both the Assyrian Empire and the Lydian Empire and succeeded in uniting much of Asia, including part of India. Through ever-greater conquests and the enormous concentration of power in the hands of one man, the king of Persia, the whole civilization committed *hybris,* leading the Persians to disaster under their kings Darius and Xerxes. Persian expansion was halted at the borders of Europe by the Greeks, who thus acted as the people chosen by the gods to teach the Persians the lesson of moderation. This is what Herodotus wanted the statesmen of the present and the future to learn from his *History*—that no nation can go beyond certain limits and survive. This concept—of cycles in history and the dangers of nations' overreaching themselves—has haunted historians ever since. Gibbon, the great author of *The Decline and Fall of the Roman Empire,* was following the theory of Herodotus when he attributed the Empire's disintegration to "the natural and inevitable effect of excessive greatness."

In the leisurely pursuit of his aims as a writer of history, Herodotus has left us classical accounts of many famous events and places. No one would want to miss his story of the rise and fall of the Lydian Empire, with his account of a conversation on human happiness between the Athenian statesman Solon and Croesus, king of Lydia, or his report of the double-edged Delphic oracle given to Croesus—that if he attacked the Persian Empire, a great empire would be destroyed. Memorable, also, are his descriptions of that marvelous land Egypt, which he calls "the gift of the Nile," and his account of its history, people, natural marvels, religion, and customs; and his account of the actual Persian invasions of Greece, including the battles of Marathon, Thermopylae (which ended in the heroic death of three hundred

Spartan expendables under Leonidas), Salamis, and Plataea.

We can easily fault Herodotus today. Sometimes he is a bit gullible, for he accepted as fact stories and explanations that are incredible or have since been proved false. It is also easy for a military expert to criticize his grasp of military strategy and for political scientists to find his understanding of politics somewhat naïve. His statistics, like most statistics in ancient writers, are unreliable, especially those he gives for the size of the Persian armies and the casualties on both sides of the war. (Part of his problem was the Greek numbering system, which, although less clumsy than the Roman, lacked the concept of zero and was unable to express very large numbers with exactness.)

Besides these matters of fact, the style of Herodotus, which adds to the interest of his narrative, may also be a source of difficulty for the modern reader. The *History* is slowed, for example, by many digressions that are not relevant to the topic under consideration. Today, a modern historian would either exclude such material or put it in an appendix. Another peculiarity of Herodotus as an historian —one that has, however, had an enormous influence on the writing of history down to modern times—is the inclusion of long speeches, debates, and conversations among the characters. These are really fictionalized speeches and conversations, not the exact words of the speaker on the particular occasion, something that Herodotus could not possibly have learned; in some cases, we know that such conversations could not have taken place at all. In his constant interest in people as individuals—a typical Greek trait—Herodotus places the greatest emphasis on trying to understand events through personal ambitions and motives. He does not find it necessary to try to take account of the broader forces that may have a controlling influence on history, such as population growth, economic developments, social movements, and the value systems of different peoples.

But despite these failings, when we read his *History,* we learn to admire Herodotus for his fairness to the Persians (he was actually attacked in ancient times as being pro-Persian), for his conscientious effort to write a true history of his times, and for his tireless curiosity. Herodotus is, above all, one of the world's great storytellers. In his search for the truth, he rebelled against blind acceptance of myths as history and found answers to historical problems in human, secular, and political terms. His *History* is indeed the product of painstaking inquiry into the past, sharpened by a high degree of skepticism and political sophistication. His breadth and scope were rarely equaled in ancient times. The English poet Wordsworth called his *History* "the most interesting and instructive book next to the Bible that has ever been written."

Thucydides

War as a central theme of history has remained dominant in the writings of historians ever since Herodotus. The classical historians concentrated their attention on this subject because among the Greeks and Romans, with rare exceptions, war was regarded as both natural and inevitable. However much we may regret their excessive interest in wars, we can understand why so many works of literature in antiquity were inspired by war. Soon after Herodotus, however, a new dominant theme in history made its appearance — politics. In the generation after Herodotus, another great war, the interminable Peloponnesian War (431–404 B.C.), which ruined Athens, inspired an even greater work of history, *The Peloponnesian War* of Thucydides (460–400 B.C.). In his treatment of this critical war, Thucydides stressed political history as primary. It was thus through the influence of the works of Herodotus and Thucydides that war and politics became the principal themes of history, not only in ancient times but for most of the modern period.

The Periclean Age of Athens did not produce any event as spectacular as the Persian Wars, and so no one considered it desirable to write an account of this great age in man's cultural history. Not until the outbreak of the Peloponnesian War did a second historian appear, the Athenian Thucydides, who recorded and studied the causes of the war, the motives of the participants, and the melancholy events that marked this total war between his own city and Sparta and her allies.

Like Herodotus, Thucydides considered that keeping a record of wars was the most important function of an historian, and he, too, was fascinated by the decline and fall of great men and nations. But unlike Herodotus, he had the advantage of witnessing the Peloponnesian War as both an active participant and an objective observer. In the early years of the conflict, Thucydides was an Athenian naval commander, elected to this public office for one year under the democratic Athenian constitution. Because of his failure to carry out a military assignment successfully, he was tried and convicted on the charge of incompetence and was exiled from Athens for twenty years. As a result, he was free to travel to all theaters of the war, using his eyes and ears, re-

ENJOY THE COMPANY OF THREE OF THE WISEST MEN WHO EVER LIVED

(Continued from other side)

The selections themselves are remarkable values. They are carefully printed on expensive paper stock. They are hard-bound in matched sand-colored buckram, worked and stamped in crimson, black, and genuine gold. And through direct-to-the public distribution, we are able to offer our members these deluxe editions for only $3.89 each, plus shipping.

Interested? We will send you the first three selections, Plato, Aristotle and Marcus Aurelius—all three for this special introductory price of $1.00, plus shipping.

We know what charmers these three wise men are. We are betting that you will be so taken by them that you will want to stay in the Club and meet some of their friends, including the greatest story tellers, philosophers, poets and historians the world has ever known.

Do not send any money now. We'll bill you later. Just fill in and mail the attached postage-paid card, today, while you are thinking about it and while the invitation still stands.

THE CLASSICS CLUB
Roslyn, New York 11576

Please enroll me as a Trial Member, and send me at once the THREE beautiful Classics Club Editions of PLATO, ARISTOTLE AND MARCUS AURELIUS. I enclose NO MONEY; within a week after receiving my books, I will either return them and owe nothing, or keep them for the special introductory price of ONLY $1.00 (plus a few cents mailing charges) for ALL THREE.

As a member, I am to receive advance descriptions of all future selections, but am not obligated to buy any. For each volume I keep, I will send you only $3.89 (plus a few cents mailing charges). I may reject any volume before or after I receive it, and cancel my membership at any time.

Mr., Mrs., Miss _____ (Please Print Plainly)

Address _____

City _____ State _____ Zip _____

In Canada: Enclose this reply card in an envelope and mail to CLASSICS CLUB OF CANADA, Pendragon House Ltd., 71 Bathurst Street, Toronto 135, Ontario

(← Continued on other side)

Do you have room in your home for three wise men? They are Plato, Aristotle, and Marcus Aurelius . . . three of the wisest, wittiest, most stimulating minds that ever lived.

They still live . . . in the Five Great Dialogues of Plato, the Meditations of Marcus Aurelius, and Aristotle's On Man in the Universe. All three books (regularly $11.67) can be yours for only $1.00 as your introduction to the Classics Club.

The Classics Club is quite unlike any other book club. The Club does not offer best sellers that come and go. Instead, it offers its members a chance to stay young through great books that never grow old. These books include Utopia by Thomas More; the complete works of Shakespeare; Benjamin Franklin's Autobiography; Omar Khayyam's Rubaiyat; Walden by Thoreau; and other fresh, spontaneous, even outspoken works that stretch your mind and sweep away the mental cobwebs that hold back most men.

You never have to buy any of these books. (To force you to buy a classic would be barbaric.) As a member, take only those books you really want to own. And, at any time, you may cancel your membership, without penalty or hurt feelings.

THE CLASSICS CLUB
Roslyn, New York 11576

Postage Will Be Paid By

BUSINESS REPLY MAIL
No postage stamp necessary if mailed in the United States

First Class
Permit No. 7
Roslyn, N. Y.

LET THESE 3 WISE MEN INTO YOUR HOME. LATER, YOU MIGHT LIKE TO INVITE THEIR FRIENDS.

cording events as they actually happened and interviewing eyewitnesses and reliable informants on both sides of the great conflict. In fact, Thucydides' political understanding was so sharp that he was able to predict the war's coming years in advance, and he began to investigate its causes long before it actually broke out.

In analyzing the causes and the events of this war, Thucydides took a more sophisticated and politically shrewd approach than Herodotus did. He had two advantages over his predecessor: He was both a general and a politician; and he had the benefit of formal higher education in the schools of the Sophists. Because of this training, Thucydides developed ways of observing and analyzing the conduct and motives of leaders and peoples that led to remarkable insights into the political behavior of man. Basic to his thinking was the view that all men everywhere always behave under the influence of a single motive—self-interest. The pursuit of personal advantage, Thucydides believed, underlies all human decisions and actions—not the principles or ideals, such as honor, altruism, or humanitarianism, that men often declare to be the reasons for their conduct. It is therefore necessary to penetrate beneath the surface of men's actions and words in order to discover the real causes of events. Nations and political leaders are driven by the desire for power; their guiding philosophy is not morality or the will to help others but the unstated certainty that "might makes right."

Why should Thucydides have taken the trouble to examine, like a skilled surgeon, the anatomy of a disastrous war and the political disease that destroyed Athens? If history cannot in fact be reconstructed, or if history never precisely repeats itself, why should anyone study it? The historian must have answers to such questions or he will not be taken seriously. The answer that Thucydides arrived at was a political one, concerned with the nature and use of political power. To his way of thinking, for political leaders who want to retain power and assure the survival of their people, the realistic understanding of a great crisis like the Peloponnesian War is eminently useful. By studying the true causes of fateful events and the hidden motives of people's behavior, the statesman equips himself for survival. Thucydides' principal aim in *The History of the Peloponnesian War* was, therefore, to provide future statesmen with the tools for predicting and controlling men and events through understanding deeply and comprehensively the behavior of leaders, states, and social classes in a great crisis.

178 Historians and Biographers

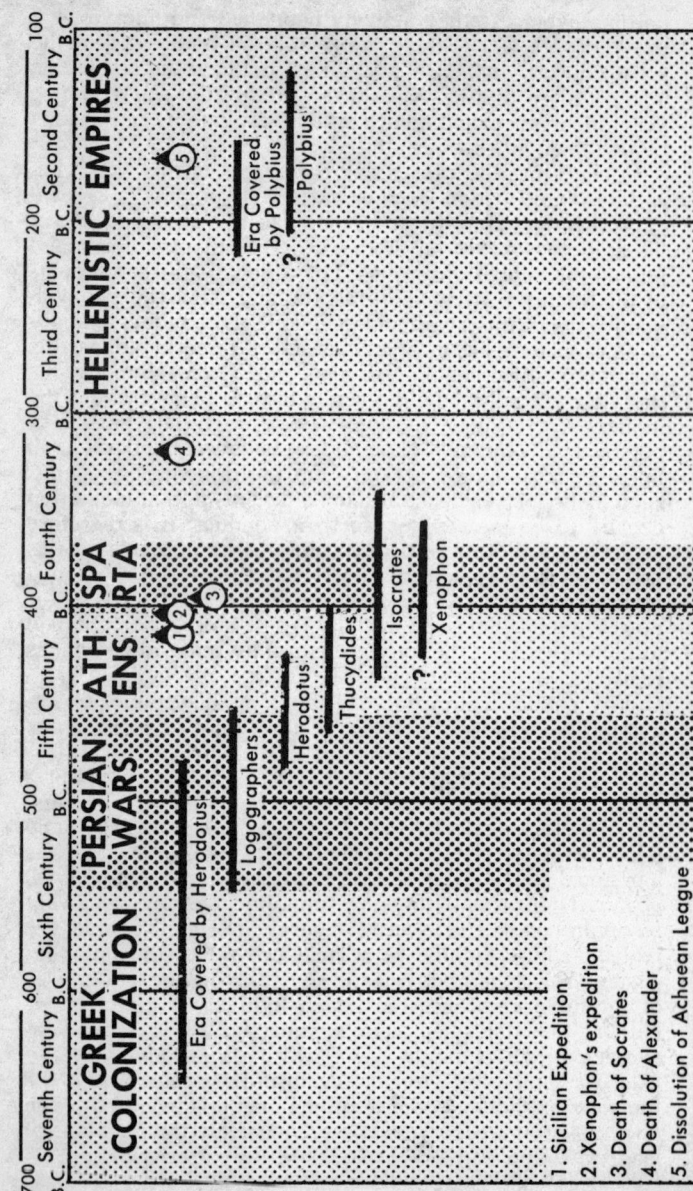

Thucydides believed that similar conditions—great wars and severe political crises—would arise in the future. He put it this way:

> If those who wish to observe the truth about events that have happened and about such events and similar ones that are likely to happen in the future in the context of human nature shall pronounce this work to be useful, then I shall be satisfied. My history is an everlasting possession. . . .

Thucydides believed that human nature is unchangeable, everywhere the same; if the circumstances are the same, then the behavior of men will always be predictably the same, also. Therefore, if one understands how men have behaved in the past, one will be better prepared to cope with crises in the present and the future.

Above all, Thucydides tried to explain the motives and behavior of political leaders and the psychology of masses of people in crises. By penetrating to the heart of human behavior, he was trying somehow to establish laws of history—general truths, stripped of local circumstances, that would apply in other times, other situations. Among the laws that Thucydides formulated are these: that all states act in their own national interest; that "might makes right" in all human affairs; that a balance of power among states is necessary to avoid conflicts, and if the balance of power is upset, war will follow; that war brutalizes all participants; that within cities harmony and strength can be maintained when there is a balance of power between rich and poor, but any disturbance of this balance to the advantage of either side will lead to internal strife, national weakness, and decay.

In many other ways, Thucydides' methods as an historian were far in advance of Herodotus'. He observed men and events with a keen critical sense; unlike Herodotus, he used some official documents, all of which were in Greek in this war; his principal source was trustworthy oral information obtained from reliable persons. Yet he was thoroughly aware of how difficult it is to attain the truth. "Of the events that happened during the war," he tells us,

> I have not ventured to write on the basis of information obtained from any chance informant, nor according to my own opinion. I have put down nothing but what I either saw in person or learned from others of whom I made the most careful inquiry possible. The investigation was a laborious one, because eyewitnesses of each occurrence gave different accounts of the same happenings, as they remembered them or were biased toward one side or the other.

In an historian as careful as Thucydides, it is strange to discover that he, too, filled his history with speeches and conversations that are not the exact words of the speakers. But unlike Herodotus, he was worried by this practice, for he warns us:

> As regards the speeches that were made on each side, either before they went to war or during the war itself, there is a problem. It was difficult for me to remember those I heard in person; and, of course, in the case of those reported to me by others from various places, it was not possible to reproduce the exact words of the speakers. Therefore, I have put into the mouth of each speaker the views especially appropriate to the particular occasion. I have expressed his views as I thought he would be likely to express them, and I have tried as nearly as I could to give the essence of what actually was said.

Thucydides used these speeches and dialogues as a device to clarify the motives on both sides of the war and to lay bare the political thinking and ethics—or lack of ethics—in the national and international affairs of his times. Like Herodotus, also, Thucydides introduced many digressions. But search as you may in Thucydides, you will not find anecdotes or human-interest stories brought in purely for their own sake, without regard to their relevance. Thucydides was not interested in entertaining his readers; he is almost grim in setting down only the essentials, in a compact, concentrated way.

Thucydides must, therefore, be read attentively, but the effort is rewarding. The many memorable parts of his history will be read as long as there are books. Outstanding are his analyses of the two competing systems of government and society, dynamic, democratic Athens and conservative, authoritarian Sparta; of the instability and inner weakness of a democracy; of the benefits of an empire and the risks of aggressive imperialism. His description of the terrible plague at Athens near the beginning of the war (430–429 B.C.), in which the great Athenian leader Pericles died, contains not only a clinical analysis of the symptoms and of the course of the disease, which Thucydides himself caught, but also an analysis of the collapse of law and order in Athens at the time. Unforgettable also is Pericles' famous Funeral Oration, delivered over the war dead in accordance with Athenian custom. This speech was actually the model for Lincoln's Gettysburg Address. Pericles presented an idealized picture of the democratic Athenian society and of the empire for which these men had laid down their lives. "I say," Pericles told the Athenians, that the city of Athens as a whole is the school of Hellas, and that each individual among us, in my opinion, proves himself to be self-sufficient in the most varied forms of action with the utmost grace and versatility. . . . There are mighty signs and witnesses of our power, and we shall be the wonder both of this and future ages; we shall need no Homer to sing our praises. . . . I want you daily to fix your eyes upon the power of Athens and become lovers of her; and when you are inspired by the vision of her greatness, reflect that these things have been acquired by men who knew their duty and, in what they had to do, acted with honor. . . . The whole world is the tomb of famous men; not only are they commemorated by inscriptions on monuments in their own land, but in foreign lands there dwells also an unwritten memorial of them, engraved not on stone, but in the heart of each and every man.

Thucydides' narrative is remarkable also for its portrayal of the revolutions that took place in Greece during the war, particularly the one on the island of Corcyra (modern Corfu), in which the democrats and the oligarchs massacred each other. "Through revolution there were visited upon the cities of Hellas," wrote Thucydides, "many terrible calamities, such as have happened and always will happen so long as human nature is the same. . . ." War brutalized everyone; the revenge motive corrupted all and turned moral principles inside out, pitting brother against brother, father against son. Force, not intelligence, prevailed; revenge and violence triumphed over justice and reason; the finer traits of human nature were overwhelmed.

In 415 B.C., in a display of her might, Athens sent an ultimatum to the neutral island of Melos, ordering her to surrender. The "Melian Dialogue" between the Athenian officials and naval officers and the leaders of Melos is one of Thucydides' masterpieces. It reveals both the desire of the Greek cities to maintain their freedom and the calculating policies of the imperial democracy of Athens, which made a cynical demonstration of the triumph of force in international affairs. When Melos rejected the ultimatum, the island was captured, the city destroyed, the men massacred, and the women and children sold into slavery—all because they refused to bow to Athens.

In the same year, in a vast new imperialist venture, the Athenian war faction set out to conquer and annex the large island of Sicily to the west. (The grounds were that Athens had treaty commitments with some Sicilians and that it was necessary for the war effort to cut off Spartan supplies from Sicily.) The attack was a total disaster, ending, in 413 B.C., in the surrender of the entire Athenian expeditionary force.

"Of all the events that took place in this war," Thucydides wrote,

and in my opinion, of all Hellenic actions of which we have record, this proved to be the greatest—the most splendid for the victors, the most disastrous for the vanquished; for they were utterly and everywhere defeated. The sufferings were enormous; it was total defeat. Fleet and infantry, everything perished. Of the many who went there, few returned home. This is what happened to the Sicilian expedition.

Thucydides managed to carry his history of the war down to the revolution in Athens in 411 B.C. It remains an unfinished work. Athens surrendered unconditionally to Sparta seven years later, in 404 B.C. Athens was never again a great power.

With Thucydides, the writing of history took a new and lasting turn. Under his influence, the serious historian now wrote about the present, concentrating henceforth on political history and on contemporary events that he could investigate himself and vouch for personally. As a consequence, Herodotus' interest in the past and his worldwide and many-faceted approach were replaced by a narrower perspective. It was like looking at history through a microscope rather than a telescope.

Thucydides has been called "the first scientific historian," but it is doubtful that history can ever be a science like chemistry or physics. The historian always selects relatively few of the almost infinite number of events that occur at any time, gives them his personal interpretation, and adds the charm of literary art. Thucydides' *History of the Peloponnesian War* is indeed a brilliant description and analysis of human behavior in the most fateful war in Greek history. Because of his concentration on the flaws of the Greek statesmen and Greek society and his grim and dramatic picture of the decline and fall of Athens from the height of the Periclean Age, Thucydides has been called "the most tragic of historians." His book has remained a manual for statesmen ever since. It was carefully studied by the American Founding Fathers and is still necessary reading in Washington today.

Other Works of History

Thucydides' young contemporary Xenophon (about 428–354 B.C.), though of lesser stature as an historian, continued the tradition of active participation in the events he wrote about. Born in Athens of an aristocratic family, Xenophon was a student of Socrates, of whom he wrote an interesting memoir that we shall discuss in a moment. Among his other books is the *Hellenica,* a history of Greece from the point where Thucydides left off to 360 B.C., when Greece lay bleeding and utterly exhausted from her ceaseless intercity warfare. Xenophon is, however, best known for his *Anabasis* (literally, "going up," called *The March Up Country* in the excellent modern translation by W.H.D. Rouse). It is a remarkable eyewitness record of a minor historical event in which he was a leading participant.

At the end of the long Peloponnesian War, an enormous number of Greeks, knowing no other occupation but war, were released from military service. In 401 B.C., Cyrus the Younger, a Persian prince plotting to overthrow his brother Artaxerxes II and seize the throne of Persia, recruited ten thousand Greek soldiers of fortune for this purpose. About thirty years of age at the time, Xenophon had several reasons for joining the expeditionary force: A friend of his was one of the mercenaries' commanders; he wanted to win fame and fortune; and he was intensely curious about Persia. He began to take notes from the very beginning and kept full records of the expedition until it was disbanded two years later. His notes became the basis for one of the great true adventure stories in world literature.

Actually, most of Xenophon's account deals not with the *anabasis*—the climb from the Aegean coast up through the mountainous terrain inland—but with the retreat of the Greek army. The ten thousand Greeks marched through Persian territory from Cyrus' headquarters at Sardis in the Persian province of Lydia toward the Persian capital at Babylon. The troops fought only one pitched battle, at Cunaxa near Babylon, and won it; but the impetuous Cyrus needlessly exposed himself to danger and was killed in the battle. As a result, the victorious Greeks, now without a purpose, were faced with the task of surviving a fifteen-hundred mile retreat through enemy territory, beset by cold, hunger, thirst, and constant attacks.

The Greek soldiers' difficulties increased immensely when most of their officers were treacherously massacred during a conference with a Persian commander. At this point, Xenophon found himself catapulted into command, and by his initiative and eloquence (as he tells the story), he succeeded in leading the Greeks through the forbidding Armenian highlands to the Black Sea, where they would find friendly Greek colonies. In a story packed with hairbreadth escapes, it is a powerful dramatic moment. A Greek scout suddenly shouts, "The sea! The sea!" and those of the ten thousand who have survived know that they have at last reached Greek waters.

The Greeks were to have other adventures before they finally returned home. For Xenophon, at least, the result was the financial independence (he held a wealthy Persian for ransom) that permitted him to devote the remainder of his life to writing.

Xenophon's almost day-by-day account of the army's advance and its great retreat is told in a simple, direct, reportorial style in which he always refers to himself in the third person. Eloquent speeches and interesting conversations enliven the narrative. In reading the *Anabasis,* we become engrossed not only in the trials and tribulations of the "marching democracy," as the Greek army under Xenophon has been called, but also in the many exotic sights, the geography, peoples, animals, and customs of the ancient Near East. Xenophon's *Anabasis* revealed to the Greeks how vulnerable the Persian Empire actually was, a weakness that, before the century was over, Alexander the Great would, by his conquest, demonstrate to the world.

Greek Biography

In any human situation, but especially in war and politics, natural leaders like Xenophon rise to prominence. Both Thucydides and the "Father of History" Herodotus included sketches of such leading historical figures as Themistocles, Pausanias, Cimon, Pericles, Cleon, Nicias, and Alcibiades. Full-scale biographies were, however, a somewhat later development, perhaps because, when history first appeared as a distinct study about the middle of the fifth century B.C., the emphasis in Greek society was more on the cities as social units than on their individual great men. Yet with their respect for individual achievement (the individual's *arete*), the Greeks had always been hero worshipers, so much so that they considered as almost divine those men who had been great benefactors of their native cities or of humanity at large—men like Ajax, Heracles, Theseus, Perseus. But such heroes belonged to the distant past, the Heroic Age commemorated in Greek myths and in *The Iliad* and *The Odyssey* of Homer.

The first beginnings of intense interest in the biographies of outstanding contemporaries became apparent at the time of the Peloponnesian War. This was due in part to a natural interest in the human personality, but more importantly to the hunger in those unstable times for information about the great individuals who were shaping events and a keen desire for examples and models of human conduct and success. Man's commemorative instinct now took a new form: For the first time, full-scale lives of famous men were written, works in which a man's entire life was recorded for posterity. Early in the fourth century B.C., the individual in Greek society began to take priority over the state as the center of interest, and more and more great men were coming to the fore in search of personal power and fame. Thus biography was born, a late creation of Greek culture.

The pioneering work in this new field—the first effort in world literature to write something approximating a biography—is the *Memorabilia* of Xenophon, a memoir of the great Athenian philosopher Socrates. Xenophon presents his teacher, who was executed by the Athenian government in 399 B.C., as a martyr to freedom of speech and the conscience of the individual. Fascinating as this book is, however, it is not a systematic life of Socrates from birth to death, as we would write a biography today. Instead, it is a series of incidents, anecdotes, and conversations loosely strung together to illustrate the thinking and greatness of Socrates. Xenophon also wrote a biographical tribute to the dead Spartan king Agesilaus, emphasizing his virtues and noble deeds. A similar eulogy was written in praise of Evagoras, a ruler on the island of Cyprus, by the Athenian writer and teacher Isocrates (436–338 B.C.). It is the first known biography of a living person in world literature.

The loose structure and special aims of these early examples were characteristic of the biographical form throughout classical times. They underline the important differences between ancient biographies and modern ones. We prefer an account of a man's life that takes us in order from his family background, birth, and youth through his mature years and achievements to his death. The ancient biographer, on the other hand, began by declaring (or having in mind) what he considered the outstanding human virtues (courage, wisdom, piety, justice, moderation, patriotism) and then proceeded to demonstrate how his hero lived up to these standards of excellence. This he did largely by relating anecdotes about the person and by reporting things he had said. We thus learn little from ancient biographies about what their subjects looked like or how they lived. The ancient biographer concentrated on the fully developed person; he does not enable us to follow the growth and changes in a man's personality and interests throughout his life.

By the end of the fourth century B.C., biography had become a standard form of literature. But so long as the biographer's aim was chiefly to praise notable individuals, there was little attention to the weaknesses and frailties of great men that would make their lives more appealing and believable. The philosopher Aristotle and his followers, however, developed a deeper psychological understanding of human types by analyzing various life styles and value systems and describing them in detail. Aristotle and his school also defined the special purpose of biography which it retained thereafter until modern times: to serve as lessons in moral conduct through famous models. Throughout antiquity, this was the principal reason why so many people read about the lives of famous people.

Aristotle and his followers made elegance of style indispensable to the writing of biography. More important, the previous practice of writing only glowing tributes to celebrities was abandoned for more balanced portrayals. Thereafter, in order to characterize the real person, biographers included intimate aspects of his private life — weaknesses, scandals, and even incidents that detracted from the greatness of the biographical hero. They did not hesitate to use biography to destroy well-known public figures. For example, a very critical biography of Socrates, written in this period by Aristoxenus of Tarentum, scandalized many people. (The book, along with so much else of classical literature, has disappeared and is known only from references by other writers.) From now on, the usual method of biography was to deal with both the virtues and the frailties of famous men.

The Hellenistic Period

The popularity of both biography and history among the Greeks from the fourth century on led to a new tendency, one with which we are quite familiar today — the writing of romanticized accounts whose main purpose was to hold the reader's interest through "good stories." Authors distorted or invented incidents in order to achieve sensational effects, sacrificing the truth in favor of tales of wonders and other remarkable occurrences. In the Hellenistic period following the death of Alexander the Great (323 B.C.), it was, in any case, difficult to write history that approached the high standards set by Herodotus and Thucydides. Alexander's conquests in the Near East opened up to the Greeks many lands full of strange sights and exotic ways of living. Confronted by such marvels, readers developed an appetite for all kinds of fantastic and improbable tales. This was especially true of the histories and biographies concerning Alexander himself, though most of these have disappeared in the wreck of ancient literature. The chaotic state of the world, disturbed by numerous wars and revolutions, added further to the difficulty of writing a true historical account of the Hellenistic period. Men found it almost impossible to discover rational principles to explain the happenings of history. In general, men reacted to this turbulent world with two fundamental explanations: that events happen by pure chance; or that they result from the workings of an inevitable fate. Neither belief provides an adequate basis for a rational view of history. As a result, from the time of Alexander the Great to the emergence of Rome as the dominant world power, the Greeks produced little history or biography that was of high quality. Almost nothing has been preserved of the works that were written in this period. The one exception, both in its quality and its survival, is the great *History* of Polybius (about 203–120 B.C.).

Polybius

As in the case of Herodotus and Thucydides, Polybius was inspired by a military conflict of tremendous proportions—the Punic Wars between Rome and Carthage, which raised Rome to the status of a world power. This struggle convulsed the western Mediterranean and was watched from all over the world, especially by the Greek leaders. Polybius, one of the heads of the Achaean League, became, like Herodotus and Thucydides, an exile from his own land. When the Romans intervened to dissolve the league in 168 B.C., Polybius and a thousand other Achaean leaders were deported to Italy. As a distinguished Greek statesman and general, Polybius soon became a close friend of some of Rome's most eminent men and was even permitted to travel. In this way, he could study the great events through direct observation, devoting his enforced leisure to seeing and hearing whatever he could of the history of his times. Thus, for example, he crossed the Alps in Hannibal's footsteps in order to "learn and see," as he tells us, and in 146 B.C. he was even at Carthage with Scipio Africanus the Younger when the Romans finally destroyed the enemy city.

Polybius decided to write a history of the entire world for the limited period from 220 to 168 B.C. He defined his subject in this way partly because, under the dynamic impact of Roman power, it was now possible to see the whole civilized world as a unified system. More importantly, Polybius was convinced that something unparalleled in world history had happened: In the roughly fifty years of which he would write, a single city had become the master of the world. Since this was achieved largely through war, Polybius devoted most of his attention to the Second Punic War (218–201 B.C.), in which the Carthaginian general Hannibal carried out his devastating Italian campaign, and to the Roman wars with Macedonia. Being himself a man of great political and military experience, Polybius sought, through the history of Rome's march to world power, to provide lessons for politicians of the future. Like Thucydides, he believed that telling how leaders had conducted affairs would make history a useful tool and training ground for statesmen. "History," he declared, "will never be properly written until either men of action undertake to write it . . . or historians become convinced that practical experience is of the first importance for historical composition."

To discover the truth about the course of historical events was the fundamental aim of Polybius. He attacked what he called "the gossip of the barber shop." In doing his research, he put less emphasis on earlier books than on painstaking personal investigations, traveling and examining witnesses and reliable informants everywhere. Although Polybius examined some official documents (treaties, inscriptions), his principal method, like that of most of the great ancient historians, was oral inquiry. And like most other ancient writers of history, Polybius included many digressions as well as artificial speeches and conversations attributed to leading historical figures.

Polybius' great predecessors Herodotus and Thucydides had discovered the guiding forces of history in the punishment of *hybris* by the gods or the clash of self-interest among the great powers. Polybius, on the other hand, concluded that human affairs are governed by a mysterious force that he called *Tyche* ("Fortune"). By this he meant something like "the unexpected" or "acts of God." But at the same time, he believed that Fortune was somehow, like a divine Providence, guiding Rome purposefully to world dominion. In this way, he offered a moral justification for Roman world rule: It was an empire that came into being for the advantage not only of the Romans themselves but also of the conquered peoples, who now enjoyed stability and order under Rome. The keys to Rome's stupendous success, Polybius believed, were to be found in the qualities of her leaders and armies, but above all in her constitution. This constitution, Polybius reasoned, was "mixed," containing elements of monarchy (the consuls), aristocracy (the Senate), and democracy (the people): Rome's remarkable internal stability resulted, in his view, from the checks and balances provided by linking these three elements in one system of government. Polybius' analysis of Rome's "mixed constitution" was very influential in the writing of the Constitution of the United States.

Polybius' *History* deserves its reputation as one of the great works of ancient history. A famous modern historian, Theodor Mommsen, who won the Nobel Prize for his studies of Rome, said of Polybius that he was "like a sun shining on the field of Roman history."

Early Roman Historians

As in literature generally, so in history the earliest serious writers about Roman affairs were all Greeks. The Romans themselves, proud of their national achievements and great men, had a strong sense of the past. Moreover, the Romans were ancestor worshipers; every family of any consequence kept records of the deeds of their ancestors and commemorated them with portrait busts which they displayed in the *atrium* of their home. The Roman national genius for recognizing and paying tribute to great men was also embodied in a very ancient Roman custom, the formal funeral oration in which the dead person was eulogized by a speaker chosen from his family. In these tributes to the deceased, the pedigrees, virtues, and deeds of both the dead person and his ancestors were described. Finally, the government also kept simple records of events, setting down year by year in a few lines the names of elected public officials and the significant happenings. These records were called *annales maximi* because they were kept by the *pontifex maximus,* the chief priest of the official state religion.

As among the Greeks, the writing of history and biography as literature was a relatively late development among the Romans. Again as with the Greeks, the earliest Roman historical writing was stirred by a great military event, the Punic Wars. As we have seen, the Romans were in general an unromantic, practical people; for centuries they regarded the writing and enjoyment of literature as a sheer waste of time. But when the Romans realized, in the third century B.C., that they had become the greatest power in the world, their attitude to literature changed. It is characteristic of them that they soon recognized the practical value of both history and biography.

When the Romans turned to history, they had few literary traditions in their own language, Latin, and little experience in the use of an attractive writing style. The first Romans to write history simply imitated the Greek historians and even wrote in the Greek language. When they finally had the experience and courage to write in Latin, for a long time the earliest Roman historians wrote *annales,* that is, simple year-by-year accounts of what had happened. They wrote in this way because they based their histories on pontifical annals, often going back to the traditional founding date of the city, 753 B.C. Only a small part of these early Roman historical writings have come down to us, but they reveal several peculiarly Roman characteristics. The Romans regarded the writing of history as a suitable occupation for a person who had had an active political career, particularly a Senator. Thus, Roman history typically was written not by a professional historian but by a member of the ruling class, taking up his leisure time or his sometimes forcible retirement from politics. For such men, the writing of history was an intensely serious matter. The Roman historians were themselves so much involved in the victories and setbacks of Rome that their patriotism and their political points of view strongly colored everything they wrote. Of one of the early Roman historians, Polybius says, "Like a man in love, he makes it appear that the Romans are always brave and wise."

The purpose of the Roman writers of history was frequently not so much to record facts as to explain Rome's greatness. This they usually attributed to Rome's national virtues: her strict moral code, the integrity of the Roman government, the Roman values of austerity, seriousness, dignity, and duty. Thus, in addition to patriotism, they were very much concerned with the relationship of morality to history; and so we find moral ideas coloring much of Roman history. When the Romans came into contact with the Greeks, they learned that history can be useful to the statesman and that one of the principal purposes of history was to provide lessons from the successes and failures of the past. This sounded reasonable to them.

The first Roman to write history in Latin was Marcus Cato the Elder (234–149 B.C.), the famous conservative

Senator whose hatred of Carthage kept alive the conflict with Rome's great rival. Cato's *Origins,* which has been lost, was a study of the founding of Rome and other Italian cities as well as of their history down to his own times, written to serve as a useful handbook for politicians. It is notable that, although he made the city of Rome the center of interest, he is said never once to have mentioned a single Roman by name in the entire work.

Revolution and Empire

With the beginnings of the Roman Revolution in the tribunates of the brothers Tiberius and Gaius Gracchus (133 and 123–122 B.C., respectively), Roman writers turned away from the annals of Rome's past. Instead, contemporary events were recorded and analyzed by men who were active participants in these fateful conflicts. Although none of these new political commentaries has survived, they mark another stage in the shaping of the special form that Roman history assumed. History now became useful as a weapon designed to capture the minds of leaders and people in the partisan politics of the times.

At the same time, the emergence of many great men fired with a new type of motivation—personal political power rather than service to Rome—led to a great interest in biography. The Romans began to write formal biographies in the first century B.C. when men like Sulla, Pompey, and Julius Caesar held the center of the stage of history. To satisfy their interest in the lives of men who had left their mark on history, the Romans imitated the Greek methods and models of biography. They were attracted mostly to the lives of political leaders and generals, from the legendary Romulus and the early dictator Fabius Maximus, the "shield of Rome" against Hannibal, to Cato and Scipio Africanus. It was only a short step to the writing of political autobiographies by prominent Roman politicians themselves, to justify their careers and win followers.

Julius Caesar

The first Roman historical writer whose works have survived and are read today is the brilliant and versatile Julius Caesar (100–44 B.C.). In the decade before his death, he wrote memoirs of his activities as a general and politician— his *Commentaries on the Gallic War* and his *Commentaries on the Civil War.* Both of these works are inspired by a politician's need to defend his official acts and his conduct as a public figure rather than by a disinterested pursuit of historical truth. We should not, therefore, expect to find in them merely a record of the facts. Caesar had actually fomented a civil war by illegally crossing the Rubicon River into Italy from the province of Cisalpine Gaul, of which he was governor. In his earlier invasion of Gaul, massive and unprovoked, Caesar had been formally accused by some Senators of treason for waging a war not authorized by the Roman government. Roman law on both counts was clearcut: A provincial governor was "forbidden to leave his province, lead an army out of it, wage war on his own initiative without the permission of the Senate and the Roman people."

From the very first sentence of his *Commentaries on the Gallic War,* a book once known to every schoolboy who studied Latin, Caesar sought both to glorify his own abilities as a military strategist and leader of men and to instill pride in Rome's might. In this firsthand account by a general in one of the greatest military conquests of world history, Caesar gives the impression of being a detached observer by writing about himself, as Xenophon had, always in the third person. ("Caesar called the men to a meeting. . . . Caesar personally led the attack. . . . Caesar conferred with ambassadors of the enemy.")

On the surface, the *Gallic War* appears to be a matter-of-fact, impersonal record of great Roman victories. There is a great deal of vivid dramatic narrative: of Roman soldiers on the march, their activities in military camps, battle scenes, conferences in the general's headquarters. Caesar's crossing of the mighty Rhine River on a bridge constructed by his engineers was a great feat and makes interesting reading, though it must be remembered that the entire action was first of all an arrogant display of Roman might and skill to the barbarians on the other side of the river and not just a hit-and-run attack. Caesar's invasion of Britain was, like the attack in force against the Germans, an adventure from which he had to withdraw. But he left a mark on history in both places, for to each he was the first to carry Roman arms. About a hundred years later, the Romans did conquer Britain and add it to the Empire; five centuries after Caesar, the Germans were to overwhelm the remains of the Roman Empire in the West.

Caesar's *Civil War* was a similar work, written in defense of his campaign against Pompey the Great, and emphasizing his policy of pardoning those political enemies who surrendered. Despite his seeming effortlessness in recording simple statements of fact, Caesar actually suppressed many details that were not favorable to his own image. It was Caesar's main purpose to guide the reader through the great events of the period as he himself wanted them to be understood. While both his historical works contain valuable information, they are as much political pamphlets as histories.

Sallust

Rome's first truly great historian was an adherent of Julius Caesar, the Roman Senator Sallust (about 86–34 B.C.). Although risen from a previously undistinguished family, he had achieved high office as a provincial governor. Sallust was a typical Roman politician of those troubled and decadent times: he was expelled from the Senate on the grounds of immorality and was even put on trial for plundering his province. After the assassination of Caesar, he decided to retire from the dangers of public life and devote to the writing of history the leisure that the profits of government had afforded him. This occupation Sallust regarded as a service to his country.

In analyzing the crisis of his times, Sallust became the historian of the death of the Roman Republic. As he saw it, in the preceding century Roman society had steadily declined from the earlier period when morality and service to the country were the hallmarks of the ruling class and of the Roman people in general. This decay had assumed the proportions of a great moral crisis: Excessive ambition for personal power, unlimited greed, and unprecedented luxury had corrupted the Roman nobles.

In the *Conspiracy of Catiline,* Sallust documented the political degeneracy of the nobility as exemplified by the Roman Senator Catiline. Until his exposure by the Consul Cicero, Rome's great orator, this ambitious man had stirred up civil strife and proclaimed a revolutionary program to seize power, destroy the Republic, redistribute all the land of Italy, and cancel all debts. Through his portrait of Catiline and analysis of his plans and his supporters, Sallust sought to show how corrupt Rome had become when eminent people would resort to violence to achieve their ends. In his *History of the Jugurthine War,* which recounts the struggle of the North African king Jugurtha against Roman imperialism, Sallust exposed the inefficiency and corruption of the Senatorial class, the bungling by Roman officials and generals in

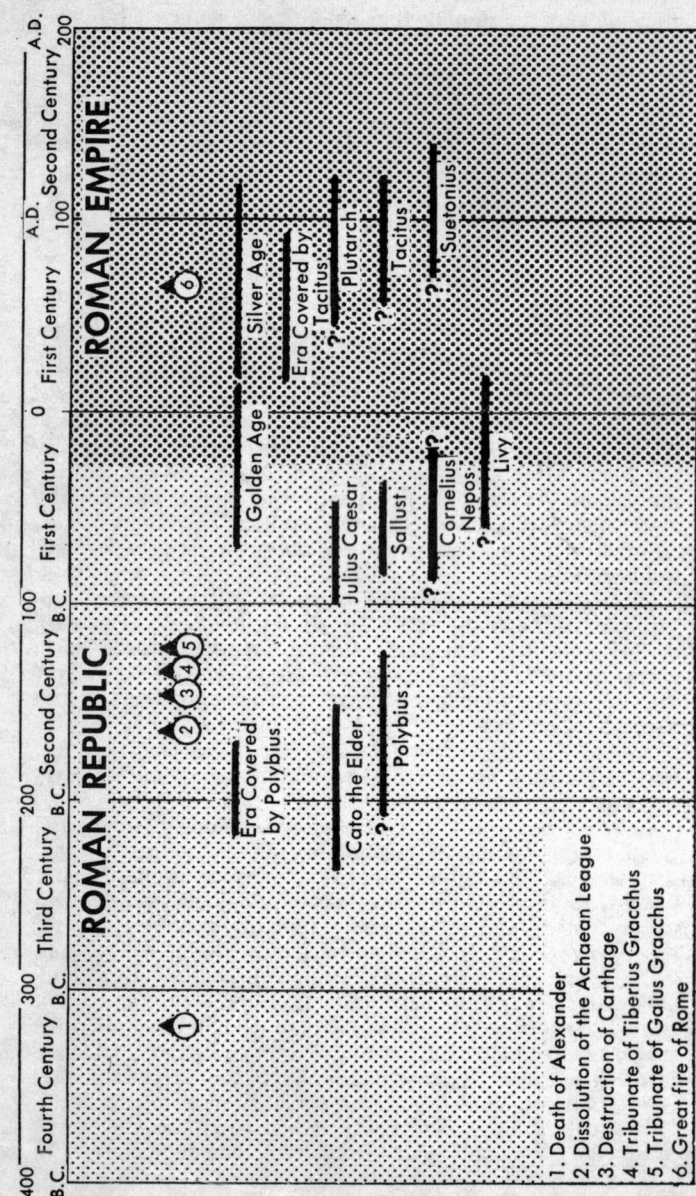

foreign policy and military matters. By documenting the corruption and faults of Roman politicians, provincial governors, and generals, Sallust was, in effect, attacking the system as a whole. The only remedy he could offer, however, was a return to an uncorrupted past.

Sallust is an obvious imitator of the Greek historian Thucydides; he was intent on the search for the truth, no matter what the consequences, no matter who was exposed. In his approach to history, Sallust revealed an awareness of the darker side of Roman society and of human nature itself, much as in the manner of his great Greek predecessor. Because of his keen understanding of human personality and motives, his realism, and his overall historical understanding, Sallust is one of the world's most interesting historians.

Biography

Cornelius Nepos is the earliest Roman biographer whose works have survived. By comparison with his contemporary Sallust, however, he is a mediocre writer. His *On Famous Men* was a collection of biographies of ancient generals, orators, statesmen, poets, philosophers, kings, scholars, and even historians. Only parts of this extensive work have come down to us, mostly lives of foreign generals. Nepos' method was the Greek model of biography; his plan was to compare Greeks and Romans in the various categories. One of his most interesting lives is that of Cicero's friend Atticus. It is unusual in that Nepos himself knew Atticus and wrote in his lifetime, mostly from firsthand knowledge.

In general, Nepos wrote eulogies of his heroes, seeking, like most other ancient biographers, to teach moral lessons through the virtues of his subjects. Typical is this brief sketch of the famous Athenian leader Alcibiades, a member of Socrates' circle of friends:

Alcibiades was unsurpassed in vices and virtues. He was born in a magnificent city of a very distinguished family; he was by far the handsomest of all those of his age; and he was versatile in everything and very resourceful. He was, for instance, chief of command of both naval and infantry forces. His eloquence was outstanding because he was so attractive in looks and spoke so charmingly as to be irresistible. Though he was rich, when circumstances demanded it, he could be hardworking and tough. He was generous, lived elegantly, was affable, courteous, and yet a shrewd opportunist. As soon as he had relaxed and there was no need for mental exertion, he proved to be luxury-loving, dissolute in behavior, lustful, and intemperate. As a result, everyone was amazed that there could be such great opposites and so varied a nature in one man.

The Augustan Age and After

With the extinction of the Roman Republic after the civil wars and the return to normal civil life under the first Roman Emperor Augustus, there came a return, also, of confidence and a resurgence of Roman patriotism. Most citizens agreed that in the last century of the Republic the Romans had been at their worst; through corruption, moral decay, internal conflict, civil war, the very existence of the Roman empire had been placed in serious jeopardy. In rebuilding their world under the Emperor Augustus, the Romans tended to look back to an earlier time when Rome rose to greatness through divine guidance and the sterling virtues of her great Republican leaders. In this time of revival of the Roman civic virtues, the Romans were fortunate in having a great historian, Livy, to record the examples of the men of old.

Livy

A northern Italian, Livy (about 59 B.C.–A.D. 17) came to Rome at the beginning of the Principate and spent the next forty years writing the history of Rome from its beginnings to the middle of Augustus' reign. His *History of Rome* was a vast work in 142 books, about a quarter of which has survived. It presented Rome's history as a grand panorama beginning with the founding of the city. Livy was unusual among Roman historians in that he was a professional writer of history. He had no political or military experience, was never a Senator, and did not even travel. Unlike most of the other great classical historians, such as Herodotus, Thucydides, and Polybius, Livy made no attempt to base his history on eyewitness evidence, even for events of his own times. He did not even go about to "see and hear" or to question authorities. He set about writing his enormous history, covering about seven hundred and fifty years, by tireless reading of earlier works about Rome's past. In many instances, Livy did not claim to know the truth. Actually, his purpose was quite different: He wanted to set down a parade of Rome's virtues and achievements, her great men and deeds, as examples of virtues to be imitated and sources of renewed pride for Romans in their national traditions.

Livy's aim, which, as we have seen (see page 153), suited the Emperor's program for literature, was to describe an ideal Rome, such as many actually believed had once existed, holding up the earlier Republic as a model. Livy's famous preface to his *History of Rome* is not only a fine

The Augustan Age and After 197

statement of his aims and attitudes as a writer of history but the classic expression of what the Romans thought history should be:

> It will be a satisfaction to have contributed as much as lies in me to the commemoration of the deeds of the foremost people of the world. . . . I do not doubt that to most readers the earliest origins and the period immediately following will afford little pleasure, for they will be in haste to reach modern times, in which the might of a people which has long been exceedingly powerful is destroying itself. On the contrary, I shall find in this an additional reward for my labors, that I may turn my eyes away from the troubles which our age has witnessed for so many years, so long, at least, as I am totally immersed in the recollections of those good old days. . . .
>
> Such traditions as belong to the time before the city was founded . . . and are adorned with poetic legends rather than based upon trustworthy records of what happened, I intend neither to affirm nor to refute. It is the privilege of antiquity to mingle divine affairs with human, and so to make the beginnings of cities more majestic; and if any people ought to be permitted to consecrate their origins and refer them to doings of the gods, such is the military glory of the Roman people that when they profess that their father and the father of their founder was none other than Mars [the god of war], the nations of the earth may well accept this also with as good a grace as they accept Rome's dominion.
>
> But to such legends as these, however they shall be judged and thought of, I shall not for my part attach any great importance. Here are the matters to which I would have every person give close attention: what life and morals were like; through what men and by what policies, in peace and in war, the empire was won and enlarged; and then let him observe how, little by little with the relaxation of discipline, morals first deteriorated . . . then sank lower and lower, and finally began the downward plunge that has brought us to the present time, when we can endure neither our vices nor their cures.
>
> What especially makes the study of history wholesome and advantageous is that you behold the lessons of every kind of example set forth as on a conspicuous monument; from these, you may choose what to imitate for yourself and your state; from these you may avoid what is shameful in the conception and shameful in the result.

Thus, Livy's central theme was the greatness of Rome, her steady march to world empire, and then her decay from her early high standards of morality. His history represents the peak of the Roman annalistic method, presenting about seven-and-a-half centuries of Roman history through a year-by-year account. Yet through Livy's vivid narrative of events and his penetration of individual and mass psychology, there emerges an overall picture of the greatness of Rome. His principal concerns were those of most classical historians since Thucydides, war and politics. His greatness lies principally in his superb dramatic narration of events. Whether he is describing a battle or a domestic political struggle, he tells a wonderful story. Among Livy's memorable passages are the legends of early Rome, such as the founding of the city by Romulus; Hannibal's march over the Alps with his vast army and his war elephants; and the great Battle of Cannae. His love of Rome and his intensely serious commentary on Rome's greatness are to be sensed everywhere in his work. In his concern for morality as a dominant theme of history, Livy pays special attention to the psychology of the leaders, their moral qualities and their abilities, and their impact on the events of their times.

Today, Livy's faults as an historian seem obvious: his moralizing, his inclusion of rhetorical speeches in words that are not the speakers', his patriotic bias, his partisan political preferences, his excessive glorification of early Roman leaders. Livy's early Rome existed only in the dreams of men who, as he did himself during the Age of Augustus, looked back to the past as an ideal time. Yet for all its faults, Livy's *History of Rome* is well worth reading. It has been called "the prose epic of Rome," and Livy himself has been hailed as "the prose Virgil" and "the Roman Sir Walter Scott."

History Under the Empire

The concept of history as a school for statesmen has meaning only when the political system permits its officials some independence of judgment and action. But in the period of the Roman Empire, beginning with Augustus, the centralization of all power and decision-making in the hands of one man, the Emperor, destroyed this major reason for writing history. Henceforward, Roman history tended to lose the qualities of honesty and truth-seeking that had been held up as ideals by such writers as Thucydides and Polybius. In place of these ideals came an emphasis on anecdotes, conversations, and praise of Rome and the Emperor rather than on military and political analysis. As a result, history was often indistinguishable from what we would call historical fiction, whose purpose is merely to entertain.

The exceptions are the writers who raised their voices in protest against the evils of the imperial system and the overwhelming and often arbitrary power of the Emperor. During the first century A.D., the Emperors silenced these voices (or else potentially serious historians kept silent through fear).

But with the new age of the good Emperors in the second century A.D., they spoke forth. It was, according to the Roman historian Tacitus, "a rarely happy time when a man thinks what he likes and says what he thinks."

Tacitus (about A.D. 55–120) was a Roman Senator who, after a long and distinguished political career, began to write history late in life. His principal interest was not contemporary history but the reigns of the ten Roman Emperors from Tiberius to Domitian (A.D. 14–96). In his two great works covering this period, the *Annals* and the *Histories,* Tacitus presents a grim picture of the decay of society, the cruelty and misgovernment of some of the Emperors, and the widespread moral sickness in the central government of the Empire. He viewed history in the manner typical of classical historians: as a storehouse of examples of virtue and vice. As a Roman Senator carrying on the traditions of the past, Tacitus had a fierce hatred of the despotism of some of the Emperors. In searching back in older histories and records, he selected mainly those incidents and acts that helped to document his prejudices. His method is the traditional Roman annalistic one, a year-by-year narrative; and like all other ancient historians, he includes speeches that he mostly composed himself to approximate what he supposed was said on each occasion.

What distinguishes Tacitus' histories is his concentration on the darker side of the Roman rulers. He debunks most of them, exaggerating evils to prove his view that there was something fundamentally wrong in the state of Rome under her earlier Emperors. He is consistently a muckraker, cynical, gloomy, ironical, sarcastic. Tacitus' purpose in both his *Annals* and his *Histories* was not to record for posterity a true picture of the Roman world state of the first century in all its varied aspects. Tacitus had a basically moral purpose: He was convinced that evil had triumphed in the heart of Rome—the Emperor, his court, his government. The evidence he brought forward highlighted mostly the oppression by the Emperors, ignoring what we know from other sources about the generally effective management of the whole Empire. By singling out examples of good and evil acts and personalities, Tacitus hoped to contribute to the improvement of the atmosphere of the central government. He was resigned to one-man rule, provided the ruler was benevolent (and he believed that things had changed for the better with the good Emperors). Yet like many other upper-class Romans, he looked back with nostalgia to the Roman Republic when there was no Emperor, a greater sharing of power among the members of the Senatorial class, and great freedom for them.

Though Tacitus claimed that he wrote "without partisanship or hatred," it was ingrained in his personality and mind to hate. Thus, he handed down an extremely distorted picture of such Emperors as Tiberius, Claudius, and Nero, creating an impression of debauchery and incompetence that has lasted until modern times. Because he kept his attention on Rome, on the Imperial court and the ruling class, Tacitus gives us a very narrow view of the Roman world. His highly prejudiced account has colored judgments of the Roman Empire and of specific Emperors ever since.

Despite his cynicism and pessimism, Tacitus' intense earnestness and extraordinary style place him among the great historians of all time. Among the most notable parts of his histories are his narratives of the funeral of Augustus, the numerous conspiracies and treason trials, the great fire of Rome in A.D. 64 under Nero, and the first persecution of the Christians. His expressions, statements of purpose, and brief judgments still capture the imagination: "I consider the principal function of history," he wrote, "to rescue virtues from oblivion and to confront evil words and deeds with the fear of censure from posterity." In the famous introduction to the *Histories,* Tacitus says:

The work I am embarking upon recounts a period rich in disasters, appalling in battles, and torn apart by mutinies—a cruel age even in the midst of peace. Four Emperors were cut down by the sword; there were three civil wars, many more foreign wars, and often wars with both combined. . . . Never before did more terrible calamities to the Roman people or clearer evidence reveal that the gods are not concerned for our peace of mind but our punishment.

Famous are the sentences, "It is characteristic of human beings to hate the people one has hurt. . . . Short-lived and unlucky are the favorites of the Roman people . . . He was luckier in the reign of other Emperors than in his own. . . . He would have been equal to the position of being Emperor —had he never been Emperor."

Of the many artificial speeches Tacitus wrote for his historical personages, the most famous is the one he put into the mouth of a chieftain of northern Britain:

It is vain to hope to escape the clutches of the arrogant Romans by obedience and self-restraint. They are the plunderers of the whole world. They have ransacked every place, and there is no more land left; so now they search the seas. If the enemy be rich, they are greedy; if he be poor, they seek glory; and neither East nor West can satisfy them. They are a unique people in that they lust for plenty and scarcity with equal passion. Empire is the name they give to a policy of stealing, bloodshed, and plunder. And when they have created a desert, they call it 'Peace.'

Apart from the many glimpses Tacitus offers of the seamy side of Roman society, what attracts the reader to his works is his style. Tacitus always makes an effort to surprise and shock the reader by startling effects and vivid phrases, many of them highly quotable because they are both clever and compact. The relaxed, rich narrative of a Herodotus or a Livy is not to be looked for in Tacitus; one must read him with constant attention. Sometimes he caters to the public taste of his times for gossip and rumor; his realism is often brutal and shocking. Above all, he is unequaled in his portrayal of character and his penetrating insights into human motives. Underlying the bitter nostalgia for a better past, there is an intensely serious concern for the decay of morality and society that is expressed in an extraordinary style. For all these qualities, Tacitus is among the greatest historians of all time.

The Great Biographers

If Tacitus made his century a notable one for history, it was also the great age of ancient biography. One of his contemporaries was the greatest of Roman biographers, Suetonius (about A.D. 69–140), whose *Lives of the Twelve Caesars* is still today among the most interesting biographical works ever written. Included are the lives of Julius Caesar and the first eleven Roman Emperors: Augustus, Tiberius, Claudius, Caligula, Nero, Galba, Otho, Vitellius, Vespasian, Titus, and Domitian. Although as a literary artist Suetonius is not in the same class as Tacitus or Livy or the Greek biographer Plutarch (see below), his *Lives* are immensely readable and entertaining. In content and method, they follow the pattern of other ancient biographies. We do not find in them a chronological treatment, but rather the deeds and traits of his subjects under various headings. For example, in the case of Augustus, he tells us, "Having set forth a summary, as it were, of his life, I will now take up the phases one by one, not in chronological order but by categories, to make the account clearer and more understandable." Sandwiched between a section dealing with Augustus' family background and birth and, at the end, an account of his death and funeral, is a detailed treatment of the highlights of his career. In all his *Lives,* Suetonius achieves his purpose by a series of brief, disconnected details—anecdotes, actions, quotations, witticisms. Rumors, scandal, and gossip, often of a cheap and sordid kind, abound. Little attention is given to the psychology and the ideas of the Emperors. Yet Suetonius has succeeded in capturing the essence of each of his subjects and in presenting them as memorable human beings. And they have held the interest of posterity ever since. Reading him anew, we can understand why Mark Twain, among many others, had a special fondness for Suetonius' *Lives*.

The greatest writer of biography in antiquity was another contemporary of Tacitus, the Greek writer Plutarch (about A.D. 47–120). A subject of the Roman Empire, Plutarch lived in the Greek town of Chaeronea, scene of the battle in which Philip of Macedon overwhelmed the Greeks. Although he taught philosophy at Rome for a time and traveled throughout the Empire, his great love was his native Greece. Plutarch was indeed very proud of the Greek tradition, of the famous Greeks of the past, and of the past greatness of his people. He also felt great respect for the Romans. It was his Greek background and the cosmopolitan culture of the Roman Empire, together with his own gentle and reflective personality, that created his outlook on life and made him one of the great biographers of all time.

Plutarch's admiration for the highest ideals and achievements of both the Greeks and the Romans led him to write his masterpiece, the *Parallel Lives,* at about the same time that Tacitus was writing his pessimistic historical works. In this book, ancient biography reached its perfection. Plutarch grouped his gallery of famous men in pairs, in each case a Greek and a Roman, followed by a brief comparison (for example, Demosthenes and Cicero, Pericles and Fabius Maximus, Alexander the Great and Caesar, Aristides and Cato the Elder, Alcibiades and Coriolanus). Of the lives he wrote, twenty-three such pairs have come down to us, together with four separate biographies.

Each of Plutarch's famous biographies is filled with little details—anecdotes, incidents, conversations, witticisms—that illuminate the hero's virtues. A modern reader may object to Plutarch's failure to arrange the facts of a life in order and to his many digressions. But there are two qualities of Plutarch's *Lives* that have endeared him to readers ever since he wrote: his eminently readable style and his respect for human nature in all its varieties. For his biographies, Plutarch selected from his subjects' known actions those that seemed to him most worthy of serving as models. He did not neglect human frailties and shortcomings, however;

he shows us vices to avoid as well as virtues to imitate. All this is done in a leisurely, kindly, artistic manner that has delighted the world ever since.

Plutarch himself explains his method and purpose thus:

The volume of deeds available is enormous.... Therefore, I shall treat in detail only the famous actions in each case, but usually in summary form.... For I am writing not history but biographies, and even in the most glorious deeds, one cannot always find clear indications of virtue or vice. In fact, often a small matter, such as some saying or jest, reveals character more clearly than battles in which thousands are killed, or vast assemblies of troops or sieges of cities.... Using history as a mirror, I try somehow to improve my own life by modeling it upon the virtues of the men I write about. In the study of and writing of history, we become familiar with famous men. In this way, we prepare ourselves to receive in our souls memorials of the best and most famous men. This enables us to drive away and put far from us all the base or corrupt or ignoble influences produced by our associations with those with whom circumstances compel us to mingle. Thus, we are enabled to discipline our thoughts and to direct them toward the finest examples of conduct.

Plutarch's *Parallel Lives* has retained a hold on the attention of modern times. A French translation in the sixteenth century by Jacques Amyot made Plutarch accessible to that era. In 1579, Thomas North translated Amyot's French version of Plutarch into English, and this translation has remained a classic of English literature in its own right. North's contemporary William Shakespeare was greatly influenced by North's Plutarch, as we can see in such plays as *Coriolanus, Julius Caesar,* and *Antony and Cleopatra.*

Plutarch's lovable personality, his high moral standards, and his charming style have endeared him to modern readers. James Boswell's *Life of Samuel Johnson,* one of the most famous biographies of all time, was consciously based on Plutarch's method of recording anecdotes, sayings, witticisms, digressions, and often trivial actions that revealed Johnson's personality. The American philosopher and essayist Ralph Waldo Emerson also treasured Plutarch. Emerson's judgment is a fitting summation not alone of Plutarch but of the long tradition of classical history and biography from which Plutarch was descended:

Plutarch's popularity will return in rapid cycles.... his sterling values will presently recall the life and thought of the best minds, and his books will be reprinted and read anew by coming generations. And thus Plutarch will be perpetually rediscovered from time to time as long as books last.

The great achievements of the Greek and Roman historians sprang from the same impulse that produced their earliest myths a thousand years earlier. That impulse today is still at the heart of our history, however changed its methods and our values: the human need to rescue, from mankind's ceaseless movement through time, something of permanence to preserve and to understand.

FOR FURTHER READING

Although Caesar, Sallust, and Nepos were quite concise, the surviving works of the ancient historians and biographers are mostly rather voluminous even when incomplete. The reader may, therefore, find it helpful to sample those writers that interest him in selected or abridged editions, which are listed in the first group. For those who wish to explore in greater depth, complete modern editions are given in the second group, followed by a few general discussions. An asterisk (*) indicates a paperback edition.

Selections

Finley, M. I., ed. *The Greek Historians; The Essence of Herodotus, Thucydides, Xenophon, Polybius.* New York: Viking, 1959. Selections from older translations revised by the editor.
* Lindeman, E. C., ed. *Life Stories of Men Who Shaped History from Plutarch's Lives.* New York: New American Library, 1950. Translated by John and William Langhorne. Six of Plutarch's longer and more interesting biographies (Lycurgus, Solon, Pericles, Alcibiades, Cicero, Alexander) in a modern translation. A complete edition of the fifty extant lives, with eighteeen of the comparisons integral to Plutarch's scheme, is available from the Modern Library in the famous seventeenth-century translation by John Dryden.
* Toynbee, Arnold J., ed. *Greek Civilization and Character; The Self-Revelation of Ancient Greek Society.* New York: New American Library, 1953. Selections from Herodotus, Thucydides, Xenophon, and Polybius, translated by the famous modern historian.

Complete Editions

Greece

* Herodotus. *The Persian Wars.* New York: Modern Library, 1942. Translated by George Rawlinson.
* Polybius. *Histories.* New York: Washington Square Press, 1966. An abridgement by E. Badian, translated by Mortimer Chambers.
* Thucydides. *The Peloponnesian War.* Baltimore: Penguin, 1954. Translated by Rex Warner.

* Xenophon. *The March Up Country*. New York: New American Library, 1959. W. H. D. Rouse's plain and vigorous version of the *Anabasis*.

Rome

Caesar. *War Commentaries*. New York: New American Library, 1960. Rex Warner's translations of *The Gallic Wars* and *The Civil War*.
* Livy. *Early History of Rome*. Baltimore: Penguin, 1960. Translated by Aubrey de Selincourt.
* Sallust. *Jugurthine War; Conspiracy of Catiline*. Baltimore: Penguin, 1964. One-volume version translated by S. A. Handford.
* Suetonius. *Twelve Caesars*. Baltimore: Penguin, 1957. Translated by Robert Graves.
* Tacitus. *The Annals*. New York: New American Library, 1966. Translated by Donald R. Dudley.

Commentary

* Bury, J. B. *The Ancient Greek Historians*. New York: Dover, 1958.

Dorey, T. A., ed. *Latin Biography*. London: Routledge & Kegan Paul, 1967.

———, ed. *Latin Historians*. London: Routledge & Kegan Paul, 1960. A scholarly collection of essays on the Roman historians, including Polybius, Caesar, Sallust, and Livy.

Grant, Michael. *The Ancient Historians*. New York: Scribner's, 1970. Summary and discussion, in context, of the chief Greek and Roman historians and biographers, from Herodotus on. Pleasant reading.

* Laistner, M. L. W. *The Greater Roman Historians*. Berkeley: University of California Press, 1963. Discussion of Roman history in general, with special attention to Sallust, Livy, Tacitus.

CHAPTER IV

The Arts of Greece and Rome

HENRY C. PITZ
PROFESSOR EMERITUS
PHILADELPHIA COLLEGE OF ART

ALTHOUGH twenty-five centuries away from us, classical Greece is still an important part of our thinking and seeing. Remote in time, it nevertheless seems familiar. We are at home with most of its artistic forms. It is so much a part of us that we tend to lose our awareness of the gigantic achievement of those remarkable people who, for the first time, saw and portrayed man and his world in a new and natural way. In sculpture and painting, the Greeks gave shape to their penetrating understanding of the human body and showed a sense of noble proportions, a knowledge of the modeling of forms, and the first command of perspective. The Greeks' artistic forms, their way of seeing things, are close to the way we see things today, as other ancient art is not. Suddenly in history, the Greek civilization reveals to us our remote ancestors as no previous civilization has been able to do.

The works of art which the Greeks produced and the techniques they discovered have been endlessly imitated, repeatedly rediscovered, by those who followed them. But the Greek legacy is more than this. The Greeks put their knowledge and skill at the service of excellence in all things. This is the classical spirit—the depiction of things in terms of an ideal. Not content with scrutinizing and reporting the world around them, the Greeks expressed an extension of it. They sensed the unseen world beyond their senses and reached for it in their art. They exalted their themes, and from that exaltation there evolved an art of nobility and dignity.

Centuries of imitation have worked changes in the original Greek classical spirit, yet it still lives in us. Mingled with a thousand other strands, changed but still discernible, the spirit of Greek classical art is woven into the texture of our thinking. It is Western man's heritage, and he uses it, most often, without question or knowledge of its origin. Classical Greece still works its enchantment over the imagination of man.

The Early Greeks

There is much mystery about the early seeds of Greek art, but we know a good deal about two earlier civilizations that waxed and waned in the lands that were to be Hellas. On the island of Crete, the southern boundary of the Aegean Sea, a civilization arose from neolithic agricultural communities that seem to have grasped the possibilities of working metals from contact with the Near East. (The neolithic period in human cultures is the late stone age, before men learned to make tools of metal instead of stone—or to keep any written records; in the Aegean area, the neolithic period may be dated some time after 10,000 B.C.) The early civilization that grew up around the shores of the Aegean—on Crete, in western Asia Minor, in parts of Hellas—is called Aegean, and the form that it took on the island of Crete is known as Minoan, from the name of Minos, a legendary Cretan king. This Minoan civilization probably began about 2500 B.C. By 2000 B.C., it was in full flower.

Crete lay midway between Asia Minor and the Greek mainland, in an advantageous position for trade in all directions. Goods and artifacts from Egypt, Asia Minor, and the many Aegean islands due north of Crete flowed through it (see map, page 42). Crete prospered greatly, and its wealth built a colorful, comfort-loving civilization.

The ruined palaces of the Cretan rulers give us a good deal of the story. The solid stone buildings were usually grouped around a central courtyard with roofs supported by heavy wooden pillars. The greatest of these, at Knossos, has been partly restored. Its columns have been repainted in rich color, fragments of old wall paintings have been replaced, and the blank areas have been filled with restorations. It imparts a feeling of sumptuous, luxurious living, but we cannot be certain how accurate the details are. Lacking sufficient evidence, the archaeologists and historians responsible for the restorations have had to rely on their imaginations for many details. Most of the discoveries at Knossos were made in this century.

Wall painting must have been a flourishing art on Crete. The fragments that have been unearthed give us revealing glimpses into the court life, the games and rituals of the people. Painted with skill and liveliness, the Cretan frescos adhere to simple conventions: Forms are painted in forceful outline, filled in with simple earth colors. Men are red, women white. It was an art of pattern and decoration.

Cretan sculpture kept pace with the wall painting. It never reached large-scale, monumental proportions, but its small figurines carved in ivory and stone or formed in baked clay are often of superb craftsmanship. Finely wrought human and animal forms appear on gold cups and inlaid dagger blades.

There are indications that the artists of the Minoan Age were numerous and important and that at an early date their work found its way beyond the boundaries of the island. It was soon sought after, and it influenced the art of a new and rival civilization.

As the Minoan civilization was moving toward its peak, the first Greek-speaking people arrived on the mainland of Greece. They appeared out of the darkness of the European continent, a horde without a history, and only as they settled, sent down roots, and began the slow climb to civilization do we begin to get glimpses of their traits and powers.

These earliest Greeks were, as we have seen in Chapter I, hardy, warlike, and capable. We call them Mycenaeans after their great fortress town of Mycenae, in the northeast corner of the Peloponnesus, and the same name is applied to the special form of the Aegean civilization which they developed on the Greek mainland. They seem to have had little or no racial kinship with the Minoans. A tougher, more pragmatic breed, they seemed invincible behind the stout stone walls of such citadel towns as Mycenae and Tiryns. Rushing out from their citadels, the Mycenaeans could strike and conquer. As merchants, they grew rich, reaching their trade routes across the mainland and out into the islands of the Aegean.

But this interesting and vigorous people seems not to have had the inherent artistic and craftsmanly gifts of the Minoans. Nevertheless, they envied those gifts, and as they grew wealthier, they imported the fine products of the older civilization. Almost certainly they imported the craftsmen, too, for the stamp of Minoan art is on much of the work that archaeologists have recovered from the Mycenaean culture. In architecture, the racial differences between Mycenaean and Minoan are clearly marked. The stern Mycenaean cita-

Plate 1. *The Lion Gate, Mycenae.* This was the main entrance in the massive, thirty-foot-high wall surrounding the fortress-castle of the Mycenaean kings, on the summit of the nine-hundred-foot Acropolis above their city. The low-relief lions above the gate were carved from a single triangular piece of stone ten feet high (their heads and the top of the column they lean against have been lost), probably in the fourteenth century B.C.

dels contrast sharply with the luxurious, brightly colored palaces of the Minoans. The great Lion Gate at Mycenae is monumental architecture, enriched with simple relief sculpture. Likewise, the great Mycenaean chamber tombs, which used corbeled vaulting* to support the high-domed circular vaults, show the Mycenaeans' sense of structural grandeur in architecture.

The story of the Mycenaeans (or Achaeans, as Homer called them) is fragmentary, and many of its details are uncertain. From the heart of this story of a people's rise from barbarism to a warrior civilization, however, one event emerges clearly: the Trojan War. With the archaeologists' rediscovery of the site of Troy where Homer said it was, *The Iliad* and *The Odyssey* have recovered their birthplace and can no longer be considered purely imaginative (as they once were). Mycenae was the home of Agamemnon; from it, the early Greeks launched the expedition against Troy, and to it they returned in victory. Mycenae was the breeding ground of the great epic themes that wove themselves into the fabric of Greek life.

At some point, probably about the fifteenth century B.C., the adjacent Minoan and Mycenaean cultures ceased to be friendly, and the tougher Mycenaeans absorbed the older civilization. As warrior conquerors, they enjoyed their domination of the Aegean world for about two centuries, until a new Greek-speaking horde came down from the northern mountains. The stone citadels were overswept, and about 1100 B.C. the thriving Mycenaean world collapsed. Only fragments of wall painting, sculpture, and pottery were left to piece out the picture, together with the memory of that lost world preserved in the epics of Homer.

The Greek Dark Age that followed this new conquest is largely blank, although bit by bit the archaeologists are finding clues. Forces were gathering. Small islands of resistance survived the barbarian tide. Individuals, families, and groups, fleeing before the invaders, found places of refuge. And, as always, the conqueror developed a taste for the things he had plundered.

The Renewal of Civilization

Gradually a new Greek world emerged from the Dark Age, a world different from the Mycenaean past but still

---

* *Corbeled vaulting:* an arched ceiling supported by *corbels,* stone brackets projecting from the wall. Technical terms of classical art and architecture are listed and explained at the end of this chapter.

haunted by memories of a time when men walked the earth with their gods, and heroes performed marvelous deeds. This reborn world inherited a tradition of epic tales that was to saturate not only its literature but its visual arts. In an outburst of creative strength, Greek art produced forms never seen before, while yet reaching backward into its Mycenaean past for many of its themes. The stories of Troy and the wanderings of Odysseus were told and retold in word, picture, and stone.

The Mycenaean collapse sent fugitives to all corners of the Aegean world. Many gathered in Athens, whose clifflike Acropolis resisted invaders. The new wave of conquerors seems to have brought in the use of iron and a new way of life but no discernible artistic impulse. The chaos and shifting of populations gradually subsided, a more settled life began to induce prosperity, and it was in Athens that a new artistic spirit began to emerge around the eleventh century B.C.

The only surviving artifacts of this new spirit are its painted pots, but they seem to indicate a coherent artistic impulse, a foundation from which the coming Golden Age of Greek art could spring. The early pottery decorations seem remote from the magnificent vase paintings and statues of the fifth century B.C. The early vases did not portray human or animal figures or other aspects of nature but were abstract and geometric; the name given this early style, protogeometric, clearly describes it. In the surviving examples, there is no hint of the superb command of the human form that Greek artists achieved in later ages, but certain basic, underlying qualities are evident. The geometric forms were firm and true, showing exact command of the brush, and the pot shapes are clean and precise. Certain qualities of the great Classical Period of the fifth century B.C.—clarity, proportion, authority, symmetry—are already present.

From its beginning, perhaps about 1000 B.C., the protogeometric style slowly changed as it moved toward the great peak of the Classical Period. The range of the designs increased, and gradually semiabstract versions of human and animal forms appeared. In sculpture, the antecedents of the great age are scanty, but from scattered places in the Greek world have come small bronze and terracotta human and animal figures. They seem to indicate the existence of many local groups of groping artisans, waiting for stable political and economic conditions to generate a coherent style. Even less evidence is available for tracing the development of architecture. Dimly we can discern the rectangular form be-

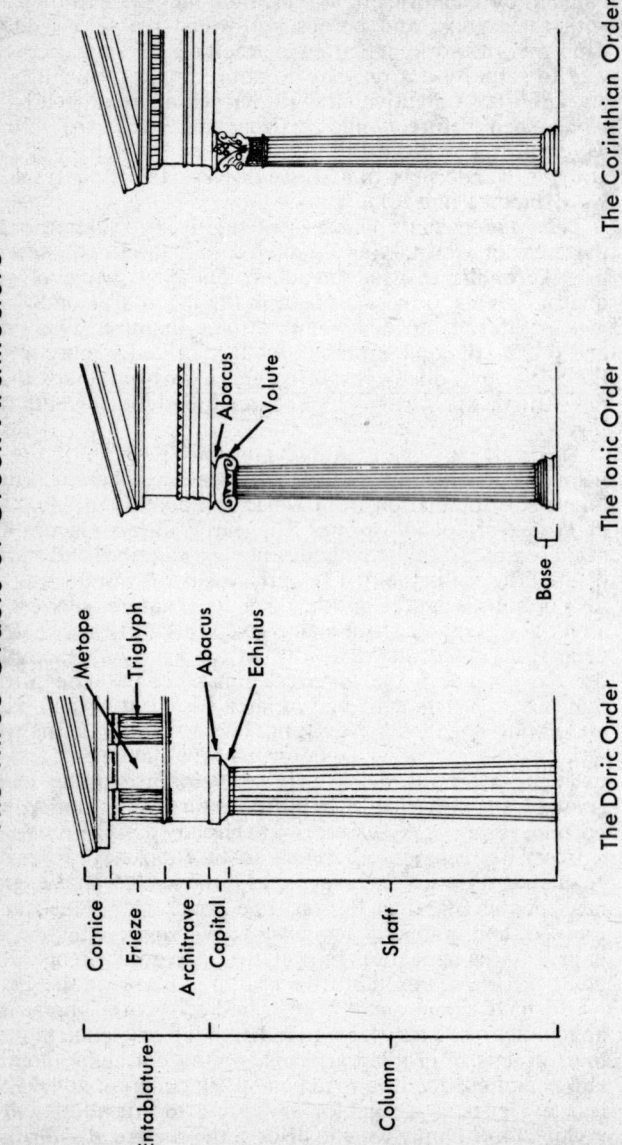

coming predominant in the plan of the temple and the use of the colonnade around the central building. The transition from clay brick and wood to stone was yet to come.

Early Greek Architecture

By about 700 B.C., change was coming more rapidly in Greek art. The period we call the Archaic Period was forming. The city-states, headed by Athens, spurred by increasing stability and prosperity, were becoming more confident and enterprising. They began to plant colonies, and new ideas were coming in from the Phoenician traders, from Egypt and from farther east. These new ideas left their traces but did not overwhelm. They were absorbed, transformed, and made a part of what was becoming Greek tradition.

The idea of the monumental—or grandiose, large-scale design—was beginning to take shape. Architecture began to develop more rapidly as the temple, the great symbol of Greek aspirations, reached a conclusive form and made the transition from brick and wood to stone. The typical Greek temple plan was a rectangle, with walls open at front and rear, surrounded on all four sides by columns that supported a wide overhanging roof. In their fully developed state, Greek temples were built in one of three orders, or architectural styles: Doric, Ionic, and Corinthian. (The difference was in the kind of column used in each and the horizontal structures resting on the columns.) The Doric was the first and basic order of Greek architecture and was firmly established by 600 B.C. It was one of the Greeks' most perfect forms and over the centuries changed only in small refinements. Austere, sparely beautiful in its proportions, the clean, massive shape of the Doric order had an effect of awesome grandeur. Built of stone and perched on the commanding elevations so common to the landscape, the Greek temples seemed a noble extension of the land from which they rose.

The Doric order was such an important artistic achievement that it should be examined in some detail. Its stone elements developed from the wooden forms of earlier temples. The massive columns rose directly from the flat temple platform and were fluted vertically their entire height. They were surmounted by broad capitals, consisting of an outward-flaring moulding (the *echinus*) and a square flat block (the *abacus*). Resting on the capitals was an unadorned *architrave* (a beam bridging the gaps between the columns), above that the *frieze* divided by a succession of panels (*triglyphs*), each of which projected three vertical strips. Between the triglyphs were other panels (*metopes*), sometimes bare, sometimes filled with relief sculpture. On the frieze rested the projecting *cornice,* creating wide eaves around the building that carried rectangular slabs dotted at intervals by projecting pegs. All these architectural details derived from the earlier wooden temples. The roof above sloped to either side from a central ridge pole, creating triangular *pediments* at front and rear. The other two Greek orders, the Ionic and Corinthian, developed somewhat later, in that sequence.

The triangular space of the temple pediment cried out for adornment, and the Greek creative mind responded. Once challenged, the Greeks solved the difficult problems of monumental sculpture with supreme skill. As always, the earliest efforts are lost to us, but an early sixth century sculptured group has survived from the pediment of a temple of Artemis on Corfu. It is a work of high accomplishment; we can only imagine the perhaps centuries of earlier experiments that lead to this splendid piece. In the center is a giant Gorgon (a female monster with snakes for hair; looking at her turned the beholder to stone) with two lionlike creatures on either side. This group is a masterpiece, but we can almost feel the exasperation of the sculptor as he dealt with the narrowing spaces on either side. Into them are squeezed small human figures imprisoned in these sloping slots.

Early Greek Sculpture

With such great opportunities and with an architectural sense in the very air, the Greek sculptor responded with high talent and genius. From the small terracotta images and some cast bronze figures of the Dark Age, the Greek sculptor now felt the intoxication of size and greatly varied scope. He had seen the great sculptural images of Egypt and at first imitated them. Soon, however, Greek sculpture had absorbed what could be learned from Egypt and was working out its own special forms.

Under the sculptor's chisel, the human figure was acquiring dignity and grandeur. He was dealing with gods and men, and they resembled each other. The primitive and near-abstract stages were behind; a new stylization was evolving. Turning from terracotta and wood to stone had confronted the Greek sculptor with a noble material that was more difficult to work, and it challenged the best in him.

This period of Greek sculpture, called the Archaic, stretched through the sixth century B.C. It is quite well documented by some complete remains and many fragments. Two idealized types of figure sculpture were evolved in the Archaic Period, the nude male *kouros* and the draped female *kore*. (The Greek words mean "youth" and "maiden," respectively, and are used to designate these two sculptural forms.) Both are standardized forms, still within the bounds of an archaic convention but showing an increased interest in human anatomy.

The *kouros* type of Archaic Greek sculpture is an erect figure, arms at its sides with the left leg slightly advanced. The body is of noble proportions and quite lifelike, now released from the cramped, boxlike form of its antecedents, the forms more rounded. It is a stage at which a beautiful convention has reached a peak. The *kore* has the same simplicity, the same serene, enigmatic smile, the same carefully braided hair, but she is clothed. The most skillful and sensitive modeling is confined to the head. The clothing, the sleeveless *peplos* over a lighter *chiton,* is treated with the utmost simplicity. The *kouros* and *kore* are two master achievements of the Archaic sixth century. They are splendid representatives of a brief moment in the story of civilization—they were undergoing transformation even as the century moved on to its end.

It is one of our contemporary limitations that we tend to think of sculpture as drab and colorless, limited to the color of the material from which it is made. But Greek sculpture was painted, and if we think of the Greek scene as vibrating with color in the clear Grecian light, we shall be closer to the truth. Greek architecture, sculpture, and painting are linked by color. It is our tragedy that so little evidence of the painting has survived. It exists almost entirely in the pottery painting. The color range of the pottery is more limited than that of the wall painting or painted stone, consisting mostly of earth colors. The colors the Greeks used were probably almost all on the warm side—red, yellow, and buff, for example.

Vase-Painting Techniques

Greek pottery painting tells us something not only about the color of Greek sculpture and architecture but about the sculptural use of human and other natural forms. The painter with brush in hand feels a greater sense of freedom than the sculptor confronting a block of stone or even a mound of clay. It is easier for the painter to experiment than for the sculptor.

One important factor curbed the inventiveness of the vase painter: his two-dimensional surface. This encouraged him to render his figures from the front or in profile, or sometimes in a makeshift combination of both viewpoints in the same figure. It could not be easy to achieve a breakthrough into three-dimensional drawing, particularly in dealing with silhouetted forms.

It is interesting to compare the stages of vase painting as it progressed toward increased freedom and three-dimensional expression. An early seventh-century mixing bowl (now in a museum in Munich, Germany) shows the early use of human and animal motifs; it is a good example of the late development of the earlier geometric forms. All the forms on this seventh-century vase are in strict profile, very nearly in pure silhouette. A band of chariots and another of lions shows some slight feeling of movement, but all the forms are arbitrary conventions. A vase from about a century later (in the National Museum in Athens) shows a running Gorgon. Movement has now arrived in vase painting. The Gorgon's head is still a fixed convention, but its features are expressive and its arms extended, its legs racing. Besides some bands of decoration, there are human figures and various animal forms that all convey movement. The touch of the brush has also become more fluent.

Then, perhaps three-quarters of a century later, the pottery painter worked out a new technique that extended his powers. For many years, he had been painting his forms in black silhouette against the red or ochre clay of his surface — the so-called black figure style. Any details of his black figures or decorative patterns were cut through the black color into the clay. But at last the painter hit upon a reversal of that process. Then he could paint in his forms in black outline with all the interior details and fill in the background areas in black. It was then red figures against black. The new technique permitted additional freedom of drawing and helped to suggest three-dimensionality. In the glow of enthusiasm over the new technique, some painters practiced both techniques on the same vase.

Another vase-painting technique was being practiced in the late years of the sixth century. The vase body was covered with a white slip (a mixture of pottery clay and water) which was allowed to dry. The design was drawn in line on this surface, and areas were filled in with color — largely red, yellow, various browns, and purple. The enlarged range of available colors was another extension of power and may well have been the same range of colors used in wall painting.

Technical advances were not confined to the vase painters. A method of hollow-casting large bronze figures opened new opportunities for the sculptors. The spread of temple building must have stimulated the Greeks to find new ways of cutting and handling large masses of stone. It was a seeking and inventing age.

The Greek architect, sculptor, and painter must have felt in closer accord than their counterparts today. Their arts were not separate, fenced in. They were related. They influenced each other. Through the centuries from the beginning of the Greek Dark Age to the beginning of the Classical Period, they must have been drawn together by their common involvement in solving the same problems. From a period of geometric design, they began to struggle with the imagery of both gods and man. From their Mycenaean heritage, they brought the narrative impulse to retell the great happenings of their past, to celebrate visually the epic legends of the Heroic Age; their deep concern with nature kept them intent on examining the living present. When an innate concern for ideal form was added to this combination, the way was open to measureless search and discovery.

If the later years of the Archaic Period had produced nothing else than the long series of the *kouros* and *kore* statues, it would have been an important age in the history of art. But as the fifth century B.C. approached, we can sense a massing of the creative powers of the Greek spirit. The high tide of one of the greatest human civilizations was close at hand.

Classical Greece: The Crest of a Civilization

The Greek Archaic Period was one of high achievement, but it was also a period of preparation. Greek art, with its deeply felt and skillfully executed conventions, might have rested content on the high cultural level it had already reached. But at the heart of the Greek artistic spirit were powerful forces of inquiry, creative energy, and racial commitment. By the later years of the sixth century B.C., the Greeks seem to have acquired a sense of racial unity and destiny.

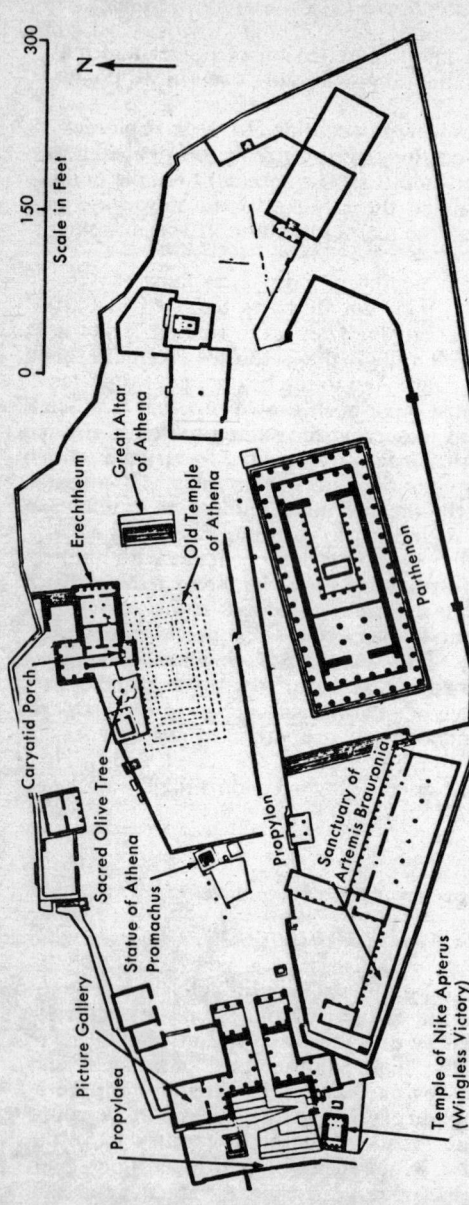

Fig. 4. *The Acropolis at Athens*. The plan above shows the Acropolis about as it was in 400 B.C., after being rebuilt under the leadership of Pericles. The Athenian statesman's great project was interrupted by the Peloponnesian War and never completed, but later rulers continued adding to it down to Christian times. The Acropolis, on a steep hill above the city, was probably the site of the earliest Athenian settlement, and the surrounding wall and the gate were ingeniously designed for defense against attackers. According to legend, the sacred olive tree near the Erechtheum commemorated Athena's victorious struggle with the sea-god Poseidon. The structures on the Acropolis were dedicated to Athena in her various aspects: as virgin (the Parthenon); as guardian of Athens (the sanctuary at the east end of the Erechtheum); as war-goddess (Athena Promachus); as victory (Nike Apteros).

Classical Greece: The Crest of a Civilization 219

It is not difficult for us to detect some of the ingredients that combined to produce the flowering of Greek civilization in the great Classical Period, but we can penetrate only so far. At the core of this marvelous civilization, we still confront mystery and miracle. On the face of it, we might easily assume a sudden leap into a supreme cultural age. The historians who must pin their labels on the stages of human history tempt us to believe in the abrupt climax of one age and the sudden birth of another. But all ages have ancestors. Man does not discard old habits and acquire new ones overnight. In the case of the merging of the Archaic into the Classical Period, we must work with the few remaining bits that time's destructiveness has left us. We do not have step-by-step evidence. We must bridge the gaps by our imagination, bringing to bear all the information that is available to us.

The fifth century B.C. was in its opening years, its art already flourishing, when disaster threatened Greek life. Two Persian invasions swept down upon the Greek mainland. Athens, the cultural heart of Hellas, was abandoned and sacked. But a series of amazing Greek victories on land and sea rescued Athens and the other city-states. As we saw in Chapter I, these dramatic victories against overwhelming odds generated enormous pride and confidence. The story of the Greek defense began to grow into a racial epic to take its place beside the tales of Troy and Odysseus. With the return of order and prosperity and a renewed release of patriotic energy, the Greek city-states, united now under the leadership of Athens, were ready to reach for the summit of their civilization.

The Rebuilt Acropolis of Athens

Athens, under the wise and energetic leadership of Pericles (about 490–429 B.C.), developed into a city of magnificent beauty. With money accumulated for the defense against the Persians, the Athenians determined to rebuild their ruined city. They had a remarkable company of great talents to call upon. Chief among them was Phidias (about 490–420 B.C.), the sculptor of the great gold and ivory statues of Athena Parthenos at Athens and of Zeus at Olympia. Pericles placed Phidias in charge of the whole ambitious building scheme.

Phidias and the other architects and sculptors involved in this ambitious project concentrated their efforts on the Acropolis and the area surrounding it. The Acropolis (it means "high city" in Greek—most Greek cities of the time had a similar focal point and stronghold, for which the same term was used) was the fortified hill, site of the earliest settlement at Athens, which after the Persian Wars was set aside for the worship of the goddess Athena and other deities. There, the Athenians planned the Propylaea, a monumental entrance to the sacred enclosure of the Acropolis. Above it rose the magnificent Parthenon, chief temple of Athena. Nearby was the Erechtheum, which replaced an earlier temple destroyed by the Persians, commemorating the legendary dispute between Athena and the sea-god Poseidon for the possession of Attica. Below the Acropolis and near the Athenian marketplace (the Agora) was, among many other notable structures, the temple of the fire god Hephaestus, the most perfectly preserved of all Greek temples (in Christian times, it became a church). This remarkable plan for the Acropolis and its environs came into being, stone by stone, over a period of perhaps half a century. Each building was itself a memorable achievement, and the whole assemblage, viewed from every angle, formed one of the greatest architectural monuments of all time. Even today, it is probably the noblest ruin in the world.

Mounting the broad steps into the Propylaea must have been a moment of pride for the Athenian citizen. It was the great gateway to the sacred places of the Acropolis, not only an entrance but a place for public meetings, an art gallery. On either side of the gateway and its porches were projecting halls. The massive lines of Doric columns were magnificent, and for a lightening touch, slender Ionic columns were used on the outer porch. The Ionic order, widely used in the Greek colonies of Asia Minor and admired for its grace and trimness, was still used with restraint on the Greek mainland, but the possibilities in the mixture of the two orders were now apparent.

From the inner porch of the Propylaea, the Parthenon came into view on the highest platform of the Acropolis. Architecturally, it was the crowning achievement of the Doric order. Spiritually, it was the heart of Athens and all she stood for. Its aspect is of great simplicity, but that effect was cunningly arrived at. The basic geometry of the Parthenon was subtly altered to accommodate the peculiarities of human sight—some perspectives were manipulated by the architects so as to appear straight or tapered to the human eye.

In an inner, shadowed chamber of the Parthenon stood the great forty-foot statue of Athena by Phidias. It was sculptured in wood, the goddess's flesh covered with a sheathing

Classical Greece: The Crest of a Civilization 221

of ivory, her garments with layers of gold. Outside, the two great pediments contained two of the most grandly conceived sculptural compositions of all time. The pediment on the east end of the Parthenon showed the birth of Athena, while that on the west depicted the struggle between Athena and Poseidon for the right to be the patron deity of Athens. Mutilated as they are, these figures are eloquent evidence of a great civilization. The problem of a large, active assemblage of figures moving within the strict confines of the flattened triangular space of the pediment, so long the goal of generations of Greek sculptors, was magnificently solved.

The marble figures, active or relaxed, fill their allotted spaces without seeming cramped by the confining diagonals of the pediment cornices. The mutilated so-called Dionysus, from the east pediment, is one of the world's great statues. The relaxed posture of the god, grandly meditative yet filled

Plate 2. *The Figure of Dionysus from the Parthenon, Athens.* The sculptures in the east pediment of the temple, which was dedicated to Athena, portrayed the myth of her birth: the goddess, among other things, of defensive warfare, she sprang, in full armor, from the head of the father-god Zeus. The relaxed, natural pose of Dionysus is a brilliant solution to the problem of the awkwardly confining pediment. The idealized form was the work of Phidias, the master sculptor of the rebuilt Acropolis.

222 The Arts of Greece and Rome

Timeline

Time axis (B.C.): 700 — Seventh Century — 600 — Sixth Century — 500 — Fifth Century — 400 — Fourth Century — 300 — Third Century — 200 — Second Century — 100

Period bands:
- GREEK COLONIZATION
- PERSIAN WARS
- ATHENS : SPARTA
- HELLENISTIC EMPIRES

Sub-periods and figures:
- Greek Trade
- Archaic Period
- Classical Period
- Pelop. War
- Pericles
- Phidias
- Simonides
- Scopas (?)
- Praxiteles (?)
- Lysippus (?)

Numbered events:
1. Earliest bronze casting
2. Building of Erechtheum (421–409 B.C.)
3. Death of Socrates
4. Monument of Lysicrates
5. Death of Alexander
6. Defeat of Gauls by Pergamum
7. Colossus of Rhodes (?)
8. Roman looting of Pergamum
9. Venus de Milo

with power, is executed with a masterful naturalism that is also guided by the Greek yearning for ideal forms. Another great reclining torso, that of the Attic river god Ilossus, from the west pediment, is a similar brilliant solution to the need for a figure designed to fill the narrow, wedge-shaped areas at either end of the pediment.*

Almost as important as the sculptures from the pediments of the Parthenon are the remains of the bas-relief frieze that encircled the building under the cornice. The theme is the Great Pan-Athenaic procession in honor of Athena.† Crowded with figures — water-bearers, horsemen, chariots, sacrificial animals, seated gods — it is a constantly moving pageant, paced with rhythmic skill, a marble narrative, an extended masterpiece of sculpture. The horses are notable, as are almost all the surviving Greek sculptures of horses. It was their favorite animal, an important part of their lives, and they gave it a magnificent ideal form that has never been surpassed. The processional frieze is another of the glories of Greek art.

There were undoubtedly free-standing statues and other sculptural elements on the Acropolis, but they are gone. The one remaining major masterpiece is the Caryatid Porch of the Erechtheum (so called from the standing female figures, or caryatids, which serve as columns). This temple of Athena Polias and Poseidon-Erechtheus is partly in ruins, but its south porch has not suffered drastically. Here, a new concept in architectural sculpture was introduced, the standing figures of maidens in place of the usual Doric or Ionic columns. Built between 421 and 409 B.C., the Erechtheum demonstrates that the creative minds of the Athenian architects and sculptors (they were often one and the same, as Phidias was) had not been trapped in their fine tradition but were still buoyant with fresh ideas. The drapery of the six

---

* Both the Dionysus and the Ilossus, along with much other sculpture from the Parthenon, have been preserved in the British Museum in London since early in the nineteenth century. They were taken there by Lord Elgin, the British ambassador to Turkey, which then ruled Greece. The Parthenon had remained nearly intact, for a time as a church and later as a mosque under the Turks (who added a minaret), until near the end of the seventeenth century. In 1687, during a war between Italians and Turks, it was used as a storehouse for gunpowder and blown up.

† This festival, held every four years, commemorated the uniting of Attica under its legendary king Theseus. Like other Greek festivals, it included athletic and other contests. The distinguishing feature was the procession itself, bringing together all ranks and ages of Athenian society as Athena's sacred garment was carried to the Parthenon.

caryatids is sheer beauty. The Greek stonecutters could now solve all their problems triumphantly.

Classical Greek Sculpture

Not all Greek sculpture was stone, despite the fact that it was usually at the service of architecture. Terra cotta, a hard, waterproof baked clay, had been used in sculpture by the Greeks since very early times. Hollow bronze casting was developed about the middle of the sixth century B.C. and soon reached a level of supreme skill. A fine lifesize figure of a bronze *kouros,* probably portraying the god Apollo, has been dated at 530 B.C. and is believed to be the earliest hollow-cast bronze figure that has survived. Although it still displays the essential pose of the earlier stone *kouros,* it shows a great advance in anatomical knowledge, in subtlety of modeling, and in command of ideal form. And it demonstrates that the technique of hollow casting had reached the expert stage.

About three-quarters of a century later than the early statue of Apollo is a magnificent bronze of Poseidon, rather recently recovered from the sea. The figure is complete, the work of a master sculptor, and one of the most impressive of all the Greek pieces. Here is a high point of sculptural art. One wonders how many works of equal greatness have vanished. The few that have come down to us seem all the more precious for their rarity.

The Apollo and Poseidon have about them the grandeur that one would expect in portrayals of gods, but the Greek sculptors were by no means limited to the world of myth and divinity. They looked at the life around them, at their fellow men, and even at the animal world, and they made their reports in stone and bronze. In the museum at Delphi is the fine figure of a youthful chariot driver, standing erect, his reins in hand. The superb youthful head, poised but charged with life, is the type the Greeks brought into the world of the arts and repeated, with slight variations, hundreds of times — the rendition of a human form with godlike qualities. And then there is the bronze figure of a young jockey (in the museum at Athens), a work of later date and of direct observation from life. The eager, tense, crouching figure touches us immediately across the centuries. We need make no mental adjustment to fit a former age — this is life as we know it. So the Greek sculptors possessed an extraordinary range, a vision both penetrating and balanced.

The grand and monumental may seem to dominate Greek

Plate 3. *Boy Jockey*. This anonymous bronze from Athens suggests the great range of subject, style, and technique that Greek sculpture had achieved by the end of the Classical Period (about 400 B.C.).

Plate 3A. *Boy Jockey* (detail). Much of Classical Greece's artistic energy in sculpture went into creating the idealized forms of gods and godlike men. Here, the unknown sculptor has captured a moment of immediate observation in the straining tenseness of the boy's pose, the individual characterization, the emphasis on texture and specific details.

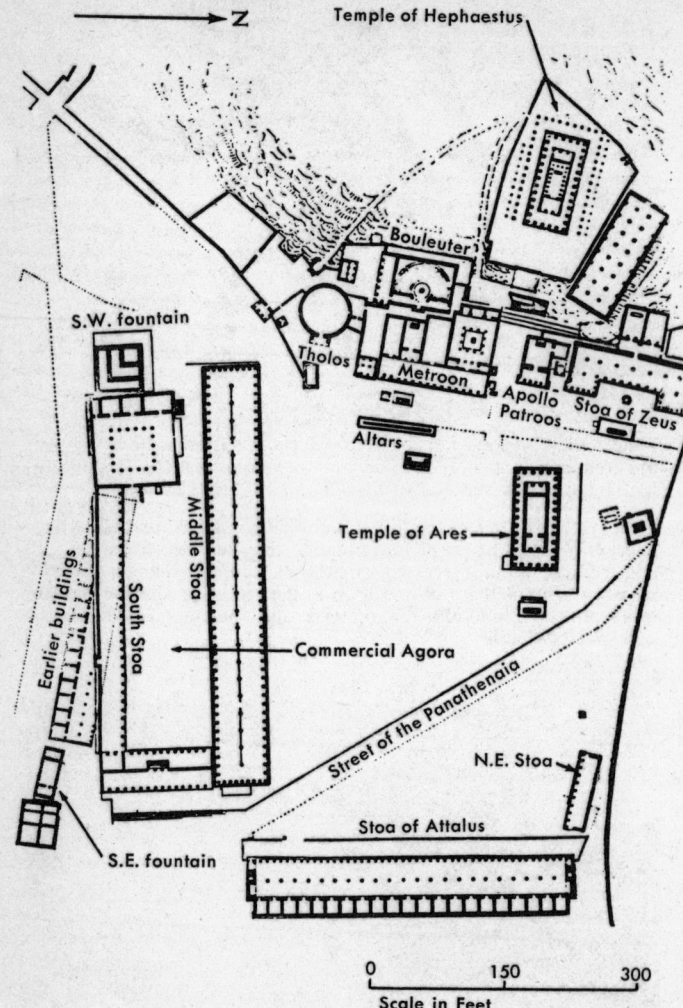

Fig. 5. *The Agora at Athens.* The Athenian Agora stood below and to the north of the Acropolis. Around this large open space were grouped buildings with a variety of public functions: for government meetings, education, worship, commerce. During the Athenian Golden Age, the Agora was embellished with many statues and other works of art given by wealthy citizens.

classical sculpture, but there was room for the small and intimate as well. Of special interest are the many carved stone pillars (called *stele*) that the Greeks used as memorials to the dead. They are characterized by tender carving in relief and an air of calm resignation. Although usually carved from a simple marble slab, sometimes these grave monuments took the form of more elaborate tombs.

Many sculptors delighted in the small and intimate. There are statuettes of animals, goats, horses, and bulls, executed with keen knowledge of animal form and character and often with playful, humorous skill. And on the smallest scale are the famous Greek coins, almost all of them miniature works of art. Akin to the coin designers were the engravers of gems, those experts who depicted so lovingly the real and imaginary beasts, birds, and fish of Greece.

Athens for some centuries was a city of sculpture, and so we must picture it. There are many written references to statues and monuments long vanished. Among the most valuable descriptions of Athens is that of Pausanias, a Greek historian and geographer of the second century A.D. Visiting the city more than five hundred years after the great century of rebuilding, he found its masterpieces still largely intact, unmarked by time and the gentle weather of Greece. His account of the sculpture in the Agora (market place) gives us some feeling for the artistic profusion that was a part of everyday Athenian life:

After the statues of the Eponymi [ancient heroes for whom the Attic tribes were named] are the statues of . . . Eirene carrying the child Plutus. Here also is a bronze figure of Lycurgus. . . . There is one of Demosthenes. . . . Near the figure of Demosthenes is the sanctuary of Ares. . . . Around the temple stand Heracles and Theseus, Apollo binding his hair with a fillet. . . .

The Agora was the bustling center of commercial and social life, and this array of their art was almost a daily experience to most Athenians. And to the scene must be added color, not only of the costumes of the people and the natural colors of stone, bronze, and vegetation but the painting of many of the statues, some with colored glass or stones for eyes, and finally the large paintings on the wall.

The Art of the Brush

Although much of classical Greek sculpture has been lost, it is well preserved compared with painting, which seems to have been an equally flourishing art. What we know of the

228   The Arts of Greece and Rome

work of the Greek painters comes to us indirectly, as in this passage from Pausanias' description of Athens where he recounts a memorable series of patriotic wall paintings:

> As one goes toward the *stoa** that the Athenians call painted on account of its paintings, there is a bronze statue of Hermes ... and a gate nearby. ... In this stoa, the first painting depicts the Athenians drawn up against the Lacedaemonians [Spartans]. ... On the middle wall, the Athenians and Theseus fighting the Amazons. ... After the Amazons are the Greeks when they captured Troy. ... The last of the paintings shows those who fought at Marathon.

Color permeated Greek art and life. Descriptions of their painting stir us to try to visualize the actual works, but all of them have vanished. Only through other sources can we attempt to reconstruct, in our minds, the Greek paintings of the Classical Period. Besides the written descriptions, we have some fragments of pictorial mosaics that we may assume have translated the themes and perhaps the actual compositions of the painters into the stiffer medium of small colored stones. Then there are later Roman copies, in paint and mosaic, of Greek originals. Finally, there is our finest source, the long line of Greek pottery painting.

From the enormous body of work represented by Greek pottery, we can form a fairly good idea of Greek painting in general. It is obvious that the problems of wall painting and vase painting are not identical, but the two fields do have many things in common. The wall painter has the excitement of size, he can satisfy a craving for large, involved compositions, and his brush stroke can be long and unimpeded. The vase painter, on the other hand, must utilize an area restricted both in size and shape, and the curved surface of the vase conditions his stroke and distorts his forms. Moreover, if he continues his compositions around the body of the vase, it can only be scanned from shifting viewpoints. So the vase painter could and did draw his subject matter from the same sources as the wall painter—the life of the gods, the wealth of myths, Greek history, and the life of his own people—but he simplified his versions to fit a limited space and the restricted color scheme of his craft. The wall painter was freer and could think in epic terms if he wished.

The vase painter and the wall painter had more than sub-

---

* *Stoa:* a covered walk with columns on either side. There were several *stoa* in Athens, built at various times under Greek and Roman rule. Pausanias here refers to the *stoa* where the philosopher Zeno taught (see page 60), which gave its name to his followers and their beliefs (Stoics, Stoicism).

ject matter in common—they had also the brush and the Greek concept of form. The vase painter handled his brush with great command, and it is impossible to believe that the wall painter's hand was less accomplished. In the hundreds of fine vase paintings that we have to study, we can see the adroit brush define its forms, relish the painter's solutions to problems in space relationships, discern his growing confidence in handling a given theme. At first essentially a two-dimensional designer, the vase painter began reaching toward the third dimension by lapping elements one over the other. He sometimes changed size to suggest shallow depth. There are some vases in which he tackled architecture and achieved receding perspectives. In all of this is evident the most skillful kind of craftsmanship, deep gifts of interpretation, and an incisive line that sprang from a long tradition of pictorial expression.

All these elements were also the heritage of the wall painter, with the additional opportunities that *his* art gave him to enlarge their scope. It is impossible to believe that he did not seize these opportunities. For evidence of the quality of Greek painting, we have, for example, the famous mosaic of Alexander the Great recovered from the ruins of Pompeii (see page 93). The mosaic, which portrays Alexander leading his army against King Darius of Persia, probably dates from the first century B.C. but is thought to be an accurate copy of a painting of the fourth century B.C. Although damaged, the mosaic shows a turbulent scene of warring men, horses, and chariots. There is great variety in the poses of the warriors. They are three-dimensional, and their foreshortened elements are handled with skill. The horses are exceptionally well done, in the sharpest perspective. If this is a reasonable copy of a Greek painting, it implies an important art.

This brief account of two of the forms of Greek painting suggests a more general point, which we must consider before taking leave of the Classical Period. The Greek mind did not put the arts in separate compartments. All the arts cultivated their own territories, but in the nature of things they had much in common. Poetry and drama, sculpture and painting spoke in their own voices, but all spoke to the inner man. At the outset of the Classical Period, the poet Simonides (556–469 B.C.) formulated this view when he wrote, "Painting is silent poetry; poetry is painting that speaks." When Plato later developed his theories of art, he applied them equally to poetry, sculpture, and painting.

Whatever medium they practiced, the Greek artists had in

230 *The Arts of Greece and Rome*

common both their fierce identification with their native cities and their sense of participation in the larger cultural life that was Hellas. Most artists placed their talents at the service of their city-state, not only from pride of citizenship but because these small political entities were important patrons, offering their artists ample scope. More and more, however, as the Classical Period drew to a close, the artist began to rove the thriving trade routes and find welcome in the new and old cities of the Mediterranean and the Near East. Greek art was fertilizing much of the known world.

If the Greek artist was proudly Greek and filled with the Greek sense of form, order, and expression, he was also and increasingly individual in his response to place and circumstance. The tension between these two sides of the Greek character—allegiance to the common culture on the one hand, the pursuit of a personal vision on the other—kept the Greek artist from slipping into repetitious and blind formalization, kept his tradition fresh and evolving. The long years of Greek art testify to its powers of renewal. Over the centuries, those powers were repeatedly tested by war and domestic turmoil. Each time, the shock was absorbed and creative activity reasserted itself.

Art in a Postwar Era

The ever-renewing vitality of Greek art was to be demonstrated in the century following the calamity of the Peloponnesian War (431–404 B.C.). The fifth century was a very high point of achievement, but Greek art did not rest there. Its development moved on.

Politically, the war was a disaster for all the free city-states, victorious Sparta and her allies no less than Athens. The war left Athens conquered, her defensive walls torn down, her trade destroyed, her citizens hungry. Pericles' grandiose plan for rebuilding the Acropolis had to be halted, and the Acropolis, though repeatedly added to through the

OPPOSITE: Plate 4. *The Alexander Mosaic* (detail). The scene is the crucial Battle of Issus, between Alexander the Great (the youthful figure on horseback, left) and Darius III of Persia (in chariot, right). The mosaic, recovered from Pompeii, dates from the first century B.C. but is thought to be a close copy of a fourth-century painting. Masterful in its own medium, the mosaic is thus evidence of the high achievement of Hellenistic painting—in its handling of color and form, its unified composition of a complex scene filled with figures in violent movement.

Plate 5. *Hermes Carrying the Infant Dionysus*. Found near the workshop of Praxiteles at Olympus, this, his most famous work, suggests the new style, the new attitude toward deity and the human form, which he brought to Greek sculpture in the fourth century B.C. As the god plays with the infant, the emphasis is no longer on heavily muscled physical force and Olympian dignity but on the relaxed and gracefully curving pose, the smooth finish of the surface, the naturalistic details of the drapery.

centuries, would always be incomplete. The city could no longer be a lavish patron of the arts. Shorn of her pride and independence, Athens no longer commanded the same devotion from her native artists. There seemed to be no loss of talent, but now the artist journeyed from place to place searching for patronage and found it.

During the fourth century B.C., while the tide of talent and new works of art flowed on, certain changes of conception and execution began to show themselves among the gifted new generation of artists. It was an era of famous sculptors, of whom the three greatest were Scopas, Praxiteles, and Lysippus. They were masterful artists, and they modified the serene classical style in subtle ways. The great concern of the sculptor with the human body was undiminished, but there was a shift in emphasis and execution. On the one hand, Scopas introduced emotional facial expression and dramatic poses into his work, in contrast to the calm of earlier Greek sculpture. Praxiteles, several of whose statues have survived, modified the classical spirit in a quite different way.

Perhaps the best-known example to illustrate the special qualities of Praxiteles' work is his *Hermes Carrying the Infant Dionysus*. Here is a god-figure that has become more human. There is little emphasis on muscularity; the muscle masses of the figure are glided over with a kind of satin smoothness from head to toe. The heroic pose is missing, and Hermes is indolent and bemused. Praxiteles was famous for the exquisite surface finish of his work, and his increased concern with the male figure offered scope for his inclinations toward the refined and graceful. As the urge for ideal form declined, an interest in individual man began to take its place, and the art of portrait sculpture developed rapidly. The stylized faces of the previous century began to give way to a wide range of Greek and other types.

While we have a good deal of direct evidence about Scopas and Praxiteles, for Lysippus we must rely on the writings of his contemporaries and a very few copies of his work made much later. None of these three fourth-century sculptors can be dated precisely, but Lysippus is known to have lived somewhat later than Scopas and Praxiteles and was associated with the court of Alexander the Great; in his lifetime, he is said to have produced fifteen hundred sculptures.

In the work of Lysippus, the classical figure proportions themselves began to undergo modification. He developed a male figure that was taller and more slender than the classical form, with a slightly smaller head. As opposed to the softly modeled figures of Praxiteles, he restored firmness to the masses and transitions, conveying a sense of lithe, imminent action and individual shape. A marble statue of a young athlete rediscovered in Rome in 1846 may be a copy of a bronze original by Lysippus. Known as the *Apoxyomenus* (the Greek word means "clean-shaven"), it certainly reflects the style and influence of the fourth-century sculptor.

We assume that the trend in sculpture toward the individual and particular, away from the ideal and general, had some counterpart in painting. Again, we are teased by some written comments but only a few scraps of second-hand pictorial evidence. Certainly, during the fourth century B.C., painting moved toward greater illusion, a closer approach to the three-dimensional appearance of things. In the famous Alexander mosaic (see page 231), however much or little it deviated from the original painting, we can see the Greek artist's capacity for organizing involved pictorial compositions, the ability to cope with the foreshortened figure and to suggest depth in space and rounded, three-dimensional form. In other works found at Pompeii—copies of Greek originals or painted by imitators of the Greek style—there is evidence of the use of landscape and other natural forms. A time of questioning and experiment was developing in the arts. One age was slipping into another.

Nor was architecture at a standstill in the fourth century. There were no new buildings to rival the Parthenon or the other remarkable structures on and around the Acropolis, but a concept of town planning was beginning to bring order and greater convenience into the life of the Greek world. New cities were springing up, and civic wisdom demanded intelligent initial planning and provision for orderly growth. The traditional market place and civic center, with open spaces, shops, arcades, and temples, was the heart of the new cities from which roads radiated to the outer gates. Often, the Greek city planners laid out their streets in the gridiron pattern that was rediscovered in the design of American cities (Philadelphia, for example, and most of those founded after the mid-nineteenth century). Paving was improved, as were drainage and water supplies. At the same time, the Greeks were building their remarkable semicircular theaters, such as the one at Epidaurus (on the Aegean coast south of Athens) with its amazing acoustics. The inhabitants of these new cities, Greeks and aliens alike, found themselves in a rational Greek framework, the beneficiaries of Greek order and competence.

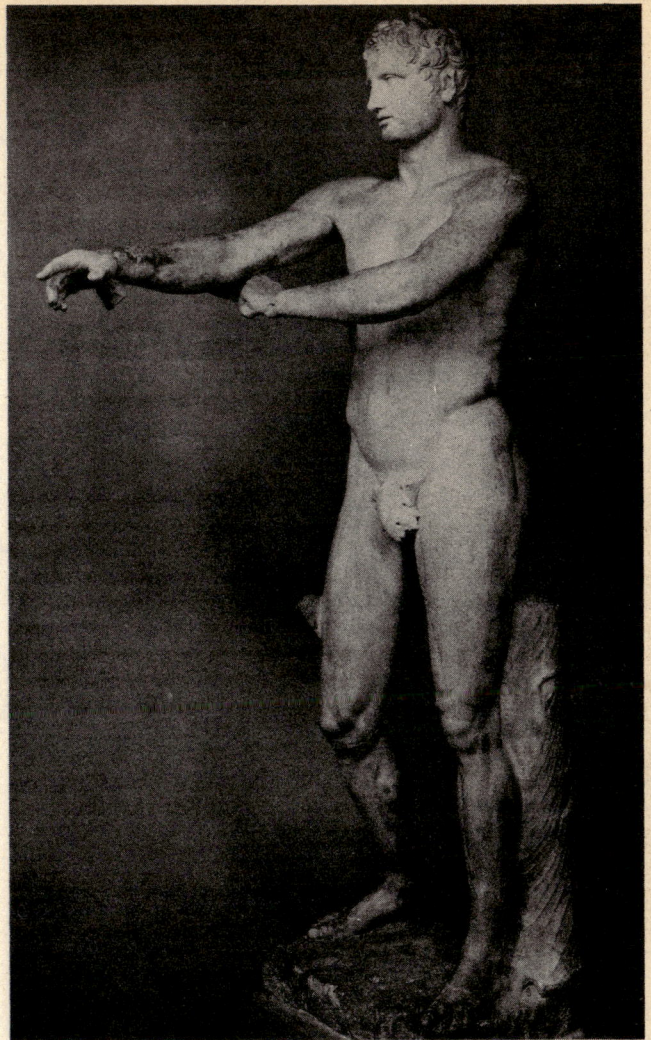

Plate 6. *Apoxyomenus*. This is a Roman copy in marble, probably from a bronze original by Praxiteles' contemporary Lysippus, who worked only in bronze; the style agrees with what is known of his contribution to the new manner of fourth-century sculpture. As in the *Hermes*, the pose is graceful and relaxed, but the underlying muscularity is emphasized, and the idealized masculine form is taller and more slender.

236 *The Arts of Greece and Rome*

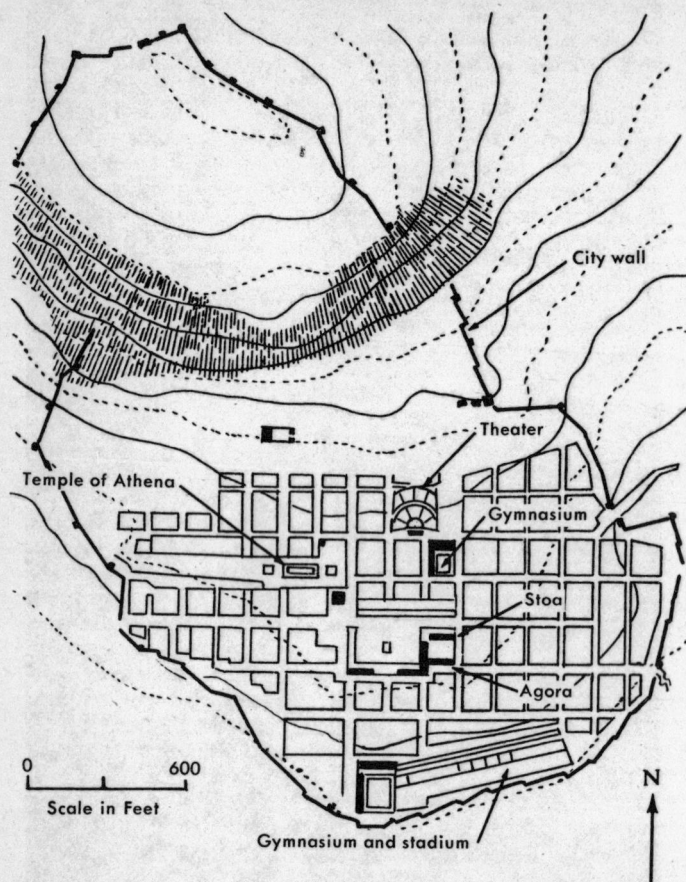

Fig. 6. *Plan of the City of Priene*. Priene was a prosperous market town near Miletus on the coast of Asia Minor. It was rebuilt in the form shown in the time of Alexander the Great, late in the fourth century B.C., and in its orderly gridiron layout it is typical of many Greek cities built from about 400 B.C. on. This plan was first devised by Hippodamus for the rebuilding of Miletus after the Persian Wars. The city was built below a steep, Acropolis-like hill with broad avenues running strictly east and west and steep, narrow streets running north and south. Each block was about 160 × 120 feet and usually held four houses. Public buildings—for education, worship, entertainment, commerce—were grouped around the center of the city as part of its original plan.

The Corinthian order, with its slender columns and leafy capitals, made its appearance in the second half of the fourth century B.C. The Monument of Lysicrates, dedicated at Athens in 335 B.C., with six Corinthian columns, is a notable example of this new architectural style. Together with the Ionic order, the ornamental Corinthian order soon superseded the simple, severe Doric. This in itself symbolizes the change of creative spirit as one age faded into the new. The simple and concentrated was giving way to the extravagant and diverse.

The Art of the Hellenistic World

For convenience, we date the Hellenistic period from the empire that Alexander created late in the fourth century B.C., mingling the Greek genius with the cultures of regions as distant as northern India (see Chapter 1, pages 57–59). Yet where the arts are concerned, this new Hellenistic age did not begin quite so abruptly as that. The seeds were sown when the first Greeks traded their pottery to alien Eastern cities or placed their first colonizing outposts on the shores of Asia Minor. Once the Greek city-states were submerged in Alexander's empire and its successors, a new culture began to seethe up everywhere in the areas where Greek and barbarian met. These areas formed the Hellenistic world.

Greek culture had marched with Alexander, fertilizing and being cross-fertilized, and scores of Greek cities were founded. Although the empire began to break up soon after Alexander's death, Greek thought and art had done their work, and they remained potent ingredients in the lives of the subject peoples. The Greeks also had changed their narrow ideas about race. As the Athenian essayist Isocrates had written prophetically, early in the fourth century B.C., "The name Greek is no longer a mark of race but of outlook and is accorded to those who share our culture as well as to those who share our blood."

In the new age, unstable political conditions, the shock of race minglings, the competition of trade rivals, the spawning of new religious and philosophical ideas, all united to create restlessness and uncertainty. But it was also an age of vitality and abundant creative talent as internal ferments

Plate 7. *Venus de Milo* (detail). Found on the island of Melos, this Venus by an unknown sculptor is dated about 100 B.C. In its exquisite finish, its skillfully realized detail, its sensuous curves, it suggests how strong the continuing influence of Praxiteles was in Greek sculpture.

sought outlet in the arts. It was a time of both exploration and exploitation. The Greek restraint and moderation were giving way to extravagance and indulgence, but with the thrust of the new and novel there was also a respect and an admiration for the old. Thousands of replicas of Greek statues were made by skilled craftsmen to satisfy the craving of rich patrons for at least an imitation of Greek classical art.

In the Hellenistic period, the historian of art is confronted by serious problems: not enough painting that has survived and both too much and too little sculpture. In the field of sculpture, we face too many examples of too many varieties, some of them contradictory, to permit neat summary. When we think we have found a school — a group of artists having artistic principles and a recognizable style in common — in one place, we promptly discover the same features elsewhere. (That is, of course, to be expected in an age of wanderlust artists who might set up shop three or four times in the course of an active life.) At the same time, there is too little sculpture to fill in all the missing links. An amazing amount of Hellenistic material has been uncovered in our own century, and we know a good deal about the art produced in some regions. But the Near East is dotted with the sites of ancient towns, scores of archaeological teams, many of them American, are digging in them, and every expert knows that tomorrow a new find may support or contradict his favorite theory. There is still large room for research in this field by the young and eager, guided by veterans, hopeful of some brilliant find or new interpretation. Around the world, there are museums eager to house each artifact that comes out of the earth or sea.

Sculpture

The large field of Hellenistic sculpture exhibits an almost uniform technical excellence. The centuries of Greek achievement had passed on their skill of hand, but that very skill was a burden. The artists of the new age were impatient to surpass their predecessors but at the same time felt overshadowed by them. They could only pour their insistent energies into a change of emphasis or into size, exaggeration, complexity, or imitation.

Although the era is complicated to sort out, we can discover a number of major trends. The classical tradition of the free-standing single figure was continued, with modifications, while the portrait head, more intensely realistic and individual, became a major sculptural form. The creation of large, complicated figure groups, both in relief and in the round, became one of the important accomplishments of the Hellenistic sculptors.

The sculpture of the free-standing single figure followed a variety of trends. Praxiteles had followers who imitated his graceful handling of the female nude and drapery and did it well, sometimes almost to the point of real mastery. Usually, however, they seem to be trying too hard, and their forms appear forced and theatrical. One of the most famous works of this productive group is the *Venus de Milo* (now in the Louvre Museum in Paris), named for the Greek island of Melos where it was uncovered a century and a half ago. It is a work of about 100 B.C., less simple than the Praxitelean ideal but also expressing more freedom of bodily pose than in the sculpture of the Classical Period. Another famous statue of the era is the *Victory of Samothrace,* or *Winged Victory,* a work of the early second century B.C. (It was found, in many pieces and incomplete, on the island of Samothrace.) This figure alone, a goddess with large, believable wings, would earn distinction for any period of sculpture. Magnificently poised, with its splendor of wings and an orchestration of drapery in movement that is almost without equal, it is one of the world's great pieces of sculptural art.

The Colossus of Rhodes makes a rather different point about the sculpture of the Hellenistic period. A gigantic statue of the sun god Apollo erected probably in the third century B.C., it towered 105 feet above the harbor of the island of Rhodes, according to ancient writers, who counted it as one of the Seven Wonders of their world. Although presently destroyed by an earthquake, the Colossus testifies both to the engineering capacities of the time and to the sheer appetite for size. More and more, as the period wore on and technical virtuosity had explored every avenue, the sculptors experimented with eclecticism, combining a number of sculptural styles in one figure. They seldom achieved more than an artificial originality.

The growing interest in sharp-eyed realism showed both in the choice of subject and the treatment of it. The whole range of human life was now possible as subject matter for sculpture, from crawling infancy to withered old age, and the human types were no longer confined to the athlete and the godlike young. The new sculptural outlook can be seen in the spread of the portrait head, with its close scrutiny of individual features. There were busy portrait sculptors in all

Plate 8. *Victory of Samothrace*. Anonymous like the *Venus de Milo*, this *Winged Victory* (as it is often known) may date from about 200 B.C. or earlier. Carved from a single block of marble, it reveals another side of the Hellenistic sculptor's mastery of his art: the ability to capture a living form in an instant of violent action; the wind-torn draperies are so sensitively executed that they seem almost transparent. The figure remains superbly convincing even though the head and arms were not among the fragments found and painstakingly reassembled.

the important centers of Hellenistic civilization, obedient to the demands of rulers, officials, and rich merchants for immortality in stone and bronze. (These patrons' wants were contradictory. They insisted on recognizable likeness, but they also wanted to be glorified. The solution was often an impressive figure or bust topped by a realistic head.)

Hellenistic mastery reached its peak in the free-standing figure groups. The technical problems of support and the involved carving were now second nature to the sculptor, freeing him to indulge his passion for theatrical composition, anatomical complexities, and emotional expression. He could be ponderous or playful, epic or anecdotal. Two of the most famous groups of the period are that of Laocoön and his sons wrapped in the coils of a serpent (a sculptural retelling of an incident from *The Iliad*) and that of a Gaulish chieftain (*The Dying Gaul*) holding his slain wife and about to plunge his sword into his own breast. Today, such sculptural groups seem melodramatic, but we can still appreciate their brilliant execution. Never before had sculpture been so grandiloquent, so free of technical and psychological restraints.

Hellenistic relief sculpture showed the same impulse toward daring technical experiment. It also shared with other sculpture the urge for depth of expression. The Hellenistic relief sculptors became experts at overlapping figures, at conveying greater illusions of roundness and depth. With the search for depth went a passion for movement, often to the point of exaggeration. The pinnacle of relief art was reached in the great frieze from the Altar of Zeus at Pergamum on the western coast of Asia Minor. The frieze commemorates the victory of Pergamum over the invading horde of Gauls who, early in the third century B.C., swept down on Greece and Asia Minor from the north. Symbolically, it represents the final triumph of Greek culture over barbarism. The whole conception is on a grand scale: a battle of gods and giants that the artist worked out in a great band of interlacing figures, straining, writhing, gesticulating, grimacing. Every inch of the frieze shows expert skill. The idea behind this remarkable work may seem pompous to us today, but that was also the reaction in the century that followed. The second century B.C. was more inclined toward the calm and restraint of the Classical Period.

The carving skills that seem so abundant in the Hellenistic world were not all at the service of creative minds, but the society could absorb any number of copies of Greek masterpieces. It had a taste for purely decorative sculpture, and

Plate 9. *Laocoön*. Several concerns of Hellenistic art come together in this famous work: the technical skill that made it possible to unify a group of figures in a single free-standing composition; the delight in violent movement and complex, writhing curves and angles for their own sake; and the story-telling quality. Here, the story is the Homeric one of the Trojan priest Laocoön, who warned the Trojans against the Greeks' Wooden Horse and was destroyed, with his sons, by a god-sent sea serpent. By tradition, the *Laocoön* was the work of the three sculptors from the island of Rhodes and belongs to the second or first century B.C. The raised arms of the priest and his younger son (left) were lost.

clever artists learned to adapt bits of classical compositions to relief panels, garden ornaments, and marble furniture. The Hellenistic artist's capable hands also learned to satisfy the growing demand for the fashioning and engraving of ivory, gold, silver, and gems.

Painting and Architecture

It is a fair assumption that Hellenistic painting kept pace with sculpture. Certainly, all the evidence, scanty though it is, points to an increasing command of technique and a vast increase in variety of subject matter. There is no question but that there were greatly increased opportunities for painters in the Hellenistic world. Houses were larger and more luxurious, affluence was more widespread, and the social climate was such that the arts were an accepted part of the individual's personal life as well as a matter of public display. Wall paintings were no longer an infrequent feature in the homes of the prosperous. In the richer homes, the walls were covered with paintings and the floors with mosaics. The subject matter was not solely the ancient myths but extended to still life, figures engaged in everyday activities, landscapes, and portraits. Architectural elements, such as marble columns or pilasters (column-like projections from a wall), were often imitated in paint. As in the days of classical Greece, color permeated the Hellenistic scene, and statues and parts of buildings were often overlaid with color.

The Hellenistic city scene now had a freshness and newness about it that contrasted with the Classical Period. In the earlier time, the awesome temples were there to capture the eye, but huddled around them were the mean, cramped dwellings of the average citizens. Most of the cities of the expansive Hellenistic period were newly built and not the result of haphazard growth. They were planned by master architects with orderly streets and open spaces. There was room for the amenities of public life, with large, well-designed civic buildings and the inevitable semicircular Greek theater. Almost as customary were the stone stadiums for sports contests and the gymnasiums, which served as secondary schools as well as providing the athletic training so important in Greek life. The palaces of the rulers were splendid to the point of extravagance, the homes of the rich large and lavish, but those of the average citizen were no longer mean by comparison.

In the new Hellenistic cities, care was taken about drainage and matters of public hygiene. The streets were well paved, and the places of public assembly were colonnaded. Commanding sites were still selected for the temples of the gods, although by now the old gods were fading and new religious concepts were forming in men's minds. In the near future, we shall probably know more about the Hellenistic cities as more sites are explored. At present, the Hellenistic city the archaeologists know best is Pergamum, the great Asia Minor capital of the inheritors of a part of Alexander's empire (see also page 242). It was a lavish city, as the ruins on its Acropolis tell us: There, we find not only the foundations of the great Altar of Zeus, whose frieze we have already discussed, but the remains of the king's palace, a huge theater, porticos, and the famous library. (Until looted by Mark Antony, who carried off two hundred thousand books as a gift for Cleopatra, the library at Pergamum rivaled that of the Museum at Alexandria in Egypt; our word *parchment*, a paper-like animal skin, derives from the name of the city, where it was first developed.)

In architecture, while the age-old method of columns-and-lintel construction was still normal for doorways and arcades, early examples of the true arch have been found from the Hellenistic period. The arch, with stones exactly tapered so that it rises in a smooth curve from either side to the keystone, is quite a sophisticated concept compared with the post-and-lintel system, in which a horizontal beam (the lintel) rests on posts or columns at either end. Although it was lavishly and elaborately used by the Romans, it seems possible that the arch was in fact a Hellenistic invention.

Meanwhile, as we noticed earlier, the steadfast Doric order, which had dominated Greek architecture for centuries, was undergoing change and losing its popularity. The Ionic order largely replaced it and then was modified in turn and its capitals elaborated. Finally, it was the Corinthian order, with its rich capitals, that answered the Hellenistic need for ornamentation. The three orders had by now lost something of their strict identities and were freely mixed with each other.

The complexity, variety, and even confusion of Hellenistic art reflects the age that produced it. It was a time of transition, when old customs, beliefs, and ideals were disintegrating and new values and voices struggling to express themselves. Whole populations were shifting and mixing, and a great new empire was gathering its forces in the West. It was necessarily a time of unease, experiment, questioning. To all this the age responded with great vigor and re-

Plate 10. *Frieze from the Altar of Zeus, Pergamum* (detail). Hellenistic half-relief sculpture reached a high point in the ceaseless movement, intertwining forms, and masterfully conveyed three-dimensional depth of this elaborate work. The scene symbolically commemorates the triumph of Greek civilization over barbarism in the warfare of the third century B.C.

markable talent. If there was a single theme that differentiated the Hellenistic Period from the lofty Classical Age, it was that of art as delight, as a partner in everyday life. Only once before have we caught a glimpse of this kind of feeling for art, and that was in the ruined palaces of Crete, twenty centuries earlier.

The Triumph of Rome

When the cycle of the centuries brought proud Greece and the whole Hellenistic world under the rule of the Romans, history had reached one of its most remarkable and crucial chapters. Shorn of political power and independence, Greece was conquered. But paradoxically, she conquered her conquerors. Greek thought, literature, and art seemed to fill up the emptiness in the Roman soul. The Romans surrendered themselves to Greek culture, absorbed it, modified it.

Plate 10A. *The Altar of Zeus, Pergamum.* This museum reconstruction of the grandiose altar at Pergamum indicates the architectural function of the frieze. It also suggests the rich public life and the wealth and power of the city it ornamented from about the end of the third century B.C. onward.

The Growth of Greek Influence

Roman power began to make itself felt in Greece early in the second century B.C. By the beginning of the Christian era, under Augustus, most of the Hellenistic cultural area rimming the eastern Mediterranean had been brought under Roman control. Yet the relations of Rome and Hellas are much older than this. To get at their roots, we must retrace our steps in time.

It still comes as a surprise to remember that as early as the seventh century B.C., Greek pottery and other artifacts were being traded throughout the Mediterranean region. From the sixth century on, this trade was a vast enterprise. Archaeological finds have made it possible to trace this great network of trade—from Marseilles and high up the Rhone valley, in the coastal settlements of Spain, along the Mediterranean edge of the African continent and the shores of the Adriatic, and, most important for our purpose, in Sicily and the Italian peninsula. In Sicily and southern Italy were some of the most important and productive of the Greek colonies. (Syracuse, in Sicily, for example, one of the earliest, was founded in 734 B.C. by colonists from Corinth and grew to rival the cities of the Greek mainland in wealth, power, and influence.) It was in this region that Greek culture first touched the Roman mind, not directly at first, but filtered through the intervening culture of the Romans' Etruscan predecessors.

The Greek craftsmen were wanderers. By the middle of the sixth century B.C., they had established pottery work-

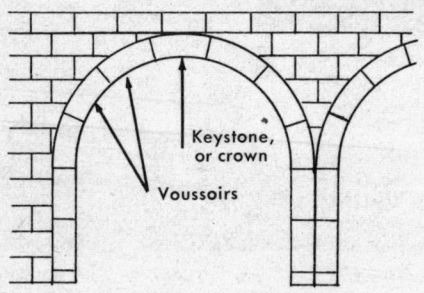

Fig. 7. *A Basic Arch Form.* The arch, invented late in the Hellenistic Period, became a basic element in Roman construction. It was used in aqueducts, bridges, huge structures like the Circus Maximus—wherever it was necessary to carry great structural weights to a height with lightness and economy of materials. The engineering principle—the wedge-shaped keystone and curving voussoirs—makes it possible to span much greater distances without separate vertical supports than did the earlier post-and-lintel system of construction.

shops in Etruria, the Etruscan heartland to the northwest of Rome; great numbers of Greek vessels have been found in Etruscan tombs. Greek art became the major foreign influence on the art of the Etruscans. Unlike the early Romans, however, the Etruscans seem, from the art of theirs that has been preserved, to have had strong native artistic gifts. Etruscan traits persist through their borrowings and adaptations from the Greeks. From the fifth century on, as Etruscan power dwindled and Roman power grew, the art tradition of central Italy showed little change for several centuries. First through peaceful trade and then through pillage of the conquered Etruscan cities, however, the Romans were coming in contact with Greek art at second hand. Presently, as Roman power spread eastward into the Hellenistic cities, the Romans came to know Greek art at first hand as well.

As Rome's empire consolidated its hold on the Mediterranean, Roman generals, returning with the spoils of conquered cities, stimulated an appetite for beautiful and sumptuous things. No matter where they originated, the pillaged treasures almost always showed the touch of Greek craftsmanship. The loot of Pergamum in 133 B.C. fired the Roman imagination. Greek art struck a chord in the practical Roman mind. The Roman upper classes grew hungry for Greek works of art, and in the Hellenistic world they found thousands of artists eager to satisfy them. From the second century B.C. onward, Greek-trained artists migrated to Rome itself and to other Roman cities, and in many Greek cities groups of artists again worked within a common style and tradition as they had in the past. The arrogant and masterful Romans had wealth to spend and victories and other great events to celebrate; the Greeks had their skills and tradition and the need to exercise them.

What has been called Greco-Roman art was ready to spread throughout the wide-flung Roman empire. Deeply immersed in the making of history, the Romans had abundant need for sculpture, painting, and buildings to commemorate their achievements. They needed new temples and the decorations for them. Roman patricians wanted portrait busts and paintings of themselves and their ancestors and stately tombs for their dead. Their homes needed mosaic floors, painted walls, fountains, and figures of the family deities. And there was an insatiable market for copies of Greek sculpture, painting, and other artifacts. So began the long years of interaction of Roman pride, imperiousness, and practicality with Greek skill and sense of form. The lingering heritage of Etruscan architecture, sculpture, and decoration was to form a part of this mixture.

Roman Architecture

The Romans seem to have taken over completely the Etruscans' building methods, which they later expanded and daringly improved to achieve a distinctive architecture of their own. In particular, they learned from the Etruscans the art of chamber vaulting similar to that of the Mycenaean domed tombs (see page 210). It is likewise probable that the Romans took over the arch from the Etruscans, although, as we have seen, this important architectural form also began to appear in Hellenistic structures in Asia Minor about the same time (the first century B.C.). In any case, the Romans

250 The Arts of Greece and Rome

B.C. Second Century 100	B.C. First Century	A.D. First Century 0	A.D. Second Century 100	A.D. Third Century 200	A.D. Fourth Century 300	A.D. 400
ROMAN REPUBLIC		ROMAN EMPIRE			EAST/WEST EMPIRE	

Timeline markers:
- ①③② (Second Century B.C.)
- ④ (First Century B.C.)
- ⑤ (First Century B.C.)
- ⑥⑦⑧⑨⑩⑪ (First Century A.D.)
- ⑫⑬ (around A.D. 100)
- ⑭ (Second Century A.D.)
- ⑮ (Third Century A.D.)
- ⑯ (Fourth Century A.D.)

Periods/events shown:
- Hellenistic Empires
- ? Development of Arch ?
- Golden Age
- Silver Age
- Egyptian Mummy Portraits
- Roman Revolution
- Virgil
- Seneca
- Terence

1. Emigration of Greek artists to Rome
2. Destruction of Carthage
3. Roman looting of Pergamum
4. Venus de Milo
5. Pompeian mosaic of Alexander (?)
6. Death of Augustus
7. Portico of Pantheon
8. Painting of Trojan Horse, Naples (?)
9. Great fire of Rome
10. Eruption of Vesuvius
11. Dedication of Colosseum
12. Column of Trajan
13. Interior of Pantheon
14. Baths of Caracalla (A.D. 211-217)
15. Palace of Diocletian (?)
16. Arch of Constantine

seized upon the arch, made it their own, and used it in ways never dreamed of before.

Already during the Republican period, Roman architecture, developing new materials and new methods, had begun to display its special characteristics. Wide use of the stone arch and then the introduction of concrete vault construction opened up a new world of architectural possibilities. The Greek orders were used with the utmost freedom, and Roman adaptation of the Corinthian order, with its rich and involved capitals, became the favorite. The severe Doric was neglected or greatly modified. From the Greeks, also, the Romans took the Greek theater form, but with an important difference. Where the Greeks had needed a steep hillside as a foundation for the semicircular tiers of seats, the Romans were able to build on a level surface, raising the auditorium on radial vaulting. Roman temples followed the Greek pattern, but not strictly, playing freely with the Greek elements. Indeed, although the Romans admired Greek culture and its art, they were not really in sympathy with the pure Greek forms. In architecture as in so much else, their natural response was toward size and elaboration.

The pride and arrogance of a conquering people naturally proclaimed itself in the Romans' architecture. They discovered the use of architecture as propaganda and invented architectural forms expressly for that purpose. The Rome of the early republican days was no longer a fitting capital for a world empire. Its rebuilding was begun by Julius Caesar and continued by Augustus, who boasted that he "found Rome brick and left it marble."

Rome in her pride we can picture quite well from present remains and old drawings. The Roman Forum, an open area near the Capitol, had been used for public meetings since the city's earliest days, but with the growth of Rome's population and international importance, Augustus built a new and larger replacement nearby. The great Forum of Augustus, its central open space flanked by long colonnades on either side and the impressive temple of Mars Ultor at one end, was a forerunner of many other forums to be found in other Roman cities. The forum area was Roman in design but largely Greek in detail. For instance, the upper stories of the long colonnades were decorated with copies of the maiden forms of the caryatids from the Erechtheum on the Acropolis at Athens (see page 223). The Forum of Augustus, in turn, was simple by comparison with those built in Rome by later Emperors—particularly the well-preserved Forum of Trajan, who employed the remarkable architect Apollodorus

252 The Arts of Greece and Rome

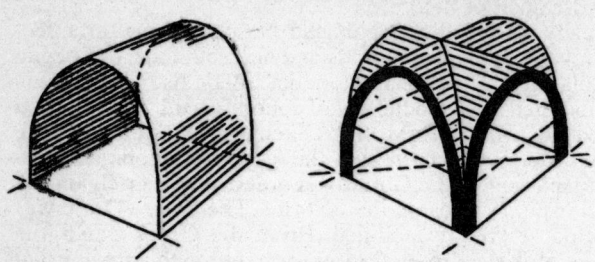

Fig. 8. *Basic Vault Forms*. These two types of vaulting (barrel vault at left, groin vault at right) were widely used by the Romans. The structural principle is similar to that of the arch (see Fig. 7). Using the various forms of arched and vaulted construction, the Romans were able to carry their buildings to great heights, covering very large areas with relatively light support—as in the Pantheon or the Baths of Caracalla at Rome.

(A.D. 60–125) from Damascus, in the Eastern part of the Empire.

After Augustus came the even more ambitious projects of the Flavian Emperors. Their most famous monument was the massive Colosseum, dedicated by the Emperor Titus in A.D. 80, the greatest of the Roman amphitheaters and a masterpiece of constructional technique. A triumph of concrete vaulting, its outer walls rose four stories, arch upon arch. It was large enough for chariot races and held fifty thousand or more spectators.

The Roman architects were masters of size, and even today, the eye travels up a remaining bit of wall with a sense of awe. As impressive for sheer size as any construction of the Empire are the Baths of Caracalla (built A.D. 211–217), with the remains of its great hall that was roofed by three concrete cross-vaults supported by huge piers. Today, the walls are weather-gnawed, but we remember that they were veneered with marble and stucco and richly decorated. Notable not so much for its size as for its splendid proportions is the famous Pantheon, a temple of "all the gods" according to its Greek name, still almost completely intact and in use as a Christian church. The marble facing has been stripped away but the classical portico entrance (built by Augustus' general Agrippa in 27 B.C.) is noble, and the high vaulted interior (added in A.D. 123 by Hadrian) has had enough restoration for us to realize the sumptuous color and detail the whole must have had.

The catalogue of Roman architecture could be almost endless. Out along the borders of the Empire, they built new cities and rebuilt old. Forums, temples, theaters, and amphitheaters, palaces and administration buildings were to be found in almost every center of any size. Two architectural forms grew out of Roman pride of conquest: the triumphal arch and the victory column. The triumphal arch, of which there were twenty-one examples in Rome alone, was essentially a large open archway, often flanked by two smaller archways as in the well known Arch of Constantine (A.D. 312). Detached or connected columns rose on either side of the archway to a heavy horizontal structure (the entablature), with a high superstructure above that. Faced with marble, most outer surfaces were encrusted with inscriptions, decorations, relief carving, and, often, sculpture in the round. The victory column was a single tall shaft rising from a solid base and covered with relief carving portraying the victory commemorated. Perhaps the best known is Trajan's Column in Rome (A.D. 114), one hundred feet high, with an ascending spiral of relief figures, hundreds of them, overlapping and intertwined. It is a greatly involved and extended work.

The Romans seemed to itch to decorate a surface. At the same time, however, they had their purely functional structures that needed no decoration and told their story in straightforward forms. Their roads, bridges, and aqueducts were some of their greatest achievements in construction. A network of stone-paved roads, making few concessions to the natural shape of the land in their passion for the straight line, ran to all the corners of the Empire. Beautifully arched bridges carried them over rivers and ravines. And cool water came sliding down from the hills into the Roman cities from great aqueducts that sometimes rose in three stories of spanning arches.

Sculpture

A prodigal amount of the sculptor's art went into the adornment of Roman architecture, but free-standing statues and statuettes were also produced in abundance, usually to glorify the person portrayed. The Hellenistic sculptor had, however, learned to scrutinize the human face and report it accurately, and this agreed with the forthright Roman vision of things, Great numbers of accomplished portrait pieces

Plate 11. *The Pantheon, Rome.* The portico was erected early in the reign of Augustus, while the rotunda behind it was added later and then rebuilt at various times over the next two hundred years. The immense columns, each cut from a single piece of marble, are in the Roman version of the Greek Corinthian order but are not fluted. The pediment and roof of the portico were originally embellished with sculpture. The rotunda, with its dome, is an ingenious solution to the architectural problem of combining curving forms with the rectangles and triangles of the portico. (For the restored interior of the Pantheon, see Plate 11A on the following page.)

have come down to us, and as we study them, we can see the individual human beings behind the stone and bronze forms. We feel we know what the Romans really looked like.

From republican generals, Emperors, and high officials down to rich patricians, there was a sustained demand for portrait sculpture. The Emperors were well aware of the propaganda value of impressive images of themselves set up in public places. In the many portraits of the Emperors, we have excellent material to acquaint ourselves with the Imperial line as it evolved through the centuries. The personal characteristics of each Emperor dictated the kind of image by which he wished to be remembered—some as victors, clad in military armor, others in the regulation Roman toga, still others in classical drapery and a pose that looks back to the high point of Greek culture. Augustus, the versatile, appears in all three guises, his individual features slightly enhanced by classical treatment. Vespasian preferred to be uncompromisingly himself, a highly successful soldier and

Plate 11A. *Interior of the Pantheon, Rome.* While the outside of the Pantheon is badly worn, the interior of the rotunda, used as a church since the seventh century A.D., has been carefully restored in multicolored stone. The rotunda is topped by the largest masonry dome in existence, dramatically lighted by high windows, and forms a nearly perfect sphere 142 feet in diameter. As a whole, it vividly illustrates both the engineering skills the Romans could call on and their passion for sheer size.

administrator. The philosopher Emperor Marcus Aurelius, modestly heroic on horseback, gives us the finest equestrian statue of Roman times. Claudius, with bare torso and a great swag of classical drapery, stands forever in the godlike pose of Jupiter.

Rich patricians, usually devoted to all things Greek, were equally fervent patrons of the portrait sculptor. The Greek tradition would not have remained such a thriving force had it not been so deeply imbedded in the consciousness of the Roman citizenry. Copies of Greek art stood in many Roman houses, and direct comparisons could be made between the old and the new. As in the case of the Imperial statues, the citizen asked for a likeness but was satisfied when this had been achieved in the face; the body and the pose were stylized and conventional. In the realistic Hellenistic fashion, the eyes were often inset with metal or semiprecious stones. In addition, various colored marbles were now sometimes used to distinguish the areas of flesh, hair, and drapery.

Painting and Mosaic

The affluent Roman citizen was as responsive to the art of painting as he was to that of sculpture, and his home was typically a colorful place. The walls were often covered with fresco paintings that now employed a greater range of colors than the early Greek painters had. Although only a few of the names of the painters of the Roman period have come down to us, we know that their subject matter was extremely varied. Often, as in earlier Hellenistic painting, architectural elements (columns, pilasters, mouldings, decorated borders) were carefully imitated in paint to frame a storytelling picture or a simulated view into the outside world. The rich history of the Empire provided much of the pictorial subject matter. Even more frequent were the retellings of the age-old Greek myths. Some of the latter paintings were certainly copies of well-known Greek originals, but others give evidence of having been painted by genuinely creative talents who must have conceived their own versions of the oft-repeated themes.

The skill of painting well-rounded forms was a common accomplishment. The flesh tones were convincing. Local colors were often modified by a feeling for light and shadow. Landscape as a setting for figures or for its own sake was common enough. Indeed, the problems of depicting the green, growing world, the sky and airy distances, led the painters to the brink of Impressionism, the school of French painting that revolutionized European art in the final third of the nineteenth century. Like the Impressionists, some of the later Roman painters seem to have discovered and become interested in the way outdoor light affects solid forms, making them seem more fluid, less sharply defined. The Impressionists painted in a high-keyed color range, using thick brushes and striving for broad, spontaneous effects rather than exact detail.

Representative of this new tendency in ancient art is a fresco of the Trojan Horse, now in the National Museum at Naples, that dates from the first century A.D. but might almost be mistaken for a work of the nineteenth century. An ambitious composition crowded with figures and with a background of city walls, it is painted with free and rapid impressionistic brush strokes. Everything is bathed in an eerie light that reveals forms but does not emphasize them. Form is subordinated to mood.

This budding "impressionism," which was to wait so many centuries before it could develop, is evident not only

Plate 12. *The Arch of Constantine, Rome.* Erected in honor of the Emperor who shifted the Empire's center of gravity permanently to the east, this typical triumphal arch provides a record both of the late Roman love of elaborate ornamentation and the decline of artistic taste and skill. Much of the sculpture was incongruously borrowed from an arch built two centuries earlier in the time of Trajan, including a portrait of Trajan himself; the new work used to fill out the design was crudely inferior.

in wall paintings but in many examples of the so-called mummy-portraits discovered principally in Egypt. (The ancient Egyptian practice of embalming the dead had persisted, first under Greek and now under Roman rule.) These portraits of the dead, dating from the first to the fourth centuries A.D., were painted in melted colored waxes on wooden panels that were placed in the wrappings of the mummified bodies. They have all the earmarks of intensely telling likenesses, and their technical freedom is close to that of the broad brush or palette-knife painting of recent times.

Wall painting had a great influence on the kindred art of mosaic. Like painting, mosaic increased its color range greatly during the Roman period; the bits of naturally colored stones were supplemented by pieces of colored glass and materials with metallic glazes. The mosaic craftsmen used the same subject matter as the painters, had the same general sense of pictorial design, and strove for the same rounded, naturalistic treatment of forms. Originally used to decorate the Roman floors, mosaic designs presently found their way onto the walls and eventually high into the vaulted ceilings. In the late years of the Empire, although mosaic craftsmanship remained at a high level, we find the hint of change, of a new outlook on art, and a dwindling interest in the realistic image. Finally, there was a return to the static, frontal figures of a much earlier time, with the emphasis on firmly enclosed shapes. The decorative art of the late Roman period already foreshadowed the new Byzantine culture that, after Rome itself fell, would flourish for another thousand years on the remains of the Eastern Roman Empire.

The Death of Classical Art

Greco-Roman art had followed the conquering legions and the civil administrators to the limits of the Empire and even beyond. There was an overall uniformity in art, as in other aspects of civilization, from one end of the Empire to the other as even the most far-flung outposts tried to imitate the mother city. Only as the Empire weakened did the provincial touch begin to assert itself again.

As the classical tradition faded, the touch of the craftsmen became less sure. The creative minds were clouded by doubts but also dimly groping toward new avenues of expression. As wealth diminished and the economy broke down in the late years of the Empire, building fell off. Even in the third century A.D., however, a number of massive structures were completed: the Baths of Caracalla in Rome, for example (see page 252), and late in the century the Palace of Diocletian at Split, on the Adriatic coast of present-day Yugoslavia. Some parts of Diocletian's edifice showed a daring and bizarre use of the classical orders, a last creative fling before the style faded.

There was a similar failure of style in painting, and in its place were only the wall paintings with which the early Christians decorated the Catacombs (underground chambers cut from solid rock in an area near Rome which they used for burials from the first to the fourth century A.D.). These earliest Christian paintings were untutored and groping,

Plate 13. *Mummy Portrait, Roman Egypt.* Portraits like this one were painted from life on wood, using a durable mixture of paint and beeswax; the portrait panel was placed over the face of the embalmed body and held in place by the burial wrappings. Nearly a hundred examples have survived from a region south of Alexandria as a record of Roman portrait painting of the first to fourth centuries A.D. The difficult medium produced a quite modern style of realistic portraiture, built up in layers with an almost sculptural effect.

partly motivated by a distaste for and a fear of pagan classical art. The Christian era in art thus began with a revolt against the themes and practices of pagan classicism.

In this and in other ways, the vast body of Greek and Roman culture, stretching in time over perhaps two thousand years and in space from the North Sea to India and Afghanistan, was beginning to die—or to be changed into something altogether new, proceeding from a radically different vision of human life. Yet it is impossible to conceive what our world would be without that triumphant civilization. Its consequences are in our blood and brain cells, its inheritances so much a part of our everyday thoughts and practices that we have forgotten their ancestry. It was one of the great fertilizing eras of human history. Not to explore it is to limit our understanding of ourselves.

Although large parts of the story of Greco-Roman civilization and its art are clear to us, much remains in shadow—the earliest beginnings of Minoan society, for example, or the first coming of the people who became the Mycenaeans. But in the continuing work of archaeologists and historians, the story adds to itself year by year—because, ultimately, out of the past the historian seeks answers that are relevant to his present, putting him in touch with the experience of the race. Perhaps, standing on the site of Troy, with its mound of seven cities one above the other, he is stabbed by the sight of the work of seven ages of city builders ground into the dust. And looking across the dry Anatolian plain, he knows of other proud cities that have risen out of the earth and attained glory, only to fall and be plowed under. But still cities are built, for man, in his irrepressible resilience, is able to start anew, to build again upon his own ruins.

FOR FURTHER READING

One of the problems in studying the visual arts of Greece and Rome is simply to see the works of art that are scattered in museums all over the world. The general works listed below, as a group, are an answer to this problem and illustrate and discuss the important works described in this chapter; in addition, several of the cultural histories recommended for Chapter I have useful illustrations. The second group of books is suggested for those who wish to pursue one aspect of Greek or Roman art in depth. The asterisk (*) indicates a paperback edition.

General Works

Becatti, Giovanni. *The Art of Ancient Greece and Rome; From the Rise of Greece to the Fall of Rome.* London: Thames and

Hudson, 1968. A sumptuously illustrated (black and white, some color) history of Greek and Roman sculpture and painting; many familiar works are shown from unusual angles, with informative captions.
* Groenewegen-Frankfort, H. A., and Ashmole, Bernard. *The Ancient World*. New York: New American Library, 1967. Concise coverage of Egypt and Mesopotamia as well as Greece and Rome.
Hawkes, Jacquetta. *Dawn of the Gods*. New York: Random House, 1968.
Richter, Gisela M. *A Handbook of Greek Art*. London and Greenwich: Phaidon/New York Graphic, 1959. Traces the development of style in each Greek art form, with a separate section for each, very fully illustrated in black and white; especially useful for sculpture.
Strong, Donald E. *The Classical World*. New York: McGraw-Hill, 1965. Brief, readable text, very full sequence of well-printed illustrations in black and white and color, including many of the surviving paintings and mosaics of the pre-Christian period.
Wegner, Max. *Greek Masterworks of Art*. New York: Braziller, 1961.

Special Subjects

Bloch, Raymond. *Etruscan Art*. Greenwich: New York Graphic, 1959.
Carpenter, Rhys. *Greek Sculpture*. Chicago: University of Chicago Press, 1960. A short, attractive, and well illustrated book by an outstanding modern scholar; emphasis on the development of Greek sculptural technique.
* Chamoux, François. *Ancient Greek Sculpture, from the Museums of Athens*. New York: New American Library, 1968.
Fyfe, Theodore. *Hellenistic Architecture*. Cambridge: Cambridge University Press, 1936.
* Laurence, A. W. *Greek Architecture*. Baltimore: Penguin, 1957.
Marinatos, Spyridon. *Crete and Mycenae*. New York: Abrams, 1960. Lavish illustrations in color and black and white.
* Richardson, Emeline. *Etruscan Sculpture*. New York: New American Library, 1966.
Scranton, Robert L. *Greek Architecture*. New York: Braziller, 1962. A very brief, well-illustrated history, including temple plans and diagrams of the orders of architecture.

SOME TECHNICAL TERMS

The technical terms used in this chapter are defined briefly as they occur. Here, their meanings will be discussed a little more fully, often in connection with related words.

abacus. *See* Order.

arch. In architecture, a structure built to cover the opening between two walls so as to form a window or doorway. An arch is built with wedge-shaped pieces of stone or brick (wider at the top than at the bottom), rising in a curve from each supporting wall, usually symmetrically, to the keystone at the highest point. Another way of doing this is by means of the earlier post-and-beam construction, in which vertical posts at either side support a horizontal beam (called the lintel) bridging the gap between the two walls. The advantage of arch construction is that it spreads the weight more evenly, in several directions, and can thus be lighter, permitting a wider opening. The arch may have been developed first by the Romans, who in any case exploited it in many kinds of construction.

architrave. *See* Entablature.

bas relief. *See* Relief.

capital. *See* Order.

caryatid. A column carved in the shape of a draped, standing female figure, a form originated by the Greeks and imitated by the Romans. The Greek word meant the priestesses of Artemis in the city of Caryae. The Erechtheum in Athens is the best example of the architectural use of caryatids.

corbel, corbeled vaulting. *See* Vault.

Corinthian. *See* Order.

cornice. *See* Entablature.

Doric. *See* Order.

echinus. *See* Order.

eclecticism. In art, the practices of selecting elements from several unrelated (often foreign) styles and combining them in a single work of art; characteristic of artists who no longer feel confident of the unified style inherited from past artists within their own culture.

entablature. The horizontal structure that rests on the top of a row of columns, supporting the roof and making a visual transition from the shape of the columns to the shape of the roof elements. In Greek architecture, the entablature consists of three parts: a projecting cornice at the top; a flat frieze in the middle; and an architrave spanning the spaces between the columns. In the Doric order, the frieze was divided into sections (metopes) by a group of three projecting vertical stripes (the triglyph); the metopes might be filled with panels of relief sculpture, as they were on the Parthenon. Loosely, any long narrow band of sculpture is called a frieze. *See also* Order.

fresco. The Italian word for the technique of painting in water colors on a plastered surface, such as a wall. (The technique developed during the Italian Renaissance involved painting while the plaster was still wet, but in classical times the paint was applied to a dry surface.) Because of their durability, Roman wall paintings are our chief source of information about Greek and Roman painting,

frieze. *See* Entablature.

geometric. An early style of Greek pottery painting that emphasized abstract, geometrical patterns rather than natural forms. The earliest form of this style, called protogeometric, dates from about 1000 B.C.

high relief. *See* Relief.

Ionic. *See* Order.

keystone. *See* Arch.

kore, kouros. Two forms of Greek figure sculpture that became common during the Archaic Period in the sixth century B.C. The *kore* sculptures portrayed a young woman, standing, in carefully arranged drapery, the *kouros* a young man, nude, also standing. Both were formal, idealized types rather than individual portraits.

lintel. *See* Arch.

low relief. *See* Relief.

metope. *See* Entablature.

mosaic. A picture made by piecing together small bits of colored stone, tile, or glass. The pieces are set in cement on a floor or wall. Artists of the Roman period made very elaborate mosaics that copied paintings and painting styles of which we would otherwise have no knowledge.

moulding. *See* Order.

order. One of the basic Greek and Roman architectural styles. The three Greek orders are the Doric, Ionic, and Corinthian, which developed in that sequence and are distinguished chiefly by the different styles of columns used in them. (The Roman orders imitated the Greek but were more elaborately ornamented.) In all three orders, the columns were fluted. The Doric column rose directly from the platform on which the building was set, without a base, while the Ionic and Corinthian columns were set on a round base. All three styles of column were surmounted by a distinctive broader capital that provided a wide, flat surface to support the entablature. The Ionic capital consisted of an outward-flaring moulding (the echinus) and a square, flat block (the abacus). The Ionic capital consisted of a carved scroll, while the Corinthian used elaborate leaf shapes (acanthus leaves). The Doric column was relatively thick—five to seven times as high as its diameter at the base; the height of the Corinthian column was about ten times its diameter, making it half as thick, relatively, as the Doric column. All three types were tapered, getting thinner as they neared the top. *See also* Entablature.

pediment. In a Greek or Roman temple, the triangle-shaped wall section at either end, formed by the sloping roof above and the horizontal entablature below. This space was often filled with sculpture, as in the Parthenon at Athens. *See also* Entablature.

pier. The heavy, vertical support, usually projecting from the wall, on which an arch rests; generally of masonry and designed to take the arch's downward thrust.

pilaster. An outward-projecting vertical element in a wall, similar in function to a pier but ornamental, in the shape of a square column with capital.

post-and-beam. *See* Arch.

protogeometric. *See* Geometric.

radial vaulting. *See* Vault.

relief, in the round. Relief sculpture is that in which the stone or other material is cut away around the figures represented so that they stand out against a flat background. The opposite is sculpture in the round, in which the figures stand free from any background and can be viewed from all directions. Different kinds of relief sculpture are defined by how far they stand out from the background: in high relief, more than half the width of the figure stands out from the background; in low relief (or bas-relief), less than half the width stands out.

school. In art, a group of artists with similar artistic style and aims.

silhouette. A painting or drawing in outline only, filled in solid without the interior detail that would suggest depth or a rounded, three-dimensional form.

slip. In pottery, a fine clay mixed with water to the consistency of cream and used to decorate or cover the surface of the pot.

stele. A free-standing slab of stone carved with sculpture or writing and set up as a memorial.

stoa. A roofed colonnade, open at the sides, used in Greek cities for various public purposes (meetings, storage, teaching). At Athens, there were several *stoas,* the most famous of which was the Painted Stoa (decorated with paintings showing Athenian achievements) where Zeno taught and from which his philosophy, Stoicism, took its name.

triglyph. *See* Entablature.

vault, vaulting. In architecture, an arrangement of structural elements so that they lean together to support each other and form a roof, historically a step toward the development of the arch. In radial vaulting (mentioned in this chapter), the structural elements lead outward symmetically from a center point like the radii of a circle. Corbeled vaulting uses stone brackets (corbels) that project from the top of the vertical walls to support the vaulting.

wall painting. *See* Fresco.

CHAPTER V

Ancient Music and Its Instruments

ROBERT DOUGLAS MEAD

TODAY'S serious European music and its American offshoot are part of a continuous tradition extending backward in time at least to Mozart and the early classical period. The music itself has been preserved in immense quantities, often in the composer's own hand, and the entire work of every important composer has been published in carefully edited editions, so that we know with great exactness what was actually written in each case. In addition, the published music of the past two hundred years is supplemented by voluminous comments by contemporary musicians and the composers themselves as to how it was actually performed. This is an important point. Written music, like written words, gives only a rather approximate notion of how it is supposed to sound: To interpret it, we depend on the tradition of performance. Moreover, the instruments themselves for which the music of the past two centuries was written still exist, and many (the Stradivarius violins, for example) are actually in use. And while the design of every orchestral instrument has been modified since the eighteenth century, many examples exist of earlier forms of these instruments, in playable condition. In the present century, musical scholarship has pushed our knowledge of early music backward in time until—despite breaks in the performance tradition, changes in the system of musical notation, the loss of accurate musical manuscripts—we know, with a fair amount of assurance, how most kinds of music written any time in the past thousand years were actually played.

In the case of Indian and Japanese music, the tradition is even more complete. It extends back, with hardly a break, to the beginning of the Christian era or earlier.

Nothing of the sort can be said for Greek and Roman music. A surprising amount is in fact known about it: There are a good many references by classical writers and a few entire books about Greek musical theory and practice; archaeologists have recovered examples of most of the known musical instruments, and they are quite fully depicted in sculpture, mosaic, and painting; even a number of fragments of Greek music in written form have survived, several of them carved in stone. Yet the fundamental question—what this music really sounded like, how it was actually performed—remains shrouded in mystery. We possess only very general ideas as to how the instruments themselves were played. Although attempts have been made to translate the Greek musical fragments (fewer than twenty in all) into modern notation and some of these have been recorded, we have no real certainty as to what they actually mean. Why, then, in a study of Greek and Roman civilization, should we try to investigate music?

If we are interested in Greek and Roman civilization in general, there are a number of reasons for wanting to know as much as can be known about these peoples' music. The position that music held in Greece and in Rome illuminates the two cultures; the contrasts underline those we have already observed in literature and art. Moreover, in Greece, particularly before the Hellenistic Age, music had an importance in daily life that it is difficult for a twentieth-century American to imagine—the kind of importance, perhaps, that ragtime and jazz had for the black society of New Orleans before World War I. Without some sense of what this music was like, of the part it played, our ideas about Greek culture are incomplete and misleading. Above all, Greek music seems to have been an integral part of Greek drama and of poetry generally, to such an extent that, having the words alone, we have only half the experience of these arts.

In Chapter II, we touched on this relation between Greek poetry and music. We noticed that lyric poetry was so called because it was sung or chanted to the music of the lyre, the musical instrument that the Greeks valued above all others. We noticed also that Greek drama of the Classical Period must have been something like modern grand opera, in the sense that it combined drama, music, and dance. But that is only a very crude comparison. It is as if the greatest English poet and writer of comedy, Shakespeare, should also have been our greatest composer—and his plays were put on in an atmosphere of patriotism and piety that combined a Fourth of July celebration with the solemnities of a state-supported religion. Yet that was the case with Aristophanes, the greatest Greek comic playwright, who was probably also the Greeks' greatest composer. In music, the writers of tragedy whose works have survived seem to have ranked only a little behind Aristophanes.

The Golden Age: How the Greeks Valued Their Music

In an early layer of Greek mythology we encounter the figure of Orpheus, the poet and musician whose songs were so compelling that animals, trees, and even stones followed after him and rivers stopped their flowing to listen. Whether or not there was ever a real poet by that name, a body of myths grew up around him, and by the fifth century B.C. he was the center of a secret religion that promised immortality to its initiates. Poetry and music, together, had a special place in Greek culture from the beginning.

Homer's epics contain many references to music and its instruments. As in other cultures dominated by a warrior aristocracy, the bard was the source both of entertainment and of traditional knowledge and history. Before they were written down in the eighth century B.C., *The Iliad* and *The Odyssey* were sung or chanted by successive generations of bards to the accompaniment of the lyre.

As in nearly every other aspect of Greek culture, the fifth century B.C.—the period between the great victories over the Persians and the end of the Peloponnesian War in 404 B.C.—is considered the high point of Greek music. And the end of the war with Sparta, with the bitter reaction that followed, was the great turning point.

By the fifth century B.C., Greek music had built up a body of traditional musical forms, styles, and melodies comparable, let us say, to the body of music that made up New Orleans jazz, though much greater in its complexity and range of expressiveness. In Athens, for several practical reasons that we'll look at shortly, music had a prominent place in the education and daily life of most citizens. The Peloponnesian War changed this. In the period of reaction and self-doubt that followed, serious Athenians questioned many of their basic ideas about themselves, and among others, they questioned their music. They wondered if one of the reasons they had lost the war was that music had become too important; perhaps they should imitate the warlike (and victorious) Spartans, who regarded music as a suitable occupation for slaves and did not permit their citizen-soldiers to be trained in it themselves. Moreover, in the fourth century B.C. there appeared a new generation of poet-musicians, such as Timotheus of Miletus, who flatly rejected the traditional musical forms and whose revolutionary new music outraged conservatives like Plato.

To a modern reader, it is both odd and revealing that the two great fourth-century philosophers, Plato (in *The Republic*, *The Laws*, and *Timaeus*) and his pupil Aristotle (in *Politics*), should have devoted significant attention to determining the role that music ought to have in the well-governed state. Both argued that the kinds of musical instruments and the forms of music should be controlled and limited — by law. While both are concerned with the function of music in education, their point of departure is the general welfare of the state. The following passage from *The Laws* reveals a number of basic characteristics of Greek music:

> The *lyra* [a form of lyre] should be used together with the voices, for the clearness of its strings, the player and the pupil producing note for note in unison. Heterophony [altering the melody with related notes] and embroidery by the *lyra* — the strings throwing out melodic lines different from the melodies which the poet composed; crowded notes where his are sparse, quick time to his slow, high pitch to his low, whether in concert or antiphony, and similarly all sorts of rhythmic complications of the *lyra* against the voices — none of this should be imposed upon pupils who have to snatch out a working knowledge of music rapidly in three years.

The passage tells us, indirectly, a good deal about the music of the Classical Period — and about the new music of Plato's own generation, to which he objected. As is so often the case, however, the most fundamental matters are not mentioned precisely because they seemed so obvious to the philosopher and his audience.

A number of vase paintings of the time help us to imagine the school scene that was in Plato's mind. The master is seated facing his pupils, *lyra* in hand. No books are in evidence. The teacher chants the poetry and plucks out the tune that goes with it; his pupils follow, line by line, note by note. The scene must have been a common one, for by this time education was the privilege of most Athenian citizens. Plato was seeking to salvage a minimum of three years of musical training in the elementary schools, from the age of nine to twelve, a reduction from the previous century. (Later, it was cut still further, to a single year.) The importance of music lay in the fact that much of the basic education was still by rote, learning the classics, particularly Homer, line by line; books were still relatively expensive and scarce, not yet common in Greek education. Learning the traditional melodies that accompanied the poetry thus had a practical function—it helped the students remember the words. Obviously, if the teacher altered the melody his pupils were trying to learn as an aide to memory, he would defeat this purpose.

The relation between melody and words was more direct than it can be in modern English. The reason for this is that classical Greek used a pitch accent rather than a stress accent: Where we accent our words by saying some syllables more loudly than others, the Greeks raised or lowered the pitch of their voices. Exactly how this sounded is only imperfectly understood, but it seems likely that Greek music, both vocal and instrumental, reflected the natural changes in pitch as well as the rhythms that were inherent in the various forms of Greek poetry. This is why Greek music of the Classical Period was always spoken of as subordinate to the words. Plato, for example, in the *Republic* writes that "the melody is composed of three things, the words, the harmony, and the rhythm.... And ... the harmony and the rhythm must follow the words." It also helps us to understand the otherwise baffling notion of music *as imitation* that appears in both Plato and Aristotle. Plato, for example, wanted to limit music to those forms that would "best imitate the utterances of men failing or succeeding, the temperate, the brave." Aristotle, in his *Politics*, makes the same point in a more extreme and abstract form:

Rhythm and melody supply imitations of anger and gentleness, and also of courage and temperance, and of all the qualities contrary to these, and of the other qualities of character which hardly fall short of the actual affections, as we know from our own experience, for in listening to such strains our souls undergo a change.

Greek music, then, was closely tied to the spoken language. From the passages quoted and others like them, we can form a fairly good general idea of what Greek music of the Classical Period must have been like—even if, finally, it proves impossible to reconstruct the music itself.

General Characteristics of Greek Music

Greek music evolved a number of basic forms, or modes, comparable to the major and minor scales of modern music except that they did not imply definite pitch. The whole question of what the modes actually meant is too complicated and uncertain for brief summary, but Greek theoretical writers at various times identified from six to fifteen different modes, by which they seem to have meant both abstract musical relationships and particular melodic forms to which these relationships lent themselves. The basic musical form was the fourth (two notes separated by three whole-note intervals); the two varying notes between determined the character of the mode. The Greeks were apparently able to distinguish much smaller note intervals than are used in European and American music today.

Harmony in the modern sense did not exist. Vocal music was sung in unison or in octaves; instrumental accompaniment might also be in unison or at a remove of an octave, although (as the passage from Plato's *Laws* implies) the instrument might engage in quite elaborate ornamentation and variation on the basic melody. Although in the fifth century B.C. the instrumental part was always subordinate to the words, by the fourth century the two had become separated, and we read of crowds of thousands gathered to witness elaborate performances of virtuosos on stringed and wind instruments.

One of the oddities of Greek music is that so little of it has survived in written form, in contrast to the relatively large number of carefully preserved and edited written texts. One reason for this may be the way in which music was used during the fifth-century Golden Age. In the drama, for example, Aristophanes wrote the music for his choruses and solo parts and almost certainly trained his singer-actors himself; the plays were intended for a single performance at one of the annual drama festivals. There was thus no need to preserve the music in a written form, and by the time the need arose, the living tradition of performance had been lost.

Moreover, it seems possible that the poetic lines themselves were considered a sufficient guide to their music: the elaborate metrical forms of Greek poetry would indicate the musical rhythms that went with them, and the pitch accents of the words would provide a melodic skeleton. Improvising within such a basic framework may well have been an essential element in Greek music. If we think of the Greek musical performer as building his accompaniment from the poetic framework the way a jazz pianist builds up melodic variations and rhythmic base from a simple sequence of abstract chords, we shall probably not be far wrong. The Greek musical notation that has been found seems to have arisen among the scholars of the Museum at Alexandria, perhaps at a time when—with the passage of time and the spread of Greek culture into alien lands—people were no longer sure how the language should be spoken and therefore needed aids to its music. In several of these musical fragments, the musical notes are written between the lines of verse, using modified forms of the Greek alphabet. (This musical notation, however, indicated position within a mode, not actual pitch.) They date from about the same time that the Alexandrians were adding signs to the Greek words to show what the pitch accent should be, quite possibly for the same reason.

There is another probable reason for the virtual disappearance of Greek music in its written form, and that is simply the perennial Greek fascination with the purely abstract and theoretical. In the fourth century B.C., for example, elaborate attempts were made to find the smallest possible interval between notes—a sort of atomic theory (see Chapter VI) applied to musical sound. This interest grew out of a practical feature of Greek music, the use of intervals of less than half a tone, referred to earlier. The fourth-century theorists, however, using mathematical formulas, defined intervals that could have had no practical value. Indeed, the only practical writer about Greek music—Aristoxenus, a student of Aristotle's—wrote in reaction against this body of theory. He pointed out that it was impossible for even the most sensitive and highly trained ear to distinguish between more than two such minute divisions of sound. After Aristoxenus, however, although a good deal was written about musical theory, all of it seems to have been purely theoretical, concerned with the nature of sound rather than the nature of music. The great astronomer Ptolemy, for example, produced such a treatise in the second century A.D., filled with mathematical formulas derived from a complicated form of lyre that he had devised for the purpose. Although he pointed out that a few of the modes he described could actually be used in the music of his day, his theories were valued precisely to the extent that they were remote from musical reality.

Greek Musical Performance

From references like those of Plato and Aristotle, we may think of Greek music as a small-scale, individual affair: the poet with his lyre, introducing each line or group of lines with an appropriate chord, emphasizing, varying, commenting on the melody of the words in the melody of the strings. Yet though it had nothing in any way comparable to the music of a modern symphonic orchestra, Greek music was capable of large effects. The dithyrambic choral lyrics discussed in Chapter II, for example, were accompanied by the wildly exciting sounds of an oboe-like wind instrument (the *aulos* — see below) played by up to fifty musicians grouped in a circle on the stage. The superb poetry of the choruses in Greek tragedies and comedies was matched by the music of the lyre. And in all probability we must imagine the choruses as accompanied not only by music in tune with the accents of the words but by dance steps underlining the rhythms. In the passages already quoted from Plato, melody and rhythm receive equal stress, both depending on the words. The Greek word for *foot* (*pous*) had the same pair of meanings as it has in English: both the physical human foot, which can stamp out complicated rhythms, move in the steps of a dance, and the metrical division of a line of verse.

The member of a Greek chorus obviously had to have an extraordinary combination of skills: the voice of an actor, the hands and ear of a musician, the feet of a dancer. And we can imagine that rehearsing for the single festival performance of such a play must have required an extraordinary amount of time. Under Pericles, the members of the festival choruses were paid for their skills and time by the government, and it was this arrangement that made possible the high reach of Athenian drama. Aristophanes in his plays comments with great subtlety on both the verse and the music of the older tragic playwrights; in the verse parodies in *The Frogs*, we can still form some idea of the radical innovations that Euripides introduced into both the music and the poetry of Greek drama. The subtlety of Aristophanes' allusions implies an equal sensitivity in his audience.

Aristophanes, who lived until 385 B.C., has left us two comedies known to have been written in the depressed years that followed the Peloponnesian War and the destruction of the Athenian Empire: *The Ekklesiazusae* (a funny, made-up word meaning "lady legislators" — a self-contradiction in terms of the male-dominated Athenian society) of 392 B.C. and *Plutus*, produced in 388 B.C. The difference in the use of the chorus between these plays and those written before the war is striking. The difference was a matter of money.

With the loss of tribute from her empire, Athens was forced to carry on her cultural life on a reduced scale. In the drama festivals, the choruses had to be smaller, with a less important part in the plays. At the same time, as we have already seen, the musical training that the average Athenian might receive in the course of his education was being debated and increasingly limited; and the music itself was becoming more complex, more difficult to perform, despite the objections of conservatives like Plato. Soon, both Plato and Aristotle would argue that there was something wrong with a citizen who was too good at music: It distracted his attention from the business of the state, made him soft; it was vulgar; only slaves and other members of the lower orders should aspire to great skill in music.

All of these factors combined to divorce Greek poetry and music from the intimate relationship that had prevailed from the beginning through the Athenian Golden Age. By the time of Menander late in the fourth century, the musical part of Greek drama had been reduced to instrumental interludes between scenes, performed by highly skilled full-time professionals. These same professionals would perform before immense crowds whose enthusiasm recalls the huge rock festivals of the American 1960s. Scholars would continue to repeat, with growing confusion and misunderstanding, the opinions of past authorities. But the popular and the serious, music with its emotional content, poetry with its ability to speak concisely and forcefully to the human mind and reason, were now split apart. Poetry and music, together, supporting each other, would never again be so near the heart of a civilization as they had been in the Athenian Golden Age.

The Instruments

In the history of musical instruments, Rome and Greece are members of the same family, start from similar levels of development. The differences and the ways in which they diverged parallel the evolution of the two cultures in other areas. It will be helpful, therefore, to consider their characteristic instruments separately, bearing in mind the original question for which we are seeking an answer—what did this music really sound like?

Greece

Stringed instruments and the lyre in particular, as we have already noticed, dominated Greek music. The lyre was the instrument most often portrayed on vases and in paintings.

In the course of Greek history, it appeared in various forms and under a variety of names, but by the fifth century B.C. the two types most widely used were the *lyra* and the *kithara*. Both had the same general shape: a curving rectangle a foot and one-half to two feet from end to end, with a sound box across the lower end, wooden arms extending up from the sides of the sound box, with a cross piece at the top; the strings were placed vertically between the arms, attached to the sound box at the lower end, to the cross piece at the top. At different times, the number of strings varied from three to twelve; seven was the typical number in the fifth century.

Both the *lyra* and the *kithara* were played upright. The *lyra* used as a sound box a tortoise shell covered with animal skin and was otherwise lightly built. It was held away from the body when played. Presumably it also had a softer sound than the *kithara*, suited to private performance rather than large audiences, and although the two instruments were basically the same, the technique associated with the *lyra* was simpler and was considered suitable for the gentleman amateur. The heavier *kithara* had to be held close to the body, against the player's left shoulder, supported by a strap attached to his left wrist. By putting together the classical references and illustrations with what is known of African tribal descendants of the *kithara*, scholars have to some extent been able to reconstruct the playing technique. The player held a large plectrum in his right hand that he drew rapidly across the strings (which would have been tuned to the intervals of the mode employed in a particular song); the fingers of the left hand silenced the strings not needed for a particular chord. Such chords might be used between lines of verse or at other pauses by way of introduction or, perhaps, as a running accompaniment to the voice. Besides damping unwanted notes in a chord, the left hand, held behind the strings, could also pluck the strings to produce a distinct melody.

From the length of the lyre strings and from other evidence, we know that both types of lyre were pitched within the range of the human voice—three octaves or so. This limitation is found in all other known Greek instruments and corresponds with the Greek views about the relation between vocal and instrumental music. In Greek music, there were no very deep or very high notes such as some instruments of a modern orchestra can produce.

In addition to the various forms of lyre, the Greeks also possessed a harp, called a *magadis*, but they regarded it as a foreign instrument and did not use it much. (The Egyptians, by contrast, brought the harp to a high level of development and made extensive use of it in their religious ceremonies.) The *magadis* was small in size compared with the modern harp, with twenty strings. The basic difference between a harp and a lyre is that the harp is designed in such a way that the strings vary regularly from short (high pitch) to long (low pitch); pitch is determined primarily by the length of the strings rather than by their tension, as with the lyre.

Among the Greek wind instruments, the most important was a very odd one called the *aulos* — often translated in English as "pipe" but actually more like the oboe, with its double reed and piercing, buzzing tone, than any other modern instrument. The typical *aulos* was presumably made of wood, and two examples in this form have been found in a fifth-century tomb near Athens, as well as several in metal and bone. Among the Greeks, it was a short instrument of narrow bore (smaller, in both dimensions, for example, than an oboe); it seems, however, to have been made in more than one size, no doubt to accompany different ranges of voice. In the Classical Period, the *aulos* had four finger holes on the front and a thumb hole behind, by means of which it could produce a complete octave, perhaps more. A few cane double reeds have been recovered from the dry land of Egypt, made, apparently, by a technique similar to that still used in making oboe reeds. These reeds, if they were indeed for an *aulos* of some kind, are rather large in relation to the size of the instrument. That fact, together with the narrow bore of the *aulos*, suggests that the instrument would have needed immense breath pressure and must have produced a loud, harsh sound — which corresponds with the kinds of things the classical writers said about it. Indeed, *aulos* players are often shown with a band of leather around the lips (with a mouth hole) and cheeks, tied by strings at the back of the head; it provided support for the terrific breath pressure needed to play the instrument.

The astonishing thing about the *aulos* was that it was nearly always played *in pairs*. Just how this worked is not known, although from surviving folk instruments in the Balkans we can get a few clues. One *aulos*, for example, might provide a drone — a continuing sound on one or two notes against which the other *aulos* would provide a melody, as is still the practice with the bagpipes and a number of other instruments. Or the two *auloi* (the Greek plural) might produce distinct melodies that would complement or contrast with one another, suggesting the feats of skill that the Greeks so admired in their professional *aulos* players. The paired *auloi* were sometimes of equal length, sometimes different. Sometimes they were attached at top and bottom, sometimes only at the top. (In the latter case, the pitch could be varied somewhat by changing the angle of the two instruments.)

Besides the solo performances and its use to accompany dithyrambic poetry (mentioned earlier), the *aulos* also provided a background for some of the Greek athletic contests, particularly the running events.

Both the lyre and the *aulos* were the sophisticated instruments of a highly developed urban culture. Shepherds and other country folk used an instrument called the *syrinx*, usually translated as "panpipes." This consisted of short lengths of hollow cane tied together in a row, each pipe of a different length to produce a different note. In Greek music, the *syrinx* had roughly the status of a mouth organ today. It had a practical function—for example, to call the sheep together in the foggy mountain weather of winter or to signal other shepherds with a distinctive sequence of notes.

Greek music made use of a number of other instruments — drums, rattles, a kind of trumpet, and, in the Hellenistic period, a single *aulos* (called a *monaulos*), with additional finger holes and an extra thumb hole. But the *aulos,* wild and penetrating, and above all the delicate and expressive lyre were the most important.

Rome

Although the native Roman instruments were similar to those of Greece, the Roman attitude toward music generally was like that of the Spartans: that it was an occupation suitable for slaves, not for serious Roman gentlemen. Complicated Roman contracts have been found between master and music teacher, spelling out the details (and the payments) for a slave's training in music. One of the things Suetonius, the Roman historian of the early Empire, found most contemptible about Nero was the Emperor's passion to excell in music. (He had a high, weak singing voice and accompanied himself on the lyre, even making a concert tour of Greece; in Rome, Nero appeared in a lyre contest organized on Greek lines, kneeling humbly at the end for the judges' verdict—which depended on the applause of an audience brought in for the purpose and kept in line by armed guards stationed at the end of each row of seats.) Indeed, in the Republican period one of the few records that we have of any special affection for music is a conservative's irritated protest at the replacement of the *tibia* (a Roman instrument like the *aulos*) by newfangled Greek instruments used to provide dinner music.

In general, the Romans' contribution to ancient music consisted of technological improvements of the instruments rather than creative artistry. Some of these instrumental refinements are of considerable interest.

Roman wall paintings exist that show elegantly designed versions of the Greek *kithara*, with an improved method of tuning the strings (wooden pegs, as in a modern violin) and a lever that made it possible to change the pitch of all the strings quickly and accurately at the same time—to suit different ranges of music or voice. To the *aulos*, the Romans added a system of rings that made it possible to adjust the pitch and the musical mode in which the instrument was played; they may also have added some spring-operated keys to this instrument. (The artistic representations are not entirely clear.)

One of the most interesting and characteristic Roman instruments was the *hydraulis* ("water organ"). It was invented at Alexandria in the third century B.C. but improved and widely used by the Romans. In essence, the *hydraulis* was a much-enlarged *syrinx*, with rows of pipes, as in a modern pipe organ, each producing a different note, and a mechanically effective, easy-operating keyboard to control the notes. The pipes were sounded by air pumped into a large, heavy chamber and released by the action of the keys; the air was held under pressure by a water seal around the bottom of the air chamber (hence the instrument's name).

The *hydraulis* must have been loud compared with other ancient instruments and relatively easy to play. The Romans used it particularly during gladiator fights and other public spectacles, such as the feeding of Christians to wild beasts— rather, one supposes, like the steam-powered calliope in an old-fashioned circus. It was probably for that reason that the Christian Church was slow to adopt this pagan instrument. It was near the end of the Middle Ages before the Christian organ attained the same level of development that the *hydraulis* had reached under the Romans.

Probably the most distinctive set of Roman instruments were the several ingenious kinds of trumpet. The Greeks had had one short, straight trumpet (the *salpinx*). The Roman version, the *tuba*, was longer (about four feet), hence deeper in pitch and probably louder, and was made of bronze. There was also the *cornu*, a shorter, gently curving trumpet with a flaring bell that, as its name implies, derived from a very widespread type of folk instrument made from an animal horn. The *lituus* was a j-shaped trumpet. Another trumpet, the *bucina,* is especially interesting. Made of the expensive and easily shaped metal brass, it was formed in a circle something like a modern French horn, with a small, flaring bell. The *bucina* fitted around the player's left shoulder and was played with the bell pointing straight ahead. Being tightly curved, the *bucina* was longer and deeper in pitch than would be practical for a straight trumpet. Its name, which combines the Latin words for dog and ox and might be translated "barking like an ox," suggests its probable sound.

It is significant that all of these Roman trumpets were military instruments; none of them had anything to do with music as such. Instead, they were used for the various signals required in battle and military camp life: the *bucina* signaled a change of guard; the *tuba* was used in battle (and also in some official religious ceremonies), so much so that the word occurs in Cicero's writings as a metaphorical synonym for war. Indeed, all of the Roman trumpets entered into the Latin literary vocabulary in various ways.

The Sound of Ancient Music

What, then, can we say about the sound of ancient music? To our modern Western ears, it might perhaps have sounded "oriental" — with the surprising intervals and complex rhythms of Middle Eastern music. Greek music in particular, from the earliest period, had important connections with other music of the eastern Mediterranean, which continued to develop independently down to modern times after the collapse of the Roman Empire. In the West, the tradition was broken; music started over, on new principles and at the service of the Church.

In this century, much has been done to resurrect the forgotten music of the Renaissance and Middle Ages, by studying musical manuscripts and written comments, comparing them with surviving folk music, above all by reconstructing the instruments of the period and putting them in the hands of skilled musicians. There was a time when it was hoped that the same kind of success could be achieved with classical Greco-Roman music, but that no longer seems possible. Yet new manuscripts continue to be found, archaeological discoveries continue to be made, and several of the ancient instruments, such as the *hydraulis,* have in fact been rebuilt and tried by modern musicians. Thus, scholars continue to hope that they may yet unravel the secrets of the early music that played so large and distinctive a part in Greek and Roman life.

FOR FURTHER READING

Curt Sachs's books on ancient music and instruments, although broader in coverage than Greece and Rome, are the only complete books on the subject; the other suggestions are for chapters in general histories of music and instruments. As usual, an asterisk indicates a paperback edition.

*Baines, Anthony, ed. *Musical Instruments Through the Ages.* Baltimore: Penguin, 1961. Chapter 9, "Ancient and Folk Backgrounds," by the editor is a brief, authoritative summary of what is known about Greek and Roman instruments. Chapter 1, "The Primitive Musical Instruments," by Klaus P. Wachsmann, is also of some interest. Line drawings and a few useful halftone illustrations.

____. *Woodwind Instruments and Their History,* 2nd ed. London: Faber, 1962. Chapter VIII, "Early Reed Instruments and Double-Piping," makes sense, by reference to similar folk instruments still in use, of the confusing matter of Greek and Roman double pipes. The author's interest is informed by concern for authentic performance of early music on the instruments for which it was written.

* Robertson, Alec, and Stevens, Dennis, eds. *The Pelican History of Music,* vol. 1: *Ancient Forms to Polyphony.* Baltimore: Penguin, 1960. Chapter 8, "Ancient Greece," is a brief, reliable account of the instruments and of what is known about the music.

Sachs, Curt. *The History of Musical Instruments.* New York: Norton, 1940. A pioneering work that emphasizes the Greek and Roman instruments. Illustrations show the main types in examples that have survived and include the evidence of vase paintings and sculpture.

____. *Our Musical Heritage; A Short History of Music,* 2nd ed. Englewood Cliffs: Prentice-Hall, 1955. The chapter on ancient music in this popular book is, in effect, a very short condensation of the author's more important book, listed next.

____. *The Rise of Music in the Ancient World, East and West.* New York: Norton, 1943. Informed by the author's worldwide knowledge and important discoveries of the instruments of primitive cultures and other ancient civilizations, such as the Chinese. His persuasive interpretation of Greek musical theory has been challenged by more recent scholars.

Wellesz, Egon, ed. *Ancient and Oriental Music;* volume 1 of *The New Oxford History of Music.* London: Oxford University Press, 1957. Chapter IX, "Ancient Greek Music," by Isobel Henderson, is an exhaustive analysis of the Greek musical theorists (often departing from Sachs) and includes possible transcriptions into modern musical notation of the more important fragments of Greek music; emphasis on the high point of the fifth century B.C. and the destructive reaction that followed. Chapter X, "Roman Music," by J. E. Scott, describes chiefly the Roman musical instruments.

CHAPTER VI

Philosophy, Religion, and Science

HAROLD L. GEISSE, JR.
WESLEYAN UNIVERSITY

Where It All Began: Classical Greek Religion

WHEN WE THINK about ancient civilization, we have to imagine what it must have been like for men and women living only a few hundred years after the discovery of writing itself, that necessary element in every civilization. Greek civilization at its greatest was just about as old as civilization in North America is now, but instead of starting as colonies of countries that were already highly developed, the Greeks started from scratch, by finding out how to write. In about the same time that it took the United States to grow from a few settlements on the Atlantic coast to its present position of power, the Greeks developed from the darkness of prehistory to the high point of one of the greatest civilizations in the history of the world. In many respects, their achievement has never been equaled since.

The Greeks were both very sophisticated and also very close to their primitive origins. At one moment, they seem strikingly modern, with attitudes much like ours, and in the next moment what they say is so obscure that we can understand it only by thinking away twenty-five-hundred years of cultural development. This is especially true of Greek religion and philosophy. Greek religion sometimes scarcely seems to us religious at all; yet there can be no doubt that it gave the Greeks a framework for all the experiences we still recognize as typically religious.

Greek Religious Ideas

As soon as they knew how, the Greeks began to write down the various traditions borne from the past by word of mouth, particularly stories about gods and heroes. The oldest Greek document is *The Iliad* of Homer, first written down sometime during the eighth century B.C. but certainly older. *The Iliad,* together with *The Odyssey,* was for the Greeks, among other things, the basic source of their religion, with something like the function that the Bible has for Christians and Jews.

Not long after the Homeric poems were written down, Hesiod was alive and working (see page 116). In his poems, he made an effort to reduce to some kind of order many of the stories about the gods that were current in his day. Later writers continued the work of writing down this oral tradition, but for the Greeks, the poems of Homer and Hesiod were the chief collections of religious ideas.

In a way, we know more about Greek religion than the Greeks did, since we can study it in the light of modern knowledge of many other primitive religions. Two ideas in particular, when applied to Greek religion, explain practices that might otherwise be puzzling. First is the concept of *mana** that anthropologists, the scientists who study all aspects of human life, customs, and development, believe to be characteristic of primitive religions everywhere. *Mana* is the notion that certain people and certain objects (such as trees or rocks) have a mysterious magical power to accomplish things not usually under the control of men. We no longer have much sense of *mana* in our religious practices, but it can be observed in all primitive religions, including the Greek. Sacrifice, for example, which was universal in the ancient world, can be explained in terms of *mana*. The *mana* of the animal sacrificed is transmitted to the god to whom the sacrifice is made. Among the Greeks, the bull, the most powerful animal available, was often the animal of sacrifice.

The other concept characteristic of primitive religions is *animism,* belief in spirits—the tendency of primitive men to see everything (rocks, rivers, trees, even the world itself) as living, as having an indwelling spirit. It took the Greeks a long time to distinguish between the animate and the inanimate. Primitive Greeks saw the weather as a manifestation of the great god Zeus, and even very late Greeks commonly thought of the heavenly bodies—the sun, moon, planets, and stars—as alive (and divine). A people influenced by animism sees gods everywhere: The belief provides an easy explana-

---

* Special words used in this chapter will be explained briefly, as they occur. Concise definitions and comparisons of all such technical terms are given at the end of the chapter.

tion for things that are otherwise mysterious. The first step toward science was taken when men no longer accepted such easy explanations.

We know something else about Greek religion that the Greeks themselves did not know or knew only dimly: that it had many different and even conflicting sources. It was the Greek habit to take stories and traditions from various sources and put them together, regardless of how incongruous the results might be. Take, for example, Poseidon, the god of the sea. In some stories, he is the brother of Zeus and lord of the ocean, just as Zeus is lord of the sky. In this role, Poseidon is often pictured with his familiar trident, rising up out of the sea, covered with seaweed and fearsome because he may whip up nasty storms without notice. Sometimes, on the other hand, Poseidon is pictured as part horse and is invoked as the deity appropriate to things horsy. The Greeks simply took two separate traditions and stuck them together; that they had nothing in common never bothered the Greeks for a moment. The Greeks were extraordinarily imaginative and cherished innumerable specific stories about their gods. The many myths and legends were contradictory and never made much connected sense, but, as we saw in Chapter II, they were immensely useful to poets and writers of tragedies.

The Greeks combined a variety of mythological traditions because Greek culture was itself a combination of several different traditions. Among the oldest traditional religious practices was the worship of the Earth-Mother, a practice common to almost all the eastern Mediterranean in very early prehistoric times. In fact, there were a great many Earth-Mothers because, while various peoples and various villages worshiped the same type of deity, they each gave her a different name. The Earth-Mother goddess thus survived in Greek religion in various guises and with various names. Worship of the Earth-Mother was what the anthropologists call a fertility cult — its main purpose was to make sure that the fields would be fertile and the crops abundant. Sacrifice to the Earth-Mother was felt to increase her *mana* and in turn ensure good harvests.

Another element of Greek religion thought to have existed from time immemorial was the worship of various earth-deities. The distinction between heavenly deities and earthly deities was well known to the ancient Greeks, who felt, quite correctly, that worship of earthly deities was a practice surviving from the times before Greek-speaking tribes arrived on the scene.

In addition to the worship of the Earth-Mother and the

various earth-deities, the third great element in Greek religion can be most clearly seen in Homer, where the sky-gods predominate. The Homeric poems reflect the life and attitudes of a group of swashbuckling conquerors who lived by their strength and skill in warfare; they were, in fact, the ruling classes descended from tribes of Indo-European invaders who swept over Greece in prehistoric times. Their chief deity was Zeus, the thunderer and bringer of storms, first and most powerful among a group of gods who had personal and intimate contact with this small group of aristocratic warriors. This explains why the Greek gods are represented as behaving in such an unseemly fashion. They act according to the code of the Indo-European warriors who worshiped them: quick-tempered, ruthless, none too scrupulous about other men's wives, and indifferent to any values except those of a warrior-hero; honor was truly a matter of life and death. Homer's heroes see themselves as motivated by the gods, who take a personal interest in what they do. Other people—farmers, merchants, craftsmen, slaves—hardly enter into the picture at all. This limitation created difficulties later when Homer's gods were supposed to function for Greeks of all classes.

Greek Gods

The Greeks' readiness to accept religious beliefs from many sources also explains their hospitality to foreign beliefs. The Greeks tended to think that every people worshiped the same gods under different names, and if some foreigner wanted to worship his own god, he was often allowed to do so. Some of these foreign gods became popular, and worship of them, together with stories about them, was simply added to the mix.

Finally, the Greeks also took into account (with varying degrees of worship) both demigods (whose parentage was half human and half divine, among whom Herakles, or Hercules, is perhaps the most notable example) and heroes, who were simply outstanding mortals remembered after their death for their remarkable accomplishments. (This may have been a survival of ancestor worship.) The lines dividing gods, demigods, and heroes are not always clear; heroes may have become demigods, and demigods may have been elevated to full divinity. Asclepius, for example, hardly even divine in Homer, became an important god in later antiquity; he was the god of healing, and innumerable miracles were held to have been worked by him at his temples. Orpheus, patron of poets and musicians, may even have been mortal originally; a group of beliefs influential during the highest period of Greek civilization centered about him (see page 304). In general, however, the Greeks made a clear distinction between gods and non-gods; the difference was immortality. What was immortal was divine, and vice versa.

In later times, writers made lists of twelve principal deities that usually included the following:

Zeus, the great Indo-European sky-god, the greatest of the gods by all accounts. He had many consorts and innumerable offspring, which made it possible for status-seekers to claim him as a distant ancestor.

Hera, the wife (and sister) of Zeus and goddess of marriage. She may possibly have been an Earth-Mother originally.

Poseidon, possibly Indo-European in origin, god of water and the sea and causer of earthquakes in one aspect, god of horses in another aspect.

Demeter, clearly an Earth-Mother, which is probably exactly what her name meant. (*Meter* becomes *mater* in Greek and Latin, *mother* in English; *de* may have meant "earth" or possibly just "grain.") She was the most important deity for farmers and one of the most widely worshiped.

Apollo, a combination of elements from many sources, thought by some scholars to be mainly Asiatic in origin. He was one of the most important gods; worship of him centered at Delphi, where he was believed to inspire oracles.

Artemis, goddess of wild animals and hunters, and also of childbearing, a function she shared with Hera.

Ares, god of war, but never an important god among the Greeks.

Aphrodite, originally probably an Earth-Mother in Cyprus but imported at a very early date. Because the first two syllables of her name sound like the Greek word for foam, she was pictured (even after the Romans changed her name to Venus) as having been born from foam, as in the famous painting by Botticelli. She was the goddess of love, beauty, and marriage, and in Sparta she was the goddess of war. (Do not expect Greek religion to be consistent.)

Hermes, one of the most complicated gods, was descended from the worship of certain stones (an example of animism), particularly milestones or those used to mark crossroads; hence, he became the god of travelers and merchants—and of the thieves who prey on travelers and merchants. He was also a general bringer of good fortune, and his rocky origin was not forgotten. *Herms* (or *Hermae*), upright stones or pillars whose tops had been carved into heads, were common religious objects in Athens, serving as good-luck charms.

Athena, the chief deity, naturally, of Athens, probably worshiped there before the Indo-European invasions. She was the goddess of weaving and spinning but also of skills and wisdom in general, and she is shown as helmeted and carrying a shield, which reflects her ancient warlike character.

Hephaestus, probably Asiatic in origin as a god of volcanoes. He became the god of craftsmen who use fire, especially smiths. Since this was a low-class occupation, Homer made fun of him, and he was never an important god.

Hestia, goddess of the hearth but not widely worshiped.

Other gods, who did not make it into any list of the twelve most important, were nevertheless among the most widely worshiped. The outstanding example is Dionysus, associated with wine and with the irrational in general; he was worshiped in ceremonies that sought to induce frenzy or ecstasy in the participants. He seems to have come from Thrace (a region immediately north of Greece proper) or Phrygia (in western Asia Minor). While barely mentioned in Homer, by the fifth century B.C. Dionysus was one of the greatest of the gods, even occupying temples at the holy city of Delphi, on Mount Parnassus, for several months of the year while Apollo was away. Dionysus was also called Bacchus.

Some of the Greeks' stories about their gods are charming, others are horrifying, and still others are so strange as to be repellent. This bothered men of later ages, who wanted to lift the whole notion of gods to a higher level. Plato, for instance, specifically rejected the traditional story about the origins of the gods. This myth said that before the gods lived, the earth was inhabited by a race of Titans, who were the sons and daughters of Earth and Heaven (Gaia, or mother earth, and Uranos, or father sky). Among the Titans were Kronos and Rhea, who were married. Kronos, however, had been told by his parents that he would be killed by his own son, and hence he simply swallowed all his children as they were born. Eventually, Rhea hid her latest offspring and gave Kronos a stone wrapped in baby clothes. He swallowed the stone, and the resulting stomach ache forced him to disgorge all the previous children he had swallowed, including Hera, Poseidon, and their brother Hades (who became god of the underworld but was never important). The son hidden by Rhea grew up to be Zeus, who in time overthrew the Titans and established the rule of the gods.

This is a very brief outline; the complete story is much more elaborate and probably reflects a conflict between the very ancient gods and the newer gods imported by the Indo-European invaders; the invading gods, those of the conquerors, naturally prevailed. But the names of the Titans, and the stories about them, survived. Among them, for instance, were Oceanus and Tethys, father and mother of the

Oceanides, the three thousand water spirits, and Hyperion, father of the sun and moon and of Eos, the dawn. In other words, the stories about the Titans constituted a *cosmogony* — an account of how the world began. Educated Greeks of later times seldom took these stories very seriously, however, and once philosophy began, it was part of its job to work out a more convincing explanation of the origins of things.

The Beginnings of Rational Thought

What is philosophy? The answer to this question depends partly on the period of history we are talking about. Today, philosophy is largely concerned with clearing away the intellectual confusions that go with almost any kind of activity that uses words. Originally, however, any kind of thinking about the universe and the mysteries of life was called philosophy; it attempted to answer not only such questions as "What is the good?" and "What is truth?" but also questions such as "What is the world made of?" and "How did it get to be that way?" As knowledge grew and better answers became possible, the subject areas of philosophy separated one by one and became independent disciplines. In the last century or so, for instance, sociology, psychology, and political science have established themselves in their own right; before that, they were all part of philosophy. The word *philosophy* was invented by the Greeks; it means "love of wisdom" — wisdom in general. The first philosophers were the first systematic thinkers of any kind.

Some technological knowledge existed before the Greeks. The Egyptians, for instance, developed the art of measuring land to a high level. The Greeks borrowed the art and turned it into the science of geometry. The Babylonians lived in a climate with clear skies and little rain for many months of the year and believed that human destinies were controlled by the stars. They accumulated an extensive knowledge of the movements of the heavenly bodies. The Greeks, using some of this knowledge, invented astronomy, a systematic attempt to account for all the observed motions of the heavenly bodies.

The Greeks, in fact, did something more. What the Egyptians and Babylonians knew was not science; it was technology. Their information was the result of unguided observation or hit-or-miss experiment; they could not, or did not try to, make a systematic account of *why* things happen as they do, except by the use of myths. The Greeks, in other words, invented theory. Explanation and proof are among the basic requirements of science, and a respect for them distinguishes the Greeks from their predecessors.

But the beginnings of Greek science were very primitive indeed. It took the Greeks generations to discover distinctions that now seem obvious and fundamental to philosophers—the difference between the abstract and the concrete, for example. This means that the thought of the first Greek philosopher-scientists can be very puzzling to us now.

The Milesian Philosophers

Philosophy began in a town called Miletus, which lay in Asia Minor near where the river Maeander flows into the Aegean Sea. (It was a very winding river, and its name survives in English as the verb *meander*.) The Greeks were a seafaring people, and in the ancient world the whole Aegean coast of Asia Minor was Greek. Miletus was founded in prehistoric times. Because it lay on a trade route into the interior, it became one of the largest and richest of the Greek cities long before Athens was important. The men traditionally regarded as the first philosophers lived there in the sixth century B.C. As a group, these philosophers are called the Milesians, after their city.

Not much is known about the Milesian philosophers. The earliest of them, according to tradition, was Thales (about 624–526 B.C.). Thales, it is thought, wrote nothing, and the earliest existing reference to him occurs in Herodotus, writing in the middle of the fifth century B.C. The second Milesian was Anaximander (about 610–547 B.C.), and the third was Anaximenes (active about 550 B.C.). Anaximander was probably a little younger than Thales, but the dates are so indefinite that we can say with assurance only that both were active in the sixth century B.C. Anaximander is known to have written a book, of which part of one sentence survives. Anaximenes also lived in the sixth century, and he also wrote a book, of which nothing survives. Fortunately, however, we have books by later writers who summarized the opinions of their predecessors (much like modern university professors). Our notions of the Milesians come almost entirely from such later writers.

The Milesians were the first men not only to express themselves as dissatisfied with the traditional accounts of the world provided by mythology but also to try to supply better accounts. Moreover, they went about it in a typically Greek way: They tried to give all-inclusive accounts using one fundamental idea to explain as much as possible. Since they tried to explain nature, for which the Greek word is *physis,* they are sometimes called "natural philosophers" or even "physicists." It must be remembered that they had no mathematics in the modern sense of the word—not even, in fact, much arithmetic.

In general, the Milesians tried to account for the world by saying that some one thing is the *arche* of all other things. *Arche* is variously translated as "beginning" or "first principle" or "starting cause"; these notions were not at all distinct in the minds of these early thinkers. Their attitude was remarkable for a number of reasons. First, it reflects a tendency to believe that there is, in fact, one substance that underlies all other substances and that everything we observe can be explained in terms of changes in that one substance—a notion not at all obviously true and with momentous consequences for Western thought. Second, it reflects a tendency toward simplification, a characteristic of Western scientific thought and quite foreign, for instance, to Indian thought.

For both these reasons, Milesian thought foreshadows science. On the other hand, it also looks backward toward myth. The Milesians did not feel it necessary to account for change because, they thought, the first principle itself is the cause of its own change. It is, in other words, alive. This is a primitive belief that later philosophers had to overcome. The Milesians had not yet clearly distinguished between living matter and inanimate matter.

The thought of the Milesians, then, is strange because it is primitive. Thales, we are told, said that the first principle of all things is water. This is not as foolish as it might seem at first glance since, as we know, there is no life without water; and water, furthermore, undergoes certain visible changes—to vapor, to ice, to rain and snow.

Anaximander, in turn, said that "the unlimited" is the first principle; this seems even more strange, but in fact the distinction between the abstract and concrete had not yet been made. Since in Greek, adjectives can serve as nouns, and the words we translate as "the unlimited" functioned grammatically just like the words for "the water," it was not apparent to Anaximander that he was dealing with a fundamentally different kind of concept. He also called his first principle "immortal" and "imperishable." The "unlimited," in other words, was alive.

Anaximenes, finally, felt that air is the first principle. He seems to have reached this conclusion mainly as a result of an emphasis on the processes of rarefaction and condensation, which he cited in an attempt to explain the world in terms of a process still going on. Rarefied air is fire; condensed air is first wind, then cloud, then water, and finally stone. This is, in a sense, an advance on Anaximander because it derives from things we can still observe instead of from activities now over and done with.

With the Milesians, a whole new era of thought began. Gone are the gods and the explanations of natural phenomena in terms of their activities. For the first time in history, there was an attempt to account for all things in terms of familiar processes or substances, and the origin of the world was seen as a natural event, not a divine act. The Milesians were the first of all men to believe that underneath the chaos of what we see there is order, and—just as important—that we are capable of understanding that order. This is the assumption of science, and its appearance marks the beginning of scientific thought.

Pythagoras

The second great tradition of Greek thought is called Pythagoreanism after its founder Pythagoras. He seems to have been born in the first third of the sixth century (about 570 B.C.) on the island of Samos, which lies off the west coast of Asia Minor not far from Miletus. He is said to have traveled extensively, perhaps to Egypt. Pythagoras apparently left Samos, perhaps about 538 B.C., because he objected to the government of the man who had seized power there. He migrated to Croton, a Greek city on the sole of the Italian boot. Hence it happened that the second great Greek philosophical tradition, like the first, centered not on Greece but along the edges of the Greek world. Pythagoras, or his followers, gained control not only of Croton but of other cities in southern Italy; when they lost power in Croton, Pythagoras fled to Metapontum, another Greek colony in Italy, where he died early in the fifth century.

The religious and political society that Pythagoras founded at Croton continued for another hundred years or so after his death. Pythagoras himself wrote nothing, but despite the fact that members of the society were sworn to secrecy, the doctrines of the movement were eventually written down and thus were preserved.

Later members of the society treated Pythagoras as though he were a god, and all sorts of miracles were attributed to him; scholars have to sift the probable out of the great body of romantic stories that have come down to us in order to arrive at some notion of what Pythagoras himself actually thought. It is certain that he mixed mathematical and religious ideas in a way that seems very strange to modern readers. His religious doctrines ranged from what seem to us irrational taboos (never stir a fire with a knife; never wear a ring; do not allow swallows in your house; never eat beans; and so forth) to the doctrine of transmigration, or reincarnation (the belief that the soul after death comes back to earth in another body, human or animal). Belief in the transmigration of souls was widely held in ancient Greece but unknown in the traditional mythology.

It is possible that there were two kinds of Pythagoreans: one group primarily interested in the religious aspects of the movement, the other in mathematics but not in religion. The goal of the religious doctrines was the salvation of the soul; like others who believe that men may be reborn as animals, some Pythagoreans seem to have been vegetarians, refusing to eat meat. But the Pythagoreans also believed in philosophy as a means of purification. They took the characteristic Greek attitude that the observable universe is divine and that the way to understand it is to cultivate what is divine in the human being: mind, or reason. The unlimited, they thought, is evil, but the limited (hence ordered and measurable) is good; the world is living and divine and accordingly limited—it is orderly and can be explained. Moreover, they said, if the divine universe is knowable only through the divine element in us, then our sense organs contribute nothing to knowledge.

This conclusion of the Pythagoreans—that only the purely rational is of value—was at once the strength and the weakness of all Greek thought. It lay behind the Greek preference for theory (which made science possible), but it also lay behind the Greek failure to develop a genuine experimental method in science. This separation of what can be perceived by the senses from what can be known only by the mind became one of the basic ideas in Greek philosophy and the backbone of Plato's philosophy; modified by early Christian theologians, the distinction became the traditional Western one between the earthly and the divine.

Philosophers are still struggling with the intellectual confusion that resulted.

The more strictly mathematical aspects of Pythagorean doctrine stemmed from the discovery that the relationships between the pitches produced by harp (or lyre) strings could be expressed in numbers. The Pythagoreans were thus the first to realize that nature can be described mathematically. Although their mathematics was entirely inadequate for the purpose, they set out to apply their discovery to every concept they could formulate. The Pythagoreans said that all of nature *is* number, and this seems to have been meant in the most literal way. Since the distinction between the abstract and the concrete had not yet been made, they thought of numbers as things, and of things as numbers. Even moral qualities were numbers: justice was the number 4, and marriage was 5. In short, numbers had a mystical significance for these early mathematicians that we find hard to grasp.

The Pythagoreans devoted enormous amounts of energy to manipulating numbers, and in the process they made some fundamental discoveries. They associated numbers with geometric figures; to this day, we talk of "squares," meaning both plane figures with four equal sides and numbers multiplied by themselves; and "cubes," meaning solid figures whose sides are squares and numbers multiplied by themselves twice. These double meanings create no difficulty for us, but for the Pythagoreans, who first formulated the concepts, the meanings were not double: A number multiplied by itself and a plane figure with four equal sides were the same thing. It seems to have come as a great shock to the Pythagoreans to find that the square roots of some numbers were precise and exact quantities (represented by the diagonal of a square) but nevertheless could not be expressed in whole numbers or rational fractions; they thus discovered irrational numbers. Having got over their shock, however, they then worked out many square roots to several decimal places.* This was a great feat. Since the Greeks had no zero—it was imported centuries later from India—in order to compute square roots the Pythagoreans had to work out a place-value notation to replace the ordi-

---

* Related to these discoveries is the so-called Pythagorean Theorem, still fundamental to geometry (though just what connection it had with Pythagoras or the Pythagoreans is not clear): that in all right-angle triangles, the square of the hypotenuse equals the sum of the squares on the other two sides. The theorem was derived from a practical Egyptian method, used in measuring land, for determining right angles.

nary Greek one, which, like Roman numerals, made simple computations difficult.

The most remarkable feature of Pythagorean ideas about the universe was their belief that the earth is not at the center of things but circles around the center like other planets. It was not, however, a heliocentric system (that is, a system based on the idea that the sun is the center around which the earth and planets revolve): The Pythagoreans believed that at the center is a fire that is never seen because our side of the earth is always turned away from it; there is also a counter-earth, invisible for the same reason. They seem to have felt that the sun's heat and light are reflected from this central fire. It is possible that they understood that eclipses of the moon are caused by the earth's shadow—a notable advance in astronomy. They also taught, finally, that the movement of the heavenly bodies produces a harmonious sound: In a later form, this belief became the famous "harmony of the spheres," which was influential in Renaissance thought. It was a rational conclusion for thinkers who began with the pitches of lyre strings, but they had to invent ingenious explanations for why we do not hear the sounds produced by the motions of the planets; there is no explanation of how they supposed that all eight notes of the musical octave (one for each of the five known planets, the moon, the sun, and the fixed stars taken together) could have produced a harmony instead of simply an awful noise.

New Ideas of the Universe

From the end of the sixth century B.C., the Greek world was full of philosophers. They can, in general, be divided into two groups: The first consists of the great cosmologists, the other of the Sophists. The *cosmologists* were those philosophers who attempted to explain the observable universe and everything in it (the Greek word is *cosmos*) and to determine the principle on which it is organized. The Sophists, on the other hand, turned their backs on scientific studies in favor of purely humanistic thought (see also page 305). We shall, for convenience, discuss the cosmologists first and then the Sophists, but the great cosmologists in fact lived at about the same time as the Sophists. The cosmologist Empedocles, for instance, died about 435 B.C. when Socrates (about 469–399 B.C.), who in some respects is usually classified with the Sophists although he opposed them, was about thirty-five years old. There is another reason for the separation, however: the cosmologists continued the tradition begun by the Milesians, but the Sophists made a break with the past and adopted a new point of view. The two streams meet and unite in Socrates' great pupil Plato (427-347 B.C.).

Heraclitus

The earliest of the cosmologists, Heraclitus (about 533-475 B.C.), was about thirty years younger than Pythagoras and perhaps fifty years younger than Anaximenes, the last of the Milesians; and nearly seventy years older than Socrates. He seems to have been a very strange man. Tradition holds that he was the hereditary king of Ephesus, a Greek city of Asia Minor, but was so proud that he could see no virtue in assuming the kingship and renounced it in favor of his brother. His surviving writings, which consist of more than a hundred sayings, exhibit great contempt for poets (including Homer), other philosophers, and mankind in general. He hated equalitarian ideas, such as democracy, and thought that there was a great deal of folly abroad in the world. He seems to have liked to express himself in paradox and metaphor, so that even in the ancient world his name was a byword for obscurity. Today, it is hard to make any sense at all out of some of the surviving fragments. He clearly supposed himself, however, to have found absolute truth, and he denied both Milesian and Pythagorean thought. Heraclitus believed the opposite of Thales: that fire is the basic, or highest, form of matter—fire thought of as a kind of invisible vapor rather than as flame. When a man is alive, his soul is fire; when he dies, his soul turns to water. Heraclitus admired the dry and thought that death (and foolishness) are connected with the damp and cold.

More important is Heraclitus' notion that everything is in continual change. His most famous saying holds that you cannot step twice into the same river—since the second time, it will not *be* the same river. Everything is always moving, and, like the change of seasons, it follows cycles: One thing changes to another and then back again. But a harmony is created by a kind of balance of opposites. The wet and the dry, the hot and the cold, and the other basic sets of opposites (so often used by the Greek philosophers) are in constant tension. Just as the string of a bow is useful only when it is under tension, so, Heraclitus thought, the entire world is what it is because of underlying tension. He calls this tension "strife" or "warfare." Those who find this baffling can take comfort in the thought that it baffled the ancients, too.

Heraclitus' saying that you cannot step twice into the same river raised a fundamental philosophical question that later Greek philosophers tried to answer: Since, obviously, everything is constantly changing, how can we know anything? What we know must be stable because the unstable is unknowable (in the Greeks' view). If what we observe changes, how can we say we know anything about it? It was almost twenty centuries before men began to formulate precise descriptions of changes that occur in repetitive and predictable ways.

The Eleatic Philosophers

The first reaction to the problem of change was formulated by a group of philosophers called the Eleatics, after the Greek colony of Elea, which lay south of Naples on the west coast of Italy. Elea was founded about 540 B.C., and Parmenides, the chief philosopher of the movement, was born there about 515 or 510 B.C. He was thus twenty or thirty years younger than Heraclitus and visited Athens when Socrates was a young man; Socrates may have had firsthand knowledge of his thought.

Parmenides expressed his ideas in a long poem divided into two parts called *The Way of Truth* and *The Way of Seeming*. It was well known in antiquity and survived intact for many centuries, but we now have only 154 lines. Most of the fragments of Parmenides' poem come from *The Way of Truth*, the more important of the two parts, which seems to have survived almost complete. *The Way of Seeming* was apparently a detailed cosmology, somewhat like those developed by earlier philosophers. The extraordinary thing about this part of the poem is that Parmenides expressly says that its views are false; the truth is contained in the first part, *The Way of Truth*.

The poem is a mixture of rational thought and myth, and the modern mind has difficulty separating the two. Parmenides said, in brief, that it is, and it is impossible for it not to be; it is false that it is not. The point of this excessively condensed statement seems to be that change and movement (or coming-to-be and perishing) are all alike impossible. What is, is what it is, and is not anything else. Parmenides, in other words, refutes Heraclitus, who saw change in everything, by flatly asserting that there is no change at all. He elaborates this doctrine of "what is" by saying that it is eternal (it never came into being) and immortal (it cannot perish). This, he said, is because nothing can be made out of nothing. In its Latin form (*ex nihilo nihil fit*), this became a famous slogan that was cited by philosophers for centuries. Parmenides said, furthermore, that what is, is continuous and indivisible: It is, in other words, one; quite literally, there is in the entire world only one thing, namely, what is. There is no void; there are no gaps in existence; there is no such thing as empty space, and movement is obviously impossible. It is also, incidentally, spherical: The Greeks always preferred the circular or spherical to the flat or straight.

Parmenides continued and extended the Greek distrust of the senses. Never trust the senses, he said; reason alone can show the way to truth. From Parmenides, it was only a step to Plato, who constructed a whole philosophy in which the world of the senses was rejected in favor of an ideal, theoretical world that he held to be more real than the observed world.

Parmenides had an important follower named Zeno (about 490–430 B.C.) who also came from Elea. Zeno is famous chiefly for having devised a series of paradoxes (seemingly self-contradictory statements and examples) to demonstrate the truth of what Parmenides said. The most famous of Zeno's paradoxes is the story of Achilles and the turtle. In a race between them, Achilles can never win if the turtle has a head start. Achilles must first get to the point where the turtle was when Achilles started, but by then the turtle will have moved on; when Achilles has run this further distance, the turtle will again have moved—and so on, indefinitely. Achilles will have to pass through an infinite number of points to catch up to the turtle, which is impossible. Zeno made a similar argument about the flight of an arrow, saying that a flying arrow does not in fact move because at every instant it can occupy only a space equal to itself and is therefore at every instant motionless. Discussion of the paradoxes leads immediately into some very tricky problems. They were cleverly formulated and difficult to refute; although everyone knows that Achilles obviously *does* win any race with a turtle, it was necessary to be very careful in accounting for his victory. Radically new approaches were necessary to get around the problem.

Other Fifth-Century Philosophers

Next in succession after the Eleatics comes the strange figure of Empedocles (about 495–435 B.C.). He was a religious mystic, a doctor, a poet, and a philosopher, and he lived entirely within the fifth century. He was thus a somewhat older contemporary of Socrates. Empedocles came from a Greek town on the south coast of Sicily, Acragas (modern Agrigento). He was rich and well-born, but even so an advocate of democracy. He had a very high opinion of himself (in the Greek fashion) and claimed to be able to cure any disease. He is also said to have favored colorful clothing (a purple robe with a golden belt and bronze shoes) and plenty of hair. He wrote two poems, one called *On Nature,* which was scientific in content, the other called *Purifications,* which was religious. Despite the fragmentary nature of what survives, it is possible to reconstruct his complex system of thought in some detail.

Building on Parmenides, Empedocles accepted the ideas that there is no void and that (since nothing can be made of nothing) the sum of being is constant and imperishable. On the other hand, he rejected the belief that there is no change and admitted, to a certain extent, the reliability of knowledge derived from the senses. He is thought to have been the first to say that there are four first principles, or elements, as they came to be called: earth, air, fire, water. This is the list that was adopted by Aristotle and generally accepted by men for many centuries afterward, down to the beginning of modern times.

Empedocles envisioned the cosmos as made up of the four elements, but since he admitted that movement could occur, the elements could mix with one another. The cosmos is involved in an eternal cycle of change—from a state in which the four elements are intermingled into a state in which they are completely separated, and then back again. This continual change is caused by Love and Strife (or Anger), conceived of as independent forces operating on the world. Love is a kind of personification of the observed phenomenon of attraction (as in magnetic action); Strife is a personification of repulsion. Empedocles did not really distinguish between natural forces and mythological conceptions; even so, he is usually cited as the first thinker to conceive of force as acting on matter; it was a basic scientific advance.

According to Empedocles, there are two stages in the world-process when human beings exist: once when the world is moving toward the domination of Love, and once when it is moving back again, toward the domination of Strife. Since the world is now moving toward the domination of Strife, it is becoming increasingly violent, which accounts for the occurrence of floods, earthquakes, volcanic eruptions, and the like. It was an imposing system that has continued to command the respect of writers and poets, even though its scientific and philosophical content was soon superseded.

Another important philosopher active in the earlier part of the fifth century B.C. was Anaxagoras (about 500–428 B.C.). A few years older than Empedocles, he came from Clazomenae, another Greek city in Asia Minor, and is taken as carrying on the tradition begun by Thales. But about 460 B.C., he moved to Athens and stayed there for most of the rest of his life, thus becoming the first important philosopher associated with the leading city of ancient Greece.

Anaxagoras was a friend and teacher of the great Athenian statesman Pericles, and this relationship got him into political difficulties. About the time the conflict with Sparta flared up again in the Peloponnesian War and Pericles himself was in deep political trouble, Anaxagoras was indicted for impiety —for saying, among other things, that the sun is a fiery stone instead of a god. Since the divinity of the sun was not a matter that people cared much about, this was clearly a trumped-up charge, and it is thought that the real target was Pericles, not Anaxagoras. Authorities disagree as to whether he was convicted and condemned to exile or was acquitted and left Athens voluntarily: in any case, he went to Lampsacus, a city on the Asian side of the Hellespont, and died soon after.

Anaxagoras lived in Athens during her greatest years and died just before her downfall and collapse. There is a tradition that he taught the playwright Euripides. Copies of his book (called the *Physics*) could easily and cheaply be bought in fifth-century Athens and are known to have survived as late as A.D. 500 (for nine hundred years, that is, which is not bad for the life of any book). Only a few fragments of the *Physics* survive today, however—almost all, apparently, from the opening chapter, so that we know more about the general nature of the book than about the details of the system expounded in it.

Anaxagoras held, with the Eleatic philosopher Parmenides, that there is no empty space and that true coming-into-being and perishing are impossible. He agreed with Empedocles that what appears to be generation is really just a new mixture of elements and perishing a separation of elements. The problem, then, is to account for the physical world as we actually experience it. Anaxagoras seems to have held that the four elements defined by Empedocles (air, fire, water, earth) are no more important than every other natural substance and that all exist just as fully. Beyond this, scholars disagree about what Anaxagoras meant by his surviving statements. The most famous of them is that "there is a portion of everything in everything," which may be an attempt to account for the fact that, for instance, digestion turns food into flesh and bone. If nothing new can come into existence, it is difficult to see how food becomes bone and muscles unless there is, in some sense, muscle already in our food (as indeed there is, in the form of protein).

To buttress his position, Anaxagoras seems to have held that all things are infinitely divisible—enunciating for the first time in Western thought, it seems, the notion of infinity that we continue to use. Over and above everything else in the universe, according to Anaxagoras, there is Mind, the purest and finest of all things, which not only started the universe into motion but also decided in what proportion things would be mingled. Mind alone has no intermixture of other things. The heavenly bodies, he said, are heavy and made of stone (the doctrine that occasioned the indictment for impiety), and in fact a large meteorite fell in Greece about 467 B.C., which astonished observers by turning out to be made of stone, since it was observably of fire before it hit the earth. Anaxagoras was among the first, and possibly the very first, to say that the moon's light is a reflection from the sun and to explain eclipses of the moon as shadows of the earth.

Anaxagoras thus had a rationalistic point of view that had little in common with the beliefs about the gods. His view of the supremacy of the mind influenced Plato and Aristotle, and the Western tradition that identifies mind with God (and vice versa) may be said to begin with him. After Anaxagoras and until very recent times, most thinkers made a sharp distinction between mind and matter, which has not yet disappeared from popular thought.

The last of the great cosmologists was slightly younger than Socrates. He was named Democritus (about 460-370 B.C.) and was born in Abdera, in Thrace. (Unlike every philosopher discussed so far, he was thus born in mainland Greece.) During his very long life, Democritus traveled extensively and wrote many books, all of which are almost entirely lost. But behind him there was an even more shadowy figure named Leucippus, of whom almost nothing whatever is known, not even where or when he was born. The titles of some of his books survive, and he is known to have been the teacher of Democritus. All later writers, however, agree that the two of them invented the famous atomic theory of matter (atomism), and, as it happens, we have a long and detailed exposition of this theory in *De Rerum Natura* (see page 319) written centuries later by the Roman poet Lucretius (94–55 B.C.). The problem is to decide which aspects of the theory were original with its inventors and which were added by later thinkers; in general, it is thought that the later additions were for the most part minor.

Atomism may be seen as an attempt to account for the physical world despite the assertions of the Eleatics that change and motion are not real. It starts with the revolutionary premise that there is empty space—an idea that ran counter to the commonsense experience of every Greek since they thought of air as filling the space it occupies and had no experience of a vacuum. Atomism also holds that there is an infinite number of very tiny but nevertheless solid entities that cannot be further divided (the Greek word for this is *atomos*, which means "uncut").

The Eleatics had said that there is no void and that the world is entirely full; this is to say, in effect, that there is only one thing, namely, the whole world. Atomism denies this entirely. It says that it is true that what exists is solid, but it does not fill the world: There is also empty space. What exist are atoms and the void. Atoms have different sizes, shapes, and weights, but no qualities that can be perceived by the senses—no color, taste, or smell. It is not clear just how the theory accounted for motion; Aristotle said that the theory of Democritus "carelessly neglected" the problem, but it is possible that Leucippus and Democritus simply regarded motion as natural to matter and did not think it necessary to account for it. In any case, the atoms are seen as in motion in empty space; this motion seems to have been thought of as aimless and headed in all directions. It has always existed and was never begun. The atoms, in motion, bump into each other, become enmeshed, and thus set up a kind of whirling movement out of which the world was created. In fact, a great many different worlds have been formed, of which ours is only one. The various worlds have different sizes and characteristics. There was no purpose behind all this; everything that exists and everything that happens is governed by necessity, although, because of our ignorance, it may seem to be a matter of chance.

The theory of Democritus was applied to every kind of scientific problem, but we can only guess at its details from what later commentators claimed the theory said. In any case, it seems to have been a thoroughgoing materialism, used to explain everything in purely physical terms, without any reference to spirit at all.

Although the theory in some respects foreshadows modern attitudes, it was not an obviously satisfactory way to account for what could be observed, and for that reason most ancient thinkers preferred other theories. Its important influence occurred at the beginning of modern times when men looking for new ways to explain careful experiments began to think their way toward modern physics and chemistry along the lines first suggested by Democritus.

The Fifth Century: The Breakdown of Values

Like our own time, the fifth century B.C. was a period of rapid change in Greece. Democracy was established at Athens toward the end of the sixth century, about 508 B.C.; during the next twenty-five years the great wars against the Persian invasions took place, ending in a triumph for the Greeks and especially for Athens (see page 44). On a great wave of self-confidence, Athens made herself the cultural capital of Greek civilization, but the wave crested and broke with great rapidity. In 499 B.C., as the Persian Wars were beginning to break out in the revolt of the Ionian cities, the earliest known play of Aeschylus was produced; Socrates was born about 469 B.C.; and in the next decade Pericles came into political prominence, and with him the city entered upon her Golden Age. The Parthenon was finished in 432 B.C., and in 431 the disastrous Peloponnesian War began, putting a halt to Pericles' magnificent plan for the Acropolis and ending in total defeat for Athens in 404. Socrates was executed in 399, and during the fourth century the Greek glory faded. The ancient world never again achieved anything like what vanished during the years after the collapse of Athens.

From our vantage point in time, we can see the trends in each period developing during the preceding period. It is clear to us, for instance, that the city-state, the basic political unit in Greece during her greatest years, had in fact outlived its possibilities; yet Plato, and even Aristotle in the generation after, who lived to witness Alexander's conquest of most of the known world, continued to talk as though no other political unit could possibly fulfill the conditions for civilized living. Similarly, we are shocked by the supersti-

302 Philosophy, Religion, and Science

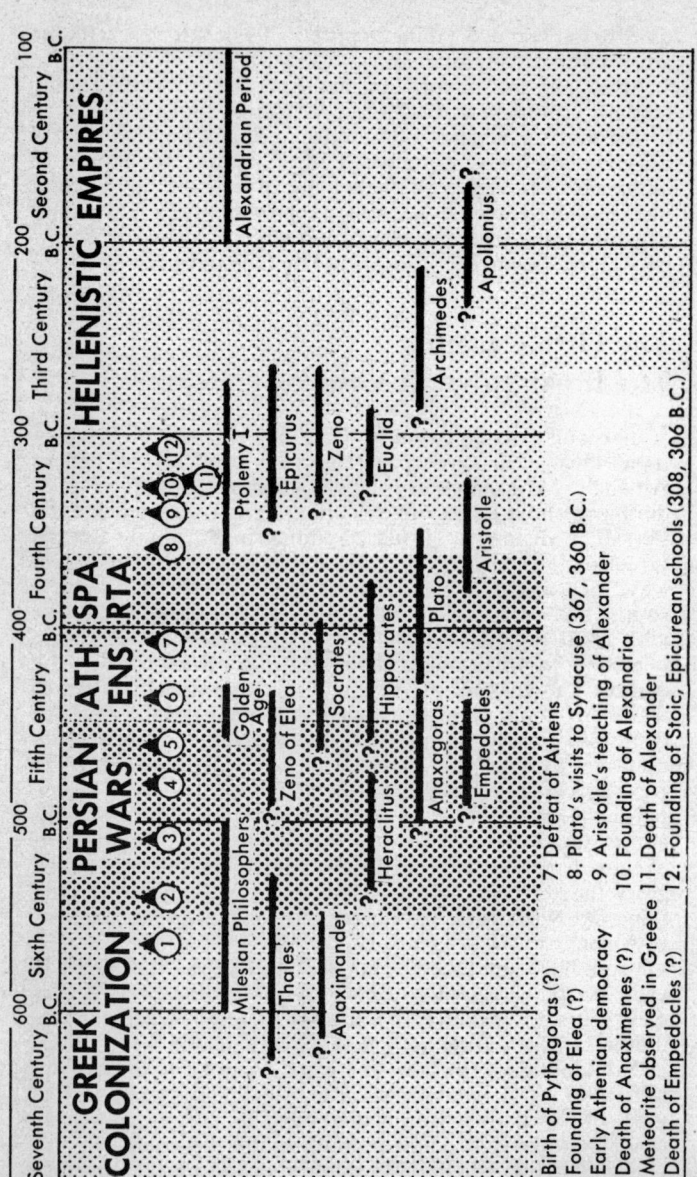

tion and credulity of educated thought in the Hellenistic world that Alexander created; yet we can see that even in the fifth century B.C., as the traditional stories about the gods satisfied fewer and fewer people, many were already turning toward the most degraded forms of religious belief (such as astrology). The scientific impulse lasted a little longer, and important advances were achieved as late as the second century B.C., but after that, most science consisted of compilations of what others had said in earlier times. The Romans produced no original philosophers and no scientists.

The Greek Mystery-Religions

The Greek culture as a whole, and above all its religion, was an unstable mixture of the rational and irrational. While rational thought developed steadily toward the high point of the fifth and fourth centuries B.C., the wild and irrational, the subjective, individual, and emotional, were also growing in importance in the lives of many Greeks. In fifth-century Athens, this side of Greek inner life was embodied in the mystery-religions, with their promise of salvation for the individual. The Greek mystery-religions seem to have developed out of the ancient fertility cults (see page 283). In many forms, they persisted throughout the long age of Greek and Greco-Roman civilization.

The most famous Athenian festival was connected with the Eleusinian Mysteries. Eleusis, a small town about twelve miles west of Athens, came under Athenian rule in the seventh century B.C. The cult there seems to have survived from pre-Homeric times, before the Indo-European invasions. The priesthood in charge of the Eleusinian Mysteries was in the hands of the members of a single family, who inherited it. The rites were dedicated to Demeter, the grain- (or earth-) mother. The myth connected with Eleusis told the story of Demeter and her daughter Kore (sometimes called Persephone), who was kidnaped by Pluto, or Hades, the god of the underworld. After a struggle, there was a compromise, and Kore was restored to her mother for two-thirds of the year but had to return to the underworld for the other third, corresponding with the Greek summer when the land lies parched and baked under the Mediterranean sun. In the fall, Kore was restored to her mother, and things could begin to grow again. This is perhaps the best known of all the fertility myths of the ancient world.

On the basis of this cult, the Greeks erected an elaborate mystery-religion: mystery because the rites were a closely guarded secret, a religion because it had to do with the immortality of the human soul. Just exactly what went on at the climax of the rites we do not know since the secret died with the religion; but we know a great deal about the preliminaries.

Candidates for initiation into the mysteries, having undergone introductory ceremonies earlier in the year, assembled in Athens on the first day of the festival; on the second day, they marched down to the sea, each with the pig he was to sacrifice to Demeter, and bathed themselves (and their pigs). On the fourth day, everyone started out in procession for Eleusis, but the trip took two days since there were frequent halts for performances by dancers and for sacrifices, libations, and hymns. Dionysus, or Bacchus, the god of the irrational (which included both religious ecstasy and mere drunkenness), in time became part of the proceedings. As we saw in an earlier chapter (see page 122), the separate Athenian festivals of Dionysus—the Dionysia—planted the seed from which Greek tragedy ultimately grew. At Eleusis, where the auditorium held three thousand people, the solemn rites of the festival took place. Just what they consisted of, no one knows; there is a possibility that at the climax the officiating priest held up a stalk of ripe wheat, symbolic of fertility, rebirth, life. The ancients, including those who had been initiated and knew, referred only to "things seen," so that we can be sure something was shown.

Another cult of the period, which attracted far fewer people but seems important to us because of its influence on Plato, was Orphism. Scholars are by no means sure what it consisted of or whether or not it had any formal organization. There seems to have been a body of poetry containing the doctrines of the belief. The author of the poems was thought to be the legendary Orpheus, a Thracian god or demigod. Its most remarkable aspect was its otherworldly point of view. Fundamental was the belief that this life is an evil and that the best possible fate for man is a permanent escape from the cycle of lives to which he is condemned. Because of transmigration (see page 291), this cycle continues until the soul has lived a pure life a sufficient number of times to break free and avoid rebirth forever. Whether or not there was an organized cult of Orphism, it does seem to be the case that some people, including Empedocles and Plato, believed in or were influenced by the notion of punishment or reward in the next life. Such a belief can offer a righteous man the hope of something better in the next incarnation.

The Orphic doctrines provided a better basis for moral

living and greater solace for unhappiness than a religion that had only the whims of unedifying gods to offer. It is also clear that Orphism regarded the human soul as divine and immortal and taught that the evil in us may be purged by participation in rites of purification. There were rules of purity that (as in any doctrine of transmigration) forbade the eating of meat and the sacrifice of animals. The doctrine apparently held that the soul, after death, is judged and goes, if wicked, to a place of punishment or, if good, to Elysium. After a time, the soul is sent to join a body again, either a man's or an animal's, depending on how good its previous life had been. Those who have been Orphics in three successive lives may hope for final salvation and escape from the wheel of reincarnation into the heavenly *aether,* the upper air that all Greeks regarded as divine. The whole story is reflected in the myth of Er that closes Plato's *Republic*.

Brief descriptions such as these can at most barely suggest the diversity of religious life in the Greece of the fifth century B.C. There were soothsayers, necromancers, and diviners who predicted the future by examining the entrails of slaughtered animals or the flight of birds. There were oracles, the most famous of which was at the great Greek religious center at Delphi. People came from all over Hellas to ask questions of the priestess through a priest who interpreted what she announced. This dizzying religious diversity persisted in the Greco-Roman world until the triumph of Christianity. Always, men were ready to welcome a new and exotic god, a secret rite of purification, that offered to the individual believer the hope of salvation from the miseries of life.

Humanism: Socrates and the Sophists

It is in the context of the rich and sophisticated culture of the fifth century B.C., at the height of Athenian wealth, power, and artistic achievement, that we must imagine the rise of the great humanistic schools of philosophy. These philosophers were called Sophists, a term derived from the Greek word for wisdom but having an unfavorable connotation even for Socrates, who opposed them. The whole movement, including Socrates, turned its back on science and concentrated its attention instead on man, on human values and human problems. By this time, as we have seen, Greek scientists had put forward many contradictory explanations of natural phenomena, none capable of proof. A certain disenchantment set in. People tended to feel that all that sort of thing was empty and useless. Aristophanes, in *The Clouds*, for example (see pages 133-4), was no doubt voicing the average Athenian's impatience with the intellectuals of the time: The arguments he puts into their mouths are "scientific" ones that fly in the face of common sense and ridicule the gods.

Furthermore, now that Athens was a democracy, the ability to make a persuasive speech commanded a high premium; for a young man who wanted to make a career in politics, it was essential. Hence, a group of men arose who taught the art of speechmaking, for a fee, and came to be known as Sophists. What was worse, in the eyes of moralists like Socrates, the Sophists claimed to be able to teach men how to make a convincing speech quite apart from the truth or justice of what the speech advocated; winning, not being right, was what counted. Students flocked to these teachers, ready to pay large fees.

The natural philosophers had created doubt about the traditional religious myths. Even worse, they tended to reject the evidence of the senses in favor of sheer reason. This had two effects: It left men adrift without satisfactory answers to basic religious questions since neither the old gods nor the new theories were convincing; and it gave men license to reach any conclusion their reasoning might lead them to, no matter how undisciplined and uncritical that reasoning might be. Nothing was sacred, anything might be questioned; and the Sophists were quick to question in particular all the traditional notions about what constituted right conduct.

The powerful can do as they please, some Sophists said; laws are made for the benefit of those with the power to enforce them. Or they said that laws are merely the device of the weak to keep the strong man from the position of power that is naturally his, and a truly strong man is therefore free to break the laws. Given enough cleverness, they announced, it is possible for an ambitious man to control the laws by arguing successfully in favor of anything at all. In a democracy, this constituted effectiveness, or skill, and so the Sophists claimed to be able to teach effectiveness. We use the word *virtue* to mean moral excellence, but the equivalent Greek word meant excellence of any kind: The excellence, or virtue, of a knife is its ability to cut; the excellence, or virtue, of a man is his ability to run well his own affairs and those of the state. Thus, the Sophists claimed to be able to teach virtue. Opposed to all of them was Socrates.

Socrates is one of the most remarkable figures in the history of Western thought. He wrote nothing, but next to Jesus he has had perhaps greater impact on Western civilization than any other single man. He was an Athenian born and bred; he never traveled except when he was serving in the army; he hated to leave Athens even to take a walk in the country. He was said to have been ugly and had a large paunch in later life. He was indifferent to food and dress; he went around with long, shaggy hair and needed a bath more often than he had one. His clothes were a joke, and he went barefoot in every kind of weather. He had a wife and family but no interest in earning a living, and therefore he was perpetually poor. (It is hardly surprising that his wife, Xantippe, became the proverbial type of the bad-tempered, nagging wife.) He was also exceedingly high-minded, almost intolerably so; but he lived up to his own elevated standards.

Socrates attracted a large following from among the well-born young of Athens; unlike the Sophists, he refused to take fees from them. On these men he made a powerful impression; Plato said of him that "of all men then living we had ever met, [he was] the noblest and the wisest and the most just." Socrates had a very long career. He was born about 469 B.C. and was executed, at the age of 70, in 399 B.C. In that year, he was accused of impiety and of corrupting the young. By then, the Athenian empire was destroyed, and with it Athenian wealth; and the unhappy citizens were ready to hunt for witches. It is thought that the indictment was intended mainly as an indirect attack on Socrates' rich and aristocratic friends. His accusers probably expected him to go quietly into exile rather than face trial or conviction, and it is clear that he could have done so. But he stuck to his principles without wavering and drank the hemlock (a painless poison used in Athens for executions), full of good humor to the end. He seems to have had an extraordinarily keen mind; he was witty and of course addicted to disputation. He was unfailingly kind and considerate, altogether a noble man both in thought and in conduct.

There is, however, a great problem about describing the thought of Socrates because most of what we know about it comes from Plato. Plato, in addition to being the greatest of philosophers, was a literary genius, and it is impossible to tell how large an element of fiction there is in his presentation of Socrates. We know, for example, that Plato attributed to Socrates philosophical doctrines that were in fact developed by Plato himself long after Socrates was dead. On the other hand, it is agreed that on other occasions Plato faithfully represented what Socrates actually said. But where is the dividing line? This is one of the most extensively argued questions in all of classical scholarship, and there is no sure answer. But there is a widely accepted feeling that certain doctrines can justly be attributed to Socrates alone.

First of all, there is the famous "Socratic method." This consisted largely of asking questions until the person questioned was led to the conclusion Socrates regarded as the correct one. It depended on a mind agile enough to anticipate the thoughts of the person giving the answers. Socrates' mother had been a midwife, and he was fond of calling himself a midwife of thoughts. He was, he said, helping the other person give birth to thoughts that had already been conceived but not yet expressed. Usually, Socrates pretended that he was ignorant and eager to learn. This pretended ignorance is called Socratic irony, and it sometimes infuriated his antagonists, for whom the reader often feels a certain sympathy. Socrates and Plato both felt that education was a matter of inducing the pupil to remember what he knew before he was born, which he forgot at the time of birth; this, it will be seen, is connected with the doctrine of reincarnation. There is a famous example of the procedure in Plato's *Meno,* where Socrates questions a slave boy so carefully that he seems to lead the boy to give the solution of a problem in geometry that he could not possibly have known.

Socrates' questions, however, had another purpose. It was one of his basic contentions that people insisted on talking about things of which they could give no rational account. Socrates was asking, in effect, "How can you talk about justice unless you can say what it is?" His questions, therefore, were designed to find out just what people meant by the words they used: a requirement for precision in thought that no one had ever made before. He would often suggest several analogies, or comparisons, and the result was rather like the process of reaching a general conclusion by examining instances, something that in philosophy is known as induction, or inductive reasoning. Socrates seems to have invented this kind of reasoning.

Socrates' claim of ignorance, he said, was a conclusion he reached when the Delphic Oracle said that he was the wisest man in Greece. This astonished him until he realized that his wisdom consisted in recognizing his own ignorance; he was aware of his own limitations, where others made large claims for themselves. This was important because he held that virtue is knowledge and that it is necessary to have knowledge in order to act in a moral fashion. Wrong actions, he said, are the result of ignorance. Nobody does wrong knowingly; on the other hand, the actions of a man who thinks he knows but does not can lead to disaster. In his opinion, any skillful (or virtuous) man is skillful because he knows how to do something; in the widest sense, a virtuous man is one who is skilled in recognizing what is good and acts accordingly.

Beginning with Aristotle, people have objected to this idea on the ground that it leaves no room for strong emotions, which may lead a man to do something he knows is wrong. But Socrates was a notably self-controlled man, and he believed that others, given true knowledge, would be similarly free from heedless impulses. The most important thing a man could do was to take care of his own soul, and the way to do this began with the famous saying written on the temple at Delphi: "Know thyself." The man who knows himself is well on the way to wisdom.

With Socrates, we move from the half-mythical statements of the early philosophers and into the ordinary world of common sense where every opinion has to be examined by reason. His aims were practical, having to do with right conduct, rather than scientific; but whereas Greek science is now a matter of history, the questions of conduct raised by Socrates have to be answered by every man for himself, and they remain as alive and relevant today as they were twenty-five centuries ago. That is why Socrates, seen in the light shed by Plato's enormous genius, continues to make an impact on every new generation.

The Fourth Century: Greatness in Defeat

One night in the summer of 405 B.C., the people of Athens heard an outcry from the harbor at Piraeus. Wailing swept along the great walls toward the city, where it went from street to street until the whole city mourned. The cry began with the arrival of a trireme carrying the news that the Athenian fleet had been destroyed and its crews massacred, and people knew they could expect no mercy at the hands of her enemies, to whom they had shown none. There was a siege, but the situation was hopeless; Athenian power, and with it Athenian confidence and enthusiasm, was gone. The Athenians had thought that anything they did was right because they had power. They acted with great cruelty toward the defeated; they listened to bad advice from ambitious leaders; and now they had to face the consequences of their actions. The principal reason for the defeat of Athens was not the strength of her enemies but her own folly. In the disillusion that followed, men began to turn away from the here and now to lay up their treasures elsewhere.

Plato

Plato was born in 427 B.C. His family was one of the richest and most aristocratic in Athens, prominent in the city's life and politics for generations. Socrates, already middle-aged by the time Plato was born, was a friend of the family, and Plato must have known him from childhood. The social prominence of his family suggests that he might have been expected to go into politics, but he was so horrified by the execution of Socrates that he turned his back on public life. Nevertheless, politics remained one of his dominant interests, and his two longest books are devoted to what we would now call political science. It is possible that he traveled to Egypt, but at some point he returned to Athens to found a school there. Since it was in or near a public park which had once belonged to a semimythical man named Academus, the school was called the *Akademeia,* or Academy—the first of all academies and the seed of the modern university. Over the door of the building were inscribed the words "Let none but geometers enter here."

The Academy was quickly recognized as the most important school in Greece and existed for centuries afterward. In 367 B.C., however, Plato went to Sicily, where a man with whom he had connections had become ruler of Syracuse, giving Plato a chance to put some of his political ideas into practice. Plato set the ruler to studying mathematics, which he held to be a necessary part of the training of every politician, but not surprisingly, the project failed. Plato visited Syracuse a second time but went back to Athens for good in 360 B.C. He died in Athens in 347 B.C.

As a very young man, according to tradition (see page 137), Plato had wanted to write plays. It seems likely that the dialogue form (see below) in which he presented his ideas grew both from that early interest and from the Socratic question-and-answer method—certainly it was a natural form in a city as fortunate in its great drama as it was passionate in argumentation. In any case, Plato, alone of all the philosophers who have ever lived, was a literary genius. Other philosophers have written well—clearly and with a clean, vigorous prose style—but only Plato created works of literary imagination that can be read with pleasure by those who are not philosophers. It is not, of course, the case that Plato can be read for amusement; he was a rigorous thinker who demands much of his readers. But for sheer literary quality, Plato is unapproached by any other philosopher.

Furthermore, Plato wrote at length on subjects of basic interest to many nonphilosophers, and what he said has remained the starting point, through all the centuries since, for almost all other discussion of the same topics. The question most important to Plato, to which he devoted his longest works, is, "How can society be arranged so that men may live the best possible lives?" He lived at a time when traditional forms of social organization were being called into question. Men were increasingly unhappy and afraid, and Plato, disgusted with what the Athenians had done to themselves and to such a superior man as Socrates, tried to work out a social system that would not be subject to the whims of mobs of inferior men and would allow superior men the fullest scope for their superiority. His prescriptions have influenced every thinker on this subject and all the subjects related to it ever since. In the course of describing the ideal state, Plato found it necessary to consider the nature of the good life for individual men, the nature of the good itself, the requirements of education, the establishment of standards of judgment, and almost every other topic associated with these questions. Unlike Socrates, he was also passionately interested in science and cosmology, and most especially in geometry. He therefore worked out a philosophy of very broad scope.

The conclusions Plato reached about all these matters are presented in a series of dialogues of varying length. He invented this form, in which two or more people hold a conversation about a given subject; the dialogue was for over two thousand years one of the basic forms of philosophical exposition. Scholars agree that Plato's dialogues were written at intervals throughout his life and that they can be arranged in rough chronological order with a fair degree of certainty. The earliest ones are mostly quite short and consider such questions as "What is courage?" or "What is piety?" or "What is poetic inspiration?" These early dialogues are generally taken to represent the thought of Socrates; they show Socrates struggling with the problem of definition and inductive reasoning. *The Apology,* which recounts the speeches Socrates made at his trial in his own defense (that is the meaning of the title, a legal term in

Greek), seems to be one of Plato's earliest dialogues and was probably written soon after the death of Socrates. *Crito,* built around the conversations between Socrates and his friends during the thirty days between his condemnation and death, explains why Socrates would not violate the decision of the jury—and the law—even to save his own life; it was evidently written somewhat later than *The Apology* but still seems to come directly out of Plato's actual experience of Socrates. Crito was the name of a wealthy friend of Socrates who is the chief speaker in the dialogue other than Socrates himself. (*Phaedo,* later still in composition, includes a moving account of Socrates' death; its title is also a man's name, one of the philosopher's devoted followers.)

Dialogues written somewhat later, although Socrates continues to be the principal speaker, are thought to include Plato's additions to the positions taken by Socrates. These dialogues (such as *The Symposium*) are longer, and some are in fact very elaborate, taking up most of the problems in which Plato was interested. The dialogues written latest (*Timaeus* and *The Laws,* for example) are pure Plato; in some of them, the conversational form was all but abandoned, and the result is nearer a written-down lecture than a dialogue. Socrates, moreover, is no longer the leading figure, and the discourses are put into the mouths of other people. In *The Laws,* a long book written toward the end of Plato's life, the principal speaker is identified only as "the Athenian stranger." Some of the last dialogues are incomplete, apparently because Plato left them that way.

Plato's thought changed over the years covered by the dialogues. In general, his thought became more mathematical in character. It is said that in his lectures at the Academy, he emphasized mathematics even more than in his dialogues. At all periods, Plato's thought shows one curious and striking feature: a readiness to resort to myths of his own invention in order to make points that he could not prove. Some scholars think, for instance, that Plato invented the myth of the lost continent of Atlantis, which first appears in literature in one of his last dialogues (*Timaeus*). He repeatedly resorts to myth to describe the life of the soul after death.

PLATO'S THEORY OF REALITY. In general, Plato set a low value on the things of this life. His works are shot through with a dislike for things as they are and a zeal for a better, higher, more real world. "More real" is his expression; he insisted that the world we know through our senses is in every way inferior to and "less real" than the ideal world.

He despised the common man and had an aristocrat's indifference to his problems. He despaired of existing forms of government and loathed democracy. Pleasures of the body were of small interest to him; thinking, and more particularly philosophizing, was the only true source of satisfaction, and an ability to think rigorously, preferably based on training in mathematics, was the true object of education.

Plato felt that what we can perceive with our senses leads at best to right opinion but never to knowledge. Sense-experience deals with appearance only; nothing but pure thought can approach reality. The world of appearance, he said, is an inferior copy of the world of reality, and this is the doctrine most widely characterized as "Platonic." The world of reality, which we can approach only by thought, is made up of pure forms of which the things we see and touch are mere copies.

This doctrine of forms has great difficulties, of which Plato himself was aware. Just what is the relationship between things and forms? Plato sometimes spoke as if things were copies of forms, but he also said that things "participate" in the forms. It is not clear just what this meant. In its earliest stages, the doctrine had a moral meaning. There are, Plato said, forms of justice, temperance, courage, and the like. This is his answer to the difficulty raised by Socrates, who asked how people could talk about justice when they could not say what it is. There is a form of justice, which we can know with our minds and which gives us a way to see the difference between just and unjust men or actions. The highest form of all is the form of the good; other forms are subordinate to it or merely aspects of the form of the good. This established a ranking of forms, from low to high, with the form of the good at the top. It was easy to identify the form of the good with God; to some extent, Plato did, and later philosophers made no qualifications about it.

Plato incorporated criticisms of his beliefs in his own writings. For example, the dialogues include speakers who point out that if there are forms of the good to account for instances of the good, there must also be forms of other things, such as chairs and beds, of which actual chairs and beds are copies. This turns the forms into patterns, which are followed when things are made; Plato developed this line of thinking into an entire cosmogony, which shows the great Creator (or "Demiurge") fashioning the world after eternal patterns—a doctrine of enormous influence in later centuries.

Similarly, as other critics pointed out in the dialogues, if we are to believe that all things are modeled after ideal forms, there must be forms of bad things as well. Plato had to admit the force of this argument, and it made him uncomfortable. He got around it, eventually, by saying that matter, from which the Demiurge fashioned the world, has a kind of resistance to it that keeps it from being worked on freely: evil exists because the world, as finished, is imperfect. Hundreds of later thinkers solved the difficulty of the goodness of God and the existence of evil by concluding that evil is a kind of built-in quality of matter.

PLATO'S SOCIAL AND POLITICAL THOUGHT. The most famous of Plato's dialogues is *The Republic*. It is a book-length dialogue in which Plato describes the constitution of the ideal state—government as he would like to see it. The book begins with the question "What is justice?" Plato's answer (put into the mouth of Socrates, as the chief speaker) is that we can best examine the nature of the truly just man by describing the nature of the truly just state, a program that is then carried out in detail. In brief, the ideal state is one in which philosophers are kings. "Those who are now called kings and potentates," he says, "must learn to seek wisdom like true and genuine philosophers, and so political power and intellectual wisdom will be joined in one."

The society within Plato's ideal state will be arranged so as to put superior men in positions of command. Craftsmen —those who are mainly interested in the pursuit of gain—are at the bottom. In the middle are the guardians, trained in warfare. There is an analogy between these three divisions of the ideal state and the three parts of the soul, as Plato imagined it. At the bottom in the human soul, corresponding to the craftsmen, are the passions, which are unruly and must be kept in check or they will drag a man down into the mud. In the middle is man's sense of honor, which when offended reacts with anger and aggressiveness; this is perfectly proper, but honor must also be kept in check lest it lead a man astray. At the top, therefore, is reason, which should be in command at all times. It is perfectly plain that Plato had small regard either for most human emotions, which he regarded as base, or for the common man, whom he also regarded as base—and, since he is entirely dominated by his emotions, sure to lead the state to disaster if given power by democracy.

Plato's ideal state has a number of extraordinary features. Women, for instance, are to be treated as complete equals of men, right up to and including training as warriors; this was a radical notion since women occupied a very lowly position in most Greek city-states, particularly in Athens. The soldier-guardians are to live together and have no wives; women and children are to be held in common by all male citizens according to their rank. The education of the soldier-guardians, from among whom the philosopher-rulers are drawn, is described at length; the discussion concludes that most poetry, most kinds of music, and all stage plays are to be excluded entirely from the ideal state. In a characteristic argument, Plato holds that plays and pictures imitate the world perceived by the senses, which in turn is an imitation of the ideal world of forms. Most works of art are thus imitations of imitations and are therefore too degraded to be useful. They are also bad because they pander to our baser instincts; in short, proper education will avoid them.

Today, although we are not likely to accept the conclusions to which Plato's social theories led him, we can read the great dialogues with the keenest interest because Plato is able to convey the intensity and passion of his beliefs by virtue of his literary genius. Almost alone of all the great philosophers, he appeals to those who have no interest whatever in more technical philosophy: What he says comes across not as cold reasoning but as the profound convictions of a deeply committed man. The force of his moral convictions bridges the gulf between ourselves and him, and whether we agree with him or not, he engages our attention and our emotions in a way no other philosopher can touch. Reading Plato, of course, is not like reading a great novel or seeing a great play. The pleasures he offers are those of the study, not those of the active world. But for the willing reader, the rewards can be great.

Aristotle

Just what is meant by the pleasure of reading Plato can be illustrated by a comparison with Aristotle (384–322 B.C.). Aristotle was a very great philosopher; he is also one of the most difficult to read. As a young man, he wrote works said to have possessed great literary merit, but they are almost entirely lost. The books that have come down to us were notes for lectures or for private use, not intended for general circulation. By any standards, Aristotle's *Metaphysics* is one of the most difficult books ever written. It is also one of the most influential.

The contrast between Plato and Aristotle goes farther. Aristotle is fair-minded and tolerant. His tone is mild and unemotional; his books are matter-of-fact and without literary frills. There is nothing whatever otherworldly about him; he rejected Plato's theory of forms, and his interests are entirely in things as they are, not as they might be. His works do not engage us as Plato's do; they appeal entirely to the mind.

Aristotle was born in Stagira in northern Greece. His father was a doctor who worked for the king of Macedonia. When Aristotle was about eighteen, he was sent to Athens to enroll in Plato's Academy, where he spent twenty years. It was during these years that he wrote the dialogues widely known in ancient times but now largely lost. When Plato died (in 347 B.C.), Aristotle left Athens for the town of Assos in Asia Minor, where he married, and then for the island of Lesbos. About 342 B.C., he received an invitation from the king of Macedonia to become tutor to his son; Aristotle was thus the student of the greatest thinker of the ancient world, and he became the teacher of its greatest ruler, for the Macedonian prince was Alexander the Great. He became king in 336 B.C. (at the age of nineteen), and Aristotle returned to Athens.

In Athens, the Academy was now under the direction of a man whose viewpoint Aristotle found unsympathetic, and he therefore set up a school of his own, possibly with financial support from the court in Macedonia; it was called the Lyceum after an existing gymnasium and exercise ground of that name. In 323 B.C., Alexander died, and the people of Athens, deluded for the moment by the hope that they could act independently of their Macedonian rulers, sought to get rid of Aristotle by bringing against him, on particularly absurd grounds, the good old Athenian charge of impiety. Aristotle simply left Athens, thus depriving her of her chief claim to importance, and went to Chalcis, not far away, where he died at the age of sixty-three. The Lyceum continued to function without him.

Aristotle's philosophy is, in general, highly technical, and every aspect of it is tightly interwoven with every other aspect. This makes it particularly difficult to summarize since it is hard to grasp the meaning of any segment until the entire system is understood. Furthermore, Aristotle's writings cover almost every conceivable theoretical topic of interest to thinking people. He made a major contribution, for instance, to the development of biology. During his years at Assos and on Lesbos, he seems to have undertaken extensive biological researches, as a result of which he was able to lay the groundwork for the scheme of genus and species according to which plants and animals are classified to this day. The accuracy and refinement of his biological descriptions were unsurpassed for centuries, in some cases right down to modern times.

Aristotle's interest in biology helps us to understand his philosophical point of view. He saw all change and motion in terms of biological growth. Just as an acorn turns into an oak tree, so, in Aristotle's thought, all change tends from potentiality to actuality. Futhermore, just as the growth of an acorn into an oak tree realizes the form of an oak tree (which the acorn is said to have potentially), so, in Aristotle's thought, all change moves toward actualization of form. He rejected Plato's notion of form as something beyond the senses and said that forms exist only in things, which are combinations of form and matter. Aristotle's scheme, therefore, is expressed in terms of movement from matter and the potential on the one hand, toward form and the actual on the other.

Aristotle held that everything tends toward the realization of an end, or purpose. An acorn has, of course, an actual form—that of an acorn—and from this point of view may be taken as the end of a process of nature. At the same time, it has, potentially, the form of an oak tree. Its purpose, or goal, is to make an oak tree by realizing the form inherent in it. The same thing is true of almost anything else: It is actual from one point of view but from another has a potentiality to be something else.

This scheme is expressed in Aristotle's statement that everything has four causes, all of which must be described in order to account for anything fully. These four causes are the formal, the material, the efficient, and the final: that is, the form of anything (what it is), the matter out of which it is made (its material), the thing or person that made it (how it was made—the efficient cause), and the purpose or end for which it was made (the final cause). A house has a form: its floor plan. It has a material cause: brick or wood. It has an efficient cause: its builder. And it has a goal, or final cause: to shelter a family. (The scheme is not always so easy to apply.)

Modern readers may find this doctrine baffling at first because we tend to think of cause and effect in terms of events: when one billiard ball strikes another and makes it move, we focus on the striking and tend to regard as irrelevant such questions as "What is the billiard ball made of?" and "Why was it made to strike another ball?" Aristotle, however, thought in terms of things, not in terms of events.

For him, the most important cause was the final cause: he wanted an answer to the question "For what purpose did the change occur?" To answer this question, he thought, you had to take into account what the thing is made of and what form it has; and the whole process is thought of as moving from a state of potentiality to a state of actuality.

Since Aristotle looked on nature as organized into genera and species, it was not difficult for him to think of the entire world as arranged in order. In theory (but not in fact), unformed, characterless matter would be at the bottom and pure form, without substance, at the top. Unformed matter is nothing but potentiality; pure form without substance is nothing but actuality. The whole direction of the cosmos is from potentiality to actuality. Pure actuality, the completely realized form at the top of the hierarchy, is God. Man is below God in the structure and animals below man. The whole strives toward God in an attempt to become more like God. Since God is completely actual already, He has no motion and undergoes no change. But the cosmos desires to be like Him, so that God causes movement without being moved: He is the unmoved mover, the final cause of the whole world, the reason why, ultimately, the acorn changes into an oak.

This is without any question the most magnificent intellectual concept of God ever reached by the mind of man. Once one grasps the scope and power of Aristotle's vision, it becomes apparent why it dominated Western thought for so many centuries. His philosophy remains to this day the backbone of Catholic thought.

Aristotle's enormous scheme is expounded in books on a variety of subjects. In addition to books on biology, there is one on nature, called by its ancient editors the *Physics*. There is one on being in general and on the nature of God, which the ancient editors placed after the *Physics* and simply called "the book that comes after the physics," for which the Greek word is *Metaphysics* (the word used ever since for speculations about the ultimate nature of things). There is a book on politics, discussing the theory of government; one on the nature of the mind, called *Psychology* — the first of all the books on the subject; one on rhetoric; and one called the *Poetics,* which is actually mostly about drama, and tragedy in particular. Finally, and of first importance, there are books on logic and two books on ethics. The books on logic were particularly influential; what Aristotle had to say on the subject constituted the main body of all books on logic right down to the twentieth century.

The Hellenistic World

The death of Alexander the Great in 323 B.C., followed the next year by the death of Aristotle, is generally taken as marking the beginning of the Hellenistic period. The one area in which definite advances continued to be made was science. During the two centuries following Aristotle's death, some thinkers (all Greek) achieved new results; but their work came to nothing. As time went by, all standards declined, and the history of the Hellenistic world, however rich and diverse it may be, is one of cultural failure, slow at first and with moments of revival, but in the end increasingly rapid, until darkness set in.

There were two important schools of Hellenistic philosophy, both of them schools in the literal sense because each was associated with an academic institution in Athens. One was the Epicurean, named for its founder Epicurus (about 342–270 B.C.); the other was the Stoic, named for the *stoa*, or porch, where the school was held (its followers were called Stoics). Of these, the Stoics were the more important. Stoicism was the most widespread single philosophical doctrine of the Hellenistic Age, and at a time when few took the old gods seriously any more, it attracted many Romans of the ruling classes.

The goal of all popular Hellenistic philosophy was to attain freedom from suffering; in their various ways, the competing doctrines all prescribed emotional and moral disciplines whose aim was to help men avoid pain. It is not surprising that so little original thinking was done.

Epicureanism

Epicurus was born on the island of Samos, studied at Athens, taught in various places, and in 306 B.C. returned to Athens to found his school in a garden outside the walls. He died in Athens about 270 B.C. He wrote extensively, but only three rather long letters and a compilation of quotations survive. But we have extensive knowledge of Epicurean doctrine from another source: During the last century before Christ, the Roman poet Lucretius, mentioned earlier, adopted the Epicurean philosophy and wrote a long poem to explain it, particularly the scientific views associated with it. This poem, called *De Rerum Natura (On the Nature of Things)*, is regarded as one of the greatest of all Latin poems. Lucretius lived in a period of unparalleled brutality, during which Rome almost succeeded in destroying herself with civil wars. He used verse, he says, in order to make the doctrine more palatable. None of what he said, however, was original, so that he is admired as a poet but not as a philosopher.

Although today we associate Epicureanism with the pursuit of pleasure, this is not what Epicurus actually recommended. In fact, he specifically opposed strong pleasures because they are disturbing. His real goal was *ataraxia*, which means peace of mind or freedom from worry. To attain it, he recommended restfulness, freedom from desires, avoidance of all strong passions. In order to provide a scientific underpinning for his position, he took over the atomism of Democritus (see page 300). Epicurus used the theory to explain away all sorts of natural phenomena that, if not understood, might upset people. His interest was not scientific; he wanted merely to provide some explanation or other so as to reassure his followers. The gods, he said, exist, but they live happily in a world far beyond ours and have no interest in mere mortals. Death is not to be feared because it is merely dissolution of the soul into the atoms of which it is made. While alive, we must try to be happy, and to be happy, one must renounce worldly position and pleasures. "Live unknown" was the great maxim of Epicureanism; an obscure, tranquil, even life was held to be the best. It was in some ways a noble and attractive doctrine that continued to draw followers throughout antiquity; but it was not a doctrine suitable to the busy life of Roman administrators working hard to govern an unruly empire.

Stoicism

There is no great body of Stoic literature comparable to the poem of Lucretius. The founder of the school was a man named Zeno (about 335–265 B.C.), who came from Citium, on Cyprus. He may have been of Phoenician descent; in any case, he does not seem to have been Greek, although he wrote and taught in Greek. Possibly about 308 B.C., he went to Athens and founded his school. In time, he attracted a great following, and at his death he was given a state funeral by the city of Athens. Only fragments of his writings survive. Our knowledge of his doctrines depends on summaries by later writers, many of them Roman. Cicero (106–43 B.C.), for instance, who wrote extensively on philosophical subjects, treated Stoic doctrines in several of his books. The

The Hellenistic World 321

chief source, however, is the *Discourses* of Epictetus (about A.D. 60–117), which are apparently stenographic reports of lectures and informal discussions taken down by the pupils of this man, who, born a slave, was freed by his master and was active in Rome until the Emperor Domitian banished all philosophers about A.D. 94. Epictetus then moved to Epirus in western Greece, where he founded a school and taught until his death. The *Discourses* is almost entirely concerned with the moral aspects of Stoicism, ignoring questions of physics.

Like Epictetus, the *Meditations* of Marcus Aurelius (A.D. 121–180) is moral in purpose. The book has the added interest of coming from the pen of the man who, as Emperor after A.D. 161, stood at the perilous summit of the Roman world. The Roman Empire was visibly in profound difficulties over which the Emperor had little control, and the *Meditations*, which does not claim to be original philosophical thinking, is a notable example of the Stoic spirit. It was written in Greek, the language of scholarship for Romans.

In the *Meditations*, Marcus Aurelius urges himself to endure with equanimity whatever may come his way: This is Stoicism in action. (Unlike *epicurean*, the word *stoic* as we use it today still means pretty much what it did in ancient times.) The philosophical doctrine was that suffering is caused not by events but by our reaction to events; more particularly, we receive through our senses impressions of the outside world, and over these we have no control; but how we react to these impressions is up to us. The goal of the Stoics was *apatheia* (literally, *unsuffering*), by which the Stoics meant a deliberate refusal to react emotionally to events — a view not at all incompatible with action. What Marcus Aurelius was experiencing when he found it, as a matter of unfortunate policy, advisable to feed Christians to the lions was *apatheia*. This notion, it will be seen, would stand by a politician in almost any distasteful situation; hence its attraction for Roman administrators.

There was more to Stoicism than *apatheia*, however. It took over from Heraclitus the notion of fire as the principal substance; fire, in Stoic teaching, is a kind of divine principle spread through the entire cosmos. This idea yielded the concept that the cosmos is both material and at the same time divine. The Stoics therefore believed that in a sense everything is God, including the divine spark in man.

The Stoics also held that the universe is cyclic: that is, that the entire history of the world repeats itself over enormous spans of time. Therefore, everything that happens is bound to happen; it has all happened before and will happen again according to the plan of an all-wise and all-good God. Evil is inevitable, and we have no choice but to put up with it. Peace of mind can be secured insofar as a man's conduct approximates the divine will. Exercise of man's free will aligns his thought with God's, and he is then in harmony with the events of the world, which are planned by God; man accepts what happens to him. This was called "living in accordance with nature," which in practice involved dislike for physical luxuries as well as efforts (such as those of Marcus Aurelius) to rise above unfortunate circumstances.

Stoic doctrine led to one more remarkable idea. Since the world was regarded as all of a piece and divine, it followed that every man in it shares in this divinity: All men, therefore, are brothers, fellow members of the city of the world. This is a truly high-minded doctrine, but men have always failed to live up to it. As an ethical creed, Stoicism was an admirable and noble teaching regardless of how open to criticism its details may be, and it is not surprising that until the rise of Christianity it attracted more adherents among the educated than any other doctrine.

The Final Flowering of Ancient Science

In view of the handicaps under which the ancient thinkers worked, it is remarkable that they achieved as much as they did in science. Among the obvious handicaps was their numbering system, which, as we noted earlier, contained no zero. This meant, for example, that the development of real algebra was impossible, so that they had no mathematical language in which to formulate the elementary laws of mechanics. They had, of course, remarkably little machinery; they designed and built some remarkably complicated war engines (for throwing rocks and the like), but, hampered by the primitive state of metallurgy, they failed to develop any but the crudest labor-saving devices. They knew, of course, about the magnetic effects of lodestone and amber but failed to develop even a speculative explanation. They were, in short, men who worked on the world with only one tool: their minds.

Hand in hand with the lack of equipment went the failure to devise an experimental method. Experiments of a sort were performed; for instance, men tried to measure the size of the earth, using shadows. But they never developed the notion that isolated parts of natural processes could be observed and measured and the results generalized. Advances were made principally in three fields that emphasized observation and reasoning alone and had no need for laboratories: geometry, medicine, and astronomy.

Students are sometimes astonished to discover that there were no Roman scientists at all, but that is the case. The Romans were not interested in mathematics; even such writers as the famous architect Vitruvius (in a book on architecture written during the reign of Augustus and dedicated to him) show a distaste for simple calculations. The Roman numbering system was, of course, cumbersome (try multiplying CLIV by LXIX without using Arabic numerals). The Romans' contribution to science was limited to compiling information based on Greek sources, and even in this they were often quite uncritical, making no distinction between confirmed facts and the wildest fairy stories. The Romans did, however, accomplish some remarkable technological feats; some of their roads and aqueducts are still in use today. Their technological ability was far in advance of what Europeans could do for centuries afterward; they knew, for instance, how to use concrete in roads and buildings, a technique entirely lost in the Middle Ages. In general, however, the Romans were simply indifferent to science, which remained a Greek monopoly.

During the Hellenistic period, Alexandria replaced Athens as the principal intellectual center of the Greek world, a position it held until long after Rome had declined. Founded in the Nile Delta by Alexander the Great in 331 B.C., it was the capital of the dynasty of Greek rulers of Egypt founded by Ptolemy I (about 367–283 B.C.), and the city's intellectual life was thoroughly Greek despite its African location. (Cleopatra was a descendant of this Ptolemy.) These rulers founded the Museum, with its famous library, which was devoted to the pursuit of contemporary knowledge of all sorts.

Mathematics

By the time Alexandria had risen to prominence, geometry had reached a very high level of development. All that the Greeks had learned about geometry over several hundred years was summed up in the *Elements* of Euclid (about 323–285 B.C.), the greatest mathematical treatise of ancient times. Almost nothing is known about the life of Euclid. He may have been trained at the Academy after Plato's death; he is thought to have started a school of his own at Alexandria in the time of Ptolemy I. Plane and solid geometry as studied in schools today has been rewritten for modern use, but all the knowledge was contained in Euclid's book. Although several original proofs are associated with Euclid, his achievement was apparently not so much in original mathematics as in the systematic presentation of a body of knowledge, an undertaking that in itself has had a vast influence on the history of mathematics.

The distinction between definitions, postulates, axioms, and propositions was a major accomplishment of Euclid and set standards for all subsequent mathematicians. The famous example is Euclid's fifth postulate about parallel lines (that they do not meet no matter how far they are extended). The fact that Euclid recognized this postulate as an unproved assumption shows great precision of thought. Although the Euclidian view of parallel lines seems obviously true, in the nineteenth century mathematicians were able to use a different set of assumptions to construct the "non-Euclidian" geometries that paved the way for Einstein, the twentieth-century physicist whose theories have helped to revolutionize modern physics.

Another great name among Greek mathematicians is Archimedes (about 287–212 B.C.). Although he studied at Alexandria, Archimedes was born and lived in the Greek city of Syracuse, in Sicily, and there he was killed by Roman soldiers when they captured the city. He is generally regarded as the greatest mathematician of antiquity. He wrote a number of books, many concerned with the areas and volumes of special curved surfaces and solids, and he developed the mathematical methods called reduction to absurdity and the method of exhaustion. Archimedes solved the ancient Greek problem of expressing very large numbers precisely when he calculated the number of grains of sand that would fill the universe. Because his work extended into so many aspects of mathematics and even led him to the threshold of calculus, it is far too technical to permit brief summary.

Alone among ancient thinkers, Archimedes is connected with several practical applications of mathematical principles that he discovered. His inventions included lever and pulley devices which, incorporated in war machines, stretched the Roman siege of Syracuse to three years. A device for raising water to a higher level, known as the screw of Archimedes, was used along the Nile until modern times.

A third great name among the Greek mathematicians is

Apollonius of Perga, who lived toward the end of the third century and the beginning of the second (200 B.C.). Like Euclid, he taught at Alexandria. His most important book is *A Treatise on Conic Sections*. Later thinkers continued the work of the major figures already mentioned, most notably the Alexandrian Diophantus of the fourth century A.D. (He seems to have had access to Babylonian knowledge and managed to deal with algebraic procedures despite the inadequate methods of notation that were all he had available to him. There was, for example, a sign for subtraction but none for addition, and only one unknown could be expressed). Apart from Diophantus, however, original mathematical thought had largely disappeared from the ancient world by the beginning of the Christian era.

Medicine

The achievements of the Greek physicians survive today in the name of Hippocrates (about 460–377 B.C.), although he did not in fact formulate the famous Hippocratic Oath still administered to new doctors. He came from the island of Cos near the southwest corner of Asia Minor. There is no way of knowing exactly what he wrote, but there grew up, associated with his name, a group of books on medical practice known as the Hippocratic *corpus*, which summed up Greek medical knowledge of the time. This knowledge was, of course, rudimentary by modern standards, although it was better than anything known until centuries later. Perhaps the most important achievement of these early doctors was the foundation of medical practice on a firm basis of observation and experience. Since there were almost no systematic methods of cure, the emphasis of medicine had to be on nutrition and a healthy regimen. The books developed the doctrine of humors (blood, phlegm, yellow bile, black bile) that was so popular during the Renaissance; Hippocratic treatment stressed the importance of establishing the proper balance of these fluids in the body. Despite their elementary knowledge of physiology, the Hippocratic doctors successfully identified and described many diseases, an important achievement even if they could not provide cures.

Cos became one of the great medical centers of the ancient world; people traveled there from all over the Mediterranean seeking relief from their symptoms. Another center grew up in the city of Cnidus in Asia Minor, and a third in Sicily. Doctors at Cnidus developed the practice of ausculation (listening while thumping—doctors still do it). Alexandria, however, eventually became the principal medical center of the ancient world and continued in that position for centuries. Among those active there was Erasistratus, who was born on Cos but practiced in Alexandria during the third century B.C. He made detailed studies of the nerves and the brain, and he was the first to say that veins and arteries are connected, although his statement was a guess that he could not prove because he had no magnifying instruments.

The last and in some ways the greatest doctor of antiquity was, with the astronomer Ptolemy (see below), one of the two great figures of the second century A.D. who summed up the scientific knowledge of the ancient world for the benefit of the centuries of scientific ignorance that followed. His name was Galen (about A.D. 130-201). He practiced at Rome, but he was born in the Greek city of Pergamum in Asia Minor where he also probably died. Galen wrote an enormous body of scientific works. His experiments in anatomy were based chiefly on dissection of animals rather than of human corpses, which was now illegal in Rome. Nevertheless, he made remarkable physiological discoveries. Unfortunately, he also entertained a variety of false notions that he allowed to distort his conclusions—and, consequently, those of generations of medieval physicians who took his books as final authorities.

Astronomy

Greek astronomy ruled the mind of Western men until the sixteenth century, when, to the outrage of the Establishment of the day, someone dared to suggest that the earth revolved around the sun. (This possibility had, in fact, been anticipated by a Greek but was rejected by other Greeks, who had no telescopes, as contrary to what can be observed.)

The greatest of ancient astronomers was Claudius Ptolemaeus, better known as Ptolemy, not to be confused with the various rulers of Egypt who had the same name. He lived and worked at Alexandria in the second century A.D. and wrote a number of books of enormous influence. The most famous of them is the *Almagest,* a name given his *Mathematical Treatise* by Arab scholars in the Middle Ages. (It means "the greatest.") This book gives a complete account of the ancient system of astronomy, which saw the earth as the center of the universe; it combines the older theories on the subject with Ptolemy's own contributions in a brilliant synthesis. The result is a monstrously complicated system, entirely sterile, although it did yield quite accurate predictions of the movements of the stars and planets. But it is a monument of ingenuity and intellect. Ptolemy also compiled a catalogue of the stars based on the work of his predecessors; it remained useful until modern times.

Religion and Philosophy Under the Romans

With Ptolemy and Galen, the scientific impulse disappeared from the ancient world. By the third century A.D., the Greco-Roman civilization was old and felt itself to be old. Most educated Romans knew nothing about Plato, and the philosophical impulses that had inspired the Greeks had been forgotten (except by specialists) in a rich and barbaric Empire that was mortally ill. Thought in the late Empire was concerned largely with grammar and education–and the gradual union of Greek traditions with the doctrines of Christianity.

Roman Religion

The Roman religion that Christianity replaced was a blend of native Roman elements, Greek elements, and strange creeds imported from the East. Greek and Roman religion had, to begin with, certain things in common. The chief Roman god, for instance, was Jupiter, whose name is merely a Latin version of *Zeus pater* ("Zeus the father"). This was not a borrowing; the two gods are descended from the same Indo-European source, and both were originally sky-gods. But because the Romans, at first not much inclined to literature, failed to write down their own traditions, it is not clear just what their native religion consisted of. By the time of the earliest documentary evidence, the Romans' borrowings from their Greek neighbors in Italy were already extensive. Much of what scholars now believe about early Roman religion was therefore established by inference rather than from direct evidence. Certain things are clear, however.

The Roman gods were much vaguer than the Greek gods. Because the comparatively unimaginative Romans were less inclined to make up stories and attribute definite characteristics to their deities, there was very little Roman mythology. (Some was invented later in imitation of the Greeks.) Almost

328 Philosophy, Religion, and Science

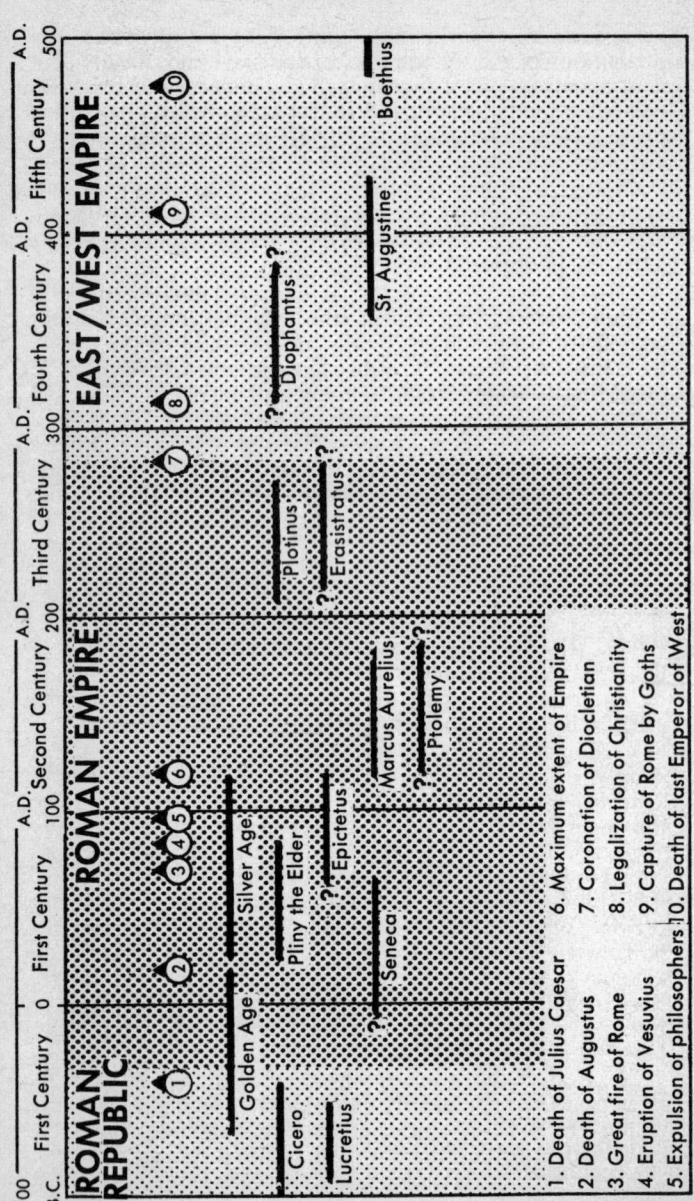

every commonplace activity was felt to be infused with religious spirit, and there were, accordingly, gods for almost every important class of objects. The Roman word for religious spirit was *numen,* which originally meant much the same as *mana* (see page 282). (The English word derived from *numen* is *numinous,* meaning, roughly, holy or awe-inspiring.) The Romans regarded anything awe-inspiring, or anything that someone hoped would be awe-inspiring, as numinous; Roman Emperors were, in later days, declared to be gods even while still living.

Originally, this idea of the numinous was applied to such important items as boundary markers (for which the word was *terminus*), which were felt to be holy. There was, accordingly, a god called Terminus, the boundary-marker god. There were similar gods for doorsteps, for crops, for doors (he was called Janus and was two-faced; January is named for him since it is the opening month of the year), and so on, in staggering profusion. The best-known deities of this kind were the Lares and Penates (almost always plural). These very common deities were also very ancient, so that their origins are not known. The Lares were simply gods of the household or even of an entire city. Pious people offered food to them at every meal. They may have begun as farmland deities or as ancestral spirits. The Penates were the gods of the storeroom or of the family wealth in general. In any case, the Romans themselves kept mixing up the Lares and Penates so that in early times they were lumped together and lost whatever differences they may once have had.

There were also several distinctively Roman presiding deities. Mars, the god of war, was an important one, far more so than his Greek equivalent Ares. Vesta, the goddess of the hearth, was given special treatment; she is a relative of the Greek Hestia, who never, however, attained the importance of Vesta. Vesta's attendants had to be maidens and are therefore known as the Vestal Virgins. There were six of them, chosen from among the daughters of the oldest aristocracy, to serve for thirty years. Their job was to tend the fire of the official hearth of the city of Rome, kept in the Temple of Vesta. The fire was never supposed to go out; if it did, there was an elaborate ritual for relighting it, starting literally from scratch. (Two pieces of wood had to be rubbed together.) There were harsh penalties for any Vestal Virgin who took a lover.

Apart from Mars and Vesta, the Roman gods tended to be overwhelmed by their Greek counterparts, so that the Romans gradually forgot their own myths. The Roman wine-god was Liber Pater, for example, but he was given the Greek name Bacchus early on, and it stuck. Apollo was borrowed from the Greeks without any Latin antecedent. Herakles, Latinized as Hercules, was borrowed and turned into a god, even though for the Greeks he had been only a hero or at most a demigod. (The Greeks admired brains, the Romans muscle.)

The chief characteristic of Roman religion was its obsession with the exact execution of sacred rites. These rites involved sacrifice, a custom the Romans had in common with the Greeks; but while it is possible for the modern mind to see at least some religious content in Greek sacrificial practice, Roman customs are remarkably unappealing. The relationship between the god and the individual was not one of worship; it was a question of "I'm doing something for you, and you've got to do something for me in return." The emphasis was always on the correct performance of the rites, down to the smallest detail; if even the slightest error was made, the whole ceremony had to be repeated. Since the ceremony might last several days and involve thousands of actions and hundreds of animals, it might be staggeringly expensive to repeat the whole business, but no matter; if some trivial detail went wrong, the whole thing had to be done over. Any inward quality of the kind we associate with religion was completely lacking.

Like the Greeks, the Romans believed in the foretelling of the future by watching the flights of birds or examining the entrails of certain animals. Just exactly how the speed, direction, number, and height of a flight of birds were interpreted is no longer known. Temple priests also developed an elaborate system for predicting events by examining the vital organs, especially the livers, of sheep and other animals; it was believed, for example, that such detailed information as the existence of a plot on the life of the Emperor could be determined from the liver of a freshly slaughtered sheep. It need hardly be added that the birds and livers could be manipulated for the benefit of any powerful person who wanted to impress the populace, and the opportunities were not overlooked. Educated persons, of course, often thought the whole business foolish.

It may be asked how so dim and repellent a religion could satisfy the spiritual needs of the Roman people. The answer is that it did not. Belief in the old religion declined rapidly after the conquering Romans were exposed to foreign notions, and by the first century B.C., Roman religion was near collapse. Under Augustus, there was a revival, but the gap between official practice and actual belief grew wider. Foreign deities were imported wholesale. Astrology became an almost universally accepted practice. The Great Mother Cybele, an ancient deity from northern Greece, was widely worshiped. Mithraism, a religion holding that the universe is the scene of an almost endless battle between the forces of good and the forces of evil, became the favorite religion of Roman soldiers; initiation seems to have included being bathed in the blood of a freshly slaughtered bull. Various forms of Gnosticism, some of them Christian heresies, were widespread. They had in common the ancient Greek belief that the soul is imprisoned in the body and seeks release from the world and a return to heaven; to a small and elite band, Gnosticism held out the promise of secret knowledge that would make the chaos of the universe intelligible. It is no wonder, in this welter of superstition and degraded religious belief, that Christianity spread so rapidly.

The End of Philosophy

In the midst of the decadent thought of the later Empire, it comes as a surprise to discover that in the third century A.D. a man of genuine philosophical stature managed to write a book of permanent philosophical interest: Plotinus (205–270 A.D.). Knowledge of Plato and study of his work had never died out in Alexandria. A group of men studying there developed Plato's thought into the religious system which we call Neo-Platonism. The school had great influence on Christian theology. Philosophers in this tradition held, in general, that Plato had answered every question and never erred, but they entertained no such attitude toward Aristotle, whose work they also knew. Plotinus was the greatest of these thinkers. Despite the fact that one of his pupils wrote a biography of him, very little is known about Plotinus simply because he refused to tell anybody about himself. It is thought that he was Greek; certainly he wrote in Greek. He may have been born in Egypt. In A.D. 232, he arrived in Alexandria where he studied the Neo-Platonism of the day. At the age of forty, he went to Rome, where he died. His writings were collected and edited by a pupil, who gave to them the name *Enneads,* from the Greek word for *nine,* since each of the six sections of the book has nine chapters.

The philosophy of Plotinus is developed from details of Plato's dialogues, especially certain late dialogues, and it is almost impossible to make sense of it in a summary apart from the dialogues in question. Plotinus was a believer in the contemplative life, the goal of which is union with God. Oriental forms of this belief, which is called mysticism, have received much attention in recent years, but the practice is as common in the West as in the East. With the exception of Plotinus, however, all the great Western mystics have been Christian. Although technically pagan, the philosophy of Plotinus exhibits no trace of any official religion of any kind. It is an account of the world in terms of mystical experience.

Inspired by Plato's dialogue *Timaeus,* Plotinus believed that the cosmos has an orderly arrangement, from lowest to highest. At the top, there is the Good, which he also calls the One. The Good is beyond the limitation of form. Below the Good is Intellect, derived from the Good by a process to which the name *emanation* is usually given; it is a kind of spontaneous overflow that then turns back on the Good in contemplation, thereby generating Intellect. Similarly, Intellect gives out Soul, which at its highest is in contact with Intellect, and at its lowest with Body. Intellect is in eternity, but Soul is in time and in continuous movement, making things that embody forms (in the Platonic sense). Man can be concerned with physical nature and usually is, but his higher impulses are concerned with Intellect, and by means of Intellect he may even rise to union with the One. The *Enneads* are not easy reading and contain many chapters of dry philosophical exposition; but when Plotinus comes to talk about the mystical union with the One, his language catches fire and sometimes rises to an impressive and moving beauty.

Plotinus was the last major figure of strictly philosophical interest in the ancient world. Roman genius devoted itself to law, not to philosophy or science, and in the late Empire the best minds were attracted by Christianity and the problems of Christian theology. But at the very end of the Western Empire, one Christian theologian cast his nets so wide that what he wrote is of lasting philosophical interest. He was St. Augustine (A.D. 354–430). Born in the small African town of Thagaste, in what is now Algeria, he had a conventional Latin education, which by this time was entirely literary. Alone among the great ancient thinkers, Augustine could not read Greek; all the philosophical thought he knew came to him in translation. He obtained an official position in the Imperial court, at that time in Milan, and there he came into contact with the work of Plotinus, which made it intellectually possible for him to adopt Christianity.

Augustine, of all the ancient thinkers, has the special appeal that comes from knowing a good deal about his life in his own words. His *Confessions,* written after his conversion to Christianity, is a moving and highly personal account of his youth as a talented Roman student searching for some truth to anchor his life to. Augustine's *City of God,* his major work of Christian theology, describes the ideal Christian commonwealth and spiritual order. In Christian thought, it parallels and is no less important or comprehensive than Plato's *Republic,* eight centuries earlier.

From Plotinus, Augustine got the idea that the world beyond the senses could be real and could form the unchanging standard against which the changing world of the senses could be judged. The realm of God, beyond the senses, was for Augustine more real than the world we know. From Plato through Plotinus to Augustine, the otherworldliness of the Greeks flowed into Christian theology and became part of the Western frame of reference, taken for granted by most people at most times and abandoned by great numbers of people only in very recent years, as history is measured. Augustine combined the Christian sense of divinity with the reality of Plato, as interpreted by Plotinus, and the result was a tool that allowed him to expound Christian doctrine systematically and lay the foundations of Christian theology.

Augustine became bishop of Hippo, a city in North Africa. He survived the sack of Rome by the Goths in A.D. 410 and the other barbarian invasions of his time; as he lay on his death bed, the Vandals were at the gates of Hippo. The Empire collapsed; for a brief period before the final dissolution, it was ruled by barbarian Emperors who, although Christian, were only slightly civilized.

We get one last echo of the Greek tradition from this time of afterglow. In the sixth century, a man named Boethius (about A.D. 480-525) set out to translate the major works of the ancients into Latin in order to make them accessible to scholars of his generation. He managed to complete a book on Aristotle's logic that became the standard logic textbook of the Dark Ages and was all they knew of Aristotle. But the Emperor Theodoric arrested Boethius for treason; in prison, awaiting execution, Boethius wrote *On the Consolation of Philosophy,* which became one of the favorite books of the Middle Ages and has, rather remarkably, enjoyed a certain popularity ever since. It is a dialogue between Boethius and Philosophia. It argues that although a man may be in chains, his mind is free to approach God, and thus he may escape the force of circumstance.

The remarkable thing about Boethius' book is its doctrinal

neutrality. Although it contains nothing offensive to Catholic doctrine, at no point does it make any Christian reference, and the Bible is never cited. Scholars have argued over whether or not Boethius, in prison, abandoned his Christian faith. No one knows. But the nonreligious character of *On the Consolation of Philosophy* makes it the last philosophical work of ancient times—or perhaps the first of the Middle Ages. In any case, as civilization slowly dissolved into the wastes of the tenth century, the little book comforted monks who, even when educated enough to know what they had lost, no longer had the ability to emulate the vigor of the Greek mind.

FOR FURTHER READING

Suggesting books to supplement this chapter presents some difficulties: the most important original works are difficult for the non-specialist; and those works that are accessible to the beginning student are not of central importance. The great exception is the early dialogues of Plato most directly concerned with Socrates. Aristotle's *Poetics*—his philosophy of art presented in terms of the classical Greek drama—is short and fairly easy to follow if one has read some Greek drama, but even this is not without difficulty; otherwise, Aristotle is best approached through commentators.

In the field of classical religion, there are a number of entertaining modern retellings of the Greek and Roman myths, but they are of limited value without interpretation in terms of specifically religious belief and practice. An interesting and different approach to the matter of Greek myth and legend is to be found in *Hercules, My Shipmate*, a witty and realistic novel by the British poet and classical scholar Robert Graves, which brings together most of Greece's pre-Homeric heroes in the exciting story of the quest for the Golden Fleece (although all of the Argonauts passed from legend into mythology and finally to deification, their ship, the *Argo*, was preserved into historic times).

In science, although there are few basic works that can be recommended for the beginning student, there are several good modern and not too technical histories.

In the following lists, an asterisk indicates a paperback edition.

Philosophy

Basic Works

* Banbrough, Remford, ed. *The Philosophy of Aristotle*. New York: New American Library, 1963. A selection, with commentary; new translations by A. E. Wardman and J. L. Creed. Includes the *Poetics* and parts of Aristotle's other important philosophical works. (For his scientific books, see, for example, *The Basic*

Works of Aristotle, edited by Richard McKeon, New York: Random House, 1941.)

* Fremantle, Anne, ed. *The Age of Belief; The Medieval Philosophers.* New York: New American Library, 1954. Includes selections from St. Augustine and Boethius.

Oates, Whitney J., ed. *The Stoic and Epicurean Philosophers.* New York: Random House, 1940. The *Meditations* of Marcus Aurelius (included) is still rewarding, though not of first importance in the history of ideas.

* O'Brien, Elmer, ed. *The Essential Plotinus; Representative Treatises from* The Enneads. New York: New American Library, 1964. Even in selections, probably too difficult for any but the most ambitious student.

* Warmington, Eric H., and Rouse, Philip G., eds. *Great Dialogues of Plato.* New York: New American Library, 1956. W. H. D. Rouse's translations. The *Crito, Apology,* and *Phaedo* are short and moving accounts of the trial and death of Socrates and represent our basic knowledge of his thought. The *Republic,* though moderately heavy going, presents Plato's ideas about the ideal state and is worth the effort of exploring.

Commentary

* Allan, D. J. *The Philosophy of Aristotle,* 2nd ed. London and New York: Oxford University Press, 1970. An excellent basic introduction. (See also the books by Lloyd and Ross, below.)

Jaeger, Werner. *Paideia; The Ideals of Greek Culture,* 3 vols. London and New York: Oxford University Press, 1939-1944. Voluminous, but fairly easy reading. The title is the Greek word for "education," taken in the broadest sense: the author discusses the essence of Greek culture in terms of the values which, by all means, the Greeks attempted to transmit from one generation to the next.

Lloyd, G. E. R. *Aristotle; The Growth and Structure of His Thought.* Cambridge: Cambridge University Press, 1968.

Ross, W. D. *Aristotle,* 5th ed. New York: Barnes & Noble, 1953. A standard commentary on the major books.

Taylor, A. E. *Plato; The Man and His Work.* London: Methuen, 1960. Commentary on each dialogue.

* Warner, Rex, ed. *The Greek Philosophers.* New York: New American Library, 1958. Selections from Plato, Aristotle, Epictetus, Marcus Aurelius, Plotinus, fragments of Thales and Epicurus.

Religion

Mythology

* Grant, Michael. *Myths of the Greeks and Romans.* New York: New American Library, 1964.
* Hamilton, Edith. *Mythology.* New York: New American Library, 1953. Norse as well as Greek and Roman myths.

* Rouse, W. H. D. *Gods, Heroes, and Men of Ancient Greece.* New York: New American Library, 1957.
Rose, H. J. *Handbook of Greek Mythology*, 6th ed. New York: Dutton, 1959.

History and Interpretation

Guthrie, William K. C. *The Greeks and Their Gods.* Boston: Beacon, 1950.
Nilsson, Martin P. *A History of Greek Religion,* 2nd ed. London and New York: Oxford University Press, 1949.
Ogilvie, R. M. *The Romans and Their Gods in the Age of Augustus.* New York: Norton, 1970.
* Rose, H. J. *Religion in Greece and Rome.* New York: Harper, 1959. One-volume edition of two concise earlier books.

Science

Roman Texts

* Lucretius. *The Way Things Are.* Bloomington: Indiana University Press, 1969. The verse compilation of the body of scientific belief that was grafted onto the Epicurean philosophy, readable and alive in this translation of *De Rerum Natura* by the poet Rolfe Humphries.
Pliny. *Natural History: A Selection.* New York and London: Oxford University Press, 1964. Edited by J. Newsome.

History and Interpretation

Clagett, Marshall. *Greek Science in Antiquity.* New York: Abelard-Schumann, 1955. Excellent and brief.
* Farrington, Benjamin. *Science in Antiquity.* London and New York: Oxford University Press, 1969. Covers Babylonia and Egypt as well as Greek and Roman science and technology. Brief.
* de Santillana, Giorgio. *The Origins of Scientific Thought; From Anaximander to Proclus, 600 B.C.–A.D. 500.* New York: New American Library, 1961.
Sarton, George. *A History of Science; Hellenistic Science and Culture in the Last Three Centuries B.C.* Cambridge: Harvard University Press, 1959. Detailed and somewhat rambling, but easy to read. Treats philosophy as well as science and technology, placing them in their cultural context.
Taton, René, ed. *History of Science,* vol. 1: *Ancient and Medieval Science.* New York: Basic Books, 1963. Excellent brief summary in topical form.

SOME TECHNICAL TERMS

In general, the small number of special words used in this chapter have been explained in context, as they occurred. Here, we shall comment a little more fully on the meanings and implications of some of the more important of these words, showing how their meanings compare with some related terms.

actuality. A key term in the philosophy of Aristotle, who held that everything is in the process of moving from a state of potentiality to a state of actuality, from a state in which its possibilities are not realized to one in which they are. A fertilized egg, for example, largely potential, is in the process of moving toward actuality, toward expressing the possibilities already present in it, but the idea is not limited to situations involving organic growth.

analogy. *See* Reasoning.

animate. Possessing spirit (from the Latin word with this meaning, *anima*), hence living; the opposite of inanimate. As this chapter has shown, the distinction between the animate and inanimate is not as obvious or as easy to make as it might seem. The related word animism means the belief, held by many primitive religions, including the Greek and Roman, that all objects and natural phenomena possess a living spirit of some kind.

arche. A Greek word meaning "beginning" or "origin." In Greek philosophy, it had a technical meaning—the one thing or being that caused or causes everything in the universe, or the one underlying substance of which everything else is made or on which it depends. The search for the *arche*, for instance, led Democritus to his theory of atomism, the idea that if you could go on dividing things up into their parts, eventually you would reach a part so small that it could not be divided, the atom, from which all things are built up.

atomism. *See* Arche.

chance. *See* Necessity.

cosmos, cosmogony, cosmology. In Greek, the primary meaning of *cosmos* is simply "order," but in time it assumed also the meaning it has in English—the observable universe as a whole—because the Greeks viewed the universe as an orderly whole, made up of parts whose relationships they could understand. A cosmogony is a theory about the nature of the universe, its origins, and the relations of its parts. Cosmology is that branch of philosophy which is concerned with cosmogony, which describes the universe in all its aspects.

deduction. *See* Reasoning.

form. *See* Reality.

free will. *See* Necessity.

geocentric. *See* Heliocentric.

heliocentric. Having the sun (*helios*) at the center of the universe, motionless, with the stars and planets revolving around it. The Greek astronomer Aristarchus, in the third century B.C., was the first to hold this theory, which was not rediscovered until the Renaissance. The majority view in ancient times was that elaborated by Ptolemy: that the universe is geocentric, with the earth (*ge*) at the center and the heavenly bodies circling it.

inanimate. *See* Animate.

induction. *See* Reasoning.

infinity. The quality of being without end or limit, boundless, an idea first put forward by Anaxagoras.

irrational. *See* Rational.

legend. *See* Myth.

mana. The peculiar power that many primitive peoples believe present in living creatures and inanimate objects of all kinds, capable of affecting events in ways not usually possible to human beings. The word derives from South Seas languages and is used by anthropologists to describe an important feature of many primitive religions, including those of the Greeks and Romans. The Latin word *numen* (adjective numinous in English) is similar in meaning, though by it the Romans meant the particular spirit dwelling in every creature and thing; *mana,* in primitive belief, may or may not be present.

metaphor. A description of one thing in terms of another that is fundamentally different but has a resemblance of some kind (especially a structural resemblance). Metaphor asserts that one thing *is* another rather than simply like it in one particular respect and thus opens the way for discovering a variety of resemblances. For example, to say that "life is a pilgrimage" suggests one kind of resemblance (movement from one point to another over a period of time) but also suggests the transference of other ideas of pilgrimage to the idea of life.

mysticism. A complex religious idea concerned with the possibility of direct and immediate communication and ultimate union between the individual human soul and the divine nature, sometimes by means of specific kinds of religious practice. Mysticism is not peculiar to any one religion; forms of mysticism have appeared in both Buddhism and Christianity as well as in the thought of Plotinus discussed in this chapter. The Greco-Roman mystery-religions were, in part, mystical in intention.

myth. A story thought of as embodying, in some way, a religious truth or group of truths about the gods or about supernatural or natural events. Myth is a more complicated matter than, let us say, simply making up a story to explain the weather; some of the more important Greek myths (those concerning Demeter and Proserpine, for example) seem to have grown up out of religious ceremonies of much earlier origin, to explain them (rather than the other way around). Legend, in contrast, always looks back to an actual historical event, something that really happened, however remote and confused the details may have become in the course of telling and retelling.

necessity. The fact of being compelled to happen, of being unavoidable. In philosophy, this idea about the causes of events ranges from a very specific application (that one thing happens, or proceeds from something else, "by necessity") to a very general one (that the entire universe is governed by necessity). Opposed to this idea are both that of chance (the idea that events cannot be predicted, in a sense that they happen without cause) and that of free will (the idea that things happen because some being, divine or human, wants them to happen and can make them happen).

paradox. A statement that seems to contradict itself, to be absurd, but that may actually be true, usually put in such a way that it is difficult to disprove by logic. A simple example: that the emphasis on individual freedom in fifth-century Athens actually produced the suppression of freedom, or tyranny.

philosophy. The love of and study of wisdom and of the knowledge of things and their causes—one of the main subjects of this chapter. Among the Greeks, philosophy included all branches of knowledge, both theoretical and practical.

potentiality. *See* Actuality.

rational. Subject to reason, the human mental power by which we understand things and events and their causes in order to be able to affect their outcomes. The opposite, the irrational, suggests active opposition to this process, reliance on powers other than those of the human mind. The mathematical meaning of *rational* derives from this: a rational number is one that can be expressed as a ratio between two whole numbers.

reasoning. The process by which one applies one's mental powers to the understanding of any particular matter or group of matters, or a description or expression of this process. There are several specific forms of reasoning. Inductive reasoning (induction) proceeds from many particular instances to a general conclusion that should be applicable to other instances not yet known (for example: a hundred insects are found to have six legs; therefore all insects have six legs). Deductive reasoning (deduction) proceeds in the opposite direction, from the general statement to the particular instance (all six-legged creatures are insects; this creature has six legs and therefore is an insect). One can also reason by analogy, that is, by starting from a metaphorical resemblance between two things and proceeding to find other resemblances that help to understand one or the other thing being compared (life is a journey, therefore long, slow, and dangerous). All forms of reasoning, of course, are risky and can lead to error if misunderstood, misapplied, or not tested against direct observation.

reality. The actual, underlying nature of something as distinct from or opposed to what it merely seems to be or is said to be. In various forms, this distinction between appearance as perceived by the senses and reality has been important in the history of philosophy since Plato, who held that for every kind of thing there is an underlying reality, or form, of which each particular instance is an inferior copy.

reincarnation. *See* Transmigration.

taboo. A prohibition, or something that is forbidden, on religious grounds, because of the spirit or nature of the thing. Like *mana*, this is a South Seas word used by anthropologists to describe a feature of many primitive religions. Taboo may apply to certain actions or persons or to animals that it would be unholy to kill or eat. In its broadest sense, it is nearly the opposite of *mana*, which implies that something is dangerous and uncanny but on the whole beneficial.

theory. A general and orderly explanation of a set of facts, arrived at by reasoning and expressed in such a way as to account for all that is known—for example, the theory of music, the theory of boat construction. This is the philosophical sense in which the word is generally used in this chapter. (Loosely in modern usage the word also means a general statement that has not been proved, expressed in a form that can be proved or disproved—a hypothesis.)

transmigration. The religious belief that the soul at death passes into a new body or other physical form, not necessarily human. Reincarnation is a specific kind of transmigration—the soul being born again in a new human body.

Index

Abdera 299
Achaean League 187
The Acharnians (Aristophanes) 132, 133
Achilles 29, 114, 115, 169
Actium, Battle of 88, 151, 157
Adriatic Sea 247, 258
Aegean Sea 21, 23, 24, 27, 57, 171, 183, 207, 211, 234, 288
Aeneas 67, 154
The Aeneid (Virgil) 91, 145, 153–55, 160
Aeschylus 49, 123–26, 127, 130, 131, 132, 140, 301
Afghanistan 75, 260
Africa 75, 164, 247. See also **North Africa**, Individual Countries, Cities
Agamemnon 27, 114, 123, 124, 125, 130, 169, 210
Agamemnon (Aeschylus) 124
Agesilaus 185
Agriculture 21: Athens 52; Crete 207; Greek 22, 27, 38, 118, 284; Rome 84, 90, 106, 153
Agrigento 297
Agrippa 252
Agrippina 93
Ajax 169, 184
Alcaeus 119, 120
Alcibiades 184, 195, 202
Alexander III. Called the Great 22, 23, 41, 54, 55–58, 60, 75, 86, 88, 119, 138, 139, 186, 187, 202, 229, 233, 234, 237, 301, 302, 316, 319, 323
Alexander Severus, Marcus Aurelius 105
Alexandria 57, 58, 62, 88, 107, 139–40, 141–43, 277, 323, 324, 325, 326, 333
Almagest (*Mathematical Treatise* – Ptolemy) 326
Alphabet 27, 170: Etruscan 65, 67; Greek 35, 115, 271; Phoenician 115; Roman 37; Semitic 35

Ambrose, Saint 163
America 19, 234, 281
Amyot, Jacques, 203
Anabasis (*The March Up Country* – Xenophon) 183–84
Anaxagoras 51, 298–99
Anaximander 288, 289–90
Anaximenes 288, 290, 294
Annals (Ennius) 79, 145
Annals (Tacitus) 102, 161, 199, 200
Anthony, Mark 88, 149, 156, 245
Antigone 127, 128, 130
Antigone (Sophocles) 127, 128
Antioch 58
Antiochus III. Called the Great 75
Antoninus Pius 95, 98
Apennine Mountains 65, 69
Aphrodite 33, 55, 62, 285
Apollo 33, 34, 125, 224, 227, 240, 285, 286, 330
Apollodorus 251–52
Apollonius 142, 155, 325
The Apology (Plato) 137, 311–12
Appian Way 69, 86
Apuleius 163–64
Arabs 57, 140
Archilochus 118
Archimedes 61, 324
Architecture 213–14: Athens 49–50, 219–24; Etruscan 66, 249; Etruscan influence on Roman 249; Greek 17, 27, 31, 37–38, 49–50, 54, 62, 219–24, 234, 237; Greek influence on Roman 249; Hellenistic 242, 244, 246, 249; Minoan 208, 210; Mycenaean 24–25, 208, 210, 249; Roman 67, 72, 80–81, 83, 249, 251–53, 258. See also **Technology**
Ares 33, 285, 329
Argonautica (Apollonius) 142, 155
Aristarchus 61
Aristides 202
Aristophanes 49, 132–34, 138, 140, 141, 266–67, 270, 272, 306
Aristoxenus 271

343

Aristotelianism 54
Aristotle 54, 57, 137–38, 139, 140, 186, 268, 269, 271, 273, 297, 299, 301, 309, 315–18, 319, 333
Ars Amatoria (*The Art of Love*—Ovid) 91, 158, 159
Artaxerxes II 183
Artemis 33, 285
Art, Glossary of Terms 261–64. See also **Architecture, Historical Writing, Literature, Music, Painting, Philosophy, Sculpture,** Individual Artists, Individual Authors
The Art of Poetry (Horace) 157
Asia 33, 55, 84, 85, 135, 138, 174. See also **Asia Minor,** Individual Countries, Individual Cities
Asia Minor 21, 25, 27, 41, 65, 75, 114, 121, 135, 144, 171, 207, 220, 237, 242, 245, 249, 286, 288, 290, 294, 298, 316, 325. See also Individual Countries, Individual Cities
Assos 316
Assyrian Empire 19, 174
Astrology 103, 303, 331. See also **Philosophy, Religion, Science**
Astronomy 61, 137, 271, 287, 293, 323, 326–27. See also **Philosophy, Science**
Athena 33, 55, 72, 219, 220, 221, 223, 285
Athens: Acropolis 219–23; Empire 45, 48, 187, 272; Empire and Peloponnesian War 52–54, 127–28; Golden Age 45–52, 135; Persian Wars 44–45; Politics 40–41. See also **Architecture, Alexander III, Delian League, Historical Writing, Literature, Painting, Peloponnesian War, Persian Wars, Philosophy, Religion, Science, Sculpture, Sparta,** Individual Citizens
Athletic Competitions (Greek) 28, 35, 119, 135
Atomism 300–01
Atreus 123
Attica 44, 52. See also **Athens**
Atticus 195
Augustan Age (Rome) 90–92, 151, 153–60, 196–204
Augustine, Saint 163, 332–33
Augustus (Octavian) 87–88, 89–90, 91, 92, 151, 153, 154, 155, 156, 157, 159, 160, 196, 198, 200, 201, 247, 251, 252, 254, 323, 331

Babylon 183
Babylonia 21, 171, 172
Babylonians 287
The Bacchae (Euripides) 131
Balkans 105, 275
Belgium 86
Bellum Poenicum (*Punic Wars*—Naevius) 79, 145
Bible 170, 176, 282
Biography 17, 168–69: Greek 184–86; Hellenistic 186–87; Roman 161, 163, 191–95, 201–04
Biology 137, 138
The Birds (Aristophanes) 132
Blacks 101
Black Sea 23, 32, 130, 159, 183
Boeotia 44, 56
Boethius 333–34
Boswell, James 203
Britain 92, 99, 102, 192, 200
British 58
Britons 14
Brutus, Marcus 87, 156
Bucolics Eclogues or *Shepherd Poems*—Virgil) 153
Buddhism 58

Caesar, Julius 86–87, 89, 149, 150, 157, 160, 191–93, 201, 202, 251
Caligula 92, 201
Callimachus 142
Calypso 115
Campania 66
Cannae, Battle of 73, 198
Caracalla (Marcus Aurelius Antoninus) 87, 101, 105, 252, 258
Carmen Saeculare (Horace) 156
Carthage 45, 66, 73, 79, 145, 146, 187, 191. See also **Hannibal, Military Power, Punic Wars**
Carthaginians 32
Cassius 87
Castor 83
Catiline 86, 149, 193
Cato, Marcus. Called the Elder 190–91, 202
Catullus 89, 150–51, 158
Chaeronea, Battle of 56, 139
Chaeronea 202
Chalcis 316
Christianity 90, 92, 104, 106, 108–10, 155, 163, 164, 200, 220, 258–59, 277, 282, 291, 305, 307, 318, 321, 322, 331, 332, 333, 334
Cicero, Marcus 76, 86, 87, 88, 147, 148–50, 193, 195, 202, 278, 320
Cimon 184
Citium 320
Citizenship (Roman) 68, 77, 84, 85, 87, 101, 105

Index 345

City-States 15, 16, 22, 25, 29–35, 37, 39, 40, 51, 53, 54, 56, 57, 59, 66, 139, 171, 213, 219, 230, 290, 315. See also Individual Cities
Civilization, defined 13
Classical Age (Greece) 25, 29, 31, 35, 219, 228, 229, 230, 242, 244, 246, 269
Cleon 184
Claudius 92–93, 200, 201, 255
Clazomenae 298
Cleisthenes 41
Cleopatra 59, 88, 156, 245, 323
The Clouds (Aristophanes) 133, 134, 138, 306
Clytemnestra 124, 130
Cnidus 325
Colonization: Greek 32–33; Roman 69
Commentaries on the Civil War (Caesar) 89, 191–92, 193
Commentaries on the Gallic War (Caesar) 89, 191, 192
Commerce 13: Athens 47, 122, 284, 288; Carthage 66, 73; Crete 207; Greek 22, 23, 32, 38, 117–18, 237, 247; Mycenean 208; Phoenicia 213; Rome 106, 248
Commodus 98
Confessions (St. Augustine) 333
Conspiracy of Catiline (Sallust) 89, 193
Constantine I. Called the Great. 108, 253
Constitution: Athens 47, 53, 176; England 69; Rome 69–70, 189; Sparta 39; U.S. 189
Cordoba 161
Corfu 181, 214
Corinth 35, 56, 59, 76, 128, 130, 248
Corinth, Congress of 56, 139
Coriolanus 202
Corsica 66, 73
Cos 325, 326
Cosmologists 294–301
Crassus, Marcus 86
Crete 23, 24, 27, 207, 208, 246
Creusa 130
Crito 137, 321
Crito (Plato) 137, 312
Croesus 174
Croton 290
Cunaxa 183
Cynicism 54, 78
Cyprus 27, 185, 320
Cyrenaicism 54
Cyrus. Called the Great or the Elder 41
Cyrus. Called the Younger 183

Dacis (Rumania) 105, 107
Daedalus 159
Damascus 252
Danube River 108
Darius 44, 174, 229
Dark Age (Greece) 27, 28, 210, 214, 217
Dark Ages 333. See also **Middle Ages**
Decius 106
The Decline and Fall of the Roman Empire (Gibbon) 174
Delian League 45, 135, 136
Delos 45
Delphi 34, 35, 224, 286, 305, 308, 309
Demeter 33, 285, 303, 304
Democracy 15, 41: Athens 47–48, 52, 53, 128, 136–37, 180, 301, 306; Greek 54
Democritus 148, 299–301, 320
Demosthenes 53, 56, 202, 225
De Rerum Natura (*On the Nature of Things* — Lucretius) 89, 147–48, 300, 319–20
Dido 155
Diocletian 101, 104, 108, 109, 258
Diogenes 54
Diomedes 169
Dionysus (Bacchus) 48–49, 78–79, 122, 123, 131, 132, 221, 286, 304, 330
Diophantus 325
Dodona 34
Domitian 93, 95, 199, 201, 321
Dorians 39

Echo 159
Ecologues (*Bucolics* or *Shepherd Poems* — Virgil) 153
Education: Athens 48, 121, 137, 140, 310; Greek 37, 78, 268–69; Rome 77–78, 160. See also Museum (of Alexandria, Philosophy
Egypt 21, 23, 24, 37, 38, 41, 57, 59, 62, 87, 107, 135, 139, 140, 172, 207, 213, 214, 245, 257, 275, 290, 310, 331
Egyptians 14, 25, 274, 287
Einstein, Albert 324
The Ekklesiazusae (Aristophanes) 272
Elea 295, 296
Eleatics 295–96, 298, 300
Electra 130
Elements of Geometry (Euclid) 61, 323
Eleusinian Mysteries 34, 303–04
Eleusis 123, 303, 304
Emerson, Ralph Waldo 203
Empedocles 293, 296–98, 304

Index

England 22, 24, 69, 86, 90, 145
English Channel 86
Enneads (Plotinus) 331
Ennius 79, 144, 145, 156
Eos 287
Ephesus 58, 294
Epictetus 321
Epicureanism 60, 78, 89, 148, 319, 320
Epicurus 51, 148, 319, 320
Epidaurus 234
Epigrams (Martial) 95
Epirus 321
Erasistratus 326
Eratosthenes 25, 61
Eretria 41, 44
Etruria 248
Etruscans 32, 65, 66, 67, 68, 248, 249
Euclid 61, 323-34, 325
The Eumenides (Aeschylus) 125
Euphrates River 108
Euripides 89, 125-26, 129-31, 132, 133, 272, 298
Europe 19, 21, 22, 65, 161, 174
Evagoras 185
Evans, Sir Arthur 23
Ex Ponto (*From Pontus* — Ovid) 159

Fasti (*Festivals* — Ovid) 159
Finance 13: Athens 122, 136; Rome 68, 76, 84, 90, 98, 103, 105, 106, 110; Roman Empire 107, 108
Flavian Dynasty 93, 252
France 14, 32, 65, 73, 86
The Frogs (Aristophanes) 132, 133, 272
Frost, Robert 18

Gaia 286
Galba 201
Galen 61, 326, 327
Gaul 87, 105, 192
Gauls 65, 66, 68, 109, 242
Generation Conflict: Athens 48; Greek 53; Rome 89
Georgics (*Agricultural Poems* — Virgil) 154
Germania (Tacitus) 102, 161
Germans 98, 102, 105, 109, 192
Germany 86
Gibbon, Edward 95, 109, 174
Gibraltar, Straits of 66, 73
The Girl from Samos (Menander) 141
Gladiators 67
Gnosticism 331
Golden Age (Greece) 45, 47-48, 55, 121-39, 170, 267-73, 301
Goths 109, 333

Gracchus, Gaius 84, 191
Gracchus, Tiberius 83, 84, 191
Gregory XIII, Pope 87

Hades (Pluto) 286, 303
Hadrian 95, 98, 160, 163, 252
Haemon 127
Halicarnassus 171, 173
Hannibal 73, 75, 84, 101, 105, 146, 187, 188, 191, 198. See also **Carthage, Punic Wars**
Hebrews 170. See also **Jews.**
Hecataeus 171
Hector 114, 115, 169
Helen 27
Hellanicus 171
Hellas, defined 14: 15, 17, 21, 22, 27, 32, 33, 41, 45, 55, 58, 59, 65, 121, 128, 136, 137, 171, 181, 207, 219, 230, 247, 305
Hellenica (Xenophon) 183
Hellenistic Age 58-63, 138, 141-43, 186-89, 242, 244, 246, 249, 266
Hellespont (Dardanelles) 25, 298
Hephaestus 33, 220, 286
Heraclitus 294-95, 321
Herakles 184, 227, 284, 330
Herculaneum 93
Hermes 33, 285
Hero 33, 72, 285, 286
Herodotus 22, 135-36, 153, 171-76, 177, 179, 180, 187, 188, 196, 201, 288
Heroic Age (Greece) 25, 28, 29, 37, 170, 184, 217
Hesiod 116-17, 154, 282
Hestia 33, 286, 329
Hipparchus 41
Hippias 41
Hippo 333
Hippocrates 325
Hippolytus 130
Hippolytus (Euripides) 130, 131
Historical Writing 15, 17, 168-69: England 95; Greek 22, 53, 135-39, 171-84; Hellenistic 186-89; Rome 79, 89, 91-92, 102, 153, 161, 163, 189-95, 196-204
Histories (Herodotus) 135, 171-76
Histories (Tacitus) 102, 161, 199, 200, 201
History (Polybius) 187-89
History of the Jugurthine War (Sallust) 89, 193
History of the Peloponnesian War (Thucydides) 53, 136-37, 176-77, 179-82

History of Rome (Livy) 196-98
Hittite Empire 19, 65
Hittites 25
Homer 25, 28-29, 61, 114, 121, 125, 135, 140, 142, 144, 145, 155, 169, 210, 267, 282, 284, 286, 294, 297, 303
Horace 91, 156-57, 162
Housman, A. E. 157
Hybris (Sin of Excess) 34, 41, 174, 188
Hyperion 287

Icarus 159
Idyls (Theocritus) 62
The Iliad (Homer) 25, 28, 29, 114, 115, 125, 155, 169, 184, 210, 267, 282
Illinois 22
Impressionism 256
India 21, 33, 41, 57, 58, 139, 174, 237, 260, 292
Indo-Europeans 284, 286, 303, 327
Institutio Oratoria (*Oratorical Principles* — Quintilian) 160
Ionian Revolt 44
Iphigenia 124
Isocrates 53, 138-39, 140, 185, 237
Istanbul (Byzantium or Constantinople) 32, 108
Italia 85
Italy 14, 22, 23, 24, 32, 39, 63, 65, 66, 68, 69, 73, 76, 83, 85, 86, 88, 91, 95, 101, 144, 146, 154, 164, 187, 247, 290, 295, 327

Janus 329
Jason 130
Jerusalem 93
Jews 58, 93, 282
Judaism 104
Judea 92, 93
Jugurtha 85, 193
Juno 72
Jupiter 67, 72, 81
Juvenal 102, 161-62

Knossos 23, 207
Kore (Persephone) 303
Kronos 286

Lampsacus 298
Languages: Chinese 21; English 13, 150; Etruscan 65; Greek 14, 21, 25, 58, 101, 143, 144, 149, 190, 321; Latin 79, 101, 143, 144, 150, 163, 164, 190, 192; Oscan 144; Western 13
Lares 329
Latins 67, 68, 69
Latium 66, 68
The Laws (Plato) 268, 270, 312
Leonidas 44
Lepidus, Marcus 87
Lesbos 119, 316
Leucippus 299, 300
Leuctra, Battle of 56
The Libation-Bearers (Aeschylus) 124
Lincoln, Abraham 180
Linear A Script 24
Linear B Script 25
Literature 13, 17: Athens 48-49, 53, 121-39; Greek 25, 28-29, 31, 35-39, 114-139, 318; Greek influence on Roman 78, 143-45, 146, 147; Hellenistic 61-63, 139-43, 164; Rome 62, 79, 88-89, 90-92, 93, 95, 102, 143-64; Sparta 40. See also **Biography, Historical Writing, Philosophy, Religion**
Lives of the Twelve Caesars (Seutonius) 163, 201, 202
Livius, Andronicus 79, 144, 145
Livy 71, 91, 153, 196-98, 201
Lucan 160, 161, 162, 175
Lucilius 91, 156, 162
Lucretius 89, 147-48, 150, 158, 300, 319-20
Lycurgus 39, 56, 227
Lydia 41, 174, 183
Lydian Empire 41, 174
Lysippus 233, 234
Lysistrata (Aristophanes) 132

Macedonia 16, 22, 55, 56, 59, 75, 76, 87, 141, 188, 316
Maecenas 91, 153-54, 156, 157
Magna Graecia 66
Mantua 153
Marathon 44, 121, 135, 171, 174, 228
Marcus Aurelius Antonius. See **Caracalla**
Marcus Aurelius 95, 98, 102, 104, 255, 321, 322
Marius, Gaius 84, 85
Mars 251, 329
Marseilles 32, 247
Martial 95, 161
Medea 130
Medea (Euripides) 130, 131
Medicine 323: Greek 61, 135, 137; Hellenistic 61, 325-26; Western 61
Meditations (Marcus Aurelius) 321

348 Index

Mediterranean Sea 14, 16, 19, 21, 23, 24, 32, 37, 45, 59, 63, 66, 67, 69, 73, 75, 85, 109, 143, 147, 154, 164, 170, 187, 230, 247, 249, 278, 283, 325
Melos 181, 239
Memorabilia (Xenophon) 185
Menander 58, 62, 63, 134, 140–41, 273
Menelaus 27
Meno (Plato) 308
Mesopotamia 22
Messenians 39, 56
Metamorphoses (*The Golden Ass*—Apuleius) 163–64
Metamorphoses (Ovid) 91, 157, 159
Metaphysics (Aristotle) 315, 318
Metapontum 290
Michelangelo 62
Middle Ages 95, 106, 277, 278, 323, 326, 333, 334. See also **Dark Ages**
Milan 332
Milesian 288–90, 294
Miletus 41, 268, 288, 290
Military Power 16: Athens 44, 48, 122; Etruscans 67; Greek 31, 44–45, 55; Macedon 56; Macedonian-Greek 57; Mycenaean 24; Persian 41, 175; Sparta 39–40, 44, 52, 136; Rome 59, 68, 69, 73, 84, 85, 90, 98, 103, 105, 106, 110. See also **Peloponnesian War, Punic Wars,** Individual Military Commanders
Mill, John Stuart 44
Minerva 72
Minoan Age 23–24, 207, 208, 260
Minos 23, 207
Mithrades 85, 86
Mithraism 104, 331
Mommsen, Theodore 189
Monaco 32
Mozart 265
Munich 216
Museum (of Alexandria) 61, 139–40, 141–43, 245, 271, 323
Music 13, 17, 265–79: American 265, 270; Athens 129; Egyptian 274–75; European 265, 270; Greek 17, 35, 78, 117, 119–20, 137, 265, 266–76; Indian 265; Japanese 265; Roman 265, 266, 276–79; Roman attitude 78, 276
Mycenae 24, 25, 115, 123, 208, 210
Mycenaean Age 24–29, 65, 117, 170, 208, 249, 260
Mystery-Religions: Greek 34; 303–05; Rome 104
Mythology. See **Literature, Philosophy, Religion,** Individual Deities

Naevius 79, 144, 145
Naples 32, 93, 256, 295
Narcissus 159
Natural History (Pliny the Elder) 95, 160
Naucratis 32
Naval Power: Athenian 44, 45, 52, 53, 136, 309; Carthage 73; Greek 44, 47; Persian 44, 53; Rome 73
Near East 19, 21, 23, 25, 27, 32, 35, 56, 57, 65, 173, 184, 187, 207, 230, 239
Nemea 35
Neo-Platonism 331
Nepos, Cornelius 195
Nero 93, 160, 200, 201, 276
Nerva 95, 101
Netherlands 86
New Orleans 266
Nicias 184
Nile River 32
North Africa 32, 66, 73, 85, 99, 105, 333. See also Individual Cities
North, Thomas 203
Numantia 76
Numidia 85

Oceanides 287
Oceanus 286
Octavia 88
Odes (Horace) 91
Odysseus 29, 115, 116, 169, 219
The Odyssey 25, 28, 29, 114, 115, 116, 117, 145, 155, 169, 184, 210, 267, 282
Oedipus 123, 127, 128, 129
Oedipus at Colonus (Sophocles) 127, 128, 129
Oedipus the King (Sophocles) 127, 129
Olympia 35, 219
On the Consolation of Philosophy (Boethius) 333–34
On Famous Men (Nepos) 195
On Nature (Empedocles) 297
On Purification (Empedocles) 297
The Oresteia (Aeschylus) 125, 129
Orestes 124, 130
Origins (Cato) 191
Orpheus 284
Orphic Mysteries 34
Orphism 304–05
Otho 201
Ovid 91, 157, 158–60

Painting 13, 17: Athens 211; Christian 258–59; Crete 208; Etruscan 66;

Greek 27, 37, 38, 206–08, 210–11, 213, 215–17, 227–28, 229, 230; Greek influence on Etruscan 248; Greek influence on Roman 80, 249; Hellenistic 62, 239, 244, 248; Mycenaean 210; Roman 109, 256–58. See also **Architecture, Sculpture**
Parallel Lives (Plutarch) 202–03
Paris (of Troy) 27
Parmenides 295–96, 297, 298
Paros 118
Parthia 86
Parthian Empire 98
Parthians 105
Patroclus 114
Paul, Saint 60
Pausanias 184
Pax Romana 16, 63, 90, 98, 99, 102, 110
Peisistratus 41, 49
Peloponnesian War 52–54, 55, 121, 129, 131, 135, 137, 138, 140, 147, 176–77, 179–82, 183, 185, 230, 267, 272, 298, 301
Peloponnesus 35, 39, 40, 208
Penates 329
Pentheus 131
Perga 325
Pergamum 58, 59, 62–63, 241, 244, 249, 326
Pericles 45, 47, 48, 49, 52, 134, 135, 136, 137, 180, 184, 202, 219, 230, 272, 298, 301
Perseus 184
Persia 53, 104, 171, 172, 174, 183, 229
Persian Empire 41, 55, 56, 57, 105, 170, 171, 173, 174
Persians 121, 122, 126, 135, 136, 170, 175, 219, 220, 267
Persians (Aeschylus) 124
Persian Wars 31, 41, 44–45, 53, 121, 131, 135, 171, 172, 173, 176, 220, 301
Petronius 93, 161, 162–63, 164
Phaedra 130
Phaeton 159
Pharsalia (Lucan) 160
Phidias 55, 219, 220, 223, 227, 228
Philip II 22, 55, 56, 138, 139, 202
Philip V 75
Philippi, Battle of 87, 153
Philosophy 17, 281–334: Athens 40, 121; Greek 17, 41, 50–52, 54, 59, 60–61, 137, 160, 287–301, 305–09; Greek influence in Rome 78, 149; Hellenistic 319–22; India 58; Roman 95, 147, 149, 331–34; Sparta 40. See also **Religion**, Individual Schools, Individual Philosophers
Philosophy, Glossary of Terms 336–40
Phoenicians 213
Phoenicia 24, 45, 66
Phrygia 286
Physics (Anaxagoras) 298
Physics (Aristotle) 318
Pindar 119–20
Piraeus 44, 45, 309
Plataea, 44, 171, 175
Plato 31, 54, 58, 137, 138, 229, 268, 269, 270, 271, 272, 273, 291, 296, 299, 301, 304, 305, 307–09, 310–15, 316, 324, 327, 331, 332, 333
Platonism 54, 138
Plautus 62, 79, 140, 144, 145–46, 147
Pliny. Called the Elder 95, 102, 160, 161
Pliny. Called the Younger 102, 161
Plotinius 331–33
Plutarch 201, 202–03
Plutus (Aristophanes) 272
Poetics (Aristotle) 138, 318
Politics (Aristotle) 268, 269
Politics (Plato) 54
Pollux 82
Polybius 187–89, 190, 196, 198
Polynices 127
Pompey. Called the Great 86, 149, 160, 191, 192
Poseidon 33, 131, 221, 223, 224, 283, 286
Praxiteles 55, 233, 234, 240
Priam 27, 169
Propertius 157, 158
Protagoras 51
Psychology (Aristotle) 318
Ptolemy 61, 271, 326–27
Ptolemy I 323, 324
Punic Wars 73, 147, 187, 189: Second Punic War 73, 146, 188
Pylos 24, 115
Pyramus 159
Pythagoras 290–93, 294
Pythagoreanism 290–93, 294

Quintilian 160

Religion 281–334: Athens 132; Egypt 164; Etruscan 66, 67; Greek 33–35, 115–16, 122–23, 173–74, 281–87, 291, 303–05; Hellenistic 303; Macedon 55; Rome 71, 72, 78–79, 90, 103–04, 105–06, 189, 327, 329–31

350 Index

Religion, Glossary of Terms 336–40
Remus 67
The Republic (Plato) 54, 268, 269
Rhea 286
Rhodes 58, 62, 239
Rome: Augustan Age 90–92, 151, 153–60, 196–204; Capital of World 83; Conquest of Seleucid Empire 75; Crisis of Empire, 104–06; Decay of Empire 102–110; Empire 14, 16, 17, 59, 92–102, 151; Founding of City 63–72; Growth of Empire 59, 73–82; Kingdom 67–68; Republic 17, 68, 72, 151, 193, 199, 251; Revolution 83–89, 160, 191; Triumvirate, First 86, 149; Triumvirate, Second 87, 153; Transformation of Society 76–79. See also **Architecture, Carthage, Historical Writing, Literature, Painting, Philosophy, Religion, Science, Sculpture, Individual Citizens**
Romulus 67, 191, 198
Romulus Augustulus 109

Sabines 67
Salamis 44, 121, 124, 126, 135, 171, 175
Sallust 89, 161, 193, 195
Samnites 69
Samos 141, 290, 319
Sappho 119, 120
Sardinia 66, 73
Sardis 183
Satires (Horace) 91
Satires (Juvenal) 102
Satyricon (Petronius) 95, 162–63, 164
Science 17, 322–23: Greek 15, 17, 41, 50, 54, 61, 137, 170, 175, 287–88, 289, 291, 292, 293, 299, 310, 312, 316–17, 318; Hellenistic 303, 323–25; Rome 95, 323
Science, Glossary of Terms 336–40
Scipio Africanus. Called the Elder 75, 83, 146
Scipio Africanus. Called the Younger 146, 187
Scopas 233
Sculpture 13: Athens 50; Crete 208; Egyptian 38; Etruscan 66; Greek 17, 27, 37–38, 54–55; 206–08, 210–11, 213, 214–15, 220–24, 227, 233, 243; Greek influence on Etruscan 248; Greek influence on Roman 80, 249; Hellenistic 62, 237–39, 241–42; Hindu 58; Mycanaean 210; Roman 63, 101–02, 109, 253–55. See also **Architecture, Literature, Painting, Religion**
Scythia 171
Seneca 95, 160–61, 162
Severus, Septimius 105
Shapur I 105
Sicily 24, 32, 45, 52, 65, 66, 73, 75, 142, 148, 181, 247, 297, 310, 324, 325
Simonides 228
Skepticism 78
Slavery 47, 70, 71, 76–77, 86, 109, 147, 154–55, 181, 276, 284, 308, 321
Socrates 35, 51–52, 54, 128, 133, 134, 137, 138, 183, 185, 186, 195, 293, 294, 295, 297, 299, 301, 305, 306, 307, 308, 309, 310, 311, 312, 314
Solon 40, 118, 174
Sophists 50–51, 133–34, 138, 139, 177, 293, 294, 305, 306, 307
Sophocles 48, 49, 126–29, 130, 136
Spain 14, 32, 66, 73, 75, 105, 247
Sparta 39–40, 44–45, 51, 52–54, 118, 129, 132, 137, 175, 180, 182, 230, 267, 298; Empire 55–56; Defeated 56; Peloponnesian League 136. See also **Athens, Education, Military Power, Peloponnesian War, Individual Citizens**
Spartacus 86
Split 258
Stagira 316
Stoicism 60–61, 78, 95, 319, 320–22
Suetonius 163, 201–02, 276
Sulla 85, 191
The Symposium (Plato) 312
Syracuse 32, 45, 58, 142, 247, 310, 324
Syria 59, 86

Tacitus 102, 161, 162, 199–201, 202
Tarentum 39, 69, 79, 144, 186
Tarquins 67
Technology: Babylonian 287–88; Egyptian 287–88; Etruscan 66; Greek 61, 117; Rome 80, 81, 99, 323
Telemachus 115
Terence 62, 79, 140, 141, 146, 147
Terminus 329
Tethys 286
Thagaste 332
Thales 288, 289, 294, 298
Thebes 56, 119, 123, 128
Themistocles 44, 184
Theogony (Hesiod) 116
Thermopylae 44, 174

Theseus 129, 130-31, 184, 227, 228
Thespis 49
Theocritus 62, 63, 142-43, 154
Theophrastus 140
Thisbe 159
Thrace 286, 299
Thucydides 53, 135, 136-37, 153, 161, 176-77, 179-82, 183, 184, 187, 188, 195, 196, 198
Tiberius 92, 199, 200, 201
Tibullus 157, 158
Timaeus (Plato) 268, 312, 332
Timon of Phlius 59
Timotheus of Miletus 268
Tiryns 24, 208
Titans 286
Titus 93, 201, 252
Tomis 160
Trajan 95, 98, 251, 252
A Treatise of Conic Sections (Apollonius) 325
Trojan War 27, 29, 45, 114, 115, 130, 135, 169, 210
Troy (Illium) 25, 67, 115, 125, 154, 210, 211, 219, 260
Tunis 73
Turkey 108, 174
Turkish Empire 14
Tyrants 39, 41, 49, 121
Tyrrhenian Sea 83

Umbria 144
Uranos 286

Valerian 105
Vandals 333
Verona 89
Vespasian 93, 101, 201, 254-55
Vesta 81, 329
Vesuvius, Mount 93, 95
Virgil 91, 145, 153-55, 156, 160, 198
Vitellius 201
Vitruvius 323

The Way of Seeming (Parmenides) 295
The Way of Truth (Parmenides) 295
Welfare System: Athens 48; Rome 17, 84, 85, 99, 103, 110; Roman Empire 101
Women, Status of: Athens 47, 48; Alexander's Empire 57; Rome, 72, 78
Works and Days (Hesiod) 116, 117

Xantippe 307
Xenophon 182-84, 185, 192
Xerxes 44, 124, 174

Yugoslavia 258

Zeno 60-61, 296, 320
Zeus 33, 34, 35, 55, 72, 219, 241, 244, 282, 283, 284, 285, 286

Other MENTOR Books About Ancient Greece and Rome

☐ **THE GREEK STONES SPEAK by Paul MacKendrick.** The glory that was Greece brought back to life through a detailed and authoritative study of archaeological finds. More than 175 photographs and drawings.
(#MW1078—$1.50)

☐ **MYTHOLOGY by Edith Hamilton.** A widely-read retelling of the Greek, Roman and Norse legends of love and adventure. "Classical mythology has long needed such a popular exposition and Miss Edith Hamilton has given us one in this volume, which is at once a reference book and a book which may be read for stimulation and pleasure."—**The New York Times.** Illustrated. Charts. Index. (#MY1196—$1.25)

☐ **THE ILIAD OF HOMER translated by W. H. D. Rouse.** A brilliant prose translation of Homer's great epic of the Trojan War, by the late distinguished scholar.
(#MT650—75¢)

☐ **THE ODYSSEY OF HOMER translated by W. H. D. Rouse.** A modern prose translation of the world's greatest adventure story, the travels of Ulysses. (#MT677—75¢)

☐ **THE PHILOSOPHY OF ARISTOTLE.** A new translation by A. E. Wardman and J. L. Creed of the basic writings of Aristotle. With Introduction and Commentary by Renford Bambrough. (#MY804—$1.25)

THE NEW AMERICAN LIBRARY, INC.
P.O. Box 999, Bergenfield, New Jersey 07621

Please send me the MENTOR BOOKS I have checked above. I am enclosing $_____ (check or money order—no currency or C.O.D.s). Please include the list price plus 25¢ a copy to cover handling and mailing costs. (Prices and number are subject to change without notice.)

Name_____

Address_____

City_____ State_____ Zip Code_____

(Allow at least 3 weeks for delivery)